DATE DUE

DEMCO 38-296

SONNETS
&
SONGS

AMS PRESS
NEW YORK

PETRARCH

SONNETS

&

SONGS

TRANSLATED BY ANNA MARIA ARMI
INTRODUCTION BY THEODOR E. MOMMSEN

PANTHEON

PQ 4496 .E23 A78 1978

Petrarca, Francesco, 1304-
1374.

Publication Data

Sonnets & songs

Translation of Rime.
Reprint of the ed. published by Pantheon, New York.
English and Italian.
1. Ascoli, Anna Maria Maddalena Paolina Giacinta Cochetti, 1899-
PQ4496.E23A78 1978   851'.1   75-41212
ISBN 0-404-14695-3

Reprinted from the edition of 1946, New York
First AMS edition published in 1978
Manufactured in the United States of America

AMS PRESS INC.
NEW YORK, N.Y.

INDEX OF FIRST LINES

Ahi, bella libertá, come tu m'hai	152
A la dolce ombra de le belle frondi	232
Al cader d'una pianta che si svelse	440
Alma felice, che sovente torni	404
Almo Sol, quella fronde ch'io sola amo	280
Amor, che meco al buon tempo ti stavi	424
Amor, che 'ncende il cor d'ardente zelo	274
Amor, che nel penser mio vive e regna	230
Amor, che vedi ogni pensero aperto	254
Amor co la man destra il lato manco	328
Amor con sue promesse lusingando	128
Amor et io sí pien di meraviglia	252
Amor, Fortuna, e la mia mente schiva	188
Amor fra l'erbe una leggiadra rete	272
Amor, io fallo, e veggio il mio fallire	336
Amor m'ha posto come segno a strale	218
Amor mi manda quel dolce pensero	260
Amor mi sprona in un tempo et affrena	270
Amor, Natura, e la bella alma umíle	276
Amor piangeva, et io con lui tal volta	36
Amor, quando fioría	450
Amor, se vuo' ch'i' torni al giogo antico	386
Anima bella, da quel nodo sciolta	426
Anima, che diverse cose tante	296
Anzi tre dí creata era alma in parte	312
A pie' de' colli ove la bella vesta	8
Apollo, s'ancor vive il bel desïo	54
A qualunque animale alberga in terra	22
Arbor vittoriosa triumfale	366
Aspro core e selvaggio, e cruda voglia	378
Aura che quelle chiome bionde e crespe	328
Aventuroso piú d'altro terreno	166
Beato in sogno e di languir contento	310
Benedetto sia 'l giorno, e 'l mese, e l'anno	96
Ben mi credea passar mio tempo omai	300
Ben sapeva io che natural consiglio	106

Cantai, or piango, e non men di dolcezza	330
Cara la vita, e dopo lei mi pare	366
Cercato ho sempre solitaria vita	362
Cesare, poi che 'l traditor d'Egitto	156
Che debb'io far? che mi consigli, Amore?	380
Che fai, alma? che pensi? avrem mai pace?	242
Che fai? che pensi? che pur dietro guardi	394
Chiare, fresche, e dolci acque	192
Chi è fermato di menar sua vita	132
Chi vuol veder quantunque pò Natura	352
Come 'l candido pie' per l'erba fresca	256
Come talora al caldo tempo sòle	230
Come va 'l mondo! or mi diletta e piace	412
Conobbi, quanto il ciel li occhi m'aperse	476
Cosí potess'io ben chiudere in versi	150
Da' piú belli occhi e dal piú chiaro viso	484
Datemi pace, o duri miei pensieri	396
Deh porgi mano a l'affannato ingegno	490
Deh qual pietá, qual angel fu sí presto	478
Del cibo onde 'l signor mio sempre abonda	478
De l'empia Babilonia, ond'è fuggita	172
Del mar Tirreno a la sinistra riva	104
Dicemi spesso il mio fidato speglio	508
Dicesette anni ha giá rivolto il cielo	186
Di dí in dí vo cangiando il viso e 'l pelo	286
Di pensier in pensier, di monte in monte	210
Discolorato hai, Morte, il piú bel vólto	404
Di tempo in tempo mi si fa men dura	240
Dodici donne onestamente lasse	326
Dolce mio caro e prezioso pegno	476
Dolci durezze, e placide repulse	488
Dolci ire, dolci sdegni e dolci paci	296
Donna, che lieta col principio nostro	484
Due gran nemiche inseme erano agiunte	418
Due ròse fresche, e còlte in paradiso	348
D'un bel, chiaro, polito e vivo ghiaccio	294
E' mi par d'or in ora udire il messo	486
È questo 'l nido, in che la mia fenice	442

Era il giorno ch'al sol si scoloraro	4
Erano i capei d'oro a l'aura sparsi	144
Far potess'io vendetta di colei	360
Fera stella (se 'l cielo ha forza in noi	266
Fiamma dal ciel su le tue treccie piova	226
Fontana di dolore, albergo d'ira	228
Fresco, ombroso, fiorito e verde colle	346
Fu forse un tempo dolce cosa amore	480
Fuggendo la pregione ove Amor m'ebbe	144
Gentil mia donna, i' veggio	116
Geri, quando talor meco s'adira	270
Giá desiai con sí giusta querela	318
Giá fiammeggiava l'amorosa stella	54
Giovene donna sotto un verde lauro	48
Giunto Alessandro a la famosa tomba	278
Giunto m'ha Amor fra belle e crude braccia	262
Gli occhi di ch'io parlai sí caldamente	414
Gloriosa Columna, in cui s'appoggia	10
Grazie ch'a pochi il ciel largo destina	312
I begli occhi ond'i' fui percosso in guisa	128
I dí miei, piú leggier che nesun cervo	440
I dolci colli ov'io lasciai me stesso	308
I' ho pien di sospir quest'aere tutto	410
I' ho pregato Amor, e 'l ne riprego	344
Il cantar novo e 'l pianger delli augelli	320
Il figliuol di Latona avea già nove	70
Il mal mi preme, e mi spaventa il peggio	348
Il mio adversario, in cui veder solete	72
Il successor di Carlo, che la chioma	38
I' mi soglio accusare, et or mi scuso	418
I' mi vivea di mia sorte contento	332
In dubbio di mio stato, or piango or canto	356
In mezzo di duo amanti onesta altèra	174
In nobil sangue vita umile e queta	316
In qual parte del ciel in quale idea	250
In quel bel viso ch'i' sospiro e bramo	360
In quella parte dove Amor mi sprona	196
In tale stella duo belli occhi vidi	364

VII

Io amai sempre, et amo forte ancóra	140
Io avrò sempre in odio la fenestra	140
Io canterei d'amor sí novamente	216
Io mi rivolgo in dietro a ciascun passo	16
Io non fu' d'amar voi lassato unquanco	136
Io sentía dentr'al cor giá venir meno	74
Io son de l'aspettar omai sí vinto	150
Io son giá stanco di pensar sí come	126
Io son sí stanco sotto 'l fascio antico	136
Io temo sí de' begli occhi l'assalto	66
I' pensava assai destro esser su l'ale	428
I' piansi, or canto; ché 'l celeste lume	330
I' pur ascolto, e non odo novella	358
Italia mia, ben che 'l parlar sia indarno	202
Ite, caldi sospiri, al freddo core	244
Ite, rime dolenti, al duro sasso	470
I' vidi in terra angelici costumi	248
I' vo pensando, e nel penser m'assale	370
I' vo piangendo i miei passati tempi	512
La bella donna che cotanto amavi	146
La donna che 'l mio cor nel viso porta	170
L'aere gravato, e l'importuna nebbia	102
La gola e 'l sonno e l'oziose piume	8
La guancia, che fu giá piangendo stanca	94
L'alma mia fiamma oltra le belle bella	410
L'alto e novo miracol ch'a' dí nostri	430
L'alto signor dinanzi a cui non vale	344
L'arbor gentil, che forte amai molt'anni	96
L'ardente nodo ov'io fui d'ora in ora	392
Lasciato hai, Morte, senza sole il mondo	474
La sera desiare, odiar l'aurora	358
L'aspettata vertú, che 'n voi fioriva	158
L'aspetto sacro de la terra vostra	106
Lassare il velo o per sole o per ombra	12
Lasso!, Amor mi trasporta, ov'io non voglio	336
Lasso!, ben so che dolorose prede	156
Lasso!, che mal accorto fui da prima	100
Lasso!, ch'i' ardo, et altri non mel crede	294

Lasso me!, ch'i' non so in qual parte pieghi	108
Lasso!, quante fiate Amor m'assale	168
L'aura celeste che 'n quel verde lauro	288
L'aura, che 'l verde lauro e l'aureo crine	350
L'aura, e l'odore, e 'l refrigerio e l'ombra	458
L'aura gentil, che rasserena i poggi	286
L'aura mia sacra al mio stanco riposo	492
L'aura serena che fra verdi fronde	288
L'aura soave al sole spiega e vibra	290
L'avara Babilonia ha colmo il sacco	226
Lá vèr' l'aurora, che sí dolce l'aura	340
La vita fugge, e non s'arresta una ora	394
Le stelle, il cielo, e gli elementi a prova	246
Levommi il mio penser in parte ov'era	424
Li angeli eletti, e l'anime beate	482
Liete, e pensose, accompagnate, e sole	322
Lieti fiori e felici, e ben nate erbe	254
L'oro e le perle, e i fior vermigli e i bianchi	72
L'ultimo, lasso!, de' miei giorni allegri	458
Mai non fui in parte ove sí chiar vedessi	402
Mai non vedranno le mie luci asciutte	444
Mai non vo' piú cantar com'io soleva	160
Ma poi che 'l dolce riso umile e piano	68
Mente mia, che presaga de' tuoi danni	436
Mentre che 'l cor da gli amorosi vermi	426
Mia benigna fortuna, e 'l viver lieto	464
Mia ventura, et Amor, m'avean sí adorno	292
Mie venture al venir son tarde e pigre	92
Mille fiate, o dolce mia guerrera	22
Mille piagge in un giorno e mille rivi	268
Mirando 'l sol de' begli occhi sereno	264
Mira quel colle, o stanco mio cor vago	346
Morte ha spento quel sol ch'abagliar suolmi	510
Movesi il vecchierel canuto e bianco	16
Né cosí bello il sol giá mai levarsi	236
Ne la stagion che 'l ciel rapido inchina	76
Ne l'etá sua piú bella e piú fiorita	400
Nel dolce tempo de la prima etade	24

Né mai pietosa madre al caro figlio	406
Né per sereno ciel ir vaghe stelle	434
Non al suo amante piú Diana piacque	82
Non da l'ispano Ibero a l'indo Idaspe	308
Non d'atra e tempestosa onda marina	242
Non fûr ma' Giove e Cesare sí mossi	246
Non ha tanti animali il mar fra l'onde	338
Non pò far morte il dolce viso amaro	494
Non pur quell'una bella ignuda mano	292
Non Tesin, Po, Varo, Arno, Adige, e Tebro	240
Non veggio ove scampar mi possa omai	166
Nova angeletta sovra l'ale accorta	164
O aspettata in ciel beata e bella	38
O bella man, che mi destringi 'l core	290
O cameretta, che giá fosti un porto	334
Occhi miei lassi, mentre ch'io vi giro	14
Occhi miei, oscurato è 'l nostro sole	396
Occhi, piangete, accompagnate il core	138
O d'ardente vertute ornata e calda	238
O dolci sguardi, o parolette accorte	356
Ogni giorno mi par piú di mill'anni	494
O giorno, o ora, o ultimo momento	460
Oimè il bel viso, oimè il soave sguardo	380
O invidia nimica di vertute	264
O misera et orribil visione!	354
Onde tolse Amor l'oro, e di qual vena	320
O passi sparsi! o pensier vaghi e pronti	252
Or che 'l ciel e la terra e 'l vento tace	256
Or hai fatto l'estremo di tua possa	456
Orso, al vostro destrier si pò ben porre	152
Orso, e' non furon mai fiumi né stagni	64
Or vedi, Amor, che giovenetta donna	184
O tempo, o ciel volubil, che fuggendo	492
Ove ch'i' posi gli occhi lassi o giri	250
Ov'è la fronte, che non picciol cenno	420
Pace non trovo, e non ho da far guerra	218
Padre del ciel, dopo i perduti giorni	98
Parrà forse ad alcun che 'n lodar quella	350

Pasco la mente d'un sí nobil cibo	284
Passa la nave mia colma d'oblio	280
Passato è 'l tempo omai, lasso!, che tanto	434
Passer mai solitario in alcun tetto	326
Per ch'al viso d'Amor portava insegna	90
Perché la vita è breve	110
Perché quel che mi trasse ad amar prima	94
Perch'io t'abbia guardato di menzogna	76
Per fare una leggiadra sua vendetta	2
Per mezz'i boschi inospiti e selvaggi	268
Per mirar Policleto a prova fiso	130
Persequendomi Amor al luogo usato	168
Piangete, donne, e con voi pianga Amore	146
Pien di quella ineffabile dolcezza	174
Pien d'un vago penser, che me desvia	260
Pióvommi amare lagrime dal viso	18
Piú di me lieta non si vede a terra	36
Piú volte Amor m'avea giá detto:—Scrivi	148
Piú volte giá dal bel sembiante umano	262
Po, ben puo' tu portartene la scorza	272
Poco era ad appressarsi a gli occhi miei	82
Poi che la vista angelica, serena	398
Poi che 'l camin m'è chiuso di mercede	214
Poi che mia speme è lunga a venir troppo	142
Poi che per mio destíno	120
Poi che voi et io piú volte abbiam provato	154
Pommi ove 'l sole occide i fiori e l'erba	236
Qual donna attende a gloriosa fama	364
Qual mio destín, qual forza, o qual inganno	322
Qual paura ho, quando mi torna a mente	352
Qual piú diversa e nova	220
Qual ventura mi fu, quando da l'uno	334
Quand'io mi volgo in dietro a mirar gli anni	420
Quand'io son tutto vòlto in quella parte	18
Quand'io veggio dal ciel scender l'Aurora	412
Quand'io v'odo parlar si dolcemente	234
Quando Amor i belli occhi a terra inchina	258
Quando dal proprio sito si rimove	68

Quando fra l'altre donne ad ora ad ora	14
Quando giugne per gli occhi al cor profondo	148
Quando giunse a Simon l'alto concetto	130
Quando il soave mio fido conforto	496
Quando io movo i sospiri a chiamar voi	6
Quando 'l pianeta che distingue l'ore	10
Quando 'l Sol bagna in mar l'aurato carro	324
Quando 'l voler che con duo sproni ardenti	238
Quando mi vène inanzi il tempo e 'l loco	266
Quanta invidia io ti porto, avara terra	422
Quante fiate al mio dolce ricetto	402
Quanto piú disiose l'ali spando	228
Quanto piú m'avicino al giorno estremo	52
Que' che 'n Tesaglia ebbe le man sí pronte	70
Que' ch'infinita providenzia et arte	4
Quel antiquo mio dolce empio signore	500
Quel che d'odore e di color vincea	474
Quel foco ch'i' pensai che fosse spento	90
Quella fenestra ove l'un sol si vede	154
Quella per cui con Sorga ho cangiato Arno	430
Quelle pietose rime, in ch'io m'accorsi	184
Quel rosigniuol che sí soave piagne	432
Quel sempre acerbo et onorato giorno	248
Quel sol che mi mostrava il camin destro	428
Quel vago, dolce, caro, onesto sguardo	460
Quel vago impallidir che 'l dolce riso	186
Questa anima gentil che si diparte	52
Questa fenice, de l'aurata piuma	276
Questa umil fera, un cor di tigre o d'orsa	244
Questo nostro caduco e fragil bene	486
Qui, dove mezzo son, Sennuccio mio	172
Rapido fiume, che d'alpestra vena	306
Real natura, angelico intelletto	340
Rimansi a dietro il sestodicemo anno	176
Ripensando a quel, ch'oggi il cielo onora	480
Rotta è l'alta colonna, e 'l verde lauro	386
S'al principio risponde il fine e 'l mezzo	132
S'Amore o Morte non dá qualche stroppio	66

S'amor non è, che dunque è quel ch'io sento?	216
S'Amor novo consiglio non n'apporta	398
Se bianche non son prima ambe le tempie	138
Se col cieco desir che 'l cor distrugge	92
Se lamentar augelli, o verdi fronde	400
Se la mia vita da l'aspro tormento	12
Se 'l dolce sguardo di costei m'ancide	274
Se l'onorata fronde, che prescrive	34
Se 'l pensier che mi strugge	188
Se 'l sasso, ond' è piú chiusa questa valle	176
Se mai foco per foco non si spense	74
Sennuccio, i' vo' che sapi in qual manera	170
Sennuccio mio, ben che doglioso e solo	408
Sento l'aura mia antica, e i dolci colli	442
Se quell'aura soave de' sospiri	408
Se Virgilio et Omero avessin visto	278
Se voi poteste per turbati segni	100
Sí breve è 'l tempo e 'l penser sí veloce	406
Sí come eterna vita è veder Dio	282
Sí è debile il filo a cui s'attene	58
S'i' fussi stato fermo a la spelunca	258
Signor mio caro, ogni pensier mi tira	378
S'i' 'l dissi mai, ch'i' vegna in odio a quella	298
S'io avesse pensato che sí care	414
S'io credesse per morte essere scarco	56
Sí tosto come aven che l'arco scocchi	142
Sí traviato è 'l folle mi' desio	6
Solea da la fontana di mia vita	462
Solea lontana in sonno consolarme	354
Soleano i miei penser soavemente	416
Soleasi nel mio cor star bella e viva	416
Solo e pensoso i piú deserti campi	56
Son animali al mondo de sí altèra	20
S'onesto amor pò meritar mercede	470
Spinse amor e dolor ove ir non debbe	482
Spirto felice, che sí dolcemente	488
Spirto gentil, che quelle membra reggi	84
Standomi un giorno solo a la fenestra	444

Stiamo, Amor, a veder la gloria nostra	284
S'una fede amorosa, un cor non finto	324
Tacer non posso, e temo non adopre	450
Tempo era omai da trovar pace o tregua	438
Tennemi Amor anni vent'uno ardendo	512
Tornami a mente, anzi v'è dentro, quella	472
Tranquillo porto avea mostrato Amore	438
Tra quantunque leggiadre donne e belle	318
Tutta la mia fiorita e verde etade	436
Tutto 'l dí piango; e poi la notte, quando	316
Una candida cerva sopra l'erba	282
Una donna piú bella assai che 'l sole	178
Vago augelletto, che cantando vai	490
Valle, che de' lamenti miei se' piena	422
Verdi panni, sanguigni, oscuri o persi	44
Vergine bella, che di sol vestita	514
Vergognando talor ch'ancor si taccia	20
Vidi fra mille donne una giá tale	472
Vincitore Alessandro l'ira vinse	332
Vinse Anibál, e non seppe usar poi	158
Vive faville uscian de' duo bei lumi	362
Voglia mi sprona, Amor mi guida e scorge	310
Voi ch'ascoltate in rime sparse il suono	2
Volgendo gli occhi al mio novo colore	98
Volo con l'ali de' pensieri al cielo	510
Zefiro torna, e 'l bel tempo rimena	432

INTRODUCTION

PETRARCH presents in his life and work a most interesting example of a complete mutation in literary fame. For there exists in critical annals a very marked and curious contrast between his reputation among his contemporaries and in subsequent periods.

In the popular imagination of today his name is indissolubly linked with that of Laura,

> "La bella giovenetta ch'ora è donna"
> *(Rime* No. 127)

This tradition reaches back many centuries; in fact it had originated shortly after his death. To the majority of the generations of his admirers, Petrarch has been primarily the lover of Laura and the author of the *Rime,* the sonnets and songs which he began in his youth and in which he never tired of singing of his love. Among Italians and non-Italians the image and fame of that Petrarch are just as much alive today as they were vivid towards the end of the fourteenth century when Geoffrey Chaucer glorified him in the *Canterbury Tales:*

> "Frauceys Petrak, the lauriat poete,
> Highte this clerk, whose rethorike sweete
> Enlumyned al Ytaille of poetrie."

Through the mastery of language in his Italian poetry Petrarch not only made an everlasting contribution to world literature, but also rendered a very specific service to the development and moulding of the language of his own country. Since the Renaissance literary historians have referred to him as "the father of the Italian language," a title which he shares with the two other great Florentines of the fourteenth century, Dante and Boccaccio.

By later generations Petrarch was considered an initiator in still another respect. Through the influence of the *Rime* he became the originator of a whole school of poetry, that of the "Petrarchists," which appeared soon after his death both inside and outside Italy. He had brought his favourite form of expression, the sonnet, to such a classical perfection that for centuries to come he remained the admired and widely imitated model of many poets who endeavoured to write in the same pattern. For the Elizabethan period witness the statement made in 1593 by Gabriel Harvey in his *Pierces Supererogation:* "All the noblest Italian, French, and Spanish poets have in their several veins Petrarchized; and it is no dishonour for the daintiest or divinest muse to be his scholar, whom the amiablest invention and beautifullest elocution acknowledge their master." Among these Petrarchists of the Renaissance we find Sir Thomas Wyatt and the Earl of Surrey in England, the group of the *Pléiade* with their leader Ronsard in France.

In marked contrast to the judgment of posterity, Petrarch's own generation, however, found his principal merit in his Latin writings, not in his Italian poetry.

This contemporary estimate is most clearly shown by the fact that it was the authorship of the Latin epic *Africa* and not that of the *Rime* which brought Petrarch, in 1341, at the age of thirty-seven, the famous crown of the poet laureateship on the Roman Capitol. According to the tradition of the fourteenth century, in antiquity this ceremony had symbolized the greatest tribute which could be given to a living poet. To Petrarch's contemporaries no one was deemed more worthy of this ancient honour than he who seemed to re-embody the classical ideal. Through the conscious imitation of the *Aeneid* and the *Eclogues* in his own *Africa* and *Carmen Bucolicum* he appeared to have become a second Vergil. Moreover his numerous treatises dealing with problems of moral philosophy and especially the content and style of his hundreds of widely circulated letters placed him in juxtaposition with Cicero. And as King Robert the Wise of Naples asked Petrarch for the dedication of the *Africa* to himself, so the German Emperor Charles IV requested later on the same honour for Petrarch's main historical work, the collection of Roman biographies entitled *De viris illustribus,* in which Petrarch recounted the lives and deeds of the great political and military leaders of ancient Rome in order to inspire his readers to similar accomplishments.

Throughout all these various Latin writings Petrarch pursued the same purpose: he wished to teach his Italian contemporaries not to regard the great Roman statesmen and writers as figures of a dead past, but to look upon them as living models for the present and as harbingers of the future. The Italians alone, not "barbarians" like the French or Germans, Petrarch asserted, had a legitimate claim to the Latin inheritance. In the acceptance of this Roman legacy Petrarch saw an instrument of spiritual unity for his fellow-countrymen. With this motive he devoted many of his Latin poems, treatises, and letters to the task of awakening the consciousness of this legacy in the hearts and minds of the Italians of his day.

In this sense, then, Petrarch again stands at the beginning of a very important evolution in Italian culture, the great movement known as "the Revival of Antiquity" or "Humanism." He was destined to direct and stimulate these new ideas in many significant ways, as for instance through his zealous effort to write in a "pure," i.e., classical, Latin style, through his tireless and often extremely successful search for ancient manuscripts, and through his gift for textual emendation. In contrast to many of the later humanists, this "father of Humanism" did not, however, study Latin primarily from an antiquarian point of view, since for him this language was the medium through which the greatest aesthetic, intellectual, and political tradition ever created had found its timeless expression. It was as the voice of this tradition that Petrarch was most admired and revered in his lifetime. This reputation of Petrarch within his own generation has been well characterized in Jakob Burckhardt's *Civilization of the Renaissance in Italy:* "Petrarch, who lives in the memory of most people of today chiefly as a great Italian poet, owed his fame among his contemporaries far more to the fact that he was a kind of living representative of Antiquity."

In view of the fact that there exists such a divergence of opinion in the evaluation of the main aspects of Petrarch's lifework and such variety in the judgments rendered by his own generation and by posterity, it seems worth asking what conceptions Petrarch had concerning himself and his work. It is quite easy to find an answer to this question. For Petrarch was fully conscious of the fact that his life and work represented a unique and interesting phenomenon. Thus he says in the first sonnet of his *Rime:*

> ". . . I have seen enough that in this land
> To the whole people like a tale I seem"

When Petrarch wrote these lines in the proem to the collection of his *Rime,* he had reached the summit of his fame. He could rightly assume that to Italian and non-Italian eyewitnesses his accomplishments and his rise to glory would appear "like a tale." Naturally he wished this "tale" to be perpetuated accurately beyond the memory of his contemporaries, and consequently around the year 1351 he wrote a letter which he addressed explicitly "To Posterity." Later he included this epistle, in a revised form, in the first collection of his letters called the *Familiares,* and thus made sure that the letter would actually come down to future generations.

The stated purpose of this letter is to tell posterity "what sort of man I was and what was the fate of my works." There is no better account of the main events during the first part of Petrarch's life than that given by himself in this "Letter to Posterity."

He introduces himself with a description of his outward appearance: "In my early days my bodily frame was of no great strength, but of great activity. I cannot boast of extreme comeliness, but only such as in my greener years would be pleasing. My complexion was lively, between fair and dark, my eyes sparkling, my sight very keen for a long time until it failed me unexpectedly after my sixtieth year, so that to my disgust I had to have recourse to glasses."

After this portrait of himself he begins the tale of his life: "I was but a mortal mannikin like yourself, with an origin neither very high nor very low ... I was of honourable parents, both natives of Florence but living in exile on a scanty fortune which was, to tell the truth, verging upon poverty. During this exile I was born at Arezzo, in the year of Christ 1304 of this present age, at dawn on Monday the 20th of July ... The first year of my life, or rather part of it, I spent at Arezzo where I first saw the light; the six following years, after my mother had been recalled from exile, at Incisa, an estate of my father's about fourteen miles from Florence. My eighth year I passed at Pisa, my ninth and following years in Transalpine Gaul on the left bank of the Rhone. The name of the city is Avignon, where the Roman Pontiff holds, and has long held, the Church of Christ in a shameful exile ... There then, on the banks of that most windy of rivers, I passed my boyhood under my parents' care, and, later, all my early manhood under my own vain fancies—not, however, without long intervals of absence. For during this time I spent four whole years at Carpentras, a small town not far east of Avignon; and in these two places I learnt a smattering of Grammar, Dialectic and Rhetoric suited to my age—as much, I mean, as is generally learnt in schools—and how little that is, dear reader, you know well enough. Then I went to Montpellier to study Law, where I spent four more years; and then three years at Bologna where I heard the whole Corpus of Civil Law, and was thought by many to be a youth of great promise if I would only persevere in what I had taken up. However, I abandoned that study altogether as soon as my parents abandoned the care of me; not because I did not respect the authority of Law, which is doubtless great and full of that Roman Antiquity in which I delight, but because it is degraded by the villainy of those who practise it. And so I revolted at learning thoroughly that what I would not turn to dishonourable, and could scarcely turn to honourable, uses; for such rectitude, if I had tried it, would have been laid to ignorance. Accordingly, in my twenty-second year (1326) I returned to Avignon—my exile home, where I had lived from the close of my childhood, for habit is second nature."

Petrarch continues to relate that there in Avignon he gained the friendship and patronage of many distinguished men. Among these patrons he mentions particularly some members of the great Roman family of Colonna who resided at that time at the papal court. He does not tell that after his renunciation of law he took minor orders which entitled him to receive ecclesiastical prebends without becoming a priest. He had now become "a worthy clerk," as Chaucer calls him in the prologue to *The Clerk's Tale*.

During that period, Petrarch's account goes on, "a youthful longing impelled me to travel through France and Germany; and though other causes were feigned to recommend my going to my superiors, yet the real reason was an eager enthusiasm to see the world. On that journey I first saw Paris; and I took delight in finding out the truth or falsehood of what I had heard about that city. Having returned thence, I went to Rome, which from my infancy I had ardently desired to see. And there I so venerated Stefano Colonna, the noble-minded father of that family, who was like one of the ancient heroes, and I was so kindly received by him in return, that you could scarcely have detected a difference between me and one of his own sons."

On his return from Rome, in 1337, Petrarch decided to establish himself in Vaucluse. According to the "Letter to Posterity" these were his reasons: "I could not overcome my natural ingrained repugnance to Avignon, that most wearisome of cities. Therefore I looked about for some bypath of retreat as a harbour of refuge. And I found a narrow valley, delightful and secluded, called Vaucluse (fifteen miles from

Avignon), where the Sorgues, king of all fountains, takes its rise. Charmed with the sweetness of the spot, I betook myself thither with my books. It would be a long story if I were to go on to relate what I did there during many, many years. Suffice it to say that nearly every one of my works was either accomplished or begun or conceived there; and these works have been so numerous that they exercise and weary me to this day."

Now Petrarch's tale comes to the supreme moment of his life, his coronation as poet laureate: "While I was spinning out my leisure in Vaucluse, on one and the same day, strange to relate, letters reached me both from the Senate of the city of Rome and from the Chancellor of the University of Paris, bringing me rival invitations to accept the laurel crown of poetry—the former at Rome, the latter at Paris. In my youthful pride at such an honour, thinking I must be worthy of it as such eminent men so thought me, but weighing their verdict instead of my own merit, I yet hesitated for a while which invitation to accept. And on this point I asked by letter for the advice of Cardinal Giovanni Colonna. He was so near that although I had written late in the day, I received his answer the next morning before nine o'clock. In accordance with his advice I decided for the dignity of the city of Rome as superior to all others, and my two replies to him applauding that advice are still extant. I set out accordingly, and though, like all young men, I was a very partial judge of my own works, I still blushed to accept the verdict upon myself even of those who had invited me. Yet no doubt they would not have done so if they had not judged me worthy of the honour so offered. I determined, therefore, first to visit Naples, and appear before that distinguished king and philosopher, Robert—as illustrious in literature as in station, the only king of our time who was a friend of learning and of virtue alike—to see what judgment he would pass upon me. I still wonder at his flattering estimate of me and the kindly welcome that he gave me; and you, reader, if you knew of it, would wonder no less. On hearing of the reason of my coming, he was marvelously delighted, and considered that my youthful confidence in him—perhaps, too, the honour that I was seeking—might be a source of glory to himself, since I had chosen him of all men as the only competent judge in such case. Need I say more? After numberless conversations on various matters, I showed him that epic of mine, the *Africa,* with which he was so delighted that he begged me as a great favour to dedicate it to him—a request which I certainly could not refuse, nor did I wish to do so. At length he fixed a day for my visit and kept me from noon to evening. And since the time proved too short for the press of subjects, he did the same on the following two days. After having fully probed my ignorance for three days, he adjudged me worthy of the laurel crown. His wish was to bestow it upon me at Naples, and he earnestly begged me to consent. But my love of Rome prevailed over even the reverend importunity of so great a king. Therefore, when he saw that my resolution was inflexible, he gave me messengers and letters to the Roman Senate in which he declared his judgment of me in flattering terms. This royal estimate was then, indeed, in accord with that of many others, and especially with my own. Today, however, I cannot approve his verdict, though it agreed with that of myself and others. Affection for me and interest in my youth had more weight with him than consideration of the facts. So I arrived at Rome, and unworthy as I was, yet with confident reliance on such a verdict, I gained the poetic laurel while still a raw scholar with great applause from those of the Romans who could be present at the ceremony. On this subject, too, there are letters of mine, both in verse and in prose."

In the retrospective view of the "Letter to Posterity" Petrarch concludes the account of this event with a rather disillusioned comment: "This laurel gained for me no knowledge, but rather much envy, but that also is too long a story to be told here."

It may be true that in the full maturity of his age Petrarch sincerely regretted his early desire for "empty glory" and his "youthful audacity" in accepting the honour of the coronation. But there is no doubt that at the time of the event itself he drew a deep inspiration for his work from his public and official acclaim as "a great poet and historian." He himself tells in the "Letter to Posterity" why it was that after his departure from Rome he resolved to finish his Latin epic *Africa* which he always considered his greatest title to fame: "I was mindful of the honour I had just received and anxious that it should not seem to be conferred on one who was unworthy of it. And so one day when, during a visit to the mountains, I had chanced upon the wood called Selvapiana across the river Enza on the confines of Reggio, I was fired by the beauty of the place and turned my pen to my interrupted poem, the *Africa*. Finding my enthusiasm, which had seemed quite dead, rekindled, I wrote a little that very day and some on each successive day until I returned to Parma. There ... in a short time I brought the work to a conclusion, toiling at it with a zeal that amazes me today." And in the last book of the *Africa* he did not hesitate to insert, in the form of a prophecy, an account of his coronation, "such as Rome has not seen for a thousand years."

While it is thus certain that Petrarch's greatest Latin poem owed its completion to the stimulus of the laurel crown, we might digress here for a moment from the account of the "Letter to Posterity," to point out that it seems at least probable that Petrarch's greatest Italian poem, the canzone "Italia mia," was conceived under the same inspiration. This fervent appeal for Italian unity is addressed to the Italian princes.

> "In whose hands Fortune has put the rein
> Of the beautiful places . . ."
> (*Rime* No. 128)

It is significant that Petrarch, a poet, not a man of politics, makes himself the mouthpiece of all his fellow countrymen when he reminds the rulers of Italy of their common inheritance of "the gentle Latin blood" and implores them not to call in "barbaric" mercenaries from abroad and not "to ruin the loveliest country of the earth." He places his hopes for the unification and pacification of contemporary Italy in the revival of the ancient *virtus Romana:*

> "Virtue will fight and soon the debt be paid:
> For the old gallantry
> In the Italian hearts is not yet dead."

It is interesting to recall that Machiavelli concludes his *Prince* with "an exhortation to liberate Italy from the barbarians," and that he ends this final chapter with the quotation of those very verses of Petrarch.

There seems to be hardly any other moment in Petrarch's life in which he could feel better entitled to utter such an exhortation than that period following his coronation when he had been acknowledged symbolically not only as the greatest living poet of Italy, but also as the resuscitator of the spirit of ancient grandeur. It is by this spirit that "Italia mia" is inspired. In this canzone Petrarch created a poem which, because of its leitmotiv of national unity, might rightly be called the first Italian anthem. But beyond that he distinguished these verses by an intensity of feeling so powerful that all his readers, regardless of their national origin, then found it and have since found it a timeless expression of their sentiments towards their native country:

> "Is not this the dear soil for which I pined?
> Is not this my own nest
> Where I was nourished and was given life?
> Is not this the dear land in which we trust,
> Mother loving and kind
> Who shelters parents, brother, sister, wife?"

It is most significant that for the first time in the history of the western world patriotic feeling had found articulate expression in poetry and had come to consciousness in a man who had grown up and lived in exile and who, therefore, could more clearly perceive the idea of supreme unity which was hidden to the resident citizens through their very entanglement in local rivalry and disunity.

The "tale" of Petrarch's life had reached its climax on the Capitoline in the spring of 1341 and during the period of the greatest productivity of his poetical genius. From the artistic point of view it appears logical, then, that in his "Letter to Posterity" Petrarch deals only very briefly with the events during the ten years following his coronation and that he breaks off his account rather abruptly with the year 1351, never to take it up again. For everything he had to narrate concerning the second half of his life would have seemed anticlimactic in comparison with the story of his dramatic rise during the first half. Even more, the account would have necessarily become a record of Petrarch's increasing pessimism and feeling of personal frustration and disillusionment. The hopes which he continued to have for the pacification and unification of Italy were destined to remain unfulfilled, whether he was to place them on the Italian princes or on the Roman Tribune of the People, Cola di Rienzo, or on the German Emperor Charles IV. The fervent exhortations which he addressed to successive popes, admonishing them to return from Avignon to Rome, met with little or no response. To his passionate feelings against Avignon as the seat of the Frenchified papal court he gave frequent expression in both his Latin and Italian writings, as for instance in the *Rime* (Nr. 138) where he denounces the hated city as:

> "Fountain of sorrow, dwelling of revolts,
> The school of errors, place of heresy,
> Once Rome, now Babylon wicked and false,
> For which the world suffers in infamy;"

The nearness of hateful Avignon poisoned even Petrarch's love for Vaucluse where since 1337 he had so often sought refuge from the turmoil of the world and found inward peace and stimulation for his work. Thus in 1353 Petrarch decided to bring to an end his sojourn of more than forty years in southern France and to go back to Italy.

It was an outwardly restless life Petrarch spent during his remaining years in northern Italy. He did not choose to take up permanent residence in any one place, not even in his native Florence where he had been offered, at the instigation of his friend and admirer Boccaccio, a professorship at the university. The Italian princes, among them the powerful Visconti family in Milan, as well as the patrician rulers of Venice, considered it a great honour when the poet accepted their hospitality. Petrarch's democratic and republican friends deplored the close relationship into which the herald of the grandeur of the Roman Republic seemed to have entered with the "tyrants" of his age. Petrarch defied these complaints, for he never considered himself the servant of any prince or the tool of any interest contrary to his own convictions. Free from all obligations of office, in complete independence, he lived solely for his literary work and for the cause of the revival of the eternal standards and universal values of classical antiquity.

If we can trust an old report, death overcame Petrarch in the midst of his studies late at night on July 18, 1374, while he was working in the library of his country house in Arquà near Padua.

An examination of Petrarch's literary opera shows that in the most complete edition, that of the year 1554, the various Latin works and letters occupy almost twenty times as much space as the Italian poetry, the *Rime* and the *Trionfi*. Thus Petrarch's Latin writings do not merely outweigh those in the vernacular in actual volume, but they seem also to have had definite preponderance in the mind and judgment of the author himself. For in the "Letter to Posterity" he speaks in some detail about most of the Latin works which he had written or begun by that time, but he does not mention specifically the collection of his Italian *Rime*. That this omission was not simply accidental becomes evident from the following passage in the same epistle: "My mind was rather well balanced than acute; and while adapted to all good and wholesome studies, its special bent was towards moral philosophy and poetry. But the latter I neglected, as time went on, because of the delight I took in sacred literature. In this I found a hidden sweetness, though at one time I had despised it, so that I came to use poetry only as an accomplishment. I devoted myself singly, amid a crowd of subjects, to a knowledge of Antiquity; for this age of ours

I have always found distasteful, so that, had it not been for the love of those dear to me, I should have preferred to have been born in any other."

This passage leaves no doubt as to which part of his work Petrarch himself considered most important. From his own point of view the judgment of his contemporaries certainly was right and that of later generations wrong. He himself desired to be renowned, above all else, for his "single devotion to the knowledge of Antiquity," and not for his Italian poetry.

The fact that Petrarch gave his personal preference to his humanistic endeavours and accomplishments ought not, however, to compel us to believe that he actually meant to disavow his Italian writings altogether. It is true that in a letter written two years before his death, he called his poems in the vernacular "little trifles" and "juvenile fooleries" and expressed the wish that "they might be unknown to the whole world and even to myself if that could be." But notwithstanding this wish for their obliteration, Petrarch, from the record of his work, actually took the greatest personal care in preserving and editing these very same poems. When in mid-life he decided to collect his "scattered rhymes" (*Rime* No. 1) in one volume, he never ceased working over them throughout the rest of his days, striving to bring them to what he considered the point of perfection.

The clearest evidence of the painstaking effort Petrarch made in this task of polishing his verse is manifestly shown by the great number of corrections and marginal notes in his working copy of the *Rime* which is preserved today in the Vatican Library. A few examples may suffice to illustrate this point. On the margin of the sonnet "Non fûr ma' Giove" (*Rime* No. 155) Petrarch remarks: "Note that I had once in mind to change the order of the four stanzas so that the first quatrain and the first terzina would have become second and vice versa. But I gave the idea up because of the sound of the beginning and the end. For (in the case of a change) the fuller sound would have been in the middle and the hollower sound at the beginning and at the end; this, however, is against the laws of rhetoric."

Another marginal note (to *Rime* No. 199) gives an interesting glimpse into Petrarch's working habits: "In 1368," he jots down, "on Friday, August the 19th, sleepless for a long time during the first watch of the night, I at last got up and came by chance upon this very old poem, composed twenty-five years ago." That Petrarch gave a great deal of thought to determining which of his earlier poems were worthy of inclusion in his final collection is well demonstrated by the following note at the end of the sonnet "Voglia mi sprona" (*Rime* No. 211): "Amazing. This poem was once crossed out by me and condemned. Now, by chance reading it again after a lapse of many years, I have acquitted it and copied it and put it in the right place. Shortly afterwards, however, on the 27th, in the evening, I made some changes in the final lines, and now I shall have finished with it."

Within the limited compass of this essay it is impossible to go into the intricate problems involving the chronology, the variant forms and arrangements of Petrarch's collection of sonnets and songs. It will be sufficient to state that despite his solemn declarations to the contrary Petrarch never, even during his old age, lost his interest in his "juvenile fooleries" but continued editing and re-editing them to the last. He worked on them until his sense of artistry was truly satisfied. There is tangible evidence of his own critical approval in the frequent recurrence of the word *placet* on the margins of his working copy. And if there is a legitimate suspicion that Petrarch was not quite candid in the denial of his personal interest in his Italian poems, the same doubt can assail our acceptance of the sincerity of his wish that "they might be unknown to the whole world." For he knew very well from the study of his beloved antiquity that glory depends solely on true distinction in whatever field of activity an individual might choose. In his own incessant striving after perfection he must, therefore, have been greatly inspired and impelled by the desire for approval of these poems by readers in his own era as well as in coming centuries.

In the final collection of his verse Petrarch included three hundred and sixty-six poems. Of this number, three hundred and seventeen were written as sonnets, twenty-nine as *canzoni,* nine as *sestine,* seven as *ballate,* and four as madrigals. The collection has no definite title but is known in Italian simply by the generic names of *Canzoniere* or *Rime,* or somewhat more specifically, *Rime Sparse.* For in contrast to Dante, who assembled his poems to Beatrice in a book named by himself *La Vita Nuova,* Petrarch never chose a precise name for his collected poems but was content to call them rather vaguely *Rerum vulgarium fragmenta,* "Fragments," or better "Pieces of matters written in the vernacular." This absence of a concrete title does not seem to be wholly fortuitous. For again in contrast to Dante's *Vita Nuova,* Petrarch's *Rime* do not form an organic unit but are in truth "scattered rhymes," as Petrarch calls them himself in the proem to the collection. The content of most of the longer poems is political, religious, or moral in nature whereas the theme of the overwhelming majority of the sonnets is Petrarch's love for Laura. The author did not arrange his poems according to their poetical form nor apparently did he attempt to divide the long series of the love sonnets to Laura into definite "sequences," although there are to be found certain groups of poems which are more closely interrelated than others.

Some of Petrarch's most beautiful verse is contained in his *canzoni,* as for instance in "Spirto gentil," "Italia mia," or "Vergine bella." But it was especially in the sonnet that his genius found the most adequate mode of expression. Petrarch did not invent the form of the sonnet. It had appeared long before his time and flourished greatly in the school of poets writing in the "dolce stil novo," which reached its climax with Dante. He surpassed, however, all his predecessors in the fashion in which he perfected the traditional form and filled it with a content at once richer and more variegated than ever before. The brevity of the fourteen lines actually permits no more than the expression of one idea or one mood or one emotion. These perceptions and feelings, however, are not allowed to remain vague and fleeting but are submitted to the discipline of rigid form. As no other poet before and only few after him, Petrarch, in many of his sonnets, succeeded in striking this delicate balance of form and content and in establishing a true harmony of feeling and thinking. As the unsurpassed master of the love sonnet of his day Petrarch became, as has been shown before, the model of innumerable sonneteers, in Italy as well as abroad, who were fully conscious of their discipleship and even proud of their denomination as "Petrarchists."

In creating the glory of the Italian sonnet Petrarch can lay claim to still another distinction, the tone colour which is one of the most outstanding characteristics of his Italian poetry. In this connection it is worth noting that the Italian terms *sonetto* and *canzone* are derived from the words for "sound" and "song." This derivation tells us very clearly that poems written in these particular two forms were meant to be intoned and that consequently their authors needed musical as well as literary talent. Petrarch in full measure possessed the gifts of the musician. His contemporary biographer, the Florentine Filippo Villani, states: "He played the lyre admirably. His voice was sonorous and overflowing with charm and sweetness." Among the few personal possessions which Petrarch deemed worthy of specific mention in his last will there appears "my good lyre."

In the working copy of his *Rime* we find the following note to one of his sonnets: "I must make these two verses over again, singing them (*cantando*), and I must transpose them. —3 o'clock in the morning, October the 19th." No better testimony than this intimate self-reminder can be found to illustrate both the importance which Petrarch attributed to the musical qualities of his verse and the method which he used to test these qualities. Whoever reads his sonnets and songs aloud in their rich Italian will immediately be impressed by their melodiousness and will readily agree with Filippo Villani who says: "His rhythms flow so sweetly that not even the gravest people can withstand their declamation and sound." Some of Petrarch's most beautiful verse, the poems in honour of the Virgin, were set to music by the greatest composer of the Italian Renaissance, Palestrina, in his *Madrigali Spirituali.*

The theme of the overwhelming majority of Petrarch's *Rime* is his love for Laura. This fact has led many editors since the sixteenth century to divide the collection up into two parts, the first containing the poems written "In vita di Madonna Laura," the second one consisting of those "In morte di Madonna Laura," beginning with the moving lamentation of the sonnet "Oimè il bel viso" (*Rime* No. 267). Although this division cannot be directly traced back to Petrarch himself there is no doubt that the main theme of the sonnets is Petrarch's love for Laura "in life and in death."

Who was Laura? With this question we come to that problem which more than almost any other has attracted the attention of scholars working on Petrarch and has, to an even greater degree, challenged and fascinated the popular imagination.

The crux of the problem is that Petrarch himself, both in his *Rime* and in his Latin writings, chose to give only very few details of a concrete nature concerning Laura and her personal circumstances. This discretion on the part of Petrarch in regard to the central figure in his life becomes particularly manifest in his "Letter to Posterity." For although in this epistle he speaks of a good many of his close friends in some detail, he condenses all he has to say about the person presumably nearest to his heart in one sentence: "In my youth I suffered from an attachment of the keenest kind, but constant to one, and honourable; and I should have suffered longer, had not death —bitter indeed, but useful—extinguished the flame as it was beginning to subside." The marked restraint and the curious detachment make it very evident that in this autobiographical record written for the perusal of later generations Petrarch was resolved to gloss over the crucial importance of Laura in his life, just as he attempted, in the same document, to belittle the significance and the value of those *Rime* whose principal theme was his love for Laura.

When not thinking of himself in the light of posterity but writing solely for his own record, Petrarch had a good deal more to say about Laura. It was his habit to make notes on the most intimate details of his personal life in the most cherished book of his library, on the fly-leaf of his manuscript of Vergil's works. There appears the following entry: "Laura, illustrious by her own virtues and long celebrated in my poems, first appeared to my eyes in the earliest period of my manhood, on the sixth day of April, anno Domini 1327, in the Church of St. Claire, at the morning hour. And in the same city at the same hour of the same day in the same month of April, but in the year 1348, that light was withdrawn from our day, while I was by chance at Verona, ignorant—alas!—of my fate. The unhappy tidings reached me at Parma in a letter from my friend Louis on the morning of May the 19th in the same year. Her chaste and lovely body was laid in the Church of the Franciscans on the very day of her death at evening. Her soul, however, I am persuaded—as Seneca says of Africanus—has returned to heaven whence it came. I have felt a kind of bitter sweetness in writing this, as a memorial of a painful matter—especially in this place which often comes under my eyes—so that I may reflect that no pleasures remain for me in this life, and that I may be warned by constantly looking at these words and by the thought of the rapid flight of years that it is high time to flee from the world. This, by God's preventing grace, will be easy to me when I keenly and manfully consider the empty, superfluous hopes of the past, and the unforeseen issue."

Neither in this most intimate record nor anywhere else does Petrarch say who Laura actually was. In truth, he kept this secret so well that apparently even among his closest friends the suspicion arose that "Laura" was merely a fictitious name for an imaginary love and that the word stood not so much for the name of a real person as for Petrarch's dearest goal in life, the "laurel," symbol of the poet's fame. Indeed Petrarch himself liked to play upon the similarity between the name of Laura and the Latin and Italian words for laurel. Against the charge of feigned love Petrarch defended himself in a letter written in 1336 to his intimate friend Giacomo Colonna,

Bishop of Lombez, as follows: "You actually say that I have invented the name of 'Laura' in order to have some one to talk about, and in order to set people talking about me, but that, in reality, I have no 'Laura' in mind, except that poetical laurel to which I have aspired, as my long and unwearied toil bears witness; and as to this breathing 'laurel,' with whose beauty I seem to be charmed, all that is 'made up'—the songs feigned, the sighs pretended. On this point would that your jests were true! Would that it were a pretense, and not a madness! But, credit me, it takes much trouble to keep up a pretense for long; while to spend useless toil in order to appear mad would be the height of madness. Besides, though by acting we can feign sickness when we are well, we cannot feign actual pallor. You know well both my pallor and my weariness; and so I fear you are making sport of my disease by that Socratic diversion called 'irony,' in which even Socrates must yield the palm to you."

This letter is a convincing proof of the genuineness of Petrarch's love, but it is again noteworthy that even in this self-defense he did not deign to reveal the identity of the actual Laura. As the result of Petrarch's silence concerning the real circumstances of Laura's life there arose soon and grew and flourished throughout the centuries almost to the present a Laura-legend which was an interesting composite of romantic and fanciful imagination, pseudo-scholarly research, and half-truth. It would lead into too many bypaths to follow the story of this legend. May it suffice to say that according to modern scholarship it seems likely that the "historical" Laura was the daughter of a Provençal nobleman, Audibert de Noves, that she was married to Hugues de Sade, and that Petrarch probably met her for the first time about two years after her marriage.

That the object of Petrarch's love was a married woman and the mother of several children was a hypothesis that ran contrary to the popular and sentimental romanticization of the two lovers and their relationship, and for that reason this thesis was long and bitterly contested. But actually the "real" Laura does not matter at all. For whatever the facts of her life might have been, they do not provide us with any "background" for a better understanding of the collection of the *Rime* in the form in which Petrarch wanted them to endure. If he had not burnt many of his earlier poems, as he did according to his own statement, the picture would perhaps be quite different. But his final collection does not present a narrative pattern or sequence, and all attempts have completely failed to crystallize an account of a romance out of the *Rime*.

Everything the more curious need know for the understanding of the nature of Petrarch's relationship with Laura, he himself has told in the self-analysis of his book called the *Secretum* which he composed in the form of a dialogue between himself and St. Augustine as his father confessor. He started writing this work in 1342 while Laura was still alive and finished it a few years after her death. Therein he states: "Whatever little I am, I have become through her. For if I possess any name and fame at all, I should never have obtained them unless she had cared with her most noble affection for the sparse seeds of virtues planted in my bosom by Nature." Laura's mind, Petrarch says, "does not know earthly cares but burns with heavenly desires. Her appearance truly radiates beams of divine beauty. Her morals are an example of perfect uprightness. Neither her voice nor the force of her eyes nor her gait are those of an ordinary human being." Petrarch asserts emphatically that he had "always loved her soul more than her body," though he has to admit that, under the compulsion of love and youth, "occasionally I wished something dishonourable."

But the purity of the relationship was saved by Laura, for "not moved by any entreaties nor conquered by any flatteries, she protected her womanly honour and remained impregnable and firm in spite of her youth and mine and in spite of many and various other things which ought to have bowed the spirit of even the most adamant. This strength of character of the woman recalled seemly conduct to the mind of the man. The model of her excellence stood before me so that in my own strife for chastity I lacked neither her example nor her reproach. And when finally she saw me break the bridle and fall (this is obviously a reference to a love affair with another woman), she left me rather than follow my course."

Eventually Petrarch succeeded in conquering himself, for in the dialogue he assures St. Augustine: "Now I know what I want and wish, and my unstable mind has become firm. She, on her part, has always been steadfast and has always stayed one and the same. The better I understand her womanly constancy, the more I admire it. If once I was grieved by her unyielding resolution, I am now full of joy over it and thankful." It was for spiritual reasons that Petrarch felt a sense of profound gratitude towards Laura, as he makes clear both in the *Secretum* and in the moving lines of thanksgiving in one of his later sonnets:

> "I thank her soul and her holy device
> That with her face and her sweet anger's bolts
> Bid me in burning think of my salvation."
>
> (*Rime* No. 289)

The autobiographical account in the *Secretum* provides the most valuable clue to the right understanding of Petrarch's conception of Laura's image and his relationship with her, as they are reflected in the *Rime*. For a clear comprehension of the passages quoted it should be remembered that they do not represent simply a personal record but are set forth in the solemn form of an imaginary dialogue with Petrarch's spiritual guide and conscience, St. Augustine. In this dialogue, which has an almost confessional character, Petrarch naturally felt bound to reveal himself fully and frankly, even if this meant his candid admission of aberrations from the right path of acting and feeling. It is purely incidental that he has satisfied our curiosity about certain external details of his relationship with Laura.

On the other hand, it is most significant that he depicted this relationship as one in which were linked together two beings who belonged to two entirely different spheres and therefore acted in an entirely different fashion. Whereas he himself was an ordinary human being with all of man's passions and desires, Laura was above earthly cares and burnt solely with heavenly desires. Whereas his own personality and sentiments underwent many radical changes, she remained always one and the same. The climax of this love was reached when Petrarch, inspired by the example of Laura's perfection, masters himself and his desires and begins, under her guidance, to strive for the salvation of his soul.

What Petrarch has recounted in the prose of his *Secretum* as his personal confession to St. Augustine, he has expressed in the lyrics of his *Rime* to all

> ". . . who hear in scattered rhymes the sound
> Of that wailing with which I fed my heart."
> (*Rime* No. 1)

For in the *Rime* he gives us the rapture of love in which there is only one subject, the man, who alone speaks and feels, acts and changes, while the woman is but the mute and passive object of this love, an ideal and therefore immutable being.

This ideal object of his love was, however, not imaginary or fictitious. As if to refute any doubt as to the existence of a "real" Laura, Petrarch makes repeatedly very specific chronological statements in the *Rime* themselves concerning the dates of his first meeting with Laura and of her death. Petrarch obviously had very good reasons for such an inclusion of dates into his verse, for his musical ear must have protested against these attempts at fitting bare figures into a rigid metre.

In other ways, too, Petrarch tries to assure his readers of Laura's reality. He describes her appearance, her golden hair and her fair eyes, or he pictures her in the beauty of nature, "walking on the green grass, pressing the flowers like a living girl." But all these descriptions are rather limited in range, for her beauty and charm are beyond the power of the poet's pen, as he himself confesses:

> ". . . I still seem to pass
> Over your beauty in my rhyme . . .
> But the burden I find crushes my frame

The work cannot be polished by my file.
And my talent which knows its strength and style
In this attempt becomes frozen and lame."
(*Rime* No. 20)

Petrarch is aware that he will be criticized for his endeavour to enshrine her above others in his song and that the temper of his praise will be considered false, but he cannot accept such criticism. For he knows that no matter what he says he will never be able to express his thoughts in verse as well as he feels them enclosed in his breast (*Rime* No. 95).

Eventually Laura assumes an ideal nature such as is disclosed in one of the sonnets in words which are almost identical with the quoted passage from the *Secretum:*

"In what part of the sky, in what idea
Was the example from which Nature wrought
That charming lovely face wherein she sought
To show her power in the upper sphere?"
(*Rime* No. 159)

This conception of Laura as the sublime ideal, expressed in terms strongly reminiscent of Platonic thought, shows most clearly the transformation which the picture of the "real" Laura had undergone in the poet's mind: she has become the image of the concept of the beautiful, and we might add from the reading of other poems in the *Rime,* the embodiment, too, of good and the right. The ultimate transfiguration of Laura is attained in one of the later sonnets where his

". . . inner eye
Sees her soar up and with the angels fly
At the feet of our own eternal Lord."
(*Rime* No. 345)

While Laura is thus elevated into "the upper sphere," Petrarch himself remains earthbound. The object of his love is an ideal, but his feelings for his beloved are human. From the time when, at the age of twenty-three, he met Laura first in the church in Avignon, to her death twenty-one years later, and from that time to his own death, this was the focusing passion of his life:

"I have never been weary of this love,
My lady, nor shall be while last my years,
(*Rime* No. 82)

Petrarch runs the whole gamut of emotions and passions of a lover, from the highest elation to the deepest despair. In this full scale only one note is missing which in ordinary love would naturally mark the supreme moment: the exaltation of physical consummation. That the love for Laura, by its very nature, was denied fulfillment in the common sense, has to be understood as the mode to which the whole tone of Petrarch's sonnets and songs is pitched. For above all the *Rime* sing of the sad and woeful beauty of love, of the longing for the unattainable, of the rebellion against denial, of the inward laceration of the lover and of his melancholic resignation. In the *Rime* all these moods of a lover have found their timeless representation. And the very fact that the figure of Laura is so idealized has made it possible for many readers of these sonnets and songs to see in the image of Laura the picture of their own beloved and to hear in the verse of the poet the expression of their own thoughts and the echoes of their own love.

While in the exalted conception of his beloved Petrarch was still bound by the tradition of the love poetry of the Provençal troubadours and the Italian poets of the "dolce stil novo," in the representation of himself and of his own humanity he was guided by a very different source of inspiration, the model of Latin poetry of classical times. There is hardly one poem in the *Rime* which does not show more or less definite traces of this influence as to form and content, figures of speech and comparisons, symbols and allegories. Petrarch went wholeheartedly (and with full consciousness of his debt) to school to the great Roman poets. And what he learned there he absorbed so completely that even in imitating he succeeded for the most part in creating something new. The splendour and richness of the *Rime* were to a large extent based on his life-long devotion to the scholarly study of antiquity. Thus the accomplishments of Petrarch the sonneteer presuppose the research of Petrarch the humanist.

Petrarch once strikingly compares himself to the statue of Janus: like the double-faced Roman god he feels himself to be looking both backward and forward. This, his own comparison, characterizes well Petrarch's personal outlook on life. For often and with profound yearning he looked back to the glory of ancient Rome and drew from its grandeur the deepest inspiration for his work. He regarded the whole epoch of a thousand years, extending from the fall of the Roman Empire to his own days, as a period of "darkness." But throughout his life he hoped that the "revival" of the past would put an end to the process of decline and would usher in a new and better era. This ardent hope for the future Petrarch has voiced in the canzone "Italia mia" and in many other pieces, but nowhere more impressively than in that work which he himself considered as his greatest, the *Africa*. At the very end of this epic he addresses his own poem as follows: "My fate is to live amid varied and confusing storms. But for you perhaps, if, as I hope and wish, you will live long after me, there will follow a better age. This sleep of forgetfulness will not last forever. When the darkness has been dispersed, our descendants can come again in the former pure radiance."

Posterity may accept Petrarch's own judgment and may agree that the figure of Janus truly symbolizes his position in history. His outlook on the world indeed included views of two different ages. Yet to posterity his choice of the image of Janus might seem a simplification. He had, it would seem, more than the two aspects of the Roman god. Witness one of the most famous incidents in his life, the ascent of Mont Ventoux near Vaucluse, which he undertook in 1336, at the age of thirty-two. In a letter written under the immediate impression of this experience Petrarch relates how he decided to climb this mountain, "induced by the sole desire of seeing the remarkable height of the place." As a student of classical authors he knows of similar undertakings in antiquity and thus, in imitation of an ancient model, he does what no man during the Middle Ages had done, he scales a mountain with the sole motive of satisfying his curiosity. He describes in great detail the difficulties which he and his brother, his only companion, found on their way. Despite the warnings which the pair received from an old shepherd, they continue their strenuous ascent and finally reach the summit. What Petrarch sees and feels on that momentous occasion, he endeavours to express in the following sentences: "First of all, braced by the nip of the keen air and the extent of the view, I stood as dazed. I looked back; the clouds were beneath my feet. And now the stories of Athos and Olympus seem less incredible to me, as I behold on a mountain of lesser fame what I had heard and read of them. I turn my eye's glance in the direction of Italy, whither my heart most inclines. . . . I confess I sighed for the skies of Italy, which I looked upon with my mind rather than with my eyes, and an irrepressible longing seized me to behold my friend and my country."

But while he was thus gazing at the beauty of the panorama of the Alps, "a new thought" suddenly possessed him which drew him from the sight of the external world towards a consideration of himself and his past life. He thinks of Laura, saying: "What I used to love, I love no longer—nay, I lie, I do love, but with more restraint, more moderately, more regretfully." He continues: "While I marveled at these things in turn, now recognizing some earthly object, now lifting my soul upwards as my body had been, I thought of looking at the book of Augustine's *Confessions* . . . which I always have with me. I opened the little volume, of handy size but of infinite charm, in order to read whatever met my eye . . . I call God to witness, and my listener too, that these were the words on which my eyes fell: 'Men go abroad to admire the heights of mountains, and the mighty billows, and the long-winding courses of rivers, the compass of the ocean, and the courses of the stars—and themselves they neglect.' I confess I was amazed; and begging my brother, who was eager to hear more, not to trouble me, I closed the book, indignant with myself that at that very moment I was admiring earthly things—I, who ought to have learnt long ago from even heathen philosophers that there is nothing admirable but the soul—in itself so great that nothing can be great beside it. Then, indeed, content with what I had seen from the mountain, I turned my eyes inward upon myself, and from that moment none heard me say a word till we reached the bottom."

By this narrative of the ascent of Mont Ventoux Petrarch revealed himself in the whole complexity of his personality and in the diversity of his thoughts, feelings, and interests. He was the man of a new age who set out to discover the beauty of the world and relive an experience forgotten for long centuries. He was the humanist who wanted not merely to devote himself to an antiquarian study of the arts and letters, the history and philosophy of Roman days, but who desired to revive the past in the present and for the future by re-enacting what the ancients had done. He was the Italian patriot whose inner eye beheld the unity and splendour of his native country. He was the lover of Laura who was still torn in his human feelings but was beginning to conquer himself. Yet at the end he found himself bound by the traditions of medieval Christianity in which he had been brought up and which he always revered in the person and work of his great guide, St. Augustine. Thus at the culminating point of his new experience Petrarch closed his eyes to the external world and turned to the spiritual problems of his soul.

All these manifold facets of Petrarch, which the account of his impressions on the peak of Mont Ventoux illumines in a most dramatic fashion, have found their expression in the *Rime*. The essential nature remains, but the colours are much more variegated and the pattern as a whole is infinitely richer. Only the most striking parallel may be pointed out. As the story of the mountain climbing ends with spiritual reflections stimulated by the reading of St. Augustine's *Confessions,* so the collection of love poetry concludes with a devout prayer to the Virgin Mary:

> "Recommend me to your Son, to the real
> Man and the real God,
> That Heaven's nod be my ghost's peaceful seal."

Petrarch lived in an era which in the history of western civilization marks the beginning of the turn from the medieval to the modern age. Petrarch's personal views and his literary work reflect fully the transitional character of his period. For if there are characteristic medieval features to be found in Petrarch, there are also just as many traits which point to a venture into a world of new ideas. Thus the English biographer of Petrarch, Edward H. R. Tatham, rightly names him "the first modern man of letters." It is Petrarch's interest in man and in the problems of human nature that makes him "modern" and differentiates him from medieval writers. All of Petrarch's works, whether they were written in verse or in prose, in Italian or in Latin, have as their main theme the spiritual and intellectual, the emotional and artistic aspects of man's life.

But Petrarch was not only concerned with "man" in general, but was also deeply engrossed in the phenomenon of man as an individual being, as he saw him in the history of the past or as a living actor on the contemporary stage. And above all Petrarch was interested in himself and in the phenomenon of his own individuality.

"In the Middle Ages," writes Jakob Burckhardt, "both sides of human consciousness—that which was turned within as that which was turned without—lay dreaming or half awake beneath a common veil. This veil was woven of faith, illusion, and childish prepossession through which the world and history were seen clad in a strange hue." Petrarch was among the first to tear this veil away by striving for a full understanding of his own individuality through continuous self-analysis and self-portrayal, as illustrated by the "Letter to Posterity" or the *Secretum* or, above all, the *Rime*. In this sense Petrarch may be called the founder of modern humanism.

Groton, Mass.
May 18, 1946   THEODOR E. MOMMSEN

I should like to thank my friend George W. Freiday, Jr., for his many valuable suggestions and for his constructive criticism.

The quotations from the "Letter to Posterity" and the letter describing Petrarch's ascension of Mont Ventoux are from the translations by Edward H. R. Tatham in Francesco Petrarca. The first modern man of letters; his life and correspondence *(1304–1347). 2 vols. 1925/26. The Sheldon Press, London.*

T. E. M.

FIRST PART
IN LAURA'S LIFETIME

I

Voi ch'ascoltate in rime sparse il suono
Di quei sospiri ond'io nudriva 'l core
In sul mio primo giovenile errore,
Quand'era in parte altr'uom da quel ch' i' sono,

Del vario stile in ch' io piango e ragiono
Fra le vane speranze e 'l van dolore,
Ove sia chi per prova intenda amore,
Spero trovar pietá, non che perdóno.

Ma ben veggio or sí come al popol tutto
Favola fui gran tempo, onde sovente
Di me medesmo meco mi vergogno;

E del mio vaneggiar vergogna è 'l frutto,
E 'l pentersi, e 'l conoscer chiaramente
Che quanto piace al mondo è breve sogno.

II

Per fare una leggiadra sua vendetta,
E punire in un dí ben mille offese,
Celatamente Amor l'arco riprese,
Come uom ch'a nocer luogo e tempo aspetta.

Era la mia virtute al cor ristretta
Per far ivi e ne gli occhi sue difese,
Quando 'l colpo mortal lá giú discese,
Ove solea spuntarsi ogni saetta.

Però, turbata nel primiero assalto,
Non ebbe tanto né vigor né spazio
Che potesse al bisogno prender l'arme,

O vero al poggio faticoso et alto
Ritrarmi accortamente da lo strazio,
Del quale oggi vorrebbe, e non pò, aitarme.

I

O you who hear in scattered rhymes the sound
Of that wailing with which I fed my heart
In my first youthful error, when in part
I was not the same man who treads this ground,

May I find mercy, also forgiveness,
Where, after trial, science of love is deep,
For all the ways in which I talk and weep
Between vain hopes, between throes of distress.

But I have seen enough that in this land
To the whole people like a tale I seem,
So that I feel ashamed of my own name;

Of all my raving the harvest is shame,
And to repent, and clearly understand
That what pleases on earth is a swift dream.

II

To make a charming vengeance of some blow
And punish in one day a long disgrace,
Surreptitiously Love resumed his bow
Like one who to do harm bides time and place.

My virtue was constrained inside my heart
To raise there its defence, and in the eyes,
When the mortal attempt struck by surprise
Where used to be defeated every dart.

Therefore, bewildered in the first assault,
It did not find enough vigour or room
To emerge all in arms and face its doom,

Or to draw me to the high, difficult
Hill shrewdly, away from the agony
From which it would but cannot rescue me.

III

Era il giorno ch'al sol si scoloraro
Per la pietá del suo fattore i rai,
Quando i' fui preso, e non me ne guardai,
Ché i be' vostr'occhi, donna, mi legaro.

Tempo non mi parea da far riparo
Contr' a' colpi d'Amor; però m'andai
Secur, senza sospetto: onde i miei guai
Nel commune dolor s' incominciaro.

Trovommi Amor del tutto disarmato,
Et aperta la via per gli occhi al core,
Che di lagrime son fatti uscio e varco.

Però, al mio parer, non li fu onore
Ferir me de saetta in quello stato,
A voi armata non mostrar pur l'arco.

IV

Que' ch'infinita providenzia et arte
Mostrò nel suo mirabil magistero,
Che criò questo e quell'altro emispero,
E mansueto piú Giove che Marte,

Vegnendo in terra a 'lluminar le carte
Ch'avean molt'anni giá celato il vero,
Tolse Giovanni da la rete e Piero,
E nel regno del ciel fece lor parte.

Di sé, nascendo, a Roma non fe' grazia,
A Giudea sí, tanto sovr'ogni stato
Umiltate essaltar sempre gli piacque;

Ed or di picciol borgo un sol n'ha dato,
Tal che natura e 'l luogo si ringrazia
Onde sí bella donna al mondo nacque.

III

It was the day when the sun's rays turned white
Out of the pity it felt for its sire,
When I was caught and taken by desire,
For your fair eyes, my lady, held me quite.

It did not seem to me a time to mind
The blows of Love; therefore I went along
Fearless, without suspicion, and my wrong
Began with the grief common to mankind.

Love found me weak, completely without arms,
With the way clear from the eyes to the heart,
For they are doors of fears and halls of harms.

Hence to my mind it was no glorious part
For him to wound me when I was so low,
To you in arms not even show his bow.

IV

He who showed plenty and art without peer
In his wonderful might among the stars,
Who made this and the other hemisphere
And made Jupiter more peaceful than Mars,

Coming upon the earth to light the set
Of volumes that had long concealed the true,
Took away John and Peter from their net
And of his kingdom gave to them their due.

With his own birth he did not honour Rome
But Judea, so much it was his choice
Above all states to praise humility;

And now sends to a small community
A sun so great that soil and place rejoice
Where such a lovely lady found her home.

V

Quando io movo i sospiri a chiamar voi,
E 'l nome che nel cor mi scrisse Amore,
LAUdando s' incomincia udir di fòre
Il suon de' primi dolci accenti suoi.

Vostro stato REal, che 'ncontro poi,
Raddoppia a l'alta impresa il mio valore;
Ma "TAci" grida il fin, ché farle onore
È d'altri omeri soma che da' tuoi.

Cosí LAUdare e REverire insegna
La voce stessa, pur ch'altri vi chiami,
O d'ogni reverenza e d'onor degna;

Se non che forse Apollo si disdegna
Ch'a parlar de' suoi sempre verdi rami
Lingua mortal presuntuosa vegna.

VI

Sí traviato è 'l folle mi' desio
A seguitar costei che 'n fuga è volta,
E de' lacci d'Amor leggiera e sciolta
Vola dinanzi al lento correr mio,

Che quanto richiamando piú l'envio
Per la secura strada men m'ascolta;
Né mi vale spronarlo, o dargli volta,
Ch'Amor per sua natura il fa restio.

E poi che 'l fren per forza a sé raccoglie,
I' mi rimango in signoria di lui,
Che mal mio grado a morte mi trasporta;

Sol per venir al lauro, onde si coglie
Acerbo frutto, che le piaghe altrui,
Gustando, afflige piú che non conforta.

V

When I summon my sighs to call you near
With the name that Love wrote within my heart,
"LAUdable," one seems suddenly to hear
The sound of its first sweet melodies start.

Your REgal state that I wish to define
Doubles my valour to the enterprise;
"TAcitly," for her honour, the end cries,
Is load for other shoulders than are thine.

Thus to LAUd and REvere teaches and vows
The voice itself, if someone tries to call,
O worthy of all praise and reverence;

Unless perhaps Apollo take offence
That mortal tongue his ever-verdant boughs
Presumptuously endeavour to extol.

VI

My mad desire is so strayed from its place
Following one who gave herself to flight,
Who, from the bands of Love quite free and light,
Flies on before my slow, encumbered race,

That the more I call it to indicate
To it the safe road, the less its concern;
Nor does it help to spur it or to turn,
For Love makes it by nature obstinate.

And since it holds the bridle with its rage,
I am left at the mercy of its power
Which against me directs me to death's grounds,

Only to reach the laurel and its sour
Fruit that applied to other people's wounds,
Will rather poison them than assuage.

VII

La gola e 'l sonno e l'oziose piume
Hanno del mondo ogni vertú sbandita,
Ond'è dal corso suo quasi smarrita
Nostra natura vinta dal costume;

Et è sí spento ogni benigno lume
Del ciel, per cui s'informa umana vita,
Che per cosa mirabile s'addita
Chi vòl far d'Elicona nascer fiume.

Qual vaghezza di lauro? qual di mirto?
—Povera e nuda vai, Filosofia—
Dice la turba al vil guadagno intesa.

Pochi compagni avrai per l'altra via;
Tanto ti prego piú, gentile spirto,
Non lassar la magnanima tua impresa.

VIII

A pie' de' colli ove la bella vesta
Prese de le terrene membra pria
La donna che colui ch'a te n'envia
Spesso dal sonno lagrimando desta,

Libere in pace passavam per questa
Vita mortal, ch'ogni animal desia,
Senza sospetto di trovar fra via
Cosa ch'al nostr'andar fosse molesta.

Ma del misero stato ove noi semo
Condotte da la vita altra serena,
Un sol conforto, e de la morte, avemo:

Che vendetta è di lui ch'a ciò ne mena,
Lo qual in forza altrui, presso a l'estremo,
Riman legato con maggior catena.

VII

Gluttony, sleep, and the leisurely way
Have banished every virtue from the world,
And our nature is almost gone astray
From its own course, by custom downward hurled;

Every kindly light up in the skies
Is so extinguished, life's informing beam,
That an astounding sight is he who tries
To draw from Helicon a newborn stream.

Is love of laurel, love of myrtle spent?
—Naked and poor thou goest, Philosophy—
The crowd pronounces, on vile lucre bent.

You will find on that road small company,
Gentle spirit; therefore I pray and ask,
Do not desert your magnanimous task.

VIII

At the foot of the hills where the fair dress
Of earthly features for the first time knew
The lady who awakes in great distress
Often the man who now sends us to you,

We used in freedom and in peace to pass
This mortal life that to all beasts is sweet,
With no suspicion to find in the grass
A thing that might be harmful to our feet.

But from the cruel state where we have been
Reduced after the other life serene,
Only one comfort, and from death, we gain:

That revenge has been made of him who caught
Us and who quite enslaved by her, distraught,
Remains imprisoned by a greater chain.

IX

Quando 'l pianeta che distingue l'ore
Ad albergar col Tauro si ritorna,
Cade vertú da l'infiammate corna
Che veste il mondo di novel colore;

E non pur quel che s'apre a noi di fòre,
Le rive e i colli di fioretti adorna,
Ma dentro, dove giá mai non s'aggiorna,
Gravido fa di sé il terrestro umore,

Onde tal frutto e simile si colga.
Cosí costei, ch'è tra le donne un sole,
In me, movendo de' begli occhi i rai,

Cria d'amor penseri, atti e parole;
Ma, come ch'ella gli governi o volga,
Primavera per me pur non è mai.

X

Gloriosa Columna, in cui s'appoggia
Nostra speranza e 'l gran nome latino,
Ch'ancor non torse del vero camino
L'ira di Giove per ventosa pioggia,

Qui non palazzi, non teatro o loggia,
Ma 'n lor vece un abete, un faggio, un pino,
Tra l'erba verde e 'l bel monte vicino,
Onde si scende poetando e poggia,

Levan di terra al ciel nostr'intelletto,
E 'l rosigniuol che dolcemente all'ombra
Tutte le notti si lamenta e piagne,

D'amorosi penseri il cor ne 'ngombra:
Ma tanto ben sol tronchi e fai imperfetto
Tu che da noi, signor mio, ti scompagne.

IX

When the planet that keeps track of the hours
Returns to Taurus and that house adorns,
A vigour falls from the resplendent horns
That dresses all the world with flaming flowers;

And not only what is before our eyes,
The shores and hills, with many blooms he fills,
But inside, where the days never arise,
He makes pregnant of him the earthly rills,

So that one fruit and the other be won.
Thus she who among women is a sun
Does in me, moving her eyes' beam that burns,

Create actions and thoughts and words of love;
Yet, no matter the way she likes to move
Them, the springtime for me never returns.

X

O glorious Column against which does lean
Our highest hope and the great Latin name,
Which has not yet been twisted from the mean
Path by Jupiter's windy rain and flame!

Here not palaces, theatre or sill,
But in their stead a fir, a beech, a pine,
Between the green grass and the neighbour hill
Whence we descend and make songs and recline,

Lift up our mind from the earth to the skies;
Also the nightingale that in the shade
Sweetly will weep every night and mourn,

Entangles all our heart in loving ties.
But so much good you break and make forlorn
Because away from us, my lord, you strayed.

XI

Lassare il velo o per sole o per ombra,
Donna, non vi vid'io,
Poi che in me conosceste il gran desio
Ch'ogni altra voglia d'entr'al cor mi sgombra.

Mentr'io portava i be' pensier celati,
C'hanno la mente desiando morta,
Vidivi di pietate ornare il vólto;
Ma poi ch'Amor di me vi fece accorta,
Fuôr i biondi capelli allor velati
E l'amoroso sguardo in sé raccolto.
Quel ch'i' piú desiava in voi m'è tolto;
Sí mi governa il velo,
Che per mia morte, et al caldo et al gielo,
De' be' vostr'occhi il dolce lume adombra.

XII

Se la mia vita da l'aspro tormento
Si può tanto schermire, e da gli affanni,
Ch'i' veggia per vertú de gli ultimi anni,
Donna, de' be' vostr'occhi il lume spento,

E i cape' d'oro fin farsi d'argento,
E lassar le ghirlande e i verdi panni,
E 'l viso scolorir, che ne' miei danni
A llamentar mi fa pauroso e lento,

Pur mi dará tanta baldanza Amore,
Ch'i' vi discovrirò de' miei martíri
Qua' sono stati gli anni e i giorni e l'ore;

E se 'l tempo è contrario a i be' desiri,
Non fia ch'almen non giunga al mio dolore
Alcun soccorso di tardi sospiri.

XI

I never saw you in the sun or shade,
Lady, remove your veil
After you knew the wish that makes me pale
By which all other wills from my heart fade.

While I was hiding the fair thoughts I bore,
That have undone my mind in this desire,
I saw compassion shine upon your face;
But when Love made you conscious of my fire
The blond hair became veiled and was no more,
The loving look closed in itself its grace.
What I most longed for finds its hiding-place
In you; the veil rules me,
Which to my death, hot or cold though it be,
Covers your eyes' sweet light as with a shade.

XII

If from the cruel anguish my life tries
To shield itself, and from the many cares,
That I may see at the end of the years,
Lady, the light extinguished of your eyes,

And the hair of fine gold to silver turn,
And garlands and green clothes all worn and spent,
And the face pale that in my sad concern
Makes me timid and slow now to lament,

Yet Love will give me such aggressive powers
That I shall tell you of my martyrdom
The years, such as they were, the days, the hours;

And when the time to kill desire is come,
At least my grief will know and recognize
The little comfort of late-coming sighs.

XIII

Quando fra l'altre donne ad ora ad ora
Amor vien nel bel viso di costei,
Quanto ciascuna è men bella di lei
Tanto cresce 'l desio che m'innamora.

I' benedico il loco e 'l tempo e l'ora
Che sí alto miraron gli occhi mei,
E dico:—Anima, assai ringraziar dêi,
Che fosti a tanto onor degnata allora:

Da lei ti vèn l'amoroso pensero,
Che, mentre 'l segui, al sommo ben t'invia,
Poco prezando quel ch'ogni uom desia;

Da lei vien l'animosa leggiadria
Ch'al ciel ti scorge per destro sentero;
Sí ch'i' vo giá de la speranza altèro.—

XIV

Occhi miei lassi, mentre ch'io vi giro
nel bel viso di quella che v'ha morti,
Pregovi siate accorti,
Ché giá vi sfida Amore, ond'io sospiro.

Morte pò chiuder sola a' miei penseri
L'amoroso camin che gli conduce
Al dolce porto de la lor salute;
Ma puossi a voi celar la vostra luce
Per meno obgetto, perché meno interi
Siete formati, e di minor virtute.
Però dolenti, anzi che sian venute
L'ore del pianto, che son giá vicine,
Prendete or a la fine
Breve conforto a sí lungo martiro.

XIII

When among other ladies now and then
Love comes into her fair physiognomy,
As much as each is less handsome than she,
So much grows the desire that is my ken.

I bless the hour and the time and the place
Where my eyes started to look up so high,
And say:—My soul, you must with thanks reply
For having been exalted to such grace:

From her the loving meditations come
That while you follow send you to the sum
Of good, not prizing much what is men's scope;

And from her comes the loving noble ray
Which leads you to the sky on the right way;
So I am proud already of my hope.—

XIV

My weary eyes, while I turn you to fly
Toward the face of one who makes you bear
Death, I beg you, beware,
For Love challenges you, who makes me sigh.

Only Death can shut off to my desire
The loving path that guides my thoughts in sight
Of the sweet haven of their blissfulness;
But to you may remain concealed your light
Through lesser object, because less entire
You have been formed and of less nobleness.
Therefore, mournful before the hours of stress
And tears have come, which are already near,
Now that the end is here
Take a brief respite from learning to die.

XV

Io mi rivolgo in dietro a ciascun passo
Col corpo stanco ch'a gran pena porto,
E prendo allor del vostr'aere conforto
Che 'l fa gir oltra, dicendo:—Oimè lasso!—

Poi ripensando al dolce ben ch'io lasso,
Al camin lungo et al mio viver corto,
Fermo le piante sbigottito e smorto,
E gli occhi in terra lagrimando abasso,

Talor m'assale in mezzo a' tristi pianti
Un dubbio: come posson queste membra
Da lo spirito lor viver lontane?

Ma rispondemi Amor:—Non ti rimembra
Che questo è privilegio de gli amanti,
Sciolti da tutte qualitati umane?—

XVI

Movesi il vecchierel canuto e bianco
Del dolce loco ov'ha sua etá fornita,
E da la famigliuola sbigottita
Che vede il caro padre venir manco;

Indi traendo poi l'antiquo fianco
Per l'estreme giornate di sua vita,
Quanto piú pò col buon voler s'aita,
Rotto da gli anni e dal camino stanco;

E viene a Roma, seguendo 'l desio,
Per mirar la sembianza di colui
Ch'ancor lassú nel ciel vedere spera.

Cosí, lasso!, talor vo cercand'io,
Donna, quanto è possibile, in altrui
La disiata vostra forma vera.

XV

I do often turn backward when I pass
By with this body that in pain I bear,
And then I receive comfort from your air
Which causes it to move, and say:—Alas!—

Then thinking of the sweet treasure I leave,
Of the long journey, of my life's short round,
I stop my walk, and pale, dismayed, I grieve
And bend my eyes in tears toward the ground.

Sometimes a doubt assails my deep distress:
How can these limbs go on living at all,
So far away from their soul's happiness?

But then Love answers me:—Don't you recall
That lovers have the privilege to be
Rid of each human trait and quality?—

XVI

The old man goes away, hoary and white,
From the sweet country where he spent his years,
And all the little family despairs
Seeing its loving father vanish quite;

Then dragging slowly on his ancient load
Through the very last days of his life's span,
He uses his good will, helps as he can,
Broken by time and weary of the road,

And comes to Rome, following his desire,
To behold here the image and the norm
Of Him whom in the sky he hopes to find.

Likewise, lady, sometimes, alas, my mind
Will try with all its power and will not tire
To seek in others your desired true form.

XVII

Pióvommi amare lagrime dal viso
Con un vento angoscioso di sospiri,
Quando in voi adiven che gli occhi giri,
Per cui sola dal mondo i' son diviso.

Vero è che 'l dolce mansueto riso
Pur acqueta gli ardenti miei desiri
E mi sottragge al foco de' martíri,
Mentr' io son a mirarvi intento e fiso;

Ma gli spiriti miei s'aghiaccian poi
Ch'i' veggio, al departir, gli atti soavi
Torcer da me le mie fatali stelle;

Largata al fin co l'amorose chiavi
L'anima esce del cor per seguir voi,
E con molto pensiero indi si svelle.

XVIII

Quand'io son tutto vòlto in quella parte
Ove 'l bel viso di madonna luce,
E m'è rimasa nel pensier la luce
Che m'arde e strugge dentro a parte a parte,

I', che temo del cor che mi si parte
E veggio presso il fin de la mia luce,
Vommene in guisa d'orbo, senza luce,
Che non sa ove si vada e pur si parte.

Cosí davanti a i colpi de la morte
Fuggo; ma non sí ratto che 'l desío
Meco non venga, come venir sòle.

Tacito vo, ché le parole morte
Farian pianger la gente, et i' desío
Che le lagrime mie si spargan sole.

XVII

A rain of bitter tears falls from my face
And a tormenting wind blows with my sighs
Whenever toward you I turn my eyes,
Whose absence cuts me from the human race.

It is true that the mild and gentle smiles
Do soothe the ardour of my strong desire
And rescue me from my martyrdom's fire
While I intently look upon your guiles;

But my spirits become suddenly cold
When I see, leaving, the acts I behold
Stolen from me by my stars' fateful ray;

Loosened at last by the amorous keys,
The soul deserts the heart to seek your breeze,
And in deep thought it tears itself away.

XVIII

When I am pulled and drawn toward that side
Where the fair visage of my lady shines,
And in my thought the light remains and shines
Which burns and consumes me from side to side,

I, fearing that my heart will leave my side,
And seeing that my light no longer shines,
Walk like a blind man on whom nothing shines,
Who knows not where to go, yet turns aside.

And so I flee before the blows of Death;
But not so rapidly that my desire
Follow me not, as it will always follow.

Silent I go, because my words of death
Would make the others cry, and I desire
That my tears be alone, with none to follow.

XIX

Son animali al mondo de sí altèra
Vista che 'n contr'al sol pur si difende;
Altri, però che 'l gran lume gli offende,
Non escon fuor se non verso la sera;

Et altri, col desio folle che spera
Gioir forse nel foco, perché splende,
Provan l'altra vertú, quella che 'ncende.
Lasso!, el mio loco è 'n questa ultima schera;

Ch'i' non son forte ad aspettar la luce
Di questa donna, e non so fare schermi
Di luoghi tenebrosi o d'ore tarde.

Però con gli occhi lagrimosi e 'nfermi
Mio destíno a vederla mi conduce;
E so ben ch'i' vo dietro a quel che m'arde.

XX

Vergognando talor ch'ancor si taccia,
Donna, per me vostra bellezza in rima,
Ricorro al tempo ch'i' vi vidi prima,
Tal che null'altra fia mai che mi piaccia.

Ma trovo peso non da le mie braccia,
Né ovra da polir colla mia lima;
Però l'ingegno, che sua forza estima,
Ne l'operazion tutto s'agghiaccia.

Piú volte giá per dir le labbra apersi;
Poi rimase la voce in mezzo 'l petto.
Ma qual sòn poría mai salir tant'alto?

Piú volte incominciai di scriver versi;
Ma la penna e la mano e l'intelletto
Rimaser vinti nel primier assalto.

XIX

There are animals here of such fierce sight
That even the sun's menace they can dare,
Others, being quite dazzled by the glare,
Never go out unless it is twilight;

And others with a mad desire that lays
Its hope in fire, perhaps because it shines,
Try the different virtue of a blaze.
Alas! my place is in these troops and lines.

I lack the strength to confront the brightness
Of this lady, and will not use the screen
Of a late hour or of a somber green,

Thus with eyes full of tears and weariness
I am led by my fate after the same,
And I know that I seek my burning flame.

XX

Feeling ashamed that I still seem to pass
Over your beauty, Lady, in my rhyme,
I remember when I for the first time
Saw you, made for my love as no one was:

But the burden I find crushes my frame,
The work cannot be polished by my file,
And my talent which knows its strength and style
In this attempt becomes frozen and lame.

Several times I moved my lips to cry;
But my voice was constrained within my lungs.
Which is the sound that can soar up so high?

Several times I began writing songs;
But pen and hand and intellect were bound
To be conquered and caught in the first round.

XXI

Mille fiate, o dolce mia guerrera,
Per aver co' begli occhi vostri pace
V'aggio proferto il cor; m'a voi non piace
Mirar sí basso colla mente altèra.

E se di lui fors'altra donna spera,
Vive in speranza debile e fallace:
Mio, perché sdegno ciò ch' a voi dispiace,
Esser non può giá mai cosí com'era.

Or s'io lo scaccio, et e' non trova in vòi
Ne l'essilio infelice alcun soccorso,
Né sa star sol, né gire ov'altri il chiama,

Poría smarrire il suo natural corso;
Che grave colpa fia d'ambeduo noi,
E tanto piú de voi, quanto piú v'ama.

XXII

A qualunque animale alberga in terra,
Se non se alquanti c'hanno in odio il sole,
Tempo da travagliare è quanto è 'l giorno;
Ma poi che 'l ciel accende le sue stelle,
Qual torna a casa e qual s'anida in selva
Per aver posa almeno in fin a l'alba.

Et io, da che comincia la bella alba
A scuoter l'ombra intorno de la terra
Svegliando gli animali in ogni selva,
Non ho mai triegua di sospir col sole;
Poi, quand'io veggio fiammeggiar le stelle,
Vo lagrimando e disiando il giorno.

Quando la sera scaccia il chiaro giorno,
E le tenebre nostre altrui fanno alba,
Miro pensoso le crudeli stelle,

XXI

A thousand times, o sweet warrior of mine,
To conclude peace with your beautiful eyes
I offered you my heart; but you decline
To look so low with your proud thoughts that rise.

And if perchance another lady longs
For it, her hope is poor, it has no cause;
My own, since I despise like you its wrongs,
It can never again be, as it was.

Now if I banish it and it finds not
In you a comfort from its grievous lot,
And cannot live alone nor answer calls,

It might be banished from its proper lairs,
Which would be a great guilt and prove us false,
And the more your own guilt, the more it cares.

XXII

To any animal that dwells on earth,
Except for but a few that hate the sun,
Is given time to toil till close of day;
But as soon as the sky lights up the stars
Some return home and some hide in the wood
To find a rest at least until the dawn.

And I, since first arrives the lovely dawn,
Shaking the shadows all around the earth
And wakening the beasts in every wood,
Never refrain from sighing in the sun;
Then when I see the kindling of the stars
I weep and long for the departed day.

When the night drives away the limpid day
And our deep gloom brings to others the dawn,
I gaze in wonder at the cruel stars

Che m'hanno fatto di sensibil terra,
E maledíco il dí ch'i' vidi 'l sole,
Che mi fa in vista un uom nudrito in selva.

Non credo che pascesse mai per selva
Si aspra fera, o di notte o di giorno,
Come costei ch'i' piango a l'ombra e al sole,
E non mi stanca primo sonno od alba;
Ché, ben ch'i' sia mortal corpo di terra,
Lo mio fermo desir vien da le stelle.

Prima ch'i' torni a voi, lucenti stelle,
O tomi giú ne l'amorosa selva,
Lassando il corpo che fia trita terra,
Vedess'io in lei pietá, che 'n un sol giorno
Può ristorar molt'anni, e nanzi l'alba
Puommi arichir dal tramontar del sole!

Con lei foss'io da che si parte il sole,
E non ci vedess'altri che le stelle,
Sol una notte, e mai non fosse l'alba,
E non se transformasse in verde selva
Per uscirmi di braccia, come il giorno
Ch'Apollo la seguia qua giú per terra!

Ma io sarò sotterra in secca selva,
E 'l giorno andrá pien di minute stelle,
Prima ch' a sí dolce alba arrivi il sole.

XXIII

Nel dolce tempo de la prima etade,
Che nascer vide et ancor quasi in erba
La fèra voglia che per mio mal crebbe,
Perché cantando il duol si disacerba,
Canterò com'io vissi in libertade,
Mentre Amor nel mio albergo a sdegno s'ebbe;
Poi seguirò sí come a lui ne 'ncrebbe
Troppo altamente, e che di ciò m'avenne,

That have created me of sentient earth,
And I curse the first time I saw the sun
Which makes me like a creature of the wood.

I do not think that ever pastured wood
Such fierce wild beast, whether by night or day,
As the one I mourn for in shade or sun
Without dreading fatigue of sleep or dawn;
For though I be a mortal thing of earth,
My unchanging desire comes from the stars.

Before I come to you, o shining stars,
Or sink again into the loving wood,
Leaving this body to be rotten earth,
Could I see mercy in her, that in one day
Can restore many years, and before dawn
Can make me rich after the setting sun!

To be with her when fades away the sun,
To be seen by no others but the stars
Only one night, and not expect the dawn,
And she never transformed into green wood
To flee my arms, as happened on the day
When Apollo pursued her on the earth!

But I shall be the earth of a dry wood
And the day will be full of tiny stars
Before such a sweet dawn will see the sun.

XXIII

In the sweet springtime of my history
Which saw the rising and becoming green
Of a desire that for my ill grew wild,
Because in singing the heart cures its spleen,
I will sing how I lived in liberty
While Love inside my dwelling was called child;
Then I will tell how he said this reviled
Him and offended, and what followed thence,

Di ch'io son fatto a molta gente essempio;
Ben che 'l mio duro scempio
Sia scritto altrove, sí che mille penne
Ne son giá stanche, e quasi in ogni valle
Rimbombi il suon de' miei gravi sospiri,
Ch'aquistan fede a la penosa vita.
E se qui la memoria non m'aita,
Come suol fare, iscusilla i martíri,
Et un penser, che solo angoscia dálle,
Tal ch' ad ogni altro fa voltar le spalle
E mi face obliar me stesso a forza,
Ch' e' tèn di me quel d'entro, et io la scorza.

I' dico che dal dí che 'l primo assalto
Mi diede Amor, molt'anni eran passati,
Sí ch'io cangiava il giovenil aspetto;
E d'intorno al mio cor pensier gelati
Fatto avean quasi adamantino smalto
Ch'allentar non lassava il duro affetto:
Lagrima ancor non mi bagnava il petto
Né rompea il sonno, e quel che in me non era
Mi pareva un miracolo in altrui.
Lasso, che son! che fui!
La vita el fin, e 'l dí loda la sera.
Ché, sentendo il crudel, di ch'io ragiono,
In fin allor percossa di suo strale
Non essermi passato oltra la gonna,
Prese in sua scorta una possente donna,
Vèr' cui poco giá mai mi valse o vale
Ingegno o forza o dimandar perdóno.
Ei duo mi trasformaro in quel ch'i' sono,
Facendomi d'uom vivo un lauro verde,
Che per fredda stagion foglia non perde.

Qual mi fec'io quando primer m'accorsi
De la trasfigurata mia persona,
E i capei vidi far di quella fronde
Di che sperato avea giá lor corona,
E i piedi in ch'io mi stetti, e mossi, e corsi,
(Com'ogni membro a l'anima risponde)

That I became a lesson to the rest,
Though my being distressed
Be written now so that a thousand pens
Are quite exhausted, and in every glade
Be thundering the sound of my deep sighs
Which are the pledges of a doleful time.
And if my memory does no more climb
As it did once, the cause in anguish lies,
And in that thought which wounds it like a blade,
So that all other thoughts vanish and fade,
And forces me to forget my own mind,
Being the inner, I the outer rind.

I say that from the day of the first blow
Thrust upon me by Love, long years had passed,
So that a change came in my youthful look;
And round my heart all thoughts were frozen fast
Making an enamel of diamond glow,
Owing to which my passion never shook;
No tear had come to run in my breast's brook
Nor had broken my sleep, and what was not
In me, I thought in others scarcely true.
Alas! I aged, I grew!
The end lauds life, the night what the day wrought.
For the hard one, whose doings I deplore,
Feeling that until then his arrow's trace
Had not gone deeper than the cloth I wore,
Took as a guardian a proud lady's face
In whose sight never was improved my case
By word or strength or repentance or more.
They both changed me from what I was before
And made out of a living man a green
Laurel whose leaves in winter can be seen.

What did I feel when I was first aware
Of the new form in which my limbs fell down,
And saw my hair become one of those boughs
From which I had once hoped to get a crown,
And the feet I stood on, moved here and there,
(As every limb responds to the soul's vows)

Diventar due radici sovra l'onde,
Non di Peneo, ma d'un piú altèro fiume,
E 'n duo rami mutarsi ambe le braccia!
Né meno ancor m'agghiaccia
L'esser coverto poi di bianche piume,
Allor che folminato e morto giacque
Il mio sperar, che tropp'alto montava.
Ché, perch'io non sapea dove né quando
Mel ritrovasse, solo, lagrimando,
Lá 've tolto mi fu, dí e notte andava,
Ricercando dallato e dentro a l'acque,
E giá mai poi la mia lingua non tacque,
Mentre poteo, del suo cader maligno;
Ond'io presi col suon color d'un cigno.

Cosí lungo l'amate rive andai,
Che volendo parlar, cantava sempre,
Mercé chiamando con estrania voce;
Né mai in sí dolci o in sí soavi tempre
Risonar seppi gli amorosi guai,
Che 'l cor s'umiliasse, aspro e feroce.
Qual fu a sentir, ché 'l ricordar mi coce?
Ma molto piú di quel che per inanzi
De la dolce et acerba mia nemica
È bisogno ch'io dica;
Ben che sia tal ch'ogni parlare avanzi.
Questa, che col mirar gli animi fura,
M'aperse il petto, e 'l cor prese con mano,
Dicendo a me:—Di ciò non far parola.—
Poi la rividi in altro abito sola,
Tal ch'i' non la conobbi, o senso umano!,
Anzi le dissi 'l ver pien di paura;
Ed ella ne l'usata sua figura
Tosto tornando, fecemi, oimé lasso!,
D'un quasi vivo e sbigottito sasso.

Ella parlava sí turbata in vista,
Che tremar mi fea dentro a quella petra,
Udendo:—I' non son forse chi tu credi.—
E dicea meco:—Se costei mi spetra,

Turn into roots over the liquid browse
Not of Peneus but of a prouder stream,
And into branches transmuted my arms!
I fear not less the charms
That covered me with a white feather's gleam
When struck by death and lightning, my hope fell
After having presumed to climb too high.
For since I did not know or where or when
I found myself, alone, weeping again
Where I was lost day and night I went by
Seeking it beside me and in that well,
And after that I never ceased to tell,
While I could do it, my grief with my tongue;
And I became a swan making my song.

Then along the beloved shores I went,
Wanting to speak and yet singing alone,
Begging for mercy with a foreign voice;
But I could never in such pleasing tone
Express the sound of my loving lament,
That the harsh, cruel heart deigned to rejoice.
What was the feeling, if the thought destroys?
But now much more than what I said before
Of my unkind and gentle enemy
I must ask you to see,
Though she is one who above words will soar.
This one, who with her looks does rob and chase,
Opened my breast, took my heart in her hands,
Telling me:—You must never speak of this.—
Then I saw her again, looking amiss,
So that I knew her not, who understands?
And I told her the truth, fearing disgrace;
She then, resuming her habitual face,
Transmuted me again as if by shock
Into a barely living baffled rock.

She was saying, in such a troubled mood
That it filled me with tremor in the stone:
—Perhaps I am not she for whom you yearn.—
I told myself:—If she makes me atone

Nulla vita mi fia noiosa o trista:
A farmi lagrimar, signor mio, riedi.—
Come, non so; pur io mossi indi i piedi,
Non altrui incolpando che me stesso,
Mezzo, tutto quel dí, tra vivo e morto.
Ma, perché 'l tempo è corto,
La penna al buon voler non pò gir presso;
Onde piú cose ne la mente scritte
Vo trapassando, e sol d'alcune parlo,
Che meraviglia fanno a chi l'ascolta.
Morte mi s'era intorno al cor avolta,
Né tacendo potea di sua man trarlo,
O dar soccorso a le vertuti afflitte:
Le vive voci m'erano interditte;
Ond'io gridai con carta e con incostro:
—Non son mio, no; s'io moro, il danno è vostro.—

Ben mi credea dinanzi a gli occhi suoi
D'indegno far cosí di mercé degno;
E questa spene m'avea fatto ardito:
Ma talora umiltá spegne disdegno,
Talor l'enfiamma; e ciò sepp'io da poi,
Lunga stagion di tenebre vestito;
Ch' a quei preghi il mio lume era sparito.
Ed io non ritrovando intorno intorno
Ombra di lei, né pur de' suoi piedi orma,
Come uom che tra via dorma,
Gittaimi stanco sovra l'erba un giorno.
Ivi, accusando il fugitivo raggio,
A le lagrime triste allargai 'l freno,
E lasciaile cader come a lor parve;
Né giá mai neve sotto al sol disparve,
Com' io sentí' me tutto venir meno,
E farmi una fontana a pie' d'un faggio.
Gran tempo umido tenni quel viaggio.
Chi udí mai d'uom vero nascer fonte?
E parlo cose manifeste e conte.

L'alma, ch'è sol da Dio fatta gentile,
Ché giá d'altrui non pò venir tal grazia,

By freeing me, life can no more be rude:
To make me weep again, my lord, return.—
I know not how; but that day I did learn
To go about blaming only my ill,
Always halfway between living and dead.
But because time is fled,
My pen cannot go after my good will;
Hence many things written within my mind
I pass in silence and talk of a few
That excite wonder in whoever hears.
Death was all fastened on my heart with fears
And I could not its punishment eschew,
Or my failing resources help and bind:
My living voices were closed and confined;
Therefore I cried with paper and with ink:
—I am not mine; yours the fault if I sink.—

I thought that in this way before her eyes
I should be found more worthy of her pain;
And in this hope I had become quite bold;
But sometimes meekness will put out disdain,
Sometimes it lights it; this I could surmise
Later on, when the dark around me rolled,
For at my prayer I did no more behold
My light. And I not finding there, alas,
Her shadow, nor a vestige of her feet,
Asleep along the street
Laid me down weary, one day, on the grass.
There in accusing the fugitive ray
I gave free rein to my desperate tears
And I let them fall down as they did please,
And never snow was seen through sun decrease
As I did then, like one who disappears,
And was a fountain where the beeches lay.
For a long time all wet I ran away.
Who ever heard of man turned into stream?
And yet I tell a truth and not a dream.

The soul that only God created fair,
Because from others cannot come such grace,

Simile al suo fattor stato ritene;
Però di perdonar mai non è sazia
A chi col core e col sembiante umíle,
Dopo quantunque offese, a mercé vène.
E se contra suo stile ella sostene
D'esser molto pregata, in lui si specchia,
E fal perché 'l peccar piú si pavente;
Ché non ben si ripente
De l'un mal chi de l'altro s'apparecchia.
Poi che madonna da pietá commossa
Degnò mirarme, e ricognovve e vide
Gir di pari la pena col peccato,
Benigna mi redusse al primo stato.
Ma nulla ha 'l mondo in ch'uom saggio si fide;
Ch'ancor poi ripregando, i nervi e l'ossa
Mi volse in dura selce; e cosí scossa
Voce rimasi de l'antiche some,
Chiamando Morte, e lei sola per nome.

Spirto doglioso errante (mi rimembra)
Per spelunche deserte e pellegrine
Piansi molt'anni il mio sfrenato ardire;
Et ancor poi trovai di quel mal fine,
E ritornai ne le terrene membra,
Credo, per piú dolore ivi sentire.
I' seguí' tanto avanti il mio desire
Ch'un dí cacciando, sí com'io solea,
Mi mossi; e quella fera bella e cruda
In una fonte ignuda
Si stava, quando 'l sol piú forte ardea.
Io, perché d'altra vista non m'appago,
Stetti a mirarla; ond'ella ebbe vergogna;
E, per farne vendetta, o per celarse,
L'acqua nel viso co le man mi sparse.
Vero dirò (forse e' parrá menzogna)
Ch'i' sentí trarmi de la propria imago,
Et in un cervo solitario e vago
Di selva in selva ratta mi trasformo;
Et ancor de' miei can fuggo lo stormo.

Keeps a condition like her Maker's state;
Therefore she does forgivingly embrace
Those who with humble heart sincerely care
After their guilt for her mercy to wait.
And if, against her style, the time grows late
While she listens to prayers, on Him she gazes
In order that the sinning be more feared;
For he cannot be cleared
Of one ill who so soon another raises.
After my lady, where pity had grown,
Began to look at me, and knew and saw
The punishment proportioned to the sin,
Gently she helped me my old state to win.
But nothing happens here that can be law
To the wise man; for as I prayed my bone
And my nerve were transformed into a stone;
And I was left a voice after my shame,
Calling for Death and only for his name.

A mournful erring spirit (I remember),
Amid deserted and outlandish caves,
I wept for many years my reckless fire;
And then my anguish found the end that saves
And I became again a living member,
Perhaps to know a torment more entire.
I went so far following my desire,
That one day, hunting as I used to do,
I walked on; and that beast charming and rude
Within a fountain, nude,
Was lying when the sun kindled the blue.
I, since for other sights I do not care,
Stopped to behold her; but shame made her shy,
And to revenge herself, or else to hide,
With her hands she threw water on my side.
I tell the truth (and it will seem a lie):
I felt my image then break up and tear
And turn into a lonely and fair
Deer, while I running go from wood to wood,
And I still flee my hounds' murderous mood.

Canzon, i' non fu' mai quel nuvol d'oro
Che poi discese in preziosa pioggia,
Sí che 'l foco di Giove in parte spense;
Ma fui ben fiamma ch'un bel guardo accense,
E fui l'uccel che piú per l'aere poggia,
Alzando lei, che ne' miei detti onoro;
Né per nova figura il primo alloro
Seppi lassar, ché pur la sua dolce ombra
Ogni men bel piacer del cor mi sgombra.

XXIV

Se l'onorata fronde, che prescrive
L'ira del ciel quando 'l gran Giove tona,
Non m'avesse disdetta la corona
Che suole ornar chi poetando scrive,

I' era amico a queste vostre dive,
Le qua' vilmente il secolo abandona;
Ma quella ingiuria giá lunge mi sprona
Da l'inventrice de le prime olive;

Ché non bolle la polver d'Etiopia,
Sotto 'l piú ardente sol, com'io sfavillo,
Perdendo tanto amata cosa propia.

Cercate dunque fonte piú tranquillo;
Ché 'l mio d'ogni liquor sostene inopia,
Salvo di quel che lagrimando stillo.

Canzone, I never was that cloud of gold
Pouring down later in a precious rain
And partly smothering the fire of Jove;
But still I was a flame lighted by love,
I was the bird that more air can sustain,
For I raise her that with my words I hold;
Nor could I leave, though novel shapes enfold
Me, the first laurel, for its lovely shade
Makes lesser pleasures from my heart to fade.

XXIV

If the illustrious branches that allay
The wrath of heaven when Jupiter roars,
Had not denied to me the wreath of bay
Adorning those who write poetic lores,

I were a friend of your Muses who are
Deserted by our heartless century;
But that offence compels me to go far
From the inventress of the olive tree;

For Ethiopia's dust will make you blink
Under the hottest sun less than I burn
From the pain of my lost beloved thing.

Go then to find a more reposeful spring;
For mine can bear the lack of any drink
Save that which I distil in tears that yearn.

XXV

Amor piangeva, et io con lui tal volta,
Dal qual miei passi non fûr mai lontani,
Mirando per gli effetti acerbi e strani
L'anima vostra de' suoi nodi sciolta.

Or ch'al dritto camin l'ha Dio rivolta,
Col cor levando al cielo ambe le mani,
Ringrazio lui, che' giusti preghi umani
Benignamente, sua mercede, ascolta.

E se, tornando a l'amorosa vita,
Per farvi al bel desio volger le spalle,
Trovaste per la via fossati o poggi,

Fu per mostrar quanto è spinoso calle,
E quanto alpestra e dura la salita,
Onde al vero valor conven ch'uom poggi.

XXVI

Piú di me lieta non si vede a terra
Nave da l'onde combattuta e vinta,
Quando la gente di pietá depinta
Su per la riva a ringraziar s'atterra;

Né lieto piú del carcer si diserra
Chi 'ntorno al collo ebbe la corda avinta,
Di me, veggendo quella spada scinta
Che fece al segnor mio sí lunga guerra.

E tutti voi ch'Amor laudate in rima,
Al buon testor de gli amorosi detti
Rendete onor, ch'era smarrito in prima;

Ché piú gloria è nel regno de gli eletti
D'un spirito converso, e piú s'estima,
Che di novanta nove altri perfetti.

XXV

Love was in tears and I sometimes with him
From whom my steps were never far apart,
Seeing after adventures strange and grim
Your soul delivered from his noose and dart.

Now that God leads it to the right again,
With my heart to the sky I raise my hands
To thank him who so kindly understands
In his mercy the just prayers of men.

And if in coming to the life of love
To make you turn your shoulders on desire
You found ditches and hills and the way rough,

That was to show you how thorny the time
And how steep and how difficult the climb,
So that a man true valour must acquire.

XXVI

Never happier than I landed a ship
Assaulted and defeated by the waves,
When the people with pity on their lip
Along the shore give thanks to Him who saves;

Nor happier he when he was freed from jail,
Who on his neck had felt a rope before,
Than I was when I saw that weapon trail
Which had made to my lord such a long war.

And you who Love in verse have praised and prayed,
To the witness of loving dictions
Give a due honour, after he had strayed;

More glory in the realm of the elect
Is shown for one converted, more respect,
Than is for ninety-nine perfected ones.

XXVII

Il successor di Carlo, che la chioma
Co la corona del suo antiquo adorna,
Prese ha giá l'arme per fiaccar le corna
A Babilonia, e chi da lei si noma;

E 'l vicario de Cristo colla soma
De le chiavi e del manto al nido torna,
Sí che s'altro accidente no 'l distorna,
Vedrá Bologna, e poi la nobil Roma.

La mansueta vostra e gentil agna
Abbatte i fieri lupi: e cosí vada
Chiunque amor legitimo scompagna.

Consolate lei dunque ch'ancor bada,
E Roma che del suo sposo si lagna;
E per Iesú cingete omai la spada.

XXVIII

O aspettata in ciel beata e bella
Anima, che di nostra umanitade
Vestita vai, non come l'altre carca,
Perché ti sian men dure omai le strade,
A Dio diletta, obediente ancella,
Onde al suo regno di qua giú si varca,
Ecco novellamente a la tua barca,
Ch'al cieco mondo ha giá volte le spalle
Per gir al miglior porto,
D'un vento occidental dolce conforto;
Lo qual per mezzo questa oscura valle,
Ove piangiamo il nostro e l'altrui torto,
La condurrá de' lacci antichi sciolta
Per dritissimo calle
Al verace oriente, ov'ella è volta.

XXVII

The successor of Charles, who with the crown
Of his ancestor now adorns his hair,
Has taken up the arms to shatter down
And Babylon and those who that name bear;

And the vicar of Christ prepares to come
With all his keys and his robe to the nest;
If by some other fate he is not pressed,
He will look at Bologna and at Rome.

Your sheep's humility and gentleness
Destroy the wolves: and let this be the doom
Of those who break a sanctified caress.

Then comfort her who still remains the same,
And Rome, who must complain of her bridegroom;
And gird the sword at last in Jesus' name.

XXVIII

O expected in heaven, blessed and fair
Soul who are clothed with our humanity,
And not weighed down as other people are,
In order that the paths less arduous be
To you, beloved by God and servant rare,
By which we go from the earth to a star,
Here comes again to your ship from afar,
After she left behind this world of force
To reach a better place,
A western wind's sweet comfort and embrace
Which from this valley that is darkness' source
Shall lead her, loosened from the ancient ties,
On a very straight course
To the true east where her direction lies.

Forse i devoti e gli amorosi preghi
E le lagrime sante de' mortali
Son giunte inanzi a la pietá superna;
E forse non fûr mai tante né tali
Che per merito lor punto si pieghi
Fuor de suo corso la giustizia eterna;
Ma quel benigno re che 'l ciel governa,
Al sacro loco ove fo posto in croce,
Gli occhi per grazia gira;
Onde nel petto al novo Carlo spira
La vendetta ch'a noi tardata nòce,
Sí che molt'anni Europa ne sospira.
Cosí soccorre a la sua amata sposa
Tal che sol de la voce
Fa tremar Babilonia e star pensosa.

Chiunque alberga tra Garona e 'l monte
E 'ntra 'l Rodano e 'l Reno e l'onde salse,
Le 'nsegne cristianissime accompagna;
Et a cui mai di vero pregio calse,
Dal Pireneo a l'ultimo orizonte,
Con Aragon lassará vòta Ispagna;
Inghilterra con l'isole che bagna
L'Oceano intra 'l Carro e le Colonne
In fin lá dove sona
Dottrina del santissimo Elicona,
Varie di lingue e d'arme e de le gonne,
A l'alta impresa caritate sprona.
Deh! qual amor sí licito, o sí degno,
Qua' figli mai, qua' donne
Furon materia a sí giusto disdegno?

Una parte del mondo è che si giace
Mai sempre in ghiaccio et in gelate nevi,
Tutta lontana dal camin del sole:
Lá, sotto i giorni nubilosi e brevi,
Nemica naturalmente di pace,
Nasce una gente a cui il morir non dole:
Questa se piú devota che non sòle
Col tedesco furor la spada cigne,

Perhaps the pious and the loving prayers
And the religious tears of mortal men
Have come before the mercy of the Lord;
Perhaps they never were of such a strain
That for their sake eternal Justice cares
To deviate, though slightly, from her word;
But that mild King who rules without a sword
Toward the holy place where rose his cross
By grace directs his eyes;
Hence in the breast of the new Charles he tries
The vengeance whose delay has been our loss,
So that after long years Europe still cries.
And thus One succours his beloved bride,
Who, simply if he toss
His voice's sound, makes Babylon to hide.

Who between mountains and Garonne has grown
And between Rhone and Rhine and the sea waves,
Will follow after the most Christian vein;
And he who for a real honour craves
From the mounts Pyrenees to the last zone
With Aragon will leave and empty Spain;
England herself, with the isles that the main
Between the Chariot and the Pillars sprays,
And the place where once won
The doctrine of the sacred Helicon,
Varied in tongues and in arms and in plays,
Charity to the high feat pushes on.
Ah, what love was so worthy, so well spent,
What sons or women's ways
Were the matter of such a just contempt?

There is a portion of the world that lies
Forever in the ice and frosted snow,
Left far away from the path of the sun:
There in the cloudy days that quickly go,
By nature alien to all peaceful ties,
Is born a people that death does not shun;
If this will more religiously run
And gird with German savagery the sword,

Turchi, arabi e caldei,
Con tutti quei che speran nelli dèi
Di qua dal mar che fa l'onde sanguigne,
Quanto sian da prezzar conoscer dèi:
Popolo ignudo, paventoso e lento,
Che ferro mai non strigne,
Ma tutt' i colpi suoi commette al vento.

Dunque ora è 'l tempo da ritrare il collo
Dal giogo antico, e da squarciare il velo
Ch' è stato avolto intorno a gli occhi nostri;
E che 'l nobile ingegno che dal cielo
Per grazia tien' de l'immortale Apollo,
E l'eloquenzia sua vertú qui mostri
Or con la lingua, or co' laudati incostri:
Perché d'Orfeo leggendo e d'Amfione
Se non ti meravigli,
Assai men fia ch'Italia co' suoi figli
Si desti al suon del tuo chiaro sermone,
Tanto che per Iesú la lancia pigli;
Che s'al ver mira questa antica madre,
In nulla sua tenzione
Fûr mai cagion sí belle o sí leggiadre.

Tu, c'hai per arricchir d'un bel tesauro
Volte l'antiche e le moderne carte,
Volando al ciel colla terrena soma,
Sai, da l'imperio del figliuol de Marte
Al grande Augusto che di verde lauro
Tre volte triumfando ornò la chioma,
Ne l'altrui ingiurie del suo sangue Roma
Spesse fiate quanto fu cortese:
Et or perché non fia,
Cortese no, ma conoscente e pia,
A vendicar le dispietate offese,
Col figliuol glorioso di Maria?
Che dunque la nemica parte spera
Ne l'umane difese,
Se Cristo sta da la contraria schiera?

Turks, Arabs and Chaldees
And those who put their hope in gods' decrees
On this side of the Red Sea of the Lord,
How much may one regard, tell, if you please,
A people bare and cowardly and slow
Who arms cannot afford
But entrusts to the wind each single blow.

Now is the time to free our neck and brace
Ourselves after the yoke, and tear the veil
That has been swaddled all around our eyes;
And that the noble mind, the holy grail,
Which from Apollo you received by grace,
And its eloquence be made manifest
Either by tongue or by the writing test:
For if you read of Orpheus, Amphion,
Call it not a surprise,
Italy and her sons will sooner rise
And wake up when resounds your orison
And bring a weapon there where Jesus lies.
If our old mother the truth will declare,
In no occasion
Of fighting did she have causes so fair.

You who to become rich with a fine treasure
Perused the ancient and the modern stories,
Flying to heaven with the earthly care,
Know from Mars' son's empire down to the glories
Of Augustus, who in his triumph's pleasure
Three times with the green bay adorned his hair,
How many times Rome courteously did share
The fights of others and did shed her blood:
And now why could not she
Not courteous any more but pious be
In avenging the foul insults she stood
With Mary's Son's glorious divinity?
What does the foe imagine can be tried
By the strength of manhood,
If Christ is standing on the other side?

Pon mente al temerario ardir di Serse,
Che fece per calcare i nostri liti
Di novi ponti oltraggio a la marina;
E vedrai ne la morte de' mariti
Tutte vestite a brun le donne perse,
E tinto in rosso il mar di Salamina.
E non pur questa misera ruina
Del popolo infelice d'oriente
Vittoria t'empromette,
Ma Maratona, e le mortali strette,
Che difese il leon con poca gente,
Et altre mille c'hai ascoltate e lette.
Per che inchinare a Dio molto convene
Le ginocchia e la mente,
Che gli anni tuoi riserva a tanto bene.

Tu vedrai Italia e l'onorata riva,
Canzon, ch'a gli occhi miei cela e contende
Non mar, non poggio o fiume,
Ma solo Amor che del suo altèro lume
Piú m'invaghisce dove piú m'incende;
Né natura può star contr'al costume.
Or movi, non smarrir l'altre compagne;
Ché non pur sotto bende
Alberga Amor, per cui si ride e piagne.

XXIX

Verdi panni, sanguigni, oscuri o persi
Non vestí donna unquanco
Né d'òr capelli in bionda treccia attorse
Sí bella, come questa che mi spoglia
D'arbitrio, e dal camin de libertade
Seco mi tira, sí ch'io non sostegno
Alcun giogo men grave.

E se pur s'arma talor a dolersi
L'anima, a cui vien manco

Call to your mind Xerxes' temerity
Who to reach and set foot upon our shores
Challenged with novel bridges our sea power;
And you will see the women leave their doors
In mourning for their husbands' agony,
And Salamis with waves red as a flower.
And not only this miserable hour
Of the poor people of the Orient
Tells us we shall prevail,
But Marathon, the deadly narrow trail
Held with a few by a lion's attempt,
And you have heard and read more than this tale.
Hence it becomes you to bend knees and mind
To God in this event,
Who so much goodness for your life designed.

You will see Italy and the honoured shore,
Song, that far from my eyes have been confined
Not by sea nor by hills or by a stream,
But by Love only, who with his proud gleam
The more seduces me, the more I mind;
Nor can we nature above custom deem.
Now go and do not lose your flock of sheep,
Because not with the blind
Alone dwells Love, for whom men laugh and weep.

XXIX

Green clothes or dark or purple or bright red
Never a woman wore
Nor golden hair in a braid wound about,
As fair as she who has taken away
My will, and from the path of liberty
Draws me to her, so that I do not bear
Other less heavy weight.

And if sometimes the soul raises its head
And mourns, having no more

Consiglio, ove 'l martír l'adduce in forse,
Rappella lei da la sfrenata voglia
Súbita vista; ché del cor mi rade
Ogni delira impresa, et ogni sdegno
Fa 'l veder lei soave.

Di quanto per Amor giá mai soffersi,
Et aggio a soffrir anco,
Fin che mi sani 'l cor colei che 'l morse,
Rubella di mercé, che pur l'envoglia,
Vendetta fia; sol che contra umiltade
Orgoglio et ira il bel passo ond'io vegno
Non chiuda e non inchiave.

Ma l'ora e 'l giorno ch'io le luci apersi
Nel bel nero e nel bianco
Che mi scacciâr di lá dove Amor corse,
Novella, d'esta vita che m'addoglia,
Furon radice, e quella in cui l'etade
Nostra si mira, la qual piombo o legno
Vedendo è chi non pave.

Lagrima dunque che da gli occhi versi
Per quelle, che nel manco
Lato mi bagna chi primier s'accorse,
Quadrella, dal voler mio non mi svoglia,
Ché 'n giusta parte la sentenzia cade:
Per lei sospira l'alma; et ella è degno
Che le sue piaghe lave.

Da me son fatti i miei pensier diversi:
Tal giá, qual io mi stanco,
L'amata spada in se stessa contorse;
Né quella prego che però mi scioglia,
Ché men son dritte al ciel tutt'altre strade,
E non s'aspira al glorioso regno
Certo in piú salda nave.

Benigne stelle che compagne fêrsi
Al fortunato fianco,
Quando 'l bel parto giú nel mondo scorse!

Support, by martyrdom exposed to doubt,
It is called back from its wishes' display
By seeing her who makes from my heart flee
Every mad desire; all scorn and snare
Her sight can palliate.

What I have borne from Love and from his dread
Now as well as before,
Until she heals my heart, who caused my rout,
The enemy of mercy though she pray,
Shall be revenged, if against modesty
Anger and pride do not shut my repair
With an invidious gate.

But the hour and the day in which I fled
The black and the white shore
That from the course of Love have cast me out
Were the new root on which my life I lay
And pain, and she, in whom our century
Is mirrored, on whom lead or wood may stare
Not fearing love or hate.

Therefore the tear that from my eyes is shed
In place of those I store
In my left side for one who wants to flout
Me, from my first desire goes not astray;
For a just cause is my defence's plea:
My soul sighs after her, for her I dare
My wounds to inundate.

My thoughts are far from me variously led:
After the grief I bore
Some plunged the sword in themselves with devout
Love; nor do I beg her to allay
My lot, for straighter road there cannot be
Leading to heaven, and no other stair,
No other ship can wait.

O kindly stars whose company has bred
The birth that I adore,
When its grace made the world joyously shout!

Ch'è stella in terra, e come in lauro foglia
Conserva verde il pregio d'onestade,
Ove non spira folgore né indegno
Vento mai che l'aggrave.

So io ben ch'a voler chiuder in versi
Suo laudi, fôra stanco
Chi piú degna la mano a scriver porse:
Qual cella è di memoria in cui s'accoglia
Quanta vede vertú, quanta beltade,
Chi gli occhi mira d'ogni valor segno,
Dolce del mio cor chiave?

Quanto il sol gira, Amor piú caro pegno,
Donna, di voi non have.

XXX

Giovene donna sotto un verde lauro
Vidi, piú bianca e piú fredda che neve
Non percossa dal sol molti e molt'anni;
E 'l suo parlare, e 'l bel viso, e le chiome
Mi piacquen sí, ch'i' l'ho dinanzi a gli occhi
Ed avrò sempre, ov'io sia, in poggio o 'n riva.

Allor saranno i miei pensieri a riva
Che foglia verde non si trovi in lauro;
Quando avrò queto il core, asciutti gli occhi,
Vedrem ghiacciare il foco, arder la neve.
Non ho tanti capelli in queste chiome
Quanti vorrei quel giorno attender anni.

Ma perché vola il tempo e fuggon gli anni,
Sí ch'a la morte in un punto s'arriva,
O colle brune o colle bianche chiome,
Seguirò l'ombra di quel dolce lauro,
Per lo piú ardente sole e per la neve,
Fin che l'ultimo dí chiuda quest'occhi.

For she is star on earth and, leaf of bay,
She preserves the green prize of honesty
Where never lightnings strike or rough winds tear
And crush her happy state.

I know well that in rhymes cannot be read
Or praised or closed her lore,
It would exhaust the worthy minds and stout:
What cell of memory can keep and say
All the virtue, the beauty that we see,
Who gazes at the eyes that truth declare,
O sweet key of my fate?

As the sun turns, Love has no pledge more fair,
Lady, to consecrate.

XXX

A young woman I saw under a laurel
Green, and she was more white and cold than snow
Deserted by the sun for many years;
And her speech and her fair face and her hair
Pleased me so that I keep her in my eyes
And always shall, whether on hill or shore.

My thoughts will only then attain a shore
When no green leaf is found upon a laurel;
When my heart will be calm and dry my eyes,
We shall see frozen fire and flaming snow.
I have not such a quantity of hair
As I would wait that day plenty of years.

But because hours go by and so do years,
And suddenly we are come to death's shore,
Whether with brown or whether with white hair,
I will follow the shade of that sweet laurel
In the most ardent sun and in the snow
Until the final day will close my eyes.

Non fûr giá mai veduti sí begli occhi
O ne la nostra etade o ne' prim'anni,
Che mi struggon cosí come 'l sol neve;
Onde procede lagrimosa riva,
Ch'Amor conduce a pie' del duro lauro
C'ha i rami di diamante e d'òr le chiome.

I' temo di cangiar pria vólto e chiome
Che con vera pietá mi mostri gli occhi
L'idolo mio scolpito in vivo lauro;
Ché, s'al contar non erro, oggi ha sett'anni
Che sospirando vo di riva in riva
La notte e 'l giorno, al caldo ed a la neve.

Dentro pur foco e fòr candida neve,
Sol con questi pensier, con altre chiome,
Sempre piangendo andrò per ogni riva,
Per far forse pietá venir ne gli occhi
Di tal che nascerá dopo mill'anni,
Se tanto viver pò ben cólto lauro.

L'auro e i topazii al sol sopra la neve
Vincon le bionde chiome presso a gli occhi
Che menan gli anni miei sí tosto a riva.

Never were seen such two beautiful eyes
In our own time or in the primal years,
As those that melt as the sun melts the snow;
Whence begins and proceeds a weeping shore
That Love leads to the feet of the hard laurel
With diamond branches and with golden hair.

I fear to change in my face and my hair
Before my idol shows to me her eyes
Full of true mercy, who is carved in laurel;
For if I do not err, now seven years
I have been sighing between shore and shore
And night and day, in the heat, in the snow.

Being inside of fire, outside of snow,
Only with these thoughts and with other hair,
I will go crying along every shore
Perhaps to stir some pity in the eyes
Of some who will be born in thousand years,
If such long time can live a well-nursed laurel.

OR and topazes in the sun and snow
Are dimmed by the fair hair around the eyes
That draw my years too quickly to the shore.

XXXI

Questa anima gentil che si diparte,
Anzi tempo chiamata a l'altra vita,
Se lassuso è quanto esser de' gradita,
Terrá del ciel la piú beata parte.

S'ella riman fra 'l terzo lume e Marte,
Fia la vista del Sole scolorita,
Poi ch'a mirar sua bellezza infinita
L'anime degne intorno a lei fíen sparte;

Se si posasse sotto al quarto nido,
Ciascuna de le tre saria men bella,
Et essa sola avria la fama e 'l grido;

Nel quinto giro non abitrebbe ella;
Ma se vola piú alto, assai mi fido
Che con Giove sia vinta ogni altra stella.

XXXII

Quanto piú m'avicino al giorno estremo
Che l'umana miseria suol far breve,
Piú veggio il tempo andar veloce e leve,
E 'l mio di lui sperar fallace e scemo.

I' dico a' miei pensier:—Non molto andremo
D'amor parlando omai, ché 'l duro e greve
Terreno incarco come fresca neve
Si va struggendo; onde noi pace avremo:

Perché co llui cadrá quella speranza
Che ne fe' vaneggiar sí lungamente,
E 'l riso e 'l pianto, e la paura e l'ira.

Sí vedrem chiaro poi come sovente
Per le cose dubbiose altri s'avanza,
E come spesso indarno sì sospira.—

XXXI

This gentle soul that from us will depart,
Called to the other life prematurely,
If she is there as dear as she must be,
Will keep of heaven the most blessed part.

If she stays between Mars and the third light,
The sun's brightness and colours will be dead,
For to admire the beauty of her sight
The holy souls around her will be spread;

If she remained under the fourth domain,
Each one of the three suns would be less pure,
And she alone would have fame and renown;

In the fifth sphere she would not settle down;
But if she flies above that, I am sure
That Jupiter and stars will shine in vain.

XXXII

The nearer I approach the extreme day
That is wont to break up the human pain,
The more swiftly I see time go away,
And what I hoped from it empty and vain.

I tell my thoughts:—Before long we shall cease
To talk of love, because the hard and slow
Terrestrial load is melting like fresh snow;
Therefore at last we shall be given peace:

For with that weight also the hope will die
Which made us rave and tremble for so long:
Laughing and weeping and anger and fear.

We shall then clearly see how often here
Through doubtful things one proceeds sure and strong,
And how often in vain some people sigh.—

XXXIII

Giá fiammeggiava l'amorosa stella
Per l'oriente, e l'altra che Giunone
Suol far gelosa nel settentrione
Rotava i raggi suoi lucente e bella;

Levata era a filar la vecchiarella,
Discinta e scalza, e desto avea 'l carbone,
E gli amanti pungea quella stagione
Che per usanza a lagrimar gli appella;

Quando mia speme giá condutta al verde
Giunse nel cor, non per l'usata via,
Che 'l sonno tenea chiusa, e 'l dolor molle;

Quanto cangiata, oimè, da quel di pria!
E parea dir:—Perché tuo valor perde?
Veder quest'occhi ancor non ti si tolle.—

XXXIV

Apollo, s'ancor vive il bel desïo
Che t'infiammava a le tesaliche onde,
E se non hai l'amate chiome bionde,
Volgendo gli anni, giá poste in oblio,

Dal pigro gielo e dal tempo aspro e rio,
Che dura quanto 'l tuo viso s'asconde,
Difendi or l'onorata e sacra fronde,
Ove tu prima, e poi fu' invescato io;

E per vertú de l'amorosa speme
Che ti sostenne ne la vita acerba,
Di queste impression l'aere disgombra:

Sí vedrem poi per meraviglia inseme
Seder la donna nostra sopra l'erba
E far de le sue braccia a se stessa ombra.

XXXIII

The star of love had just begun to glare
Throughout the east, and the other that makes
Juno jealous, and in the north awakes,
Whirled round its beams all luminous and fair;

The poor old woman, with bare feet, undressed,
Had just got up to spin and stirred the coal,
And lovers by that season were distressed
Which always seems to cause their tears to fall;

When the hope that by now was turning green
Came in my heart, not by the usual way
That sleeping closed and suffering made wet;

How changed, alas! from what she had once been!
—Why do you lose your strength?—she seemed to say,
—To see my eyes is not denied you yet.—

XXXIV

Apollo, if still lives the sweet desire
That made you yearn on the Thessalian wave,
If you have not forgotten to suspire,
With time, for the fair hair you used to crave,

From the slow frost and from the weather's grief
Which lasts as long as your face is not bare,
Defend the honoured and the sacred leaf
That once held you and holds me in a snare;

And by virtue of those amorous ties
That sustained you in your life's cruel harms,
Make the menace of these impressions pass:

Then we shall see together with surprise
Our lady sitting down amid the grass,
Casting a shade around her with her arms.

XXXV

Solo e pensoso i piú deserti campi
Vo mesurando a passi tardi e lenti,
E gli occhi porto per fuggire intenti
Ove vestigio uman l'arena stampi.

Altro schermo non trovo che mi scampi
Dal manifesto accorger de le genti;
Perché ne gli atti d'allegrezza spenti
Di fuor si legge com'io dentro avampi:

Sí ch'io mi credo omai che monti e piagge
E fiumi e selve sappian di che tempre
Sia la mia vita, ch'è celata altrui.

Ma pur sí aspre vie né sí selvagge
Cercar non so ch'Amor non venga sempre
Ragionando con meco, et io co llui.

XXXVI

S'io credesse per morte essere scarco
Del pensiero amoroso che m'atterra,
Colle mie mani avrei giá posto in terra
Queste membra noiose e quello incarco;

Ma perch'io temo che sarrebbe un varco
Di pianto in pianto e d'una in altra guerra,
Di qua dal passo ancor che mi si serra
Mezzo rimango, lasso!, e mezzo il varco.

Tempo ben fôra omai d'avere spinto
L'ultimo stral la dispietata corda,
Ne l'altrui sangue giá bagnato e tinto.

Et io ne prego Amore, e quella sorda
Che mi lassò de' suoi color depinto,
E di chiamarmi a sé non le ricorda.

XXXV

Alone and pensive, the most desert strand
I tread and measure with steps slow and dark,
My eyes ever intent to flee the mark
Of human feet imprinted in the sand;

I find no other screen to protect me
From men's knowledge that has nothing to learn,
For in my gestures bleak, without gaiety,
People can read how inwardly I burn:

So much, that I think now mountain and plain
And woods and rivers must know of what stuff
My life is made, that is concealed and dim.

Yet there is not a wild or rough terrain
Where I am not accompanied by Love
Always talking to me and I to him.

XXXVI

If I believed that death would free my chest
Of the amorous thought that crushes me,
With my own hands I should have laid to rest
These tiresome limbs and calmed this misery;

But since I fear that it would be a change
From war to war, from woe to other woe,
On this side of the pass that marks my range
I half remain, alas, and half I go.

It is now time that the merciless string
Should press and push the arrow that remained,
With other people's blood all wet and stained.

And I pray Love for this, and that deaf thing
Who left me with his colours splashed and dyed,
And does not care to call me to his side.

XXXVII

Sí è debile il filo a cui s'attene
La gravosa mia vita,
Che s'altri non l'aita,
Ella fia tosto di suo corso a riva;
Però che dopo l'empia dipartita
Che dal dolce mio bene
Feci, sol una spene
È stato in fin a qui cagion ch'io viva;
Dicendo:—Perché priva
Sia de l'amata vista,
Mantienti, anima trista:
Che sai s'a miglior tempo anco ritorni,
Et a piú lieti giorni?
O se 'l perduto ben mai si racquista?—
Questa speranza mi sostenne un tempo;
Or vien mancando, e troppo in lei m'attempo.

Il tempo passa, e l'ore son sí pronte
A fornire il viaggio,
Ch'assai spazio non aggio
Pur a pensar com'io corro a la morte.
A pena spunta in oriente un raggio
Di sol, ch' a l'altro monte
De l'adverso orizonte
Giunto il vedrai per vie lunghe e distorte.
Le vite son sí corte,
Sí gravi i corpi e frali
De gli uomini mortali,
Che quando io mi ritrovo dal bel viso
Cotanto esser diviso,
Col desio non possendo mover l'ali,
Poco m'avanza del conforto usato,
Né so quant'io mi viva in questo stato.

Ogni loco m'atrista ov'io non veggio
Quei begli occhi soavi
Che portaron le chiavi
De' miei dolci pensier, mentre a Dio piacque;

XXXVII

So feeble is the thread by which is held
My torments' living sum,
That if help does not come,
My life will soon at journey's end arrive:
Because after I left in tears the home
Of my good unexcelled,
Only a hope impelled
Me until now to continue to live;
Saying:—Though days deprive
You of her lovely sight,
Be firm in your sad plight:
Who knows but better times return and stay
Or else a happier day?
Or if lost love can again be our right?—
This hope comforted me some time ago;
Now it declines, I must not let it grow.

Time passes and the hours have so well tried
To provide for the trip,
That I may stop or slip
Before I think how fast my life decays.
As soon as in the east you see a strip
Of light, the ray will slide
To the opposite side,
Reaching the other hill by tortuous ways.
So short are our life's days,
So heavy and so vain
Are the bodies of men,
That when I find myself from the sweet face
Separated by space,
Unable with my wish to fly again,
My usual comfort I seek and I miss,
Nor do I know how long I live like this.

All place is sad in which she does not move
Those gentle lovely eyes
That held the keys and ties
Of all my thoughts as long as God was pleased;

E perché 'l duro essilio piú m'aggravi,
S'io dormo, o vado, o seggio,
Altro giá mai non cheggio,
E ciò ch'i' vidi dopo lor mi spiacque.
Quante montagne et acque,
Quanto mar, quanti fiumi
M'ascondon que' duo lumi,
Che quasi un bel sereno a mezzo 'l die
Fêr le tenebre mie,
A ciò che 'l rimembrar piú mi consumi,
E quanto era mia vita allor gioiosa
M'insegni la presente aspra e noiosa!

Lasso!, se ragionando si rinfresca
Quel ardente desio
Che nacque il giorno ch'io
Lassai di me la miglior parte a dietro,
E s'Amor se ne va per lungo oblio,
Chi mi conduce a l'ésca,
Onde 'l mio dolor cresca?
E perché pria tacendo non m'impetro?
Certo cristallo o vetro
Non mostrò mai di fòre
Nascosto altro colore,
Che l'alma sconsolata assai non mostri
Piú chiari i pensier nostri,
E la fera dolcezza ch'è nel core,
Per gli occhi, che di sempre pianger vaghi
Cercan dí e notte pur ch'i' glie n'appaghi.

Novo piacer che ne gli umani ingegni
Spesse volte si trova,
D'amar qual cosa nova
Piú folta schiera di sospiri accoglia!
Et io son un di quei che 'l pianger giova;
E par ben ch'io m'ingegni
Che di lagrime pregni
Sien gli occhi miei sí come 'l cor di doglia;
E perché a cciò m'invoglia
Ragionar de' begli occhi,

And to make my exile more pain comprise,
Whether I sleep or rove
Or sit, I nothing love
Of what I see, by all I am displeased.
How many hills have seized,
How many seas and streams
Have robbed from me those beams
That made my darkness almost crystal clear
As when noonday is here,
So that remembering I may be more teased,
And that the present life, made to annoy,
May teach me how the other was a joy!

Alas! if by this talking is renewed
That impatient desire
Born when I did retire,
Leaving my better part behind, alone,
And if forgetfulness quenches love's fire,
What traitor has pursued
Me, why is grief accrued?
And why does silence not turn me to stone?
Crystal or glass alone
Show as clearly outside
The shades they cannot hide,
As our sorrowful soul makes manifest
The thoughts within our breast;
And the sour bitterness that my heart tried
Glows through my eyes always ready to weep
And day and night seeking their fruit to reap.

The novel pleasure that to a man's mind
Oftentimes will be found
In loving on new ground,
Be welcomed by a thicker swarm of sighs!
And I am one in whom the tears abound;
As if I had designed
That my eyes should be blind
From tears, just as my heart in anguish lies;
Since talking of her eyes
Provokes me to that state,

(Né cosa è che mi tocchi,
O sentir mi si faccia cosí a dentro),
Corro spesso a rientro
Colá donde piú largo il duol trabocchi,
E sien col cor punite ambe le luci,
Ch' a la strada d'Amor mi furon duci.

Le treccie d'òr che devrien fare il sole
D'invidia molta ir pieno,
E 'l bel guardo sereno,
Ove i raggi d'Amor sí caldi sono
Che mi fanno anzi tempo venir meno,
E l'accorte parole,
Rade nel mondo o sole,
Che mi fêr giá di sé cortese dono,
Mi son tolte; e perdóno
Piú lieve ogni altra offesa,
Che l'essermi contesa
Quella benigna angelica salute,
Che 'l mio cor a vertute
Destar solea con una voglia accesa:
Tal ch'io non penso udir cosa giá mai
Che mi conforte ad altro ch'a trar guai.

E per pianger ancor con piú diletto,
Le man bianche sottili
E le braccia gentili,
E gli atti suoi soavamente altèri,
E i dolci sdegni alteramente umíli,
E 'l bel giovenil petto,
Tórre d'alto intelletto,
Mi celan questi luoghi alpestri e feri;
E non so s'io mi speri
Vederla anzi ch'io mora;
Però ch'ad ora ad ora
S'erge la speme, e poi non sa star ferma;
Ma ricadendo afferma
Di mai non veder lei che 'l ciel onora,
Ov'alberga onestate e cortesia
E dov'io prego che 'l mio albergo sia.

(There is no other bait
That catches me or makes my love so deep),
I often run and leap
There where grief overflows with greater weight,
And let my heart be punished with the lights
That led me to Love's road and to his rites.

The golden hair that should make the sun, stirred
By a great envy, stare,
The glance serene and fair
Where love's beams are so full of burning heat
That they before my time make me despair,
And the discerning word
That the world seldom heard,
And that gave me itself as a rare treat
Are denied me; I meet
Any wrong with more ease
Than this, by which will cease
For me the comfort of that saving art
Which used to wake my heart
To virtue by my own desire's release:
So that I do not hope ever to hear
A thing that helps me better than a tear.

And to move me to weep with greater zest,
The hands so white and slender,
And the arms pure and tender,
And her manner so beautifully proud,
And the sweet scorn chastising the offender,
And the fair youthful breast
Where the high mind has rest,
Have been concealed by these wild places' shroud;
I know not if I vowed
To see her ere I die;
Because all the hours fly
And hope arises and cannot stay there,
But falling will declare
That it shall not see one praised by the sky,
Where dwell charm, courtesy,
And where I pray that my abode may be.

Canzon, s'al dolce loco
La donna nostra vedi,
Credo ben che tu credi
Ch'ella ti porgerá la bella mano,
Ond'io son sí lontano.
Non la toccar; ma reverente ai piedi
Le di' ch'io sarò lá tosto ch'io possa,
O spirto ignudo od uom di carne e d'ossa.

XXXVIII

Orso, e' non furon mai fiumi né stagni,
Né mare, ov'ogni rivo si disgombra,
Né di muro o di poggio o di ramo ombra,
Né nebbia che 'l ciel copra e 'l mondo bagni,

Né altro impedimento, ond'io mi lagni,
Qualunque piú l'umana vista ingombra,
Quanto d'un vel che due begli occhi adombra,
E par che dica:—Or ti consuma e piagni.—

E quel lor inchinar ch'ogni mia gioia
Spegne, o per umiltate o per argoglio,
Cagion sará che nanzi tempo i' moia.

E d'una bianca mano anco mi doglio,
Ch'è stata sempre accorta a farmi noia,
E contra gli occhi miei s'è fatta scoglio.

Song, if in that sweet place
Our lady you will see,
You think perhaps like me
That she will offer you her lovely hand
From which so far I strand.
Do not go near; kneeling respectfully,
Tell her:—I come as soon as can be done,
Either bare soul or man of flesh and bone.—

XXXVIII

Orso, there never was a pond or rill,
Nor sea where every river lies unfurled,
Nor shadow of a wall or branch or hill,
Nor fog that hides the sky and wets the world,

Nor other obstacle that I will blame,
Whatever most annoys the human eye,
As a veil that obscures her look's dear flame
And seems to say:—Now weep until you die.—

And that lowering of eyes which smothers all
My joy—be it humility or pride—
Will be the cause of my early downfall.

And a white hand I also want to chide,
Which has always been quick to bring me grief,
Rising against me like an angry cliff.

XXXIX

Io temo sí de' begli occhi l'assalto,
Ne' quali Amore e la mia morte alberga,
Ch'i' fuggo lor come fanciul la verga;
E gran tempo è ch'i' presi il primier salto.

Da ora inanzi faticoso od alto
Loco non fia dove 'l voler non s'erga,
Per no scontrar chi miei sensi disperga,
Lassando, come suol, me freddo smalto.

Dunque, s'a veder voi tardo mi volsi,
Per non ravvicinarmi a chi mi strugge,
Fallir forse non fu di scusa indegno.

Piú dico, che'l tornare a quel ch'uom fugge,
E 'l cor che di paura tanta sciolsi,
Fûr de la fede mia non leggier pegno.

XL

S'Amore o Morte non dá qualche stroppio
A la tela novella ch'ora ordisco,
E s'io mi svolvo dal tenace visco,
Mentre che l'un coll'altro vero accoppio,

I' farò forse un mio lavor sí doppio,
Tra lo stil de' moderni e 'l sermon prisco,
Che, paventosamente a dirlo ardisco,
In fin a Roma n'udirai lo scoppio.

Ma però che mi manca a fornir l'opra
Alquanto de le fila benedette
Ch'avanzaro a quel mio diletto padre,

Perché tien' verso me le man sí strette
Contra tua usanza? I' prego che tu l'opra,
E vedrai riuscir cose leggiadre.

XXXIX

I fear so much the onslaught of the eyes
In which my death and Love lodge, live and last,
That I fly as a child from flogging flies;
And since I first took flight, much time has passed.

From now on there is not a tiring, steep
Place where my will is not arrived and gone
In order to avoid who makes me weep,
And then deserts me changed into cold stone.

Therefore if to see you I have come late,
Not to be near the one who is my death,
My fault perhaps is not without excuse.

I say more: to return to what we hate,
And a heart free from fear and from abuse
Were not too slight a warrant of my faith.

XL

If Love or Death will waste not or undo
The new weaving whose warp I laid with care,
If I can clear myself from the thick glue
While the one truth with the other I pair,

I shall perhaps make a work that will come
Between the modern style and the old tongue,
And then, I say it fearfully, my strong
Thoughts will resound from here as far as Rome.

But since I lack, to finish what I wove,
A great part of those blessed yarns and strands
That have been left to the father I love,

Why do you keep so tightly closed your hands
Against your custom? Please, untie the strings,
You will see as an outcome some fair things.

XLI

Quando dal proprio sito si rimove
L'arbor ch'amò giá Febo in corpo umano,
Sospira e suda a l'opera Vulcano,
Per rinfrescar l'aspre saette a Giove;

Il qual or tona, or nevica, et or piove,
Senza onorar piú Cesare che Giano;
La terra piange, e 'l Sol ci sta lontano,
Ché la sua cara amica ved'altrove.

Allor riprende ardir Saturno e Marte,
Crudeli stelle; et Orione armato
Spezza a' tristi nocchier governi e sarte;

Eolo a Nettuno et a Giunon turbato
Fa sentire, et a noi, come si parte
Il bel viso da gli angeli aspettato.

XLII

Ma poi che 'l dolce riso umíle e piano
Piú non asconde sue bellezze nove,
Le braccia a la fucina indarno move
L'antiquissimo fabbro ciciliano;

Ch'a Giove tolte son l'arme di mano
Temprate in Mongibello a tutte prove,
E sua sorella par che si rinove
Nel bel guardo d'Apollo a mano a mano.

Del lito occidental si move un fiato
Che fa securo il navigar senz'arte,
E desta i fior tra l'erba in ciascun prato;

Stelle noiose fuggon d'ogni parte,
Disperse dal bel viso inamorato,
Per cui lagrime molte son giá sparte.

XLI

When from its proper place is seen to move
The tree that Phoebus loved in human form,
Vulcan over his work does sweat and storm
To renew the fierce lightnings dealt by Jove,

Who now thunders, now sends snow and now rain,
No more Caesar than Janus is his care,
The earth sheds tears, the sun cannot remain,
Because he sees his beloved elsewhere.

Then Mars and Saturn their boldness resume,
The cruel stars; and Orion in arms
The luckless pilots' shrouds and rudders breaks;

Aeolus is felt by us in all his gloom,
By Juno, Neptune too, when she forsakes
Us with that face that even angels charms.

XLII

But when the gentle laughter's humble charms
No longer hide their beauty rare to see,
In vain around the furnace moves his arms
The very ancient smith of Sicily;

Without those weapons is left Jupiter,
That Mongibello made of tempered power,
And his sister appears to grow more fair
In Apollo's sweet look hour by hour.

From the western horizon comes a breeze
That makes unskilful sailing full of ease,
And wakes up flower and grass in every place;

Malignant stars from every side have fled,
Defeated by the fair, enamoured face
For which so many tears have now been shed.

XLIII

Il figliuol di Latona avea già nove
Volte guardato dal balcon sovrano
Per quella ch'alcun tempo mosse in vano
I suoi sospiri, et or gli altrui commove.

Poi che cercando stanco non seppe ove
S'albergasse, da presso o di lontano,
Mostrossi a noi qual uom per doglia insano,
Che molto amata cosa non ritrova.

E cosí tristo standosi in disparte,
Tornar non vide il viso, che laudato
Sará, s'io vivo, in piú di mille carte:

E pietá lui medesmo avea cangiato,
Sí che' begli occhi lagrimavan parte;
Però l'aere ritenne il primo stato.

XLIV

Que' che 'n Tesaglia ebbe le man sí pronte
A farla del civil sangue vermiglia,
Pianse morto il marito di sua figlia,
Raffigurato a le fattezze conte;

E 'l pastor ch'a Golía ruppe la fronte
Pianse la ribellante sua famiglia,
E sopra 'l buon Saúl cangiò le ciglia,
Ond'assai può dolersi il fiero monte.

Ma voi, che mai pietá non discolora,
E ch'avete gli schermi sempre accorti
Contra l'arco d'Amor, che 'ndarno tira,

Mi vedete straziare a mille morti,
Né lagrima però discese ancóra
Da' be' vostr'occhi, ma disdegno et ira.

XLIII

Latona's son had raised nine times his eyes
Already from his sovereign domain
To look for her who once had moved in vain
His sighs, and now excites some other sighs.

Because, weary of seeking, he did not
Know where she lived, near, far, before, behind,
He showed himself like one by grief distraught,
Who a much beloved thing can no more find.

Therefore, absconding far apart to fret,
He did not see the face that, if I live,
By more than thousand sheets shall praise receive:

And he himself was grown compassionate,
So that the limpid eyes were partly wet;
But the air still retained its previous state.

XLIV

That man whose hands to Thessaly brought slaughter
And made her red with civil blood and bold,
Mourned the death of the husband of his daughter,
Recognized by the features known of old;

And the shepherd who broke Goliath's brow
For his rebellious family did spill
Tears from his eyes, and to good Saul did bow,
Whence great must be the grief of the wild hill.

But you, whom pity does not make more pale,
Who always have your screens cunningly set
Against the aims of Love that always fail,

Can see me by a thousand tortures torn,
And not a tear is fallen down as yet
From your fair eyes, but only wrath and scorn.

XLV

Il mio adversario, in cui veder solete
Gli occhi vostri ch'Amore e 'l ciel onora,
Colle non sue bellezze v'innamora,
Piú che 'n guisa mortal soavi e liete.

Per consiglio di lui, donna, m'avete
Scacciato del mio dolce albergo fòra:
Misero essilio! avegna ch'i' non fòra
D'abitar degno ove voi sola siete.

Ma s'io v' era con saldi chiovi fisso,
Non devea specchio farvi per mio danno,
A voi stessa piacendo, aspra e superba.

Certo, se vi rimembra di Narcisso,
Questo e quel corso ad un termine vanno;
Ben che di sí bel fior sia indegna l'erba.

XLVI

L'oro e le perle, e i fior vermigli e i bianchi,
Che 'l verno devria far languidi e secchi,
Son per me acerbi e velenosi stecchi,
Ch'io provo per lo petto e per li fianchi.

Però i dí miei fíen lagrimosi e manchi;
Ché gran duol rade volte aven che 'nvecchi.
Ma piú ne 'ncolpo i micidiali specchí,
Che 'n vagheggiar voi stessa avete stanchi:

Questi poser silenzio al signor mio,
Che per me vi pregava, ond'ei si tacque,
Veggendo in voi finir vostro desio;

Questi fuôr fabbricati sopra l'acque
D'abisso, e tinti ne l'eterno oblio;
Onde 'l principio de mia morte nacque.

XLV

My adversary in which you can see
Your eyes that Love and heaven praise and seal,
With beauties not its own does your love steal,
That have more than a mortal quality.

Following its advice, Lady, you did
Cast me out of my habitation:
Grievous exile! though justly you forbid
Me to reside there where you dwell alone.

But if I was attached by nails so firm,
You should not have, to please your proud and sour
Self, raised a mirror against my sore need.

If you remember Narcissus, indeed,
One and the other road have the same term,
Though the grass is not worthy of that flower.

XLVI

Gold and pearls, a vermilion, a white flower
That winter ought to make drooping and dry,
Are to me only twigs poisonous, sour,
That on my breast and on my sides I tie.

Therefore my days will be tearful and void;
For seldom a great grief is seen to age.
But I blame more the mirrors that destroyed
Me and are tired to be your flattering cage:

These commanded my lord to hold his breath
While he was praying you, and he did so,
Seeing that you desired yourself alone;

These were constructed on the waves that flow
On the abyss, with forgetfulness' tone,
Whence arose the beginning of my death.

XLVII

Io sentía dentr'al cor giá venir meno
Gli spirti che da voi ricevon vita,
E perché naturalmente s'aita
Contra la morte ogni animal terreno,

Largai 'l desio, ch'i' teng' or molto a freno,
E misil per la via quasi smarrita;
Però che dí e notte indi m'invita,
Et io contra sua voglia altronde 'l meno.

E mi condusse vergognoso e tardo
A riveder gli occhi leggiadri, ond'io,
Per non esser lor grave, assai mi guardo.

Vivrommi un tempo omai, ch' al viver mio
Tanta virtute ha sol un vostro sguardo;
E poi morrò, s'io non credo al desio.

XLVIII

Se mai foco per foco non si spense,
Né fiume fu giá mai secco per pioggia,
Ma sempre l'un per l'altro simil poggia,
E spesso l'un contrario l'altro accense,

Amor, tu che 'pensier nostri dispense,
Al qual un'alma in duo corpi s'appoggia,
Perché fai in lei con disusata foggia
Men, per molto voler, le voglie intense?

Forse sí come 'l Nil, d'alto caggendo,
Col gran suono i vicin d'intorno assorda,
E 'l sole abbaglia chi ben fiso 'l guarda,

Cosí 'l desio, che seco non s'accorda,
Ne lo sfrenato obieto vien perdendo,
E per troppo spronar la fuga è tarda.

XLVII

My heart already felt from itself flee
The spirits that by you are made alive,
And because against death naturally
Every earthly beast will fight and strive,

I freed Desire, that I keep in control,
And put him where I almost went astray;
Therefore and day and night he sends his call
And I against his will take him away.

And he led me, very slow and ashamed,
To see again the fair eyes from whose fire
I always guard myself, not to be blamed.

Now I will live, because to bring me light
Only a look from you has such a might,
Then I will die if I trust not Desire.

XLVIII

If fire by fire was never made to cease,
Nor river ever was dried up by rain,
But always things alike themselves sustain,
And often contrasts each other increase,

Love, you who minister to our thoughts' course,
On whom one soul within two bodies leans,
Why do you cause, with unaccustomed means,
Her wishes to grow less by greater force?

Perhaps just as the Nile falling from high
Deafens the neighbours all around with sound,
As the sun dazzles the unblinking eye,

So a desire that with itself will fight
In a reckless devotion loses ground
And a too eager spurring checks a flight.

XLIX

Perch'io t'abbia guardato di menzogna
A mio podere et onorato assai,
Ingrata lingua, giá però non m'hai
Renduto onor, ma fatto ira e vergogna;

Ché quando piú 'l tuo aiuto mi bisogna
Per dimandar mercede, allor ti stai
Sempre piú fredda, e se parole fai,
Son imperfette, e quasi d'uom che sogna.

Lagrime triste, e voi tutte le notti
M'accompagnate, ov'io vorrei star solo,
Poi fuggite di nanzi a la mia pace;

E voi sí pronti a darmi angoscia e duolo,
Sospiri, allor traete lenti e rotti:
Sola la vista mia del cor non tace.

L

Ne la stagion che 'l ciel rapido inchina
Verso occidente, e che 'l dí nostro vola
A gente che di lá forse l'aspetta,
Veggendosi in lontan paese sola
La stanca vecchiarella pellegrina
Raddoppia i passi, e piú e piú s'affretta;
E poi cosí soletta,
Al fin di sua giornata
Talora è consolata
D'alcun breve riposo, ov'ella oblía
La noia e 'l mal de la passata via.
Ma, lasso!, ogni dolor che 'l dí m'adduce,
Cresce, qualor s'invia
Per partirsi da noi l'eterna luce.

Come 'l sol volge le 'nfiammate rote

XLIX

Although I always guarded you from lie,
As was my power, always honoured you best,
Ungrateful tongue, from you never did I
Receive an honour, but shame and unrest.

When I am most in need of assistance
To beg for mercy, then your hostile chords
Grow colder still, and if you know some words,
They are imperfect, of a man in trance.

Sorrowful tears, you that every night
Remain with me when I would be alone,
And desert me when I expect relief,

And you, so quick in bringing anguish, grief,
Slow, broken sighs that leave me half undone:
Only my look does not betray my plight.

L

At that time when the sky rapidly bends
Toward the west, and our day starts to fly
Beyond, to people who wait for the sun,
Feeling in distant lands alone and dry,
The tired old woman to her journey lends
A doubled step, and hurries, hurries on;
And as she is, alone,
At the end of her day
Sometimes is glad to stay
A little while, and rest and so forget
The pain by which her past road was beset.
Alas! for any grief the day brings me
Grows when the heavens let
Fade out from us their blessed clarity.

When the sun turns its incandescent wheels

Per dar luogo a la notte, onde discende
Da gli altissimi monti maggior l'ombra,
L'avaro zappador l'arme riprende,
E con parole e con alpestri note
Ogni gravezza del suo petto sgombra;
E poi la mensa ingombra
Di povere vivande,
Simili a quelle ghiande
Le qua' fuggendo tutto 'l mondo onora.
Ma chi vuol si rallegri ad ora ad ora;
Ch'i' pur non ebbi ancor, non dirò lieta,
Ma riposata un'ora,
Né per volger di ciel né di pianeta.

Quando vede 'l pastor calare i raggi
Del gran pianeta al nido ov'egli alberga,
E 'nbrunir le contrade d'oriente,
Drizzasi in piedi, e co l'usata verga,
Lassanda l'erba e le fontane e i faggi,
Move la schiera sua soavemente;
Poi lontan da la gente
O casetta o spelunca;
Di verdi frondi ingiunca;
Ivi senza pensier s'adagia e dorme.
Ahi, crudo Amor, ma tu allor piú m'informe
A seguir d'una fera che mi strugge
La voce e i passi e l'orme,
E lei non stringi che s'appiatta e fugge.

E i naviganti in qualche chiusa valle
Gettan le membra, poi che 'l sol s'asconde,
Sul duro legno e sotto a l'aspre gonne.
Ma io, perché s'attuffi in mezzo l'onde,
E lasci Ispagna dietro a le sue spalle
E Granata e Marrocco e le Colonne,
E gli uomini e le donne
E 'l mondo e gli animali
Aquetino i lor mali,
Fine non pongo al mio obstinato affanno;
E duolmi ch'ogni giorno arroge al danno,

To give room to the night, and greater then
Falls down the shadow from the mountain crest,
The greedy sapper takes his tool again
And with some country songs and words he heals
And clears away the burden of his breast.
And then he fills with zest
His table with poor food
Like those acorns of wood
That the world, shunning, still worships as power.
Let anyone find joy from hour to hour:
I have not had, I will not say a gay,
But a comforting hour,
Either from wheeling sky or planet's ray.

When the shepherd has seen the beams decrease
Of the great sun on the nest which he trod,
And in the east dark the horizon,
He stands erect and with the usual rod
Leaving the grass, the fountain, the beech-trees,
He softly leads his little army on;
Then, far from people gone,
A little hut he weaves
And covers with green leaves:
There without worries he lies down to sleep.
Ah, cruel Love, then you drive me to creep
And follow the wild beast that I adore,
Footsteps and voice and leap;
You do not catch her, and she flees the more.

The sailors too, in some protected valley
Drop down their limbs, after the sun is set,
On the hard wood, retaining their rough clothes;
But I, though it is sunk in the waves' net,
And though Spain has been left alone to dally,
And Granada, Morocco and Pillars' rows
And mankind, friends and foes,
And world and animals
Solace with rest their galls,
I never cease to languish in my song
And lament that each day augments the wrong,

Ch'i' son giá pur crescendo in questa voglia
Ben presso al decim'anno,
Né poss' indovinar chi me ne scioglia.

E perché un poco nel parlar mi sfogo,
Veggio la sera i buoi tornare sciolti
Da le campagne e da' solcati colli.
I miei sospiri a me perché non tolti
Quando che sia? perché no 'l grave giogo?
Perché dí e notte gli occhi miei son molli?
Misero me, che volli,
Quando primier sí fiso
Gli tenni nel bel viso,
Per iscolpirlo, imaginando, in parte
Onde mai né per forza né par arte
Mosso sará, fin ch'i' sia dato in preda
A chi tutto diparte!
Né so ben anco che di lei mi creda.

Canzon, se l'esser meco
Dal matino a la sera
T'ha fatto di mia schiera,
Tu non vorrai mostrarti in ciascun loco;
E d'altrui loda curerai sí poco,
Ch'assai ti fia pensar di poggio in poggio
Come m'ha concio 'l foco
Di questa viva petra, ov'io m'appoggio.

For I have been consumed by a complaint
Now nearly ten years long,
And do not know who will ease my constraint.

If I relieve with talk my pain a bit,
I see at night the oxen come back free
Out of the pastures and the laboured hills.
Why are not then my sighs taken from me
At any time? Why does the yoke still fit?
Why day and night are my wet eyes two rills?
Remorse my conscience fills,
For I with stubborn glance
Watched her face in a trance,
To carve it, as I thought, at least in part
Where neither by coercion nor by art
It shall be moved, until I am a prey
Of Death who all does part,
Nor do I know whether to trust his play.

Song, if being with me
From morning unto night
Made you my company,
You will not show yourself in any light:
You will not care for other people's praise,
You will think it enough that you have seen
How I faint from the blaze
Of that animate stone on which I lean.

LI

Poco era ad appressarsi a gli occhi miei
La luce che da lunge gli abbarbaglia,
Che, come vide lei cangiar Tesaglia,
Cosí cangiato ogni mia forma avrei.

E s'io non posso transformarmi in lei
Piú ch'i' mi sia (non ch'a mercé mi vaglia),
Di qual petra piú rigida s'intaglia,
Pensoso ne la vista oggi sarei,

O di diamante, o d'un bel marmo bianco
Per la paura forse, o d'un diaspro,
Pregiato poi dal vulgo avaro e sciocco;

E sarei fuor del grave giogo et aspro,
Per cui i'ho invidia di quel vecchio stanco
Che fa co le sue spalle ombra a Marrocco.

LII

Non al suo amante piú Diana piacque,
Quando per tal ventura tutta ignuda
La vide in mezzo de le gelide acque,

Ch'a me la pastorella alpestra e cruda
Posta a bagnar un leggiadretto velo,
Ch'a l'aura il vago e biondo capel chiuda,

Tal che mi fece, or quand'egli arde 'l cielo,
Tutto tremar d'un amoroso gielo.

LI

The light that from afar dazzles my eyes
Was coming toward me at closer range,
When, as Thessaly saw her aspect change,
So would I have transmuted shape and size.

And if I cannot be transformed and shut
In her more than I am (she does not care),
I would as thoughtful and impassive stare
As the hardest of stones that can be cut,

Either a diamond or a marble white
Perhaps from fear, or a jasper displayed
Later and prized by stingy, foolish folk;

And I would be out of the heavy yoke
Which makes me grudge that elderly man's plight
Whose shoulders on Morocco throw a shade.

LII

Diana never pleased her lover more,
When by some chance he saw her naked lie
Among the chilly waters, from the shore,

Than did me the small shepherdess and shy,
Intent to bathe a fascinating veil
That the aura's fair hair is wont to tie,

So that it made me in the torrid dale
Tremble all over, like a loving gale.

LIII

Spirto gentil, che quelle membra reggi
Dentro a le qua' peregrinando alberga
Un signor valoroso, accorto e saggio,
Poi che se' giunto a l'onorata verga
Colla qual Roma e suoi erranti correggi,
E la richiami al suo antiquo viaggio,
Io parlo a te, però ch'altrove un raggio
Non veggio di vertú, ch'al mondo è spenta,
Né trovo chi di mal far si vergogni.
Che s'aspetti non so, né che s'agogni,
Italia, che suoi guai non par che senta;
Vecchia, oziosa e lenta,
Dormirá sempre, e non fia chi la svegli?
Le man l'avess'io avolto entro ' capegli.

Non spero che giá mai dal pigro sonno
Mova la testa per chiamar ch'uom faccia,
Sí gravemente è oppressa e di tal soma.
Ma non senza destíno a le tue braccia,
Che scuoter forte e sollevar la ponno,
È or commesso il nostro capo Roma.
Pon man in quella venerabil chioma
Securamente e ne le treccie sparte,
Sí che la neghittosa esca del fango.
I' che dí e notte del suo strazio piango,
Di mia speranza ho in te la maggior parte;
Che se 'l popol di Marte
Devesse al proprio onore alzar mai gli occhi,
Parmi pur ch' a' tuoi dí la grazia tocchi.

L'antiche mura ch'ancor teme et ama
E trema 'l mondo, quando si rimembra
Del tempo andato e 'n dietro si rivolve,
E i sassi dove fûr chiuse le membra
Di ta' che non saranno senza fama
Se l'universo pria non si dissolve,
E tutto quel ch'una ruina involve,
Per te spera saldar ogni suo vizio.

LIII

O gentle spirit who those members rule
Inside which like a pilgrim dwelt and trod
A gallant lord, as discerning as wise,
Since you have reached the honourable rod
By which you chastise Rome and every fool,
And remind her of her historic ties,
I speak to you because there does not rise
Elsewhere a ray of valour, which is gone,
And men are not ashamed of being knaves.
What Italy waits for, or what she craves
I do not know, she feels less than a stone;
Old and idle and prone,
Will she forever sleep and none will care?
Could I entwist my hands within her hair!

I do not hope that from her lazy sleep
She will turn round, however loud one calls,
So heavy is her burden, of such weight.
But not by chance the task to your arms falls,
That can shake her and raise out of the deep;
Our head, Rome, is entrusted you by fate.
Lay your hand on that venerable plait
Firmly, and in the braids loosened and lewd,
So that the slothful from the mud emerge.
I who repeat and day and night her dirge,
Have put in you all my solicitude,
For if Mars' people should
Ever look at their honour with their eyes,
I think that to your days belongs the prize.

The ancient walls that the world fears and loves
Still, and trembles, recalling to its mind
The time that was, turning to give a glance,
And the stones where were closed in and confined
The limbs of some of whom honour approves,
Unless the universe fall to mischance,
And all the things on which ruins advance
Through you hope to reform each vice and lust.

O grandi Scipioni, o fedel Bruto,
Quanto v'aggrada, s'egli è ancor venuto
Romor lá giú del ben locato offizio!
Come cre' che Fabrizio
Si faccia lieto udendo la novella!
E dice:—Roma mia sará ancor bella.—

E se cosa di qua nel ciel si cura,
L'anime che lassú son citadine
Et hanno i corpi abandonati in terra,
Del lungo odio civil ti pregan fine,
Per cui la gente ben non s'assecura,
Onde 'l camin a' lor tetti si serra;
Che fûr giá sí devoti, et ora in guerra
Quasi spelunca di ladron son fatti,
Tal ch'a' buon solamente uscio si chiude,
E tra gli altari e tra le statue ignude
Ogni impresa crudel par che se tratti.
Deh quanto diversi atti!
Né senza squille s'incommincia assalto,
Che per Dio ringraziar fûr poste in alto.

Le donne lagrimose, e 'l vulgo inerme
De la tenera etate, e i vecchi stanchi
C'hanno sé in odio e la soverchia vita,
E i neri fraticelli e i bigi e i bianchi,
Coll'altre schiere travagliate e 'nferme,
Gridan:—O signor nostro, aita, aita!—
E la povera gente sbigottita
Ti scopre le sue piaghe a mille a mille,
Ch'Anibale, non ch'altri, farian pio.
E se ben guardi a la magion di Dio,
Ch'arde oggi tutta, assai poche faville
Spegnendo, fíen tranquille
Le voglie, che si mostran sí 'nfiammate,
Onde fíen l'opre tue nel ciel laudate.

Orsi, lupi, leoni, aquile e serpi
Ad una gran marmorea colonna
Fanno noia sovente, et a sé danno.

O you great Scipios, loyal Brutus, how
Happy you are, if the rumour by now
Has come below, of the well-given trust!
How Fabricius must
Rejoice when the good news catches his ears!
He says:—My Rome still beautiful appears.—

And if the sky cares for some earthly things,
The souls that have received a high estate
And let their bodies languish in the soil,
Beg you to stop this endless civil hate
Which does not soothe the people's sufferings
And closes against them their homes of toil;
These were once so devout, now they recoil
Like dark caverns of thieves that a war breeds,
So that only the good cannot find rest,
And among altars and statues undressed
Every cruel plot seems to sow seeds.
Ah, what different deeds!
Nor without trumpets does a charging shove,
Which to give thanks to God were placed above.

The weeping women and the unarmed crowd
Of children, and the old who cannot fight,
Who loathe themselves and life's wearisome pass,
And the black little monks, the grey, the white,
With all the ailing masses cry aloud,
Saying:—O kindly lord, help us, help us!—
And the poor folk bewildered, tired, alas,
Open to you their more than thousand sores
That would move others and Hannibal too.
And if you look at the house of the true
God, that now blazes, who few sparks abhors
To peacefulness restores
The wills that such a glowing flame have raised,
Whence your works up in heaven will be praised.

The bears, the wolves, the lions, eagles, snakes,
To a column of marble often are
Just a nuisance and to themselves a wrong.

Di costor piange quella gentil donna,
Che t'ha chiamato, a ciò che di lei sterpi
Le male piante, che fiorir non sanno.
Passato è giá piú che 'l millesimo anno
Che 'n lei mancâr quell'anime leggiadre
Che locata l'avean lá dov'ell'era.
Ahi nova gente oltra misura altèra,
Irreverente a tanta et a tal madre!
Tu marito, tu padre;
Ogni soccorso di tua man s'attende;
Ché 'l maggior padre ad altr'opera intende.

Rade volte adiven ch'a l'alte imprese
Fortuna ingiuriosa non contrasti,
Ch'a gli animosi fatti mal s'accorda:
Ora sgombrando 'l passo onde tu intrasti,
Famisi perdonar molt'altre offese,
Ch'almen qui da se stessa si discorda;
Però che, quanto 'l mondo si ricorda,
Ad uom mortal non fu aperta la via
Per farsi, come a te, di fama eterno,
Che puoi drizzar, s'i' non falso discerno,
In stato la piú nobil monarchia.
Quanta gloria ti fia
Dir:—Gli altri l'aitâr giovene e forte;
Questi in vecchiezza la scampò da morte!—

Sopra 'l monte Tarpeio, canzon, vedrai
Un cavalier, ch'Italia tutta onora,
Pensoso piú d'altrui che di se stesso.
Digli:—Un che non ti vide ancor da presso,
Se non come per fama uom s'innamora,
Dice che Roma ogni ora,
Con gli occhi di dolor bagnati e molli
Ti chier mercé da tutti sette i colli.—

For them weeps the good woman, from afar
Begging you to uproot and tear with rakes
The evil plants that for blooms do not long.
The thousandth year has passed since she was strong,
Since those beautiful souls went to another
Place, who had raised her where she was seen then.
Ah, new-made people measurelessly vain,
Who feel no reverence for such a mother!
You husband and you father,
All comforts are expected from your hands;
For the great Father fills other demands.

It seldom happens that a noble feat
Is not contrasted by insulting Chance
Who ill agrees with a spirited deed:
Now since she clears the step whence you advance,
I must forgive her, though she likes to cheat,
For this time with herself she disagreed;
Because, after the world had known our seed,
To a mortal the way was never free
To acquire as you will eternal fame,
Being able to raise, the truth I claim,
To great estate the noblest monarchy.
What glory will it be
To say:—The others helped her young and bold;
This one saved her from death when she was old!—

On the Tarpeian height, song, you will see
A knight whom all of Italy admires,
To whom our good beyond his own is dear.
Tell him:—One who has not yet seen you near,
Except as by hearsay we feel love's fires,
Says that Rome who suspires,
Every hour, with tears that grief distils,
Begs for your mercy from her seven hills.—

LIV

Per ch'al viso d'Amor portava insegna,
Mosse una pellegrina il mio cor vano,
Ch'ogni altra mi parea d'onor men degna.

E lei seguendo su per l'erbe verdi,
Udí' dir alta voce di lontano:
—Ahi, quanti passi per la selva perdi!—

Allor mi strinsi a l'ombra d'un bel faggio,
Tutto pensoso; e rimirando intorno,
Vidi assai periglioso il mio viaggio;

E tornai in dietro quasi a mezzo 'l giorno.

LV

Quel foco ch'i' pensai che fosse spento
Dal freddo tempo e da l'etá men fresca,
Fiamma e martír ne l'anima rinfresca.

Non fûr mai tutte spente, a quel ch'i' veggio,
Ma ricoperte alquanto le faville;
E temo no 'l secondo error sia peggio.
Per lagrime, ch'i' spargo a mille a mille,
Conven che 'l duol per gli occhi si distille
Dal cor, c'ha seco le faville e l'ésca;
Non pur qual fu, ma pare a me che cresca.

Qual foco non avrian giá spento e morto
L'onde che gli occhi tristi versan sempre?
Amor, avegna mi sia tardi accorto,
Vòl che tra duo contrarî mi distempre;
E tende lacci in sí diverse tempre,
Che quand'ho piú speranza che 'l cor n'èsca,
Allor piú nel bel viso mi rinvesca.

LIV

Because she wore Love's signs upon her face,
A pilgrim woman moved my foolish heart,
Every other seeming of less grace.

And in following her on the green grass,
I heard a voice cry from a distant part:
—How many steps lost in the woods, alas!—

Then I clung to the shadow of a beech
In meditation; and, watching my way,
I saw my journey's aim too hard to reach;

And I came back almost at noon of day.

LV

That fire which I believed had been put out
By the cold weather and the years that run,
Anguish and flame renew with passion.

It never was extinguished, as I see,
It only stifled just a bit its spark;
And this second mistake may ruin me.
Though I shed thousand and more tears, the mark
Of grief comes to the eyes out of the dark
Where the heart keeps concealed and spark and stone;
Not as it was before, but mightier grown.

What fire would not be stilled and forced to die
By the water that from my sad eyes falls?
Love—I noticed too late that he is sly—
Wants me to waste between two extreme poles;
And he deceives me with such warring goals,
That the more I dare hope my heart has won,
The more that fair face blinds me like a sun.

LVI

Se col cieco desir che 'l cor distrugge,
Contando l'ore no m'inganno io stesso,
Ora, mentre ch'io parlo, il tempo fugge
Ch' a me fu inseme et a mercé promesso.

Qual ombra è sí crudel che 'l seme adugge
Ch'al disiato frutto era sí presso?
E dentro dal mio ovil qual fera rugge?
Tra la spiga e la man qual muro è messo?

Lasso!, no 'l so; ma sí conosco io bene
Che per far piú dogliosa la mia vita
Amor m'addusse in sí gioiosa spene.

Et or di quel ch'i' ho letto mi sovene,
Che nanzi al dí de l'ultima partita
Uom beato chiamar non si convene.

LVII

Mie venture al venir son tarde e pigre,
La speme incerta, e 'l desir monta e cresce,
Onde e 'l lassare e l'aspettar m'incresce;
E poi al partir son piú levi che tigre.

Lasso!, le nevi fíen tepide e nigre,
E 'l mar senz'onda, e per l'alpe ogni pesce,
E corcherassi il sol lá oltre ond'esce
D'un medesimo fonte Eufrate e Tigre,

Prima ch'i' trovi in ciò pace né triegua,
O Amore o madonna altr'uso impari,
Che m'hanno congiurato a torto incontra.

E s'i' ho alcun dolce, è dopo tanti amari,
Che per disdegno il gusto si dilegua.
Altro mai di lor grazie non m'incontra.

LVI

If with this blind desire that tears my heart
Counting the hours I am not deceived,
Now while I speak all the minutes depart
Which had promised to pity one so grieved.

What shadow is so cruel to hate the seed
That is so near to fruit, to being born?
And, in my fold, what of such roaring need?
What wall between the hand and the ear of corn?

Alas! I do not know, but I perceive
That in order to make my life more dread
Love urged me in this gladness to believe.

And I remember now what I have read,
That we cannot, before the parting day,
Call a man blessed in his earthly stay.

LVII

My lucky chances are lazy to come,
Hope is uncertain, desires mount and heave,
Hence to go and to wait will make me glum,
And they run like a tiger when they leave.

Alas! the snows will be lukewarm and black,
And the sea without waves, the Alps with fish,
The sun will set in the same spring and track
Where Tigris and Euphrates have one wish,

Before I find from this peace or relief,
Or Love or else my lady learn to see,
Who have conspired against me by mischief.

And if I have some sweet after so much
Bitter, the taste will tire and not be such.
Nothing else of their grace is given me.

LVIII

La guancia, che fu giá piangendo stanca,
Riposate su l'un, signor mio caro;
E siate ormai di voi stesso piú avaro
A quel crudel che ' suoi seguaci imbianca;

Coll'altro richiudete da man manca
La strada a' messi suoi ch'indi passaro,
Mostrandovi un d'agosto e di genaro,
Per ch'a la lunga via tempo ne manca;

E col terzo bevete un suco d'erba
Che purghe ogni pensier che 'l cor afflige,
Dolce a la fine e nel principio acerba.

Me riponete ove 'l piacer si serba
Tal ch'i' non téma del nocchier di Stige,
Se la preghiera mia non è superba.

LIX

Perché quel che mi trasse ad amar prima
Altrui colpa mi toglia,
Del mio fermo voler giá non mi svoglia.

Tra le chiome de l'òr nascose il laccio,
Al qual mi strinse, Amore;
E da' begli occhi mosse il freddo ghiaccio,
Che mi passò nel core,
Con la vertú d'un súbito splendore,
Che d'ogni altra sua voglia,
Sol rimembrando, ancor l'anima spoglia.

Tolta m'è poi di que' biondi capelli,
Lasso!, la dolce vista;
E 'l volger de' duo lumi onesti e belli
Col suo fuggir m'atrista;
Ma perché ben morendo onor s'acquista,
Per morte, né per doglia,
Non vo' che da tal nodo Amor mi scioglia.

LVIII

Your cheek that has become weary of tears
Lay upon this, my lord, be self-controlled
Now and more avaricious of your years
Toward someone who makes his courtiers old;

With the other shut off at the left side
The road whence come his messengers to carry
News, one in August and in January,
Because we have no time for the long ride;

And with the third drink up a juice of grass
That purifies each thought ailing the heart,
Sweet in the end and bitter at the start.

Lay me where pleasure lasts and does not pass,
So that I may not fear the Stygian shroud,
If this prayer of mine is not too proud.

LIX

Though what caused me to love her at first sight
By her fault seems to wane,
From my desire I will never refrain.

Into her golden hair Love hid and tossed
The snare that fastened me;
And from her lovely eyes came the hard frost
That is my penalty,
With the might of a sudden brilliancy
Which does in me remain
Until from other wishes I abstain.

Then the blond head which was my lovely sight
Was denied to my sense;
And the dear turning of her eyes' pure light
That is no more, torments;
But since those who die well are honoured thence,
Be it death, be it pain,
I do not want to be freed from my chain.

LX

L'arbor gentil, che forte amai molt'anni,
Mentre i bei rami non m'ebber a sdegno
Fiorir faceva il mio debile ingegno
A la sua ombra, e crescer ne gli affanni.

Poi che, securo me di tali inganni,
Fece di dolce sé spietato legno,
I' rivolsi i pensier tutti ad un segno,
Che parlan sempre de' lor tristi danni.

Che porá dir chi per Amor sospira,
S'altra speranza le mie rime nove
Gli avessir data, e per costei la perde?

—Né poeta ne colga mai, né Giove
La privilegi; et al Sol venga in ira,
Tal che si secchi ogni sua foglia verde.—

LXI

Benedetto sia 'l giorno, e 'l mese, e l'anno,
E la stagione, e 'l tempo, e l'ora, e 'l punto,
E 'l bel paese, e 'l loco ov'io fui giunto
Da' duo begli occhi, che legato m'hanno;

E benedetto il primo dolce affanno
Ch'i' ebbi ad esser con Amor congiunto,
E l'arco, e le saette ond'i' fui punto,
E le piaghe che 'n fin al cor mi vanno.

Benedette le voci tante ch'io
Chiamando il nome de mia donna ho sparte,
E i sospiri, e le lagrime, e 'l desio;

E benedette sian tutte le carte
Ov'io fama l'acquisto, e 'l pensier mio,
Ch'è sol di lei, sí ch'altra non v'ha parte.

LX

The gentle tree that I loved many years
When the fair branches did not spurn my eyes,
Caused my weak mind to blossom and to rise
Under her shade, and to grow among cares.

When, having sheltered me from her deceits,
The wood which had been sweet became malign,
I turned my thoughts always toward one sign,
And now they only speak of their defeats.

What will be the retort of those who sigh,
If my new rhymes had made them hope in love
And now, because of her, have lost their path?

—May neither poet pluck her boughs, nor Jove
Honour her; and the sun display his wrath,
So that all her green leaves be dead and dry.—

LXI

Blessed may be the day, the month, the year,
And the season, the time, the hour, the point,
And the country, the place where I was joined
By two fair eyes that now have tied me here.

And blessed be the first sweet agony
That I felt in becoming bound to Love,
And the bow and the arrows piercing me,
And the wounds that go down so deep to move.

Blessed the many voices that I raised,
Calling my lady, to scatter her name,
And blessed be my tears, my sighs, my heart;

Blessed may be the paper where more fame
I earn for her, my thought by which she is praised,
Only her own: no one else has a part.

LXII

Padre del ciel, dopo i perduti giorni,
Dopo le notti vaneggiando spese,
Con quel fero desio ch'al cor s'accese,
Mirando gli atti per mio mal sí adorni,

Piacciati omai col tuo lume ch'io torni
Ad altra vita, et a piú belle imprese,
Sí ch'avendo le reti indarno tese,
Il mio duro adversario se ne scorni.

Or volge, Signor mio, l'undecimo anno
Ch'i' fui sommesso al dispietato giogo,
Che sopra i piú soggetti è piú feroce.

Miserere del mio non degno affanno;
Redúci i pensier vaghi a miglior luogo;
Ramenta lor come oggi fusti in croce.

LXIII

Volgendo gli occhi al mio novo colore,
Che fa di morte rimembrar la gente,
Pietá vi mosse; onde, benignamente
Salutando, teneste in vita il core.

La fraile vita ch'ancor meco alberga,
Fu de' begli occhi vostri aperto dono,
E de la voce angelica soave.
Da lor conosco l'esser ov'io sono;
Ché, come suol pigro animal per verga,
Cosí destaro in me l'anima grave.
Del mio cor, donna, l'una e l'altra chiave
Avete in mano; e di ciò son contento,
Presto di navigare a ciascun vento;
Ch'ogni cosa da voi m'è dolce onore.

LXII

Father of heaven, after the wasted days,
After the nights spent in a raving mind
With that cruel desire, my heart's mad chase
After the beauty for my grief designed,

Let it please your pure light that I return
To other life and to more worthy ends:
So that, having in vain snared me to burn,
My adversary resent this offence.

Now approaches, dear Lord, the eleventh year
That I have spent under the ruthless weight
Which to the more oppressed is more severe;

Have pity of my guilty pain and loss,
Lead my distracted thoughts to better state,
Tell them today you were nailed to the cross.

LXIII

Turning your eyes to my poor colour's blight
Which reminds people of the death they see,
Pity moved you; hence kindly greeting me,
You kept alive my heart by that delight.

The fragile life that within me remains
Was the generous gift of your fair eyes
And of the angel-soft, melodious voice.
From them my station I can realize;
For as a lazy beast when whipped regains
Speed, so they spurred my soul's delaying choice.
Lady, you hold the keys—hence I rejoice—
Of my own heart in your sweet hands that bind;
I am ready to sail by any wind,
Everything from you is sweet and right.

LXIV

Se voi poteste per turbati segni,
Per chinar gli occhi, o per piegar la testa,
O per esser piú d'altra al fuggir presta,
Torcendo 'l viso a' preghi onesti e degni,

Uscir giá mai, o ver per altri ingegni,
Del petto, ove dal primo lauro innesta
Amor piú rami, i' direi ben che questa
Fosse giusta cagione a' vostri sdegni;

Ché gentil pianta in arido terreno
Par che si disconvenga, e però lieta
Naturalmente quindi si diparte.

Ma poi vostro destíno a voi pur vieta
L'esser altrove, provedete almeno
Di non star sempre in odiosa parte.

LXV

Lasso!, che mal accorto fui da prima
Nel giorno ch'a ferir mi venne Amore,
Ch'a passo a passo è poi fatto signore
De la mia vita, e posto in su la cima!

Io non credea per forza di sua lima
Che punto di fermezza o di valore
Mancasse mai ne l'indurato core;
Ma cosí va chi sopra 'l ver s'estima.

Da ora inanzi ogni difesa è tarda,
Altra che di provar s'assai o poco
Questi preghi mortali Amore sguarda.

Non prego giá, né puote aver piú loco
Che mesuratamente il mio cor arda,
Ma che sua parte abbi costei del foco.

LXIV

If you could ever, by your troubled air,
By looking down, or bending not to see,
By seeming more than others swift to flee,
Turning your face away from a just prayer,

If you could thus or in another way
Part from my breast where Love from the first-born
Laurel grafts many boughs, then I would say
That this might be the cause of all your scorn;

A gentle plant in a barren terrain
Is not at home, and therefore it is fain
Naturally from that soil to depart.

But since your destiny seems to deny
That you be somewhere else, you might well try
Not to be always in a hateful part.

LXV

Alas! I was too heedless the first day
When Love came down to wound me with a sword,
Who step by step has now become the lord
Of all my life, and from its top holds sway!

I did not think that his sharp-cutting dart
Would take away and overcome and beat
Firmness or valour in my hardened heart;
This is what happens to human conceit.

From now on all defence-move is too slow,
Except trying how little or how much
Love intends to respect a mortal prayer.

Not a prayer can there be, nor a place such
That let my heart more moderately glow,
Only that of this fire she get her share.

LXVI

L'aere gravato, e l'importuna nebbia
Compressa intorno da rabbiosi vènti
Tosto conven che si converta in pioggia;
E giá son quasi di cristallo i fiumi,
E 'n vece de l'erbetta per le valli
Non se ved'altro che pruine e ghiaccio.

Et io nel cor via piú freddo che ghiaccio
Ho di gravi pensier tal una nebbia,
Qual si leva talor di queste valli,
Serrate incontra a gli amorosi vènti,
E cincundate di stagnanti fiumi,
Quanto cade dal ciel piú lenta pioggia.

In picciol tempo passa ogni gran pioggia,
E 'l caldo fa sparir le nevi e 'l ghiaccio,
Di che vanno superbi in vista i fiumi;
Né mai nascose il ciel sí folta nebbia
Che sopragiunta dal furor di vènti
Non fugisse da i poggi e da le valli.

Ma, lasso!, a me non val fiorir de valli;
Anzi piango al sereno et a la pioggia,
Et a' gelati et a' soavi vènti:
Ch'allor fia un dí madonna senza 'l ghiaccio
Dentro, e di fòr senza l'usata nebbia,
Ch'i' vedrò secco il mare, e' laghi, e i fiumi.

Mentre ch' al mar descenderanno i fiumi
E le fiere ameranno ombrose valli,
Fia di nanzi a' begli occhi quella nebbia
Che fa nascer di ' miei continua pioggia,
E nel bel petto l'indurato ghiaccio
Che tra' del mio sí dolorosi vènti.

Ben debbo io perdonare a tutt'i vènti,
Per amor d'un che 'n mezzo di duo fiumi
Mi chiuse tra 'l bel verde e 'l dolce ghiaccio,
Tal ch'i' depinsi poi per mille valli

LXVI

The heavy air and the untimely fog,
Concentrated and pressed by raging winds,
Will soon fall upon us turned into rain;
And now almost of crystal seem the rivers,
And instead of small grass throughout the valleys
One sees nothing but hoary frost and ice.

And in my heart that grows colder than ice
I have amassed from heavy thoughts a fog
Such as will rise at times out of these valleys
Gathered and closed against the loving winds
And all encircled by stagnating rivers,
When from the sky slowly descends the rain.

In a small time is gone the greatest rain,
And the heat melts away the snows and ice,
Whence full of pride appear the flowing rivers;
The sky never concealed so thick a fog
That, overreached by the wrath of the winds,
Did not hurriedly run from hills and valleys.

But not for me, alas, the blooming valleys;
I must weep in the sun and in the rain,
Under the frozen and the gentle winds;
For my lady will be left without ice
Inside and free outside from the old fog,
When I behold dry seas and lakes and rivers.

But till toward the sea flow down the rivers
And the beasts love the shadows of the valleys,
There will remain before her eyes that fog
Which distils out of mine an endless rain,
And in the charming breast the hardened ice
That draws out of my own such woeful winds.

I must nevertheless forgive the winds,
For love of one who once between two rivers
Placed me amid the green and the sweet ice,
So that I painted in a thousand valleys

L'ombra, ov'io fui; che né calor, né pioggia,
Né suon curava di spezzata nebbia.

Ma non fuggío giá mai nebbia per vènti,
Come quel dí, né mai fiumi per pioggia,
Né ghiaccio, quando 'l sole apre le valli.

LXVII

Del mar Tirreno a la sinistra riva,
Dove rotte dal vento piangon l'onde,
Súbito vidi quella altèra fronde,
Di cui conven che 'n tante carte scriva.

Amor che dentro a l'anima bolliva,
Per rimembranza de le treccie bionde,
Mi spinse; onde in un rio che l'erba asconde
Caddi, non giá come persona viva.

Solo, ov'io era, tra boschetti e colli,
Vergogna ebbi di me; ch'al cor gentile
Basta ben tanto, et altro spron non volli.

Piacemi almen d'aver cangiato stile,
Da gli occhi a' pie'; se del lor esser molli
Gli altri asciugasse un piú cortese aprile!

The shadow where I was; nor heat, nor rain,
Nor sound I heeded of a broken fog.

But never did fog flee before the winds
As on that day, nor rivers under rain,
Nor ice, when the sunlight opens the valleys.

LXVII

On the left shore of the Tyrrhenian sea
Where broken by the wind the billows rant,
I saw all of a sudden that proud plant
Of which I write with such tenacity.

Love that was boiling deep down in my soul
For the remembrance of her golden beam,
Pushed me; and I fell down into a stream
Amid the grass, as when dying fall.

Alone, finding myself by wood and hill,
I was ashamed; for to a gentle heart
This will suffice, no other spur I met.

It pleases me that I have changed my part
From eyes to feet; would that when these are wet,
The first were dried up by a sweet April!

LXVIII

L'aspetto sacro de la terra vostra
Mi fa del mal passato tragger guai,
Gridando:—Sta su, misero; che fai?—
E la via de salir al ciel mi mostra.

Ma con questo pensier un altro giostra,
E dice a me:—Perché fuggendo vai?
Se ti rimembra, il tempo passa omai
Di tornar a veder la donna nostra.—

I', che 'l suo ragionar intendo, allora
M'agghiaccio dentro, in guisa d'uom ch'ascolta
Novella che di súbito l'accora.

Poi torna il primo, e questo dá la volta:
Qual vincerá, non so; ma 'n fino ad ora
Combattuto hanno, e non pur una volta.

LXIX

Ben sapeva io che natural consiglio,
Amor, contra di te giá mai non valse,
Tanti lacciuol, tante impromesse false,
Tanto provato avea 'l tuo fiero artiglio.

Ma novamente, ond'io mi meraviglio
(Dirol, come persona a cui ne calse,
E che 'l notai lá sòpra l'acque salse,
Tra la riva toscana e l'Elba e Giglio),

I' fuggia le tue mani, e per camino,
Agitandom' i vènti e 'l ciel e l'onde,
M'andava sconosciuto e pellegrino;

Quando ecco i tuoi ministri, i' non so donde,
Per darmi a diveder ch'al suo destíno
Mal chi contrasta e mal chi si nasconde.

LXVIII

The venerable aspect of your land
Reminds me of the sorrows of my past,
Crying:—Awake, poor wretch, why do you stand?—
And shows to me the saving way at last.

But with this thought another comes to fight
And says to me:—Why do you want to run?
Remember that the time is almost gone
To call and see again our dear delight.—

Listening to its arguments I freeze
Inside, like one who is given by chance
Some news that suddenly darkens his brow.

Then the other comes back and the last flees:
Which will win, I know not; but until now
They have been jousting and not only once.

LXIX

I was aware that a natural law
Has never been of help, Love, against you,
So many snares and promises untrue,
So often had I tried your savage claw.

But lately, and I must marvel therefore,
(I will say it as one to whom it matters,
And that I noticed it on the salt waters
Between the Giglio and the Tuscan shore),

I escaped from your hands and on my way,
Upset by winds and heaven and the sea,
I was going, a pilgrim and astray;

When came your ministers I know not whence,
To let me know that to thwart destiny
Is as bad as to hide behind a fence.

LXX

Lasso me!, ch'i' non so in qual parte pieghi
La speme, ch'è tradita omai piú volte,
Che se non è chi con pietá m'ascolte,
Perché sparger al ciel sí spessi preghi?
Ma s'egli aven ch'ancor non mi si nieghi
Finir, anzi 'l mio fine,
Queste voci meschine,
Non gravi al mio signor perch'io il ripreghi
Di dir libero un dí tra l'erba e i fiori:
"Drez et rayson es qu'ieu ciant e 'm demori".

Ragion è ben ch'alcuna volta io canti,
Però c'ho sospirato sí gran tempo
Che mai non incomincio assai per tempo
Per adequar col riso i dolor tanti.
E s'io potesse far ch'a gli occhi santi
Porgesse alcun diletto
Qualche dolce mio detto,
O me beato sopra gli altri amanti!
Ma piú, quand'io dirò senza mentire:
"Donna mi priega, per ch'io voglio dire".

Vaghi pensier, che cosí passo passo
Scorto m'avete a ragionar tant'alto,
Vedete che madonna ha 'l cor di smalto
Sí forte, ch'io per me dentro no 'l passo.
Ella non degna di mirar sí basso
Che di nostre parole
Curi; ché 'l ciel non vòle,
Al qual pur contrastando i' son giá lasso;
Onde, come nel cor m'induro e 'naspro,
"Cosí nel mio parlar voglio esser aspro".

Che parlo? o dove sono? e chi m'inganna,
Altri ch'io stesso e 'l desiar soverchio?
Giá, s'i' trascorro il ciel di cerchio in cerchio,
Nessun pianeta a pianger mi condanna.
Se mortal velo il mio veder appanna,

LXX

Alas! I do not know from what side fly
My hopes that many times have been betrayed,
For if no one is touched by what I said,
Why do I send all these prayers to the sky?
But if no powers happen to deny
My little sounds their end,
Before I find my end,
May my lord allow me again to cry
One day, free among flowers, the poem's story:
"Drez et rayson es qu'ieu ciant e 'm demori."

There is a reason why sometimes I sing,
Because I have been sighing for so long
That I can never start too soon a song
To make my laughter balance suffering.
And if to her pure eyes I were to bring
Some pleasurable sign
By any word of mine,
Above all lovers' then blessed my string!
But more when truthfully I sing the lay:
"A lady begs me to be pleased to say."

Delightful thoughts that everywhere I go
Have guided me and my reason so high,
See how my lady's heart is hard and dry
Like enamel, inside I cannot go.
She does not deign to cast her eyes so low
That she may hear our voice;
This is not heaven's choice,
And I am tired to fight against it so;
As in my heart I become harsh and blind,
"So in my speech I want to be unkind."

What say I? Where am I? and who cheats me
But my own self and my desire's despair?
Though I run through the sky from sphere to sphere,
No planet dooms me to this misery.
And if a veil makes me too dull to see,

Che colpa è de le stelle,
O de le cose belle?
Meco si sta chi dí e notte m'affanna,
Poi che del suo piacer mi fe' gir grave
"La dolce vista e 'l bel guardo soave".

Tutte le cose, di che 'l mondo è adorno,
Uscir buone de man del mastro eterno;
Ma me, che cosí a dentro non discerno,
Abbaglia il bel che mi si mostra intorno;
E s'al vero splendor giá mai ritorno,
L'occhio non pò star fermo;
Cosí l'ha fatto infermo
Pur la sua propria colpa, e non quel giorno
Ch'i' volsi in vèr' l'angelica beltade
"Nel dolce tempo de la prima etade".

LXXI

Perché la vita è breve,
E l'ingegno paventa a l'alta impresa,
Né di lui né di lei molto mi fido;
Ma spero che sia intesa
Lá dov'io bramo e lá dove esser deve
La doglia mia, la qual tacendo i' grido.
Occhi leggiadri dove Amor fa nido,
A voi rivolgo il mio debile stile,
Pigro da sé, ma 'l gran piacer lo sprona;
E chi di voi ragiona
Tien dal soggetto un abito gentile,
Che con l'ale amorose
Levando il parte d'ogni pensier vile;
Con queste alzato vengo a dire or cose,
C'ho portate nel cor gran tempo ascose.

Non perch'io non m'aveggia
Quanto mia laude è 'ngiuriosa a voi;

Are the stars to be blamed?
Or what is nobly framed?
Day and night they require my company
To hurt me, since their pleasure was my chance,
"The lovely presence and the fair sweet glance."

Everything that gives the world delight
Was made good by the master of the sheep,
But I who cannot see so far and deep,
Am dazzled by the beauty in my sight.
Whenever I return to the true light
My eyes cannot be still;
And they suffer this ill
By their own fault and not by that day's plight
When I turned them that angel's face to see
"In the sweet springtime of my history."

LXXI

Because our life is brief
And the mind is appalled by its great task,
Nor the one nor the other I trust much;
But I hope what I ask
Will resound there where must be heard my grief,
A silent one, and yet not really such.
O charming eyes that Love comes home to touch,
To you I dedicate my feeble mind
Slow in itself, but spurred by deep delight:
Who speaks of you with right,
Takes from his subject a sense more refined,
For on amorous wings
Soaring, he parts from all thought mean and blind:
Lifted by those I now come to tell things
That I have long concealed in my heart's strings.

Not that I do not see
How injurious my praise will be to you;

Ma contrastar non posso al gran desio,
Lo quale è 'n me da poi
Ch'i' vidi quel che pensier non pareggia,
Non che l'avagli altrui parlar o mio.
Principio del mio dolce stato rio,
Altri che voi so ben che non m'intende.
Quando a gli ardenti rai neve divegno,
Vostro gentile sdegno
Forse ch'allor mia indignitate offende.
Oh, se questa temenza
Non temprasse l'arsura che m'incende,
Beato venir men! ché 'n lor presenza
M'è piú caro il morir che 'l viver senza.

Dunque ch'i' non mi sfaccia,
Sí frale obgetto a sí possente foco,
Non è proprio valor che me ne scampi;
Ma la paura un poco,
Che 'l sangue vago per le vene agghiaccia,
Risalda 'l cor, perché piú tempo avampi.
O poggi, o valli, o fiumi, o selve, o campi,
O testimon de la mia grave vita,
Quante volte m'udiste chiamar morte!
Ahi, dolorosa sorte!
Lo star mi strugge, e 'l fuggir non m'aita.
Ma se maggior paura
Non m'affrenasse, via corta e spedita
Trarrebbe a fin questa aspra pena e dura;
E la colpa è de tal che non ha cura.

Dolor, perché mi meni
Fuor di camin a dir quel ch'i' non voglio?
Sostien ch'io vada ove'l piacer mi spigne.
Giá di voi non mi doglio,
Occhi sopra 'l mortal corso sereni,
Né di lui ch'a tal nodo mi distrigne.
Vedete ben quanti color depigne
Amor sovente in mezzo del mio vólto,
E potrete pensar qual dentro fammi,
Lá 've dí e notte stammi

But I cannot resist the strong desire
That was mine hitherto
Since I once saw what passes fantasy,
What mine or other words does not require.
Beginning of my sweet and bitter fire,
I know none but yourself will understand:
When in those ardent rays I turn to snow,
Your gentle scorn does show
That my low state displeases your command.
O if a constant fear
Did not restrain the burning of their brand,
Bliss it would be to fall! for to die near
Them more than living far from them is dear.

Not to succumb to pain,
A fragile object of a mighty flame,
'Tis not my virtue which is of avail;
But rather fear or shame
That freezes the swift blood inside the vein,
Remoulds my heart and heats it without fail.
O hills, o streams, o wood, o plain, o dale,
O witnesses of my burdensome life,
How many times you heard me mourn my state!
What agonizing fate!
Staying consumes, fleeing wounds like a knife.
But if a greater fear
Did not check me, this hard and cruel strife
Would come to end by speedy means and near;
And the fault is of one who does not hear.

Grief, why do you lead me
Out of my path to say what is not right?
Let me walk on the road my pleasure craves.
I do not blame your light,
Eyes more serene than our mortality,
Nor him who by such fetters made men slaves.
You see how many shades Love paints, engraves
So often in the middle of my face,
And you can guess how I become inside,
When day and night he's tied

A dosso col poder c'ha in voi raccolto,
Luci beate e liete,
Se non che 'l veder voi stesse v'è tolto;
Ma quante volte a me vi rivolgete,
Conoscete in altrui quel che voi siete.

S'a voi fosse sí nota
La divina incredibile bellezza
Di ch'io ragiono, come a chi la mira,
Misurata allegrezza
Non avria 'l cor; però forse è remota
Dal vigor natural che v'apre e gira.
Felice l'alma che per voi sospira.
Lumi del ciel, per il quali io ringrazio
La vita che per altro non m'è a grado!
Oimè! perché sí rado
Mi date quel dond'io mai non son sazio?
Perché non piú sovente
Mirate qual Amor di me fa strazio?
E perché mi spogliate immantanente
Dal ben ch'ad ora ad or l'anima sente?

Dico ch'ad ora ad ora,
Vostra mercede, i' sento in mezzo l'alma
Una dolcezza inusitata e nova,
La qual ogni altra salma
Di noiosi pensier disgombra allora,
Sí che di mille un sol vi si ritrova:
Quel tanto a me, non piú, del viver giova.
E se questo mio ben durasse alquanto,
Nullo stato aguagliarse al mio porrebbe;
Ma forse altrui farrebbe
Invido, e me superbo l'onor tanto:
Però, lasso!, convensi
Che l'estremo del riso assaglia il pianto,
E 'nterrompendo quelli spiriti accensi,
A me ritorni, e di me stesso pensi.

L'amoroso pensero
Ch'alberga dentro, in voi mi si discopre

To me with all the power of your grace.
O blissful lights and gay,
You cannot see yourselves from your own place,
But each time that to me you turn and stray,
Recognize in another your own ray.

If to yourself were known
The divine, unimagined loveliness
Of which I speak, as to one who admires
It, a boundless gladness
Would fill your heart: thus it may not be sown
In the vigorous soil of your desires.
Blissful the soul that after you suspires,
Heavenly lights for which I want to thank
A life that for no other thing I prize!
Why in such meager wise
Do you give me what never fills this blank?
Why do you not more oft
Look on and see how Love pierces my flank?
Why do you rob at once my soul that loved
A bliss which grows hour after hour more soft?

I say hour after hour
Sent by your mercy I feel in my soul
A sweetness so unusual and new,
That any clumsy role
Of tiresome thoughts is shattered in its power,
Until of thousand only one is true:
This is, and nothing else, my comfort's clue,
And if this good of mine would last some time
No other state could be compared to mine,
But rather would incline
Others to envy, me to vaunt my climb.
But, alas! grief requires
That crying break across the laughing chime,
And interrupting those ardent desires,
That I return to my thoughts' old attires.

The loving argument
Which dwells inside, in you stands out revealed

Tal che mi tra' del cor ogni altra gioia;
Onde parole et opre
Escon di me sí fatte allor ch'i' spero
Farmi immortal, perché la carne moia.
Fugge al vostro apparire angoscia e noia,
E nel vostro partir tornano insieme.
Ma perché la memoria innamorata
Chiude lor poi l'entrata,
Di lá non vanno da le parti estreme;
Onde s'alcun bel frutto
Nasce di me, da voi vien prima il seme:
Io per me son quasi un terreno asciutto,
Cólto da voi, e 'l pregio è vostro in tutto.

Canzon, tu non m'acqueti, anzi m'infiammi
A dir di quel ch'a me stesso m'invola;
Però sia certa de non esser sola.

LXXII

Gentil mia donna, i' veggio
Nel mover de' vostr'occhi un dolce lume
Che mi mostra la via ch'al ciel conduce;
E per lungo costume
Dentro lá dove sol con Amor seggio,
Quasi visibilmente il cor traluce.
Questa è la vista ch'a ben far m'induce,
E che mi scorge al glorioso fine;
Questa sola dal vulgo m'allontana.
Né giá mai lingua umana
Contar poría quel che le due divine
Luci sentir mi fanno,
E quando 'l verno sparge le pruine,
E quando poi ringiovenisce l'anno
Qual era al tempo del mio primo affanno.

Io penso: se lá suso,

Such that it drives from me all other joy;
Hence words and deeds are sealed
And formed in such a shape that my intent
Is to become immortal, though Death's toy.
When you appear, things cannot hurt, annoy,
And when you leave both ills remain to stay.
But since the recollection of my love
Closes the entrance of
My self, beyond the bounds they find no way;
Therefore if some sweet fruit
Is born of me, from you the seed and clay:
I in myself am like a barren root
Nurtured by you, yours the gift of the shoot.

Song, you do not appease me but inflame
To say what of myself from me is flown:
Be sure at least that you are not alone.

LXXII

My sweet Lady, I see
In your eyes' motion an enchanting light
Showing the way that toward heaven tends;
And after its old rite,
Inside, where Love and I keep company,
The heart almost apparently resplends.
This is the sight that my good deeds defends,
The sight that leads to glorious ends the lost;
Only this can divide me from the throng.
Never a human tongue
Will be able to tell what those two most
Divine lights make me feel
When winter scatters all around the frost,
And when the year glows with a young appeal
As it did when I first bore sorrow's seal.

I think:—If up above,

Onde 'l motor eterno de le stelle
Degnò mostrar del suo lavoro in terra,
Son l'altr'opre sí belle,
Aprasi la pregione, ov'io son chiuso,
E che 'l camino a tal vita mi serra.
Poi mi rivolgo a la mia usata guerra,
Ringraziando Natura e 'l dí ch'io nacqui
Che reservato m'hanno a tanto bene,
E lei ch'a tanta spene
Alzò il mio cor; ché 'n sin allor io giacqui
A me noioso e grave,
Da quel dí inanzi a me medesmo piacqui,
Empiendo d'un pensier alto e soave
Quel core ond'hanno i begli occhi la chiave.

Né mai stato gioioso
Amor o la volubile Fortuna
Dieder a chi piú fûr nel mondo amici,
Ch'i no 'l cangiassi ad una
Rivolta d'occhi, ond'ogni mio riposo
Vien come ogni arbor vien da sue radici
Vaghe faville, angeliche, beatrici
De la mia vita, ove 'l piacer s'accende,
Che dolcemente mi consuma e strugge;
Come sparisce e fugge
Ogni altro lume dove 'l vostro splende,
Cosí de lo mio core,
Quando tanta dolcezza in lui discende,
Ogni altra cosa, ogni penser va fòre,
E solo ivi con voi rimanse Amore.

Quanta dolcezza unquanco
Fu in cor d'aventurosi amanti, accolta
Tutta in un loco, a quel ch'i' sento, è nulla,
Quando voi alcuna volta
Soavemente tra 'l bel nero e 'l bianco
Volgete il lume in cui Amor si trastulla:
E credo, de la fasce e da la culla
Al mio imperfetto, a la Fortuna adversa
Questo rimedio provedesse il cielo.

Whence the Eternal Mover of each sphere
Deigned to reveal his work to us on earth,
All his acts are so fair,
Let the prison be opened where I move
And which prevents my going to such mirth.—
Then I come back to my accustomed dearth
To thank Nature, the day that I was born,
Which have reserved my life to so much good,
And her who understood
And gave hope to my heart; distressed and torn
Till then I used to be,
But from that day I was no more forlorn,
And filled up with one thought's felicity
The heart of which those fair eyes are the key.

Never a joyful state
Love or a fickle Fortune gave to those
Who have been in this world their favoured friends,
That I did not soon lose
When those eyes turned, on which my comforts wait
As every tree upon its roots attends.
Delightful sparks, angelic, blessed ends
Of my whole life, where that pleasure ignites
Which sweetly consumes me and wears me out;
As quick as is the rout
Of any other gleam where shine your lights,
So out of my own heart,
When such a sweetness over it alights,
All other things, all other thoughts depart,
And Love alone remains there and your art.

Whatever deep delight
Was in the heart of gallant lovers, all
Poured in one place is nothing when compared
To the throbs that enthral
Me when you turn between the black and white
Softly sometimes the light where Love is snared;
And I think, from the crib where I was reared
To my imperfect self, to adverse Chance
This remedy was sent by Providence.

Torto mi face il velo
E la man che sí spesso s'atraversa
Fra 'l mio sommo diletto
E gli occhi, onde dí e notte si rinversa
Il gran desio per isfogare il petto,
Che forma tien dal variato aspetto.

Perch'io veggio, e mi spiace,
Che natural mia dote a me non vale
Né mi fa degno d'un sí caro sguardo,
Sforzomi d'esser tale
Qual a l'alta speranza si conface,
Et al foco gentil ond'io tutto ardo.
S'al ben veloce, et al contrario tardo,
Dispregiator di quanto 'l mondo brama
Per solicito studio posso farme,
Porrebbe forse aitarme
Nel benigno iudicio una tal fama.
Certo il fin de' miei pianti,
Che non altronde il cor doglioso chiama,
Vèn da' begli occhi al fin dolce tremanti,
Ultima speme de' cortesi amanti.

Canzon, l'una sorella è poco inanzi,
E l'altra sento in quel medesmo albergo
Apparechiarsi; ond'io piú carta vergo.

LXXIII

Poi che per mio destíno
A dir mi sforza quell'accesa voglia
Che m'ha sforzato a sospirar mai sempre,
Amor, ch'a ciò m'invoglia,
Sia la mia scorta, e 'nsignimi 'l camino,
E col desio le mie rime contempre;
Ma non in guisa che lo cor si stempre
Di soverchia dolcezza, com'io temo,

I am torn from my sense
When the veil and the hand rise to advance
Between my happy rest
And my eyesight, hence day and night desire
Flows out and rushes to relieve my breast,
Taking form from the aspect of its nest.

Since I remark and grieve
That my natural gifts do not avail
To make me worthy of those looks that turn,
I try hard not to fail
And to be such as never to deceive
The high hope and the fire that makes me burn.
If quick to good and against evil stern,
Scornful of what is the world's greedy aim,
I can become by my assiduous care,
It might help me to wear
In their kindly opinion such a fame.
The end of my lament
That of no other origin I claim,
Comes from the eyes so tremblingly intent,
The highest hope of lovers gently bent.

My song, one sister is not far ahead
And the other is there in the same place
Ready to go; hence more letters I trace.

LXXIII

Because it is my fate
To be compelled to speak by that desire
Which forces me to sigh ever and ever,
Love that makes me suspire
Shall show me where to walk and where to wait,
And temper with my wish my words' endeavour;
But not so as to cause my heart to waver
From too much sweetness, which is what I dread,

Per quel ch'i' sento ov'occhio altrui non giugne;
Ché 'l dir m'infiamma e pugne,
Né per mi 'ngegno, ond'io pavento e tremo,
Sí come talor sòle,
Trovo 'l gran foco de la mente scemo;
Anzi mi struggo al suon de le parole,
Pur com'io fusse un uom di ghiaccio al sole.

Nel cominciar credía
Trovar parlando al mio ardente desire
Qualche breve riposo e qualche triegua.
Questa speranza ardire
Mi porse a ragionar quel ch'i' sentia;
Or m'abbandona al tempo, e si dilegua.
Ma pur conven che 'alta impresa segua
Continuando l'amorose note,
Sí possente è 'l voler che mi trasporta;
E la ragione è morta,
Che tenea 'l freno, e contrastar no 'l pôte.
Mostrimi almen ch'io dica
Amor in guisa che se mai percote
Gli orecchi de la dolce mia nemica,
Non mia, ma di pietá la faccia amica.

Dico: se 'n quella etate
Ch'al vero onor fûr gli animi sí accesi,
L'industria d'alquanti uomini s'avolse
Per diversi paesi,
Poggi et onde passando, e l'onorate
Cose cercando el piú bel fior ne colse,
Poi che Dio e Natura et Amor volse
Locar compitamente ogni virtute
In quei be' lumi, ond'io gioioso vivo,
Questo e quell'altro rivo
Non conven ch'i' trapasse e terra mute.
A llor sempre ricorro,
Come a fontana d'ogni mia salute;
E quando a morte disiando corro,
Sol di lor vista al mio stato soccorro.

Feeling so deep where others cannot see;
For this reasoning kindles, pierces me,
Nor does my talent, hence I am afraid,
As it did oftentimes,
Abate the strength of the fire in my head;
Rather I melt at the sound of my rhymes
As if I were an ice in sunny climes.

When I began, I thought
To find in words for my ardent affair
A little comfort and a brief delay.
This hope led me to dare
Express by language my emotions' knot;
Now it abandons me and fades away.
But still I must pursue my task and play
And sing my amorous music again,
So mighty is the will that drives me on;
Reason is dead and gone
That held the check, it cannot use a rein.
Let it at least teach me
To speak of love so well that if I gain
The ears of my sweet, bitter enemy,
She may befriend not me, but sympathy.

I say, if in that age
When true honour some breasts did understand,
The industry of men was all displayed
Across many a land,
Over mountains and waves, and on the stage
Of honoured things the best flower was arrayed,
Since God, Nature and Love together laid
Every virtue in perfection
On those fair eyes that make me live and dream,
This or the other stream
I need not cross nor from my country run.
To them I always go
As to the fountain of salvation.
And when toward death all my yearnings flow,
Their sight alone brings solace to my woe.

Come a forza di vènti
Stanco nocchier di notte alza la testa
A' duo lumi c'ha sempre il nostro polo,
Cosí ne la tempesta
Ch'i' sostengo d'amor, gli occhi lucenti
Sono il mio segno e 'l mio conforto solo.
Lasso!, ma troppo è piú quel ch'io ne 'nvolo
Or quinci, or quindi, come Amor m'informa,
Che quel che vèn da grazioso dono;
E quel poco ch'i' sono
Mi fa di loro una perpetua norma.
Poi ch'io li vidi in prima,
Senza lor a ben far non mossi un'orma:
Cosí gli ho di me posti in su la cima
Che 'l mio valor per sé falso s'estima.

I' non poria giá mai
Imaginar, non che narrar gli effetti,
Che nel mio cor gli occhi soavi fanno:
Tutti gli altri diletti
Di questa vita ho per minori assai,
E tutte altre bellezze in dietro vanno.
Pace tranquilla, senza alcuno affanno,
Simile a quella ch'è nel ciel eterna,
Move da lor inamorato riso.
Cosí vedess'io fiso
Come Amor dolcemente gli governa,
Sol un giorno da presso,
Senza volger giá mai rota superna,
Né pensasse d'altrui né di me stesso,
E 'l batter gli occhi miei non fosse spesso.

Lasso!, che disiando
Vo quel ch'esser non puote in alcun modo;
E vivo del desir fuor di speranza.
Solamente quel nodo
Ch'Amor cerconda a la mia lingua, quando
L'umana vista il troppo lume avanza,
Fosse disciolto, i' prenderei baldanza
Di dir parole in quel punto sí nove,

As when a windstorm cries,
The weary pilot at night lifts his head
Toward the two lights that stay fixed at our pole,
Thus in the tempest's dread
That I endure for love, her shining eyes
Are the true sign and comfort of my soul.
Alas! because much more is what I stole
Now here, now there, as Love guided my bark,
Than what was given me by her consent;
And my humble content
Puts them before me as a saving mark.
Since I first heard their calls,
I never did some good without their spark;
Therefore I placed them above my life's walls,
Because my strength alone seems to me false.

It could never be said
In words, the deep sensation they excite,
Those charming eyes, and in my heart impress:
Any other delight
Of life I deem of much inferior grade,
And any other beauty is much less.
A tranquil peace, without any distress,
Like to the one eternal of the sky,
Flows from their love-inspired and lovely laughter.
Could I perceive hereafter
How Love gently directs their going-by,
Could I be near their wells
Without the turning of a wheel on high,
Not thinking of myself or someone else,
And not with eyelids blinking under spells!

Alas! for I desire
What can never come true in any way;
And live by this desire, having no hope.
If that noose made to prey,
Which Love ties on my tongue when the great fire
Of that light overcomes my human scope,
Were loosened, I should have courage to cope
With it and I should utter words so new

Che farian lagrimar chi le 'ntendesse.
Ma le ferite impresse
Volgon per forza il cor piagato altrove;
Ond'io divento smorto,
E 'l sangue si nasconde, i' non so dove,
Né rimango qual era; e sommi accorto
Che questo è 'l colpo di che Amor m'ha morto.

Canzone, i' sento giá stancar la penna
Del lungo e dolce ragionar co llei,
Ma non di parlar meco i pensier mei.

LXXIV

Io son giá stanco di pensar sí come
I miei pensier in voi stanchi non sono,
E come vita ancor non abbandono
Per fuggir de' sospir sí gravi some;

E come a dir del viso e de le chiome
E de' begli occhi, ond'io sempre ragiono,
Non è mancata omai la lingua e 'l suono
Dí e notte chiamando il vostro nome;

E che ' pie' miei non son fiaccati e lassi
A seguir l'orme vostre in ogni parte,
Perdendo inutilmente tanti passi;

Et onde vien l'enchiostro, onde le carte
Ch'i' vo empiendo di voi: se 'n ciò fallassi,
Colpa d'Amor, non giá defetto d'arte.

That they would make all those who hear them cry.
But my sores never dry
Compel my wounded heart to turn to rue;
Hence I faint and despair
And my blood creeps I cannot say whereto,
I am not what I was; I am aware
That by this trick Love has become my slayer.

Canzone, I feel my pen already tired
Of this long and sweet reasoning with her,
But my thoughts are not tired my talk to share.

LXXIV

I am as tired of thinking as my thought
Is never tired to find itself in you,
And of not yet leaving this life that brought
Me the too heavy weight of sighs and rue;

And because to describe your hair and face
And the fair eyes of which I always speak,
Language and sound have not become too weak
And day and night your name they still embrace.

And tired because my feet do not yet fail
After following you in every part,
Wasting so many steps without avail,

From whence derive the paper and the ink
That I have filled with you; if I should sink,
It is the fault of Love, not of my art.

LXXV

I begli occhi ond'i' fui percosso in guisa
Ch'e' medesmi porian saldar la piaga,
E non giá vertú d'erbe, o d'arte maga,
O di pietra dal mar nostra divisa,

M'hanno la via sí d'altro amor precisa,
Ch'un sol dolce penser l'anima appaga;
E se la lingua di seguirlo è vaga,
La scorta pò, non ella esser derisa.

Questi son que' begli occhi che l'imprese
Del mio signor vittoriose fanno
In ogni parte, e piú sovra 'l mio fianco;

Questi son que' begli occhi che mi stanno
Sempre nel cor colle faville accese;
Per ch'io di lor parlando non mi stanco.

LXXVI

Amor con sue promesse lusingando
Mi ricondusse a la prigione antica,
E die' le chiavi a quella mia nemica
Ch'ancor me di me stesso tène in bando.

Non me n'avídi, lasso!, se non quando
Fui in lor forza; et or con gran fatica
(Chi 'l crederá, perché giurando i' 'l dica?)
In libertá ritorno sospirando.

E come vero pregioniero afflitto,
De le catene mie gran parte porto;
E 'l cor ne gli occhi e ne la fronte ho scritto.

Quando sarai del mio colore accorto
Dirai:—S'i' guardo e giudico ben dritto,
Questi avea poco andare ad esser morto.—

LXXV

The lovely eyes which have so wounded me,
That they alone could heal their stinging smart,
Not a virtue of herbs or magic art,
Or of a stone divided from our sea,

Have so precluded any other side
To Love, that one sweet thought is my content;
And if my tongue likes to follow its bent,
The leader, not the follower, deride.

These are those lovely eyes that make the deeds
Of my lord be the winners everywhere,
And the more so when my own body bleeds;

These are those lovely eyes whose sparkling gem
Is always in my heart with its strong glare;
Hence I never grow tired to speak of them.

LXXVI

Love with his promises and flattery
Directed me again to my old prison,
And gave the keys to that same enemy
Who keeps me locked, divided from my reason.

I noticed it, alas! only when I
Was in their power; and now in agony
(Who will believe it, though I will not lie?)
And weary I return to liberty.

Like to a true, afflicted captive, now
I carry a great number of my chains,
And my heart is imprinted on my brow.

When you observe how all my colour wanes,
You will say:—If I can judge from his head,
He has not far to go before he's dead.—

LXXVII

Per mirar Policleto a prova fiso
Con gli altri ch'ebber fama di quell'arte
Mill'anni, non vedrian la minor parte
De la beltá che m'have il cor conquiso.

Ma certo il mio Simon fu in paradiso,
Onde questa gentil donna si parte;
Ivi la vide, e la ritrasse in carte,
Per far fede qua giú del suo bel viso.

L'opra fu ben di quelle che nel cielo
Si ponno imaginar, non qui tra noi,
Ove le membra fanno a l'alma velo.

Cortesia fe'; né la potea far poi
Che fu disceso a provar caldo e gielo,
E del mortal sentiron gli occhi suoi.

LXXVIII

Quando giunse a Simon l'alto concetto
Ch'a mio nome gli pose in man lo stile,
S'avesse dato a l'opera gentile
Colla figura voce ed intelletto,

Di sospir molti mi sgombrava il petto,
Che ciò ch'altri ha piú caro a me fan vile;
Però che 'n vista ella si mostra umíle
Promettendomi pace ne l'aspetto.

Ma poi ch'i' vengo a ragionar co llei,
Benignamente assai par che m'ascolte:
Se risponder savesse a' detti miei!

Pigmalion, quanto lodar ti dêi
De l'imagine tua, se mille volte
N'avesti quel ch'i' sol una vorrei!

LXXVII

If Polycletus put it to a test,
With all the other masters of his art,
A thousand years, they would not see the best
Part of that beauty which conquered my heart.

But certainly Simon saw paradise
Wherein this gentle lady had her place;
There he saw her and portrayed in such guise
That is the witness here of her fair face.

The work is one of those that in the sky
Can be conceived, and not in our sheepfold
Where the flesh throws a shadow on the soul.

Courtesy is the work; nor could he try
It when he was exposed to heat and cold,
And when his eyes aimed at a mortal goal.

LXXVIII

When Simon was inspired by the elect
Idea that to his hand the brush consigned,
If he had given to the fair object
With a figure a voice too and a mind,

He would have freed my heart of many sighs,
That depreciate for me what others love;
Because she looks as humble as a dove
And she promises comfort with her eyes.

And when I come and try to speak to her
She seems to listen with benignity;
If she could only answer to my prayer!

Pygmalion, how happy you must be
With your image, who thousand times have had
From her what only once would make me glad!

LXXIX

S'al principio risponde il fine e 'l mezzo
Del quartodecimo anno ch'io sospiro,
Piú non mi pò scampar l'aura né 'l rezzo;
Sí crescer sento 'l mio ardente desiro.

Amor, con cui pensier mai non amezzo,
Sotto 'l cui giogo giá mai non respiro,
Tal mi governa, ch'i' non son giá mezzo,
Per gli occhi, ch'al mio mal sí spesso giro.

Cosí mancando vo di giorno in giorno,
Sí chiusamente, ch'i' sol me n'accorgo,
E quella che guardando il cor mi strugge.

A pena in fin a qui l'anima scorgo,
Né so quanto fia meco il suo soggiorno;
Ché la morte s'appressa, e 'l viver fugge.

LXXX

Chi è fermato di menar sua vita
Su per l'onde fallaci e per li scogli
Scevro da morte con un picciol legno
Non pò molto lontan esser dal fine;
Però sarrebbe da ritrarsi in porto
Mentre al governo ancor crede la vela.

L'aura soave, a cui governo e vela
Commisi entrando a l'amorosa vita
E sperando venire a miglior porto,
Poi mi condusse in piú di mille scogli;
E le cagion del mio doglioso fine
Non pur d'intorno avea, ma dentro al legno.

Chiuso gran tempo in questo cieco legno
Errai, senza levar occhio a la vela
Ch'anzi al mio dí mi trasportava al fine;

LXXIX

If the beginning, middle, and the end
Are alike in my fourteenth year of sighs,
Neither a breeze nor a shade can defend
Me, for I feel that my wish multiplies.

Love, with whose thoughts I never quite agree,
Under whose yoke I cannot breathe the air,
So rules me that I am unfit to see
With the eyes that I turn to my despair.

Therefore I grow more faint from day to day,
So quietly that no one knows it but I
And she who looking has worn out my heart.

I led my soul with pain since the first start,
Nor do I know how long it likes to stay;
For death is coming and life hurries by.

LXXX

Who is determined to conduct his life
On the deceitful waves and on the cliffs,
Sheltered from death by a small piece of wood,
Cannot be far divided from his end:
Therefore one should withdraw inside the port
While to the rudder still responds the sail.

The gentle air to which I gave both sail
And rudder when I started my love life,
Hoping to reach some time a better port,
Drove me across more than a thousand cliffs;
And the reasons of my distracting end
Were not only round me, but in the wood.

Enclosed for a long time in this blind wood
I roamed without once looking at the sail
Which carried me so early to my end;

Poi piacque a lui che mi produsse in vita
Chiamarme tanto in dietro da li scogli
Ch'almen da lunge m'apparisse il porto.

Come lume di notte in alcun porto
Vide mai d'alto mar nave né legno,
Se non gliel tolse o tempestate o scogli,
Cosí di su da la gonfiata vela
Vid'io le 'nsegne di quell'altra vita,
Et allor sospirai verso 'l mio fine.

Non perch'io sia securo ancor del fine;
Ché volendo col giorno esser a porto
È gran viaggio in cosí poca vita;
Poi temo, ché mi veggio in fraile legno,
E piú che non vorrei piena la vela
Del vento che mi pinse in questi scogli.

S'io èsca vivo de' dubbiosi scogli,
Et arrive il mio essilio ad un bel fine,
Ch'i' sarei vago di voltar la vela,
E l'ancore gittar in qualche porto!
Se non ch'i' ardo come acceso legno,
Sí m'è duro a lassar l'usata vita.

Signor de la mia fine e de la vita,
Prima ch'i' fiacchi il legno tra li scogli,
Drizza a buon porto l'affannata vela.

Then it seemed good to him who gave me life
To draw me to such distance from the cliffs
That far away I might perceive the port.

As in the night a light shines in a port
Across the sea to reach a ship or wood
If not prevented by tempests or cliffs,
So did I see above the swelling sail
The revelations of that other life,
And then I sighed, aspiring to my end.

Not because I am certain of this end;
For within the day's length to be in port
Is a great voyage for a little life:
And I fear, for I float on fragile wood
And see more than I wished swollen the sail
By the wind which has thrust me on these cliffs.

If I come back alive from the dread cliffs,
And my exile can reach a happy end,
How eager I shall be to turn the sail
And to throw down the anchors in some port!
But I am heated like a burning wood,
So much I hate to part with my old life.

O you, Lord of my end, Lord of my life,
Before I break this wood among the cliffs,
Lead to a blessed port my troubled sail.

LXXXI

Io son sí stanco sotto 'l fascio antico
De le mie colpe e de l'usanza ria,
Ch'i' temo forte di mancar tra via,
E di cader in man del mio nemico.

Ben venne a dilivrarmi un grande amico
Per somma et ineffabil cortesia;
Poi volò fuor de la veduta mia,
Sí ch'a mirarlo indarno m'affatico.

Ma la sua voce ancor qua giú rimbomba:
"O voi che travagliate, ecco 'l camino;
Venite a me, se 'l passo altri non serra".

Qual grazia, qual amore, o qual destíno
Mi dará penne in guisa di colomba,
Ch'i' mi riposi, e levimi da terra?

LXXXII

Io non fu' d'amar voi lassato unquanco,
Madonna, né sarò mentre ch'io viva;
Ma d'odiar me medesmo giunto a riva,
E del continuo lagrimar so' stanco;

E voglio anzi un sepolcro bello e bianco,
Che 'l vostro nome a mio danno si scriva
In alcun marmo, ove di spirto priva
Sia la mia carne, che pò star seco anco.

Però, s'un cor pien d'amorosa fede
Può contentarve, senza farne strazio,
Piacciavi omai di questo aver mercede.

Se 'n altro modo cerca d'esser sazio,
Vostro sdegno erra; e non fia quel che crede;
Di che Amor e me stesso assai ringrazio.

LXXXI

I am so tired under the ancient load
Of my own guilt and of the daily woe,
That I fear to succumb along the road
And to fall in the power of my foe.

True, a great Friend did come to rescue me
By a sublime, indescribable grace,
But then he flew higher than I could see,
And now in vain I strive to find his face.

Yet his voice here below does still resound:
—O you who suffer, come, this is the way,
Come unto me if none bid you to stay.—

What blessing or what destiny, what love
Will give to me the feathers of a dove,
That I may rest and rise up from the ground?

LXXXII

I have never been weary of this love,
My Lady, nor shall be while last my years,
But of hating myself I have enough,
And I am tired of my continuous tears;

And I demand a grave handsome and white,
That your name for my punishment be writ
Into the marble where without delight
My flesh will be, to remain still with it.

Then if a heart full of amorous sighs
Can make you glad, without tearing your prey,
Be kind enough to pity my soul's breath.

If your contempt wants in some other way
To vent itself, it will remain a blank;
For which Love and myself I have to thank.

LXXXIII

Se bianche non son prima ambe le tempie
Ch'a poco a poco par ch' 'l tempo mischi,
Securo non sarò, ben ch'io m'arrischi
Talor ov'Amor l'arco tira et empie.

Non temo giá che piú mi strazi o scempie,
Né mi ritenga, perch'ancor m'invischi,
Né m'apra il cor, perché di fuor l'incischi,
Con sue saette velenose et empie.

Lagrime omai da gli occhi uscir non ponno
Ma di gire in fin lá sanno il viaggio;
Sí ch'a pena fia mai ch'i' 'l passo chiuda.

Ben mi pò riscaldare il fiero raggio,
Non sí ch'i' arda; e può turbarmi il sonno,
Ma romper no l'imagine aspra e cruda.

LXXXIV

—Occhi, piangete, accompagnate il core,
Che di vostro fallir morte sostene.—
—Cosí sempre facciamo; e ne convene
Lamentar piú l'altrui che 'l nostro errore.—

—Giá prima ebbe per voi l'entrata Amore,
Lá onde ancor come in suo albergo vène.—
—Noi gli aprimmo la via per quella spene
Che mosse d'entro da colui che more.—

—Non son, come a voi par, le ragion pari;
Ché pur voi foste ne la prima vista
Del vostro e del suo mal cotanto avari.—

—Or questo è quel che piú ch'altro n'atrista;
Che 'perfetti giudicii son sí rari,
E d'altrui colpa altrui biasmo s'acquista.—

LXXXIII

Until the temples of my brow are white
That slowly time is mixing with grey hair,
I shall not be secure, though I still dare
To go where Love stretches his bow more tight.

I do not fear to be more torn or maimed,
Nor to be caught, though he still threatens me,
Nor to see my heart split, though he has framed
It with his poisonous, foul archery.

Tears do not fall from my eyes any more,
But they know very well how to go there;
So that no one can try to shut the door.

I can be heated by the furious glare,
But not inflamed; my sleep it can erase,
But never break the harsh and cruel face.

LXXXIV

—Weep still, my eyes, and wait upon my heart
That for your fault must suffer death and break.—
—And so we do; and it becomes our part
To mourn another's more than our mistake.—

—From you Love had the entrance where he flies
And settles down and stays as in his home.—
—We opened him the way through hopes that come
From the inner desire of him who dies.—

—The reasons that you give seem to me lame;
For you have always been, since you began,
Too desirous of yours and of his ill.—

—Now this is what makes us more furious still;
That justice is so rare and that one can
For others' sins receive the others' blame.—

LXXXV

Io amai sempre, et amo forte ancóra,
E son per amar piú di giorno in giorno
Quel dolce loco, ove piangendo torno
Spesse fiate, quando Amor m'accora.

E son fermo d'amare il tempo e l'ora
Ch'ogni vil cura mi levâr d'intorno;
E piú colei, lo cui bel viso adorno
Di ben fa co' suoi essempli m'innamora.

Ma chi pensò veder mai tutti insieme
Per assalirmi il core, or quindi or quinci,
Questi dolci nemici, ch'i' tant'amo?

Amor, con quanto sforzo oggi mi vinci!
E se non ch'al desio cresce la speme,
I' cadrei morto, ove piú viver bramo.

LXXXVI

Io avrò sempre in odio la fenestra
Onde Amor m'aventò giá mille strali,
Perch'alquanti di lor non fûr mortali;
Ch'è bel morir, mentre la vita è destra.

Ma 'l sovrastar ne la pregion terrestra
Cagion m'è, lasso!, d'infiniti mali:
E piú mi duol che fíen meco immortali,
Poi che l'alma dal cor non si scapestra.

Misera!, che devrebbe esser accorta,
Per lunga esperienzia, omai che 'l tempo
Non è chi 'n dietro volga, o chi l'affreni.

Piú volte l'ho con ta' parole scorta:
—Vattene, trista; ché non va per tempo
Chi dopo lassa i suoi dí piú sereni.—

LXXXV

I always loved and I love dearly still,
And to love even more each day I learn,
That darling place where weeping I return
Time and again when Love disrupts my will.

And I will always love the day and hour
That took away from me each sordid care;
And especially one, whose face so fair
And whose example have on me such power.

But who had thought to see them all arrive
To smite my heart in this and in that way,
The handsome enemies that I love so?

Love, with what force you conquer me today!
If with desire hope did not also grow,
I should fall dead where I most wish to live.

LXXXVI

I feel hate for the window from which Love
Thrust against me more than a thousand spears,
Because a few were not deadly enough:
Since it is well to die when life appears.

But in this earthly prison to survive
Makes me suffer, alas, unending woes,
And more because they will forever live,
The soul being entrapped in the heart's throes.

Unhappy soul! She ought to be aware
From long experience now that no one may
Turn back or check the galloping of time.

Several times with these words I warned her:
—Go, miserable one; they cannot climb,
Who leave behind them their most cloudless day.—

LXXXVII

Sí tosto come aven che l'arco scocchi,
Buon sagittario di lontan discerne
Qual colpo è da sprezzare e qual d'averne
Fede ch'al destinato segno tocchi;

Similemente il colpo de' vostr'occhi,
Donna, sentiste a le mie parti interne
Dritto passare; onde conven ch'etterne
Lagrime per la piaga il cor trabocchi.

E certo son che voi diceste allora:
—Misero amante! a che vaghezza il mena?
Ecco lo strale onde Amor vol ch'e' mora.—

Ora, veggendo come 'l duol m'affrena,
Quel che mi fanno i miei nemici ancóra
Non è per morte, ma per piú mia pena.

LXXXVIII

Poi che mia speme è lunga a venir troppo,
E de la vita il trappassar sí corto,
Vorreimi a miglior tempo esser accorto,
Per fuggir dietro piú che di galoppo;

E fuggo ancor cosí debile e zoppo
Da l'un de' lati, ove 'l desio m'ha storto;
Securo omai, ma pur nel viso porto
Segni ch'io presi a l'amoroso intoppo.

Ond'io consiglio voi che siete in via,
Volgete i passi; e voi ch'Amore avampa,
Non v'indugiate su l'estremo ardore;

Ché, perch'io viva, de mille un no scampa:
Era ben forte la nemica mia,
E lei vid'io ferita in mezzo 'l core.

LXXXVII

As soon as a good archer draws the bow,
He sees from far away which is the shot
That must be spurned, and which he hopes will go
Toward the destined goal and mark the spot;

Likewise the shooting that came from your eyes,
Lady, was felt by you to travel straight
And reach my bowels; hence an endless spate
Of tears flows from my heart where the wound lies.

And I am sure that at this point you said:
—Unhappy lover, how he was betrayed!
There goes the spear by which he will be slain.—

Now, seeing that by grief I am made tame,
What my enemies do, always the same,
Is not to make me die, but suffer pain.

LXXXVIII

Because my hope is slow to come and late,
And the allotted span of life is brief,
I would be conscious of a better state
To flee and gallop after like a thief;

And I do flee, somewhat feeble and lame,
From the side where desire crippled my race;
Now quite secure, but wearing on my face
The signs impressed in me by my past shame.

Hence I warn you who begin now to move,
Turn back at once; and you, kindled by Love,
Do not delay in the last flare, but flee;

For though I live, no one escapes his dart:
Great was the power of my enemy,
And yet I saw her wounded in the heart.

LXXXIX

Fuggendo la pregione ove Amor m'ebbe
Molt'anni a far di me quel ch'a lui parve,
Donne mie, lungo fôra a ricontrarve
Quanto la nova libertá m'increbbe.

Diceami il cor che per sé non saprebbe
Viver un giorno; e poi tra via m'apparve
Quel traditore in sí mentite larve
Che piú saggio di me inganato avrebbe.

Onde piú volte sospirando in dietro
Dissi:—Oimè!, il giogo e le catene e i ceppi
Eran piú dolci che l'andare sciolto.—

Misero me, che tardo il mio mal seppi!
E con quanta fatica oggi mi spetro
De l'errore ov'io stesso m'era involto!

XC

Erano i capei d'oro a l'aura sparsi,
Che 'n mille dolci nodi gli avolgea;
E 'l vago lume oltra misura ardea
Di quei begli occhi, ch'or ne son sí scarsi;

E 'l viso di pietosi color farsi,
Non so se vero o falso, mi parea:
I' che l'ésca amorosa al petto avea,
Qual meraviglia se di súbito arsi?

Non era l'andar suo cosa mortale,
Ma d'angelica forma; e le parole
Sonavan altro che pur voce umana:

Uno spirto celeste, un vivo sole
Fu quel ch'i' vidi; e se non fosse or tale,
Piaga per allentar d'arco non sana.

LXXXIX

Fleeing the prison where Love made me wait
So many years, only his whim to please,
Ladies, it would be tedious to relate
How the new freedom deepened my unease.

The heart was telling me that such a task
It could not bear; then I saw him go by,
The betrayer, in such deceptive mask,
That would have seduced one wiser than I.

Hence often sighing behind him I said:
—Ah me! the yoke, the fetters and the chains
Were sweeter than to go without your reins.—

Unlucky, that too late I knew my ill!
How painfully I try to free my will
From the pitfall that I myself have laid.

XC

The golden hair was loosened in the breeze
That in many sweet knots whirled it and reeled,
And the dear light seemed ever to increase
Of those fair eyes that now keep it concealed:

And the face seemed to colour, and the glance
To feel pity, who knows if false or true;
I who had in my breast the loving cue,
Is it surprising if I flared at once?

Her gait was not like that of mortal things,
But of angelic forms; and her words' sound
Was not like that which from our voices springs;

A divine spirit and a living sun
Was what I saw; if such it is not found,
The wound remains, although the bow is gone.

XCI

La bella donna che cotanto amavi
Subitamente s'è da noi partita,
E, per quel ch'io ne speri, al ciel salita,
Sí furon gli atti suoi dolci soavi.

Tempo è da ricovrare ambe le chiavi
Del tuo cor, ch'ella possedeva in vita,
E seguir lei per via dritta espedita;
Peso terren non sia piú che t'aggravi.

Poi che se' sgombro de la maggior salma,
L'altre puoi giuso agevolmente porre,
Salendo quasi un pellegrino scarco.

Ben vedi omai sí come a morte corre
Ogni cosa creata, e quanto all'alma
Bisogna ir lieve al periglioso varco.

XCII

Piangete, donne, e con voi pianga Amore;
Piangete, amanti, per ciascun paese;
Poi ch'è morto collui che tutto intese
In farvi, mentre visse al mondo, onore.

Io per me prego il mio acerbo dolore
Non sian da lui le lagrime contese,
E mi sia di sospir tanto cortese
Quanto bisogna a disfogare il core.

Piangan le rime, ancor piangano i versi,
Perché 'l nostro amoroso messer Cino
Novellamente s'è da noi partito.

Pianga Pistoia, e i citadin perversi
Che perduto hanno sí dolce vicino;
E rallegresi il cielo ov'ello è gito.

XCI

The gracious lady that you have loved so
Is suddenly departed from this place,
And I know that to heaven she will go
Because her actions were so full of grace.

It is time to recover the two keys
Of your heart that she guarded while she lived,
And follow her there where she is arrived:
Let no terrestrial weight weaken your knees.

When you are rid of the essential tie,
The others you can easily let fall,
Mounting up like a pilgrim without load.

You can see how all things toward death fly,
That were created, and how light the soul
Must be when it begins that dangerous road.

XCII

Be weeping, women, and with you weep Love;
Be weeping, lovers, throughout every land;
For he is dead, who spent his life to prove
That he could honour you and understand.

As to myself, I pray my cruel grief
Not to begrudge and deny me my tears,
But kindly to allow me the relief
Of all the sighs I need to calm my fears.

Let our rhymes weep and also poems weep,
Because our Cino, Love's devoted friend,
Has been taken away to journey's end.

Let Pistoia and her bad citizens weep,
Who have lost such a sweet companion,
And let the sky rejoice, where he is gone.

XCIII

Piú volte Amor m'avea giá detto:—Scrivi,
Scrivi quel che vedesti in lettre d'oro,
Sí come i miei seguaci discoloro,
E 'n un momento gli fo morti e vivi.

Un tempo fu che 'n te stesso 'l sentivi,
Volgare essempio a l'amoroso coro;
Poi di man mi ti tolse altro lavoro;
Ma giá ti raggiuns'io mentre fuggivi.

E se 'begli occhi, ond'io me ti mostrai
E lá dove era il mio dolce ridutto
Quando ti ruppi al cor tanta durezza,

Mi rendon l'arco ch'ogni cosa spezza,
Forse non avrai sempre il viso asciutto;
Ch'i' mi pasco di lagrime, e tu 'l sai.—

XCIV

Quando giugne per gli occhi al cor profondo
L'imagin donna, ogni altra indi si parte,
E le vertú che l'anima comparte,
Lascian le membra, quasi immobil pondo.

E del primo miracolo il secondo
Nasce talor, che la scacciata parte
Da se stessa fuggendo arriva in parte
Che fa vendetta e 'l suo essilio giocondo.

Quinci in duo vólti un color morto appare;
Perché 'l vigor che vivi gli mostrava
Da nessun lato è piú lá dove stava.

E di questo in quel dí mi ricordava
Ch'i' vidi duo amanti trasformare,
E far qual io mi soglio in vista fare.

XCIII

Love had already often told me:—Write,
Write what you saw in clear letters of gold,
How my disciples' colour I make white
And in one moment warm with life and cold.

There was a time when in yourself you felt
My strength, and were a sample of my choirs;
Then you were flattered by other desires,
But I overtook you when you rebelled.

And if the eyes where I showed you my spell
And where I used to settle and to fly
When I shattered the hardness of your soul,

Return to me the bow that conquers all,
Perhaps your face will not always be dry;
For I feed on your tears, you know it well.—

XCIV

When through the eyes reaches the secret heart
A high image, the others dissipate,
And the virtues that are our soul's best part
Desert the members, leaving a dead weight.

And from this wonder a second sometimes
Derives its birth, and the excluded thing
Fleeing itself arrives in other climes
That revenge it and make its exile sing.

Hence in two faces comes a look of death;
Because the vigour that gave them life's breath
In neither place can stay where it had been.

And I remembered this a certain day
When I beheld two lovers' cheeks decay
And suddenly assume my usual mien.

XCV

Cosí potess'io ben chiudere in versi
I miei pensier, come nel cor gli chiudo;
Ch'animo al mondo non fu mai sí crudo,
Ch'i' non facessi per pietá dolersi.

Ma voi, occhi beati, ond'io soffersi
Quel colpo, ove non valse elmo né scudo,
Di fòr e dentro mi vedete ignudo,
Ben che 'n lamenti il duol non si riversi.

Poi che vostro vedere in me risplende,
Come raggio di sol traluce in vetro,
Basti dunque il desio senza ch'io dica.

Lasso!, non a Maria, non nocque a Pietro
La fede, ch'a me sol tanto è nemica;
E so ch'altri che voi nessun m'intende.

XCVI

Io son de l'aspettar omai sí vinto,
E de la lunga guerra de' sospiri,
Ch'i' aggio in odio la speme e i desiri,
Et ogni laccio onde 'l mio cor è avinto.

Ma 'l bel viso leggiadro che depinto
Porto nel petto, e veggio ove ch'io miri,
Mi sforza; onde ne' primi empii martíri
Pur son contra mia voglia risospinto.

Allor errai quando l'antica strada
Di libertá mi fu precisa e tolta,
Ché mal si segue ciò ch'a gli occhi agrada;

Allor corse al suo mal libera e sciolta;
Ora a posta d'altrui conven che vada
L'anima che peccò sol una volta.

XCV

I wish I could enclose my thoughts in verse
As well as I can close them in my breast;
Because there never was soul so perverse
That would not pity my cruel unrest.

But you, o blissful eyes whence came the blow
That neither shield nor helmet can defend,
Outwardly and inside my bare self know,
Although my heart does not break up and rend.

Since your power of seeing in me shines
As a sunbeam reflected in a glass,
Let my desire dispense with words and lines.

Mary and Peter were not harmed, alas,
By a faith that is so hostile to me;
And I know that no one but you can see.

XCVI

I am so overcome by the long wait
And by the endless battle of my sighs,
That my desire and hope I come to hate,
And every snare in which my passion lies.

But the enchanting face that in my breast
Is painted, that I see where'er I gaze,
Curbs me; and to my first consuming quest
Against my will I am pushed back always.

I erred once, long ago, when the old way
Of freedom was cut off and barred to me,
For it is wrong to follow what we crave;

That time she ran to ruin loose and free,
Now of another will she is made slave,
My soul whose sin was once to disobey.

XCVII

Ahi, bella libertá, come tu m'hai
Partendoti da me mostrato quale
Era 'l mio stato, quando il primo strale
Fece la piaga ond'io non guerrò mai!

Gli occhi invaghiro allor sí de' lor guai,
Che 'l fren de la ragione ivi non vale,
Perc'hanno a schifo ogni opera mortale:
Lasso!, cosí da prima gli avezzai!

Né mi lece ascoltar chi non ragiona
De la mia morte; e solo del suo nome
Vo empiendo l'aere, che sí dolce sona.

Amor in altra parte non mi sprona,
Né i pie' sanno altra via, né le man come
Lodar si possa in carte altra persona.

XCVIII

Orso, al vostro destrier si pò ben porre
Un fren, che di suo corso in dietro il volga;
Ma 'l cor chi legherá che non si sciolga,
Se brama onore, e 'l suo contrario aborre?

Non sospirate: a lui non si pò tôrre
Suo pregio, per ch'a voi l'andar si tolga;
Ché, come fama publica divolga,
Egli è giá lá, che null'altro il precorre.

Basti che si ritrove in mezzo 'l campo
Al destinato dí, sotto quell'arme
Che gli dá il tempo, amor, vertute e 'l sangue,

Gridando:—D'un gentil desire avampo,
Co' 'l signor mio, che non pò seguitarme,
E del non esser qui si strugge e langue.—

XCVII

Ah, beloved liberty, how well you did,
When you left me, my condition reveal,
Such as it was when the first arrow hid
That wound within my heart which does not heal!

My eyes were so seduced by suffering,
That the control of reason held no sway,
For they abhor every mortal thing:
Alas! that I have trained them in this way.

Nor can I follow those who do not talk
Of my own death, and only with her name
I fill the ether that so sweetly sounds.

Love in no other region leads my walk,
No other path I know, no other fame
My hand can shape where so much praise abounds.

XCVIII

Orso, to your war-horse that forward runs
You can apply a bit and change his course,
But the heart, who can tie and hold by force
If he craves honour and dishonour shuns?

Do not complain: he will be worth his prize,
Though it is not permitted you to go;
For like a public rumour he will rise
And be already there, never too slow.

Enough for him to be among the lines
On the appointed day, and in those arms
Given to him by time, love, virtue, blood,

Crying aloud:—A gentle desire warms
Me and my master who was left to brood
And at not being here mourns and repines.—

XCIX

Poi che voi et io piú volte abbiam provato
Come 'l nostro sperar torna fallace,
Dietro a quel sommo ben che mai non spiace
Levate il core a piú felice stato.

Questa vita terrena è quasi un prato,
Che 'l serpente tra 'fiori e l'erba giace;
E s'alcuna sua vista a gli occhi piace,
È per lassar piú l'animo invescato.

Voi dunque, se cercate aver la mente
Anzi l'estremo dí queta giá mai,
Seguite i pochi, e non la volgar gente.

Ben si può dire a me:—Frate, tu vai
Mostrando altrui la via, dove sovente
Fosti smarrito, et or se' piú che mai.—

C

Quella fenestra ove l'un sol si vede,
Quando a lui piace, e l'altro in su la nona,
E quella dove l'aere freddo suona
Ne' brevi giorni, quando borrea 'l fiede;

E 'l sasso, ove a' gran dí pensosa siede
Madonna, e sola seco si ragiona;
Con quanti luoghi sua bella persona
Coprí mai d'ombra o disegnò col piede;

E 'l fiero passo ove m'agiunse Amore;
E lla nova stagion che d'anno in anno
Mi rinfresca in quel dí l'antiche piaghe;

E 'l vólto, e le parole che mi stanno
Altamente confitte in mezzo 'l core,
Fanno le luci mie di pianger vaghe.

XCIX

Since you and I have often realized
How all our hoping is deceived by fate,
Toward that good which is forever prized
Lift up your heart, to a more blissful state.

This earthly life is almost like a field
Where serpents hide among the flowers and grass,
And if some of its aspects have appealed
To us, it was to snare our souls to pass.

Then you, if you aspire to keep your mind
Before the parting day somewhat secure,
Follow the few and not the vulgar kind.

Someone might say to me:—Brother, you show
A way to others, that you do not know,
Where you got lost, and now worse than before.—

C

That window where one of the two suns shows
When it pleases, the other marking nones,
And that in which the frozen windstorm blows
In the short days when angry Boreas groans;

And the stone where, when days are long and warm,
My lady sits left to her own conceit,
And all the places that her lovely form
Wrapped with her shadow or pressed with her feet;

And the fierce spot where Love began his part;
And the new season that, year after year,
Awakens on that day my ancient sore;

And the face and the words that remain here
Magnificently carved inside my heart,
Make my eyes fond of weeping more and more.

CI

Lasso!, ben so che dolorose prede
Di noi fa quella ch'a nullo uom perdona,
E che rapidamente n'abandona
Il mondo, e picciol tempo ne tien fede;

Veggio a molto languir poca mercede,
E giá l'ultimo dí nel cor mi tuona:
Per tutto questo Amor non mi spregiona,
Che l'usato tributo a gli occhi chiede.

So come i dí, come i momenti, e l'ore,
Ne portan gli anni; e non ricevo inganno,
Ma forza assai maggior che d'arti maghe.

La voglia e la ragion combattuto hanno
Sette e sette anni; e vincerá il migliore,
S'anime son qua giú del ben presaghe.

CII

Cesare, poi che 'l traditor d'Egitto
Li fece il don de l'onorata testa,
Celando l'allegrezza manifesta
Pianse per gli occhi fuor, sí come è scritto;

Et Anibál, quando a l'imperio afflitto
Vide farsi fortuna sí molesta,
Rise fra gente lagrimosa e mesta,
Per isfogare il suo acerbo despitto;

E cosí aven che l'animo ciascuna
Sua passion sotto 'l contrario manto
Ricopre co la vista or chiara or bruna.

Però, s'alcuna volta io rido o canto,
Facciol perch'i' non ho se non quest'una
Via da celare il mio angoscioso pianto.

CI

Alas! I know, we are the piteous preys
Of one who never pardons human dust,
I know the world quickly deserts, betrays
Us, and a little time will keep our trust;

I see that anguish gets a small reward,
Already the last day thunders in me;
Nevertheless Love keeps me under guard
And asks my eyes to pay their usual fee.

I know the days, the moments and the hours
Carry the years; nor do I earn deceit,
But greater vigour than of magic powers.

Desire and reason fought against defeat
Seven and seven years: the best will stand,
If some of us down here can guess their land.

CII

Caesar, when the betrayer of Egypt
Gave to him as a gift the honoured head,
Hiding the joy that in his spirit spread,
Wept in his outward show, as says the script.

And Hannibal when to his torn empire
He saw fortune declare her enmity,
Laughed among those who were in agony,
To vent his anger for a lost desire.

And so it happens that our souls betray
Each passion and conceal it with their sight,
With a behaviour that is dark or light.

Therefore if I sometimes will laugh or sing,
It is because I have no other way
To conceal my distressful suffering.

CIII

Vinse Anibál, e non seppe usar poi
Ben la vittoriosa sua ventura;
Però, signor mio caro, aggiate cura
Che similmente non avegna a voi.

L'orsa, rabbiosa per gli orsacchi suoi,
Che trovaron di maggio aspra pastura,
Rode sé dentro, e i denti e l'unghie endura
Per vendicar suoi danni sopra noi.

Mentre 'l novo dolor dunque l'accora,
Non riponete l'onorata spada;
Anzi seguite lá dove vi chiama

Vostra fortuna dritto per la strada
Che vi può dar, dopo la morte ancóra
Mille e mille anni, al mondo onor e fama.

CIV

L'aspettata vertú, che 'n voi fioriva
Quando Amor cominciò darvi battaglia,
Produce or frutto, che quel fiore aguaglia,
E che mia speme fa venire a riva.

Però mi dice il cor ch'io in carte scriva
Cosa onde 'l vostro nome in pregio saglia;
Ché 'n nulla parte sí saldo s'intaglia
Per far di marmo una persona viva.

Credete voi che Cesare o Marcello
O Paolo od Affrican fossin cotali
Per incude giá mai né per martello?

Pandolfo mio, quest'opere son frali
Al lungo andar, ma 'l nostro studio è quello
Che fa per fama gli uomini immortali.

CIII

Hannibal won and then he could not use
His victory with rightful means and true;
Therefore, my lord, you must know how to choose,
That the same thing may not be said of you.

The she-bear, angry because her small bears
Found the pastures in May not good enough,
Rages and makes her fangs and claws more tough
To revenge upon us her anxious cares.

Though this resentment crushes you, my lord,
Do not neglect your honourable sword,
But rather answer where resounds your name

Called by your fortune that travels ahead
On the way which, long after you are dead,
Can give you thousand years of earthly fame.

CIV

The rooted virtue that blossomed in you
When Love began to battle at your door,
Now bears the fruit where once the flower grew,
And so my hope can come and touch the shore.

Therefore my heart begs me to write and tell
On paper what brings glory to your name;
For in no other stuff we carve so well
To make a marble of a living frame.

Think you that Caesar or Marcellus then,
And Paul and Africanus were such men
Thanks to a hammer's or an anvil's strength?

My Pandolfo, those works have no great length,
They are too frail, our own studies are what
Makes men immortal and famous their lot.

CV

Mai non vo' piú cantar   com'io soleva,
Ch'altri non m'intendeva,   ond'ebbi scorno,
E puossi in bel soggiorno   esser molesto.
Il sempre sospirar   nulla releva;
Giá su per l'Alpi neva   d'ogn'intorno;
Et è giá presso al giorno;   ond'io son desto.
Un atto dolce onesto   è gentil cosa:
Et in donna amorosa   ancor m'aggrada,
Che 'n vista vada   altèra e disdegnosa,
Non superba e ritrosa:
Amor regge suo imperio senza spada.
Chi smarrita ha la strada,   torni in dietro;
Chi non ha albergo, posisi in sul verde;
Chi non ha l'auro, o 'l perde,
Spenga la sete sua con un bel vetro.

I' die' in guarda a san Pietro;   or non piú, no.
Intendami chi pó,   ch'i' m'intend io.
Grave soma è un mal fio   a mantenerlo:
Quando posso, mi spetro, e sol mi sto.
Fetonte odo che 'n Po   cadde, e morio;
E giá di lá dal rio   passato è 'l merlo;
Deh, venite a vederlo.   Or i' non voglio:
Non è gioco uno scoglio   in mezzo l'onde,
E 'ntra le fronde   il visco. Assai mi doglio
Quando un soverchio orgoglio
Molte vertuti in bella donna asconde.
Alcun è che risponde   a chi no 'l chiama;
Altri, chi 'l prega, si delegua e fugge;
Altri al ghiaccio si strugge;
Altri dí e notte la sua morte brama.

Proverbio "ama chi t'ama"   è fatto antico.
I' so ben quel ch'io dico.   Or lass'andare;
Ché conven ch'altri impare   a le sue spese.
Un'umil donna grama   un dolce amico.
Mal si conosce il fico.   A me pur pare
Senno a non cominciare   tropp'alte imprese;

CV

I no more want to sing   as then and there,
Because she did not care,   to my disgrace,
And in a charming place   one can displease.
Sighs are a useless thing,   a wasted prayer;
It snows everywhere   in the Alps' trace,
And the day starts to race,   I wake and freeze.
Honest acts full of ease   are praised above,
And in a ladylove   they can be dear,
But her look should appear   scornful and haughty,
Not arrogant and naughty:
Love governs his empire without a spear.
Who lost power to steer   must leave that pass;
Who has no home, let him shut up his door;
Who laurel has no more,
Let him satiate his thirst with a clear glass.

I called Peter, alas;   but no more now.
Let who can, figure how;   I understand.
A heavy load's demand   is hard to keep:
No more the stone I was: a lonely bough.
Phaëton, I do avow,   fell in Po's sand;
And to another land   the blackbirds sweep.
Will you please come and leap.   I am unbent:
By a rock to be rent   among the waves
Is hard, and to be slaves   of leaves and spent
When too great a contempt
So many virtues in women depraves.
There is someone who raves   in speechless groves,
Others who hunted disappear and fly,
Some in ice melt and lie,
And someone day and night toward death moves.

The proverb "Love who loves you" is grown old.
I mean what I have told.   Now let it go;
For one must learn to know   to his own cost.
A humble woman proves   how she can hold.
A fig who can unfold?   One does not show
Good sense striving to grow   and reach the most;

E per ogni paese è bona stanza.
L'infinita speranza occide altrui;
Et anch'io fui alcuna volta in danza.
Quel poco che m'avanza,
Fia chi no 'l schifi, s'i' 'l vo' dare a lui.
I' mi fido in colui che 'l mondo regge
E che 'seguaci suoi nel bosco alberga,
Che con pietosa verga
Mi meni a passo omai tra le sue gregge.

Forse ch'ogni uom che legge non s'intende;
E la rete tal tende che non piglia;
E chi troppo assotiglia si scavezza.
Non sia zoppa la legge ov'altri attende.
Per bene star si scende molte miglia.
Tal par gran meraviglia, e poi si sprezza.
Una chiusa bellezza è piú soave.
Benedetta la chiave che s'avvolse
Al cor, e sciolse l'alma, e scossa l'have
Di catena sí grave,
E 'nfiniti sospir del mio sen tolse!
Lá dove piú mi dolse, altri si dole;
E dolendo adolcisce il mio dolore;
Ond'io ringrazio Amore
Che piú no 'l sento; et è non men che suole.

In silenzio parole accorte e sagge,
E 'l suon che mi sottragge ogni altra cura,
E la pregione oscura ov'è 'l bel lume;
Le notturne viole per le piagge,
E le fere selvagge entr' a le mura,
E la dolce paura, e 'l bel costume,
E di duo fonti un fiume in pace vòlto
Dov'io bramo, e raccolto ove che sia,
Amor e gelosia m'hanno il cor tolto,
E i segni del bel vólto,
Che mi conducon per piú piana via
A la speranza mia, al fin de gli affanni.
O riposto mio bene, e quel che segue,
Or pace, or guerra or triegue,

Wherever we are lost   we find a nest.
Too much hope in our breast   will make us die;
And I myself did try   to be life's guest.
What has been scorned, suppressed,
Someone will like unless I am too shy.
I will beg the most High   who rules and leads
The world and wood where his disciples trod,
With a merciful rod
To guide my steps where his flock always feeds.

Perhaps someone who reads   can't grasp it yet;
And some drop down a net   they cannot fill;
Those too subtle and still   will never learn.
There are no crooked creeds   when they are met.
To live well and forget   we go downhill;
And a beauty we will   admire and spurn.
To remote charms we turn   that are more sweet.
Blest be the keys that meet   the heart and save
The soul made free and brave,   and hail and greet
Her when she flouts defeat,
And deliver the sighs that made us rave!
Where I once used to crave,   others feel pain;
And their sorrow diminishes my grief;
I thank Love for relief,
I do not feel it, yet it will remain.

In my silent domain   words keen and wise,
And the sounds that disguise   all other care,
And the dark prison bare   where shines that light;
The violets in the plain   when stars arise,
And the wild beast that lies   in the walled lair,
My sweet fright and despair   and the dear rite,
And of two streams one bright   turned toward peace
Where I must go, to cease   in any place;
Jealousy and that face   are my disease,
And the two signs of ease
That lead me on the way of softened pace
To my hope's only grace,   to my grief's end.
O my hidden delight and what comes after,
Or peace or war or laughter,

Mai non m'abbandonate in questi panni.

De' passati miei danni piango e rido,
Perché molto mi fido in quel ch'i' odo;
Del presente mi godo, e meglio aspetto,
E vo contando gli anni, e taccio e grido;
E 'n bel ramo m'annido, et in tal modo,
Ch'i' ne ringrazio, e lodo, il gran disdetto,
Che l'indurato affetto al fine ha vinto,
E ne l'alma depinto: "I' sare' udito,
E mostratone a dito": et hanne estinto
(Tanto inanzi son pinto,
Ch'i' 'l pur dirò): "Non fostú tant'ardito".
Chi m'ha 'l fianco ferito e chi 'l risalda,
Per cui nel cor via piú che 'n carta scrivo;
Chi mi fa morto e vivo,
Chi 'n un punto m'agghiaccia e mi riscalda.

CVI

Nova angeletta sovra l'ale accorta
Scese dal cielo in su la fresca riva,
Lá 'nd'io passava sol per mio destino:

Poi che senza compagna e senza scorta
Mi vide, un laccio che di seta ordiva
Tese fra l'erba ond'è verde il camino:

Allor fui preso; e non mi spiacque poi,
Sí dolce lume uscía di gli occhi suoi.

You never desert me, I am your friend.

At my past I intend   to laugh and cry,
Because I must comply   with what I hear;
I enjoy what is near   and what is sent,
And my years I defend,   or bold or shy;
On a fair branch I fly,   and in such gear
That I thank and revere   the great contempt
Which my love and lament   at last has stilled.
My soul's words are fulfilled,   "I shall be heard,
As example referred":   my life was chilled
(So far they stretched my guilt
That I will say): "Your courage was not stirred."
She who slew me, interred,   who makes me whole,
Because of whom I do not write but sigh,
Who makes me live and die,
Who in one point freezes and heats my soul.

CVI

A new small angel balanced on her wings
Descended from the sky on the cool shore
Where I walked all alone as is my fate:

Seeing me without company or things
To trust, she threw a woven silk before
Me in the grass that makes a green estate;

Then I was caught; and I was not afraid,
So lovely was the light that her eyes spread.

CVII

Non veggio ove scampar mi possa omai:
Sí lunga guerra i begli occhi mi fanno,
Ch'i' temo, lasso!, no 'l soverchio affanno
Distruga 'l cor che triegua non ha mai.

Fuggir vorrei; ma gli amorosi rai,
Che dí e notte ne la mente stanno,
Risplendon sí, ch'al quintodecimo anno
M'abbaglian piú che 'l primo giorno assai;

E l'imagine lor son sí cosparte
Che volver non mi posso ov'io non veggia
O quella o simil indi accesa luce.

Solo d'un lauro tal selva verdeggia
Che 'l mio adversario con mirabil arte
Vago fra i rami, ovunque vuol, m'adduce.

CVIII

Aventuroso piú d'altro terreno,
Ov'Amor vidi giá fermar le piante
Vèr' me volgendo quelle luci sante
Che fanno intorno a sé l'aere sereno,

Prima poría per tempo venir meno
Un'imagine salda di diamante,
Che l'atto dolce non mi stia davante,
Del qual ho la memoria e 'l cor sí pieno;

Né tante volte ti vedrò giá mai,
Ch'i' non m'inchini a ricercar de l'orme
Che 'l bel pie' fece in quel cortese giro.

Ma se 'n cor valoroso Amor non dorme,
Prega, Sennuccio mio, quando 'l vedrai,
Di qualche lagrimetta, o d'un sospiro.

CVII

I do not see from where I can escape:
Such a long war those eyes against me wage,
That I begin to fear this cruel rage
Will rob my heart of peace, my life of shape.

I would flee them, but the amorous rays
Which day and night remain within my mind,
Sparkle so well that the fifteenth year's blaze
Shines more than the first day and makes me blind:

Their image so pervades every part,
That I can never turn without remarking
Either that light or one equally sparking.

From one laurel such wood grows and increases,
That my foe with an admirable art
Can draw me through the branches where he pleases.

CVIII

More delightful than any other ground,
Where I saw Love press on the earth his feet,
Turning to me those lights that heaven greet
And make the air unclouded all around,

Time could sooner destroy, reduce to nought
A solid image made of diamond,
Than her sweet action will cease to be brought
Before my eyes to make me feel my bond;

Nor can I see you so regularly
That I forget to bend and seek the trace
Her fair foot left in such a gentle place.

But if in gallant hearts love does not die,
O my Sennuccio, when that ground you see,
Beg it to shed some tears or just to sigh.

CIX

Lasso!, quante fiate Amor m'assale,
Che fra la notte e 'l dí son piú di mille,
Torno dov'arder vidi le faville
Che 'l foco del mio cor fanno immortale.

Ivi m'acqueto; e son condotto a tale,
Ch'a nona, a vespro, a l'alba et a le squille
Le trovo nel pensier tanto tranquille
Che di null'altro mi rimembra o cale.

L'aura soave che dal chiaro viso
Move col suon de le parole accorte
Per far dolce sereno ovunque spira,

Quasi un spirto gentil di paradiso
Sempre in quell'aere par che mi conforte;
Sí che 'l cor lasso altrove non respira.

CX

Persequendomi Amor al luogo usato
Ristretto in guisa d'uom ch'aspetta guerra,
Che si provede, e i passi intorno serra,
De' miei antichi pensier mi stava armato.

Volsimi, e vidi un'ombra che da lato
Stampava il sole, e riconobbi in terra
Quella che, se 'l giudicio mio non erra,
Era piú degna d'immortale stato.

I' dicea fra mio cor:—Perché paventi?—
Ma non fu prima dentro il penser giunto,
Che i raggi, ov'io mi struggo, eran presenti.

Come col balenar tona in un punto,
Cosí fu' io de' begli occhi lucenti
E d'un dolce saluto inseme aggiunto.

CIX

Alas! as often as Love throws his dart
Which night and day has left so many marks,
I return where I saw ignite those sparks
That make immortal the fire of my heart.

There I am calm; and I am so resigned,
That at vesper and nones, dawn's or night's chimes,
I find them in my thought where such peace climbs
That nothing else I keep inside my mind.

The gentle aura that from that clear face
Moves with the sound of her words full of grace
To make a limpid climate everywhere,

Almost like a pure soul of paradise
In such air always makes me glad and wise,
So that the weary heart breathes only there.

CX

While Love was chasing me in the same ground,
I stood there like a man ready for war,
Who measures and defines his steps around,
Armed with my thoughts and with their ancient law.

Turning, I saw a shadow that near me
Blotted the sun, and I looked up to find
A lady who, if I know well my mind,
Should have been given immortality.

I was asking my heart:—What do you fear?—
But this thought had not yet begun to rise
When the consuming rays were shining here.

As to the lightning the thunder is joined,
So was I reached by her luminous eyes
And by her sweet salute at the same point.

CXI

La donna che 'l mio cor nel viso porta,
Lá dove sol fra bei pensier d'amore
Sedea, m'apparve; et io per farle onore
Mossi con fronte reverente e smorta.

Tosto che del mio stato fussi accorta,
A me si volse in sí novo colore
Ch'avrebbe a Giove nel maggior furore
Tolto l'arme di mano, e l'ira morta.

I' mi riscossi; et ella oltra, parlando,
Passò, che la parola i' non soffersi,
Né 'l dolce sfavillar de gli occhi suoi.

Or mi ritrovo pien di sí diversi
Piaceri, in quel saluto ripensando,
Che duol non sento, né sentí' ma' poi.

CXII

Sennuccio, i' vo' che sapi in qual manera
Trattato sono, e qual vita è la mia:
Ardomi e struggo ancor com'io solia;
L'aura mi volve; e son pur quel ch'i' m'era.

Qui tutta umile, e qui la vidi altèra,
Or aspra, or piana, or dispietata, or pia;
Or vestirsi onestate, or leggiadria,
Or mansueta, or disdegnosa e fera;

Qui cantò dolcemente, e qui s'assise;
Qui si rivolse, e qui rattenne il passo;
Qui co' begli occhi mi trafisse il core;

Qui disse una parola, e qui sorrise;
Qui cangiò 'l viso. In questi pensier, lasso!,
Notte e di tiemmi il signor nostro, Amore.

CXI

The lady in whose face my heart is set
Appeared to me where among thoughts of love
I was sitting alone; I rose to move
And honour her, looking pale and upset.

When she became aware of my condition,
She turned to me a face of such new shade
That would rob Jove of his menacing mission
And steal his arms and make his anger fade.

I was shaken; she went on to converse
And passed, I could not bear the words she said,
Nor the sweet sparkling that from her eyes spread.

I find myself so full now of diverse
Pleasures in thinking of that greeting's bliss,
That I nothing regret and nothing miss.

CXII

Sennuccio, you must hear in what a way
I have been treated and what life is mine:
I burn as I used to and I repine,
The air sweeps me, and where I stayed I stay.

I saw her humble and I saw her proud,
Now harsh, now soft, now merciless, now kind;
Now honestly, now gracefully inclined,
Now meek and now disdainful as a cloud.

Here she sang sweetly, here sat on the grass,
Here she turned backward, here she did not move,
Here her eyes pierced my breast as with a shaft.

Here she uttered a word and here she laughed,
Here she changed colour; with these thoughts, alas,
Night and day crushes me our master, Love.

CXIII

Qui, dove mezzo son, Sennuccio mio,
(Cosí ci foss'io intero, e voi contento)
Venni fuggendo la tempesta e 'l vento
C'hanno súbito fatto il tempo rio.

Qui son securo: e vo' vi dir perch'io
Non, come soglio, il folgorar pavento,
E perché mitigato, non che spento,
Né mica trovo il mio ardente desio.

Tosto che giunto a l'amorosa reggia
Vidi onde nacque l'aura dolce e pura,
Ch'acqueta l'aere e mette i tuoni in bando,

Amor ne l'alma, ov'ella signoreggia,
Raccese 'l foco, e spense la paura:
Che farei dunque gli occhi suoi guardando?

CXIV

De l'empia Babilonia, ond'è fuggita
Ogni vergogna, ond'ogni bene è fòri,
Albergo di dolor, madre d'errori,
Son fuggito io per allungar la vita.

Qui mi sto solo; e, come Amor m'invita,
Or rime e versi, or colgo erbette e fiori,
Seco parlando, et a tempi migliori
Sempre pensando: e questo sol m'aita.

Né del vulgo mi cal, né di fortuna,
Né di me molto, né di cosa vile,
Né dentro sento né di fuor gran caldo.

Sol due persone cheggio; e vorrei l'una
Col cor vèr' me pacificato umíle,
L'altro col pie', sí come mai fu, saldo.

CXIII

Here where I am by half, Sennuccio kind,
(Could I be there entire, you glad enough),
I came fleeing the tempest and the wind
That suddenly have made the weather rough.

Here I am safe: and I must tell you why
I do not dread the lightning as before,
And why I find the ashes almost dry
Of my desire that used to burn and roar.

When I arrived in my love's paradise
I saw whence sprang the aura's lovely wonder
Which calms the air and banishes the thunder.

Love in the soul where she has her domain
Put out my fear and lit the fire again:
What would I do if I looked in her eyes?

CXIV

From that dire Babylon, from where is run
Away all shame, from where all good is gone,
Dwelling of misery, mother of strife,
I fled to lengthen the course of my life.

Here I am all alone: and by Love's powers
Now I pluck rhymes, now the small grass and flowers,
Talking to him, and of a better station
Forever thinking, this is my salvation.

I do not care for men, nor for luck's tide,
And not much for myself or trivial jumble,
I am not cold or warm inside, outside.

I only want two people: and one ready
To bring to me a heart peaceful and humble,
The other feet now more than ever steady.

CXV

In mezzo di duo amanti onesta altèra
Vidi una donna, e quel signor co lei
Che fra gli uomini regna, e fra li dèi;
E da l'un lato il Sole, io da l'altro era.

Poi che s'accorse chiusa de la spera
De l'amico piú bello, a gli occhi miei
Tutta lieta si volse; e ben vorrei,
Che mai non fosse in vèr' di me piú fera.

Súbito in allegrezza si converse
La gelosia che 'n su la prima vista
Per sí alto adversario, al cor mi nacque.

A lui la faccia lagrimosa e trista
Un nuviletto intorno ricoverse;
Cotanto l'esser vinto li dispiacque.

CXVI

Pien di quella ineffabile dolcezza
Che del bel viso trassen gli occhi miei
Nel dí che volentier chiusi gli avrei
Per non mirar giá mai minor bellezza,

Lassai quel ch'i' piú bramo; et ho sí avezza
La mente a contemplar sola costei
Ch'altro non vede, e ciò che non è lei
Giá per antica usanza odia e disprezza.

In una valle chiusa d'ogni 'ntorno,
Ch'è refrigerio de' sospir miei lassi,
Giunsi sol con Amor, pensoso e tardo.

Ivi non donne, ma fontane e sassi,
E l'imagine trovo di quel giorno
Che 'l pensier mio figura ovunque io sguardo.

CXV

Between two lovers I saw her go by,
My proud, grave lady, and part of her train
The lord who governs among gods and men;
The sun on one side, on the other I.

When she found out that she had been beguiled
By the handsomer friend, toward my eyes
Gaily she turned; I would she were so wise
Always in my respect, and reconciled.

The jealousy was turned into delight
At once, that had consumed me at first sight,
When I had noticed such a rivalry.

A little cloud surrounded the sun's face
Full of sadness because of his disgrace;
So great was his resentment against me.

CXVI

Full of that indescribable sweetness
Which my eyes from her face had seen to pour
The day when I had wanted to suppress
Them not to see a beauty any more,

I left what I desire; I have so trained
My mind to contemplate only one good,
That it sees nothing else, for its ingrained
Will is to hate and scorn all other mood.

Here in a valley all enclosed around,
The only solace of my weary way,
I slowly came with Love, pensive, alone.

Not ladies I find here, fountain and stone,
And the remembered image of a day
Which my thought represents in every ground.

CXVII

Se 'l sasso, ond'è piú chiusa questa valle,
Di che 'l suo proprio nome si deriva,
Tenesse vòlto, per natura schiva,
A Roma il viso et a Babel le spalle,

I miei sospiri piú benigno calle
Avrian per gire ove lor spene è viva:
Or vanno sparsi, e pur ciascuno arriva
Lá dov'io il mando, che sol un non falle;

E son di lá sí dolcemente accolti,
Com'io m'accorgo, che nessun mai torna,
Con tal diletto in quelle parti stanno.

De gli occhi è 'l duol; che tosto che s'aggiorna
Per gran desio de' be' luoghi a lor tolti,
Dànno a me pianto, et a' pie' lassi affanno.

CXVIII

Rimansi a dietro il sestodicemo anno
De' miei sospiri, et io trapasso inanzi
Verso l'estremo; e parmi che pur dianzi
Fosse 'l principio di cotanto affanno.

L'amar m'è dolce, et util il mio danno,
E 'l viver grave; e prego ch'egli avanzi
L'empia fortuna; e temo no chiuda anzi
Morte i begli occhi che parlar mi fanno.

Or qui son, lasso!, e voglio esser altrove;
E vorrei piú volere, e piú non voglio;
E per piú non poter fo quant'io posso;

E d'antichi desir lagrime nove
Provan com'io son pur quel ch'i' mi soglio,
Né per mille rivolte ancor son mosso.

CXVII

If the rock of this valley closed and stable,
From which has been derived its proper name,
Would turn, out of reserve or out of shame,
Its face to Rome and its shoulders to Babel,

My sighs would find a more propitious vault
To go there where their hope is still alive;
Now they are scattered, and yet they arrive
Where I send them, there is not a default;

And they are there so graciously received,
As I remark, that none of them regress,
With so much pleasure they have been retrieved.

The pain is in the eyes, that when day comes,
Out of their longing for their stolen homes,
Give tears to me and to my limbs distress.

CXVIII

Now I have left behind the sixteenth year
Of my heart's yearning and soon I shall be
At the last step; and yet it seems quite near,
The beginning of this long agony.

Loving is sweet to me, useful this rut,
And life is hard and I hope it survive
The wicked fortune, and Death never shut
Before then the fair eyes for which I strive.

Ah! I am here, and I want to be there;
I would wish even more, and wish no more;
And since I cannot do, do what I can;

And from an old desire a newborn tear
Proves that I am what I have been before,
And though tried to leave, I never ran.

CXIX

Una donna piú bella assai che 'l sole,
E piú lucente, e d'altrettanta etade,
Con famosa beltade,
Acerbo ancor, mi trasse a la sua schiera.
Questa in penseri, in opre et in parole
(Però ch'è de le cose al mondo rade),
Questa per mille strade
Sempre inanzi mi fu leggiadra, altèra.
Solo per lei tornai da quel ch'i' era,
Poi ch'i' soffersi gli occhi suoi da presso;
Per suo amor m'er'io messo
A faticosa impresa assai per tempo;
Tal che s'i' arrivo al disiato porto,
Spero per lei gran tempo
Viver, quand'altri mi terrá per morto.

Questa mia donna mi menò molt'anni
Pien di vaghezza giovenile ardendo,
Sí come ora io comprendo,
Sol per aver di me piú certa prova,
Mostrandomi pur l'ombra, o 'l velo, o' panni
Talor di sé, ma 'l viso nascondendo;
Et io, lasso!, credendo
Vederne assai, tutta l'età mia nova
Passai contento, e 'l rimembrar mi giova,
Poi ch'alquanto di lei veggi' or piú inanzi.
I' dico che pur dianzi,
Qual io non l'avea vista in fin allora,
Mi si scoverse; onde mi nacque un ghiaccio
Nel core; et evvi ancóra,
E sará sempre fin ch'i' le sia in braccio.

Ma non mel tolse la paura o 'l gielo,
Che pur tanta baldanza al mio cor diedi,
Ch'i' le mi strinsi a' piedi
Per piú dolcezza trar de gli occhi suoi:
Et ella, che remosso avea giá il velo
Dinanzi a' miei, mi disse:—Amico, or vedi
Com'io son bella; e chiedi

CXIX

A lady much more gorgeous than the sun,
And more resplendent, and of equal age,
With beauty did engage
And draw me still unripe among her crowd.
This, in thought and in word and action
(Since she is rare and made to assuage)
Through life's multiple stage
Stood always before me charming and proud.
Only for her I renounced what I vowed,
After I let her eyes follow me close;
For love of her I chose
A tiring enterprise early in time;
And if I reach the port where I am led,
I hope in her own clime
To live long after others think me dead.

This lady guided me many a year
Full of a youthful ardour and desire,
Determined to require
From me, as now I see, a surer proof,
Showing to me her shadow, veil or gear,
From time to time, never her face entire;
Thinking I could admire
Enough, alas! I spent my youth aloof
And satisfied. I rejoice in this move,
For a great deal of her I learned to store.
I say that just now more
Than I ever discovered became known
To me, whence in my heart an ice rose high,
An ice that here is grown
And here shall grow till in her arms I lie.

But neither fear nor frost prevented me
From giving to my heart so much conceit,
That I embraced her feet
To draw out more compassion from her eyes:
And she who had already made me see
Her eyes out of their veil, said:—Friend, now greet
My beauty and entreat

Quanto par si convenga a gli anni tuoi.—
—Madonna—dissi—giá gran tempo in voi
Posi 'l mio amor, ch'i' sento or sí infiammato;
Ond'a me in questo stato,
Altro volere o disvoler m'è tolto.—
Con voce allor di sí mirabil tempre
Rispose, e con un vólto,
Che temer e sperar mi fará sempre:

—Rado fu al mondo, fra cosí gran turba,
Ch'udendo ragionar del mio valore,
Non si sentisse al core,
Per breve tempo almen, qualche favilla;
Ma l'adversaria mia, che 'l ben perturba,
Tosto la spegne; ond'ogni vertú more,
E regna altro signore
Che promette una vita piú tranquilla.
De la tua mente Amor, che prima aprilla,
Mi dice cose veramente, ond'io
Veggio che 'l gran desio
Pur d'onorato fin ti fará degno;
E come giá se' de' miei rari amici,
Donna vedrai per segno,
Che fará gli occhi tuoi via piú felici.—

I' volea dir—quest'è impossibil cosa—
Quand'ella:—Or mira (e leva' gli occhi un poco
In piú riposto loco)
Donna ch'a pochi si mostrò giá mai.—
Ratto inchinai la fronte vergognosa,
Sentendo novo dentro maggior foco.
Et ella il prese in gioco,
Dicendo:—I' veggio ben dove tu stai.
Sí come 'l sol con suoi possenti rai
Fa súbito sparire ogni altra stella,
Cosí par or men bella
La vista mia, cui maggior luce preme.
Ma io però da' miei non ti diparto;
Ché questa e me d'un seme,
Lei davanti e me poi, produsse un parto.—

From me whatever you may call a prize.—
—My lady—I replied—in yourself lies
The goal of all my love burning like fire;
To me in such desire
All other wish or refusal is base.—
Then with a voice so marvellously clear,
She said, and with a face
That forever shall make me hope and fear:

—There hardly was a man in the great crowd
Of the world, who in learning of my art
Did not feel in his heart
For a small time at least a little spark;
But my foe who abhors good and is proud,
Soon smothers it, and all virtues depart;
A new lord's powers start
To rule, which promise a securer ark.
Of your mind Love, who took it from the dark,
Truly tells me such things that I foresee
How your heart's constancy
Will make you worthy of a noble death;
And since you are of my few friends on earth,
You shall see by your faith
A lady who shall give your eyes more mirth.—

I was going to say:—It cannot be—
When she:—Behold (and lift your eyes a bit
Where the secret ones sit)
A lady who appears seldom to few.—
Quickly I bent my head from modesty,
Feeling by new and warmer feeling hit:
She began mocking it
And said:—I know what this has done to you.
Just as the sun's irradiating view
Extinguishes at once all other beams,
So now less charming seems
My countenance oppressed by greater light.
But I do not exclude you from my breed;
For we have one birthright,
First she, then I, were born from the same seed.—

Rúpessi in tanto di vergogna il nodo
Ch'a la mia lingua era distretto intorno
Su nel primiero scorno,
Allor quand'io del suo accorger m'accorsi;
E 'ncominciai:—S'egli è ver quel ch'i' odo,
Beato il padre, e benedetto il giorno
C'ha di voi il mondo adorno,
E tutto 'l tempo ch'a vedervi io corsi!
E se mai da la via dritta mi torsi,
Duolmene forte, assai piú ch'i' non mostro.
Ma se de l'esser vostro
Fossi degno udir piú, del desir ardo.—
Pensosa mi rispose, e cosí fiso
Tenne il suo dolce sguardo,
Ch'al cor mandò co le parole il viso:

—Sí come piacque al nostro eterno padre,
Ciascuna di noi due nacque immortale.
Miseri! a voi che vale?
Me' v'era che da noi fosse il defetto.
Amate, belle, giovani e leggiadre
Fummo alcun tempo; et or siam giunte a tale
Che costei batte l'ale
Per tornar a l'antico suo ricetto;
I' per me sono un'ombra. Et or t'ho detto,
Quanto per te sí breve intender puossi.—
Poi che i pie' suoi fûr mossi,
Dicendo—Non temer ch'i' m'allontani—
Di verde lauro una ghirlanda colse,
La qual co le sue mani
Intorno intorno a le mie tempie avolse.

Canzon, chi tua ragion chiamasse obscura,
Di':—Non ho cura, perché tosto spero
Ch'altro messaggio il vero
Fará in piú chiara voce manifesto.
I' venni sol per isvegliare altrui,
Se, chi m'impose questo,
Non m'ingano, quand'io partí da lui.—

Meanwhile the tangle snapped that full of shame
Had been fastened and tied around my tongue
In the first sting of wrong,
When I saw her awareness of my play;
And I began:—If I heard your true fame,
Blest be the father and the day ever young
That gave the world your song,
And all the time I ran after your ray!
And if I ever turned from the right way,
I regret it more deeply than appears.
But if of your careers
I may beg to know more, I burn with zeal.—
Thoughtfully then she answered, and such grace
Did her firm look reveal,
That she sent to my heart and words and face:

—As it seemed fit to our Eternal Sire,
Each one of us was of immortal blood.
Unhappy ones, what good
Does that to you? Better it were our fault.
Beloved and lovely, young and full of fire
We were sometime; and now such is our mood
That she has not withstood
The beating of her wings toward her vault;
As to me I am a shade. But here I halt,
For I have said the little you can hear.—
Then, moving:—Do not fear—
She said—to see me go far from your ground.—
She plucked a garland of green laurel, and
She entwined it all around
My temples and my forehead with her hand.

Song, if somebody calls your speech obscure,
Say:—I am sure and do not worry, for
I hope the clearer law
Of a new word will show you what you seek.
I only came to give others a light,
If he who made me speak
Did not deceive me when I left his sight.—

CXX

Quelle pietose rime, in ch'io m'accorsi
Di vostro ingegno, e del cortese affetto,
Èbben tanto vigor nel mio conspetto
Che ratto a questa penna la man porsi,

Per far voi certo che gli estremi morsi
Di quella ch'io con tutto 'l mondo aspetto,
Mai non sentí, ma pur, senza sospetto,
In fin a l'uscio del suo albergo corsi;

Poi tornai in dietro, perch'io vidi scritto,
Di sopra 'l limitar, che 'l tempo ancóra
Non era giunto al mio viver prescritto;

Ben ch'io non vi legessi il dí né l'ora.
Dunque s'acqueti omai 'l cor vostro afflitto,
E cerchi uom degno, quando sí l'onora.

CXXI

Or vedi, Amor, che giovenetta donna
Tuo regno sprezza e del mio mal non cura,
E tra duo ta' nemici è sí secura.

Tu se' armato, et ella in treccie e 'n gonna
Si siede, e scalza, in mezzo i fiori e l'erba,
Vèr' me spietata, e 'n contra te superba.

I' son pregion; ma se pietá ancor serba
L'arco tuo saldo, e qualcuna saetta,
Fa di te, e di me, signor, vendetta.

CXX

Those pious rhymes in which I understand
And recognize your mind and courtesy,
Had such a power on my sympathy
That I at once took this pen in my hand

To make you sure that the last biting pain
Of a death human beings must expect
I did not feel, but I did not suspect
That I had touched the wall of its domain;

I came back here when I read on the door
Some words that said the time was not yet spent
Allotted me to act my living part.

Which is my day or hour I still ignore.
Then let your sad affection be content,
And look for a man worthy of your heart.

CXXI

Love, you must know how a certain young maid
Disdains your rule, and my pain does not see,
And is safe between either enemy.

You are in arms, and she in gown and braid
Sits down with naked feet on grass and flower,
Merciless toward me, toward you sour.

I am a captive; but if pity's power
Stays in your bow, and perhaps still an arrow,
Take revenge for your self and for my marrow.

CXXII

Dicesette anni ha giá rivolto il cielo
Poi che 'mprima arsi, e giá mai non mi spensi;
Ma quando aven ch'al mio stato ripensi,
Sento nel mezzo de le fiamme un gielo.

Verò è 'l proverbio, ch'altri cangia il pelo
Anzi che 'l vezzo; e per lentar i sensi,
Gli umani affettti non son meno intensi:
Ciò ne fa l'ombra ria del grave velo.

Oi me lasso!, e quando fia quel giorno
Che mirando il fuggir de gli anni miei,
Èsca del foco, e di sí lunghe pene?

Vedrò mai il dí che pur quant'io vorrei
Quel'aria dolce del bel viso adorno
Piaccia a quest'occhi, e quanto si convene?

CXXIII

Quel vago impallidir che 'l dolce riso
D'un'amorosa nebbia ricoperse,
Con tanta maiestade al cor s'offerse
Che li si fece incontr'a mezzo 'l viso.

Conobbi allor sí come in paradiso
Vede l'un l'altro; in tal guisa s'apperse
Quel pietoso penser ch'altri non scerse;
Ma vidil io, ch'altrove non m'affiso.

Ogni angelica vista, ogni atto umíle
Che giá mai in donna, ov'amor fosse, apparve,
Fôra uno sdegno a lato a quel ch'i' dico.

Chinava a terra il bel guardo gentile,
E tacendo dicea, come a me parve:
—Chi m'allontana il mio fedele amico?—

CXXII

Seventeen years heaven has turned and tossed
Since I burned, and the fire does not abate;
But when I begin thinking of my state,
I feel among the flames a chilly frost.

The old saying is true: we lose our hair
But not our vice; and though the senses fail,
Human emotions are still hard to bear.
This is caused by the shadow of that veil.

Alas! when shall I see that day of grace
When, watching the dispersion of my years,
I go out of this fire and of my fears?

Shall I behold the day when, as I would,
That charming aura of her lovely face
Will please my eyes exactly as it should?

CXXIII

That fetching pallor which spread on her sweet
Smile, veiling it as with a loving haze,
Came to my heart, calling forth such a praise,
That it showed on my face, my love to greet.

Then I knew how the souls in paradise
See one another; no one was aware
Of that pitiful thought shown in such guise.
But I saw it, for I look not elsewhere.

Any angelic sight or humble act
That ever was in woman full of love,
Compared to this, I cannot comprehend.

She looked down on the ground, my gentle dove,
Silently saying, and it seemed a fact:
—Who takes away from me my faithful friend?—

CXXIV

Amor, Fortuna, e la mia mente schiva
Di quel che vede, e nel passato volta,
M'affligon sí, ch'io porto alcuna volta
Invidia a quei che son su l'altra riva.

Amor mi strugge 'l cor; Fortuna il priva
D'ogni conforto; onde la mente stolta
S'adira e piange: e cosí in pena molta
Sempre conven che combattendo viva.

Né spero i dolci dí tornino in dietro,
Ma pur dí male in peggio quel ch'avanza;
E di mio corso ho giá passato 'l mezzo.

Lasso!, non di diamante, ma d'un vetro
Veggio di man cadermi ogni speranza,
E tutt'i miei pensier romper nel mezzo.

CXXV

Se 'l pensier che mi strugge,
Com'è pungente e saldo,
Cosí vestisse d'un color conforme,
Forse tal m'arde e fugge,
Ch'avria parte del caldo,
E desteriasi Amor lá dov'or dorme;
Men solitarie l'orme
Fôran de' miei pie' lassi
Per campagne e per colli,
Men gli occhi ad ogn'or molli,
Ardendo lei che come un ghiaccio stassi,
E non lascia in me dramma
Che non sia foco e fiamma.

Però ch'Amor mi sforza
E di saver mi spoglia,

CXXIV

Love, Fortune, and my intellect retiring
From what it sees, and turned toward the past,
Distress me so that I have been desiring
The lot of those who cross the stream at last.

Love eats my heart; Fortune leaves it without
Any comfort; therefore the foolish brain
Is full of wrath and weeps; with grief about,
I must live always in the combat's strain.

No hope to see those days come back, alas!
From bad to worse goes the rest of the rope;
And of my course I left behind the middle.

Ah, not substance of diamond but of glass
Now drops down from my hand with every hope,
And all my thoughts are broken in the middle.

CXXV

If the thought melting me,
As it is firm and neat,
Could also be clothed in a fitting shade,
She who burns me to flee
Away, might feel some heat,
And Love would wake up from where he is laid;
Less lonely would be made
My tired footsteps that go
Among meadows and hills,
Less tears would run in rills,
If she would burn, who is as cold as snow,
And does not leave a drop
In me this fire to stop.

Because Love crushes me
And nullifies my mind,

Parlo in rime aspre e di dolcezza ignude.
Ma non sempre a la scorza
Ramo, né in fior, né 'n foglia,
Mostra di fòr sua natural vertude.
Miri ciò che 'l cor chiude,
Amor e que' begli occhi,
Ove si siede a l'ombra.
Se 'l dolor che si sgombra
Avèn che 'n pianto o in lamentar trabocchi,
L'un a me noce, e l'altro
Altrui, ch'io non lo scaltro.

Dolci rime leggiadre
Che nel primiero assalto
D'Amor usai, quand'io non ebbi altr'arme,
Chi verrá mai che squadre
Questo mio cor di smalto,
Ch'almen, com'io solea, possa sfogarme?
Ch'aver dentro a lui parme
Un che madonna sempre
Depinge, e de lei parla:
A voler poi ritrarla,
Per me non basto; e par ch'io me ne stempre.
Lasso!, cosí m'è scorso
Lo mio dolce soccorso.

Come fanciul ch'a pena
Volge la lingua e snoda,
Che dir non sa, ma 'l piú tacer gli è noia,
Cosí 'l desir mi mena
A dire; e vo' che m'oda
La dolce mia nemica anzi ch'io moia.
Se forse ogni sua gioia
Nel suo bel viso è solo,
E di tutt'altro è schiva,
Odil tu, verde riva,
E presta a' miei sospir sí largo volo,
Che sempre si ridica
Come tu m'eri amica.

I only speak in rhymes unsweet and rough.
But not always a tree
In flower or leaf or rind
Does outwardly reveal its inner stuff.
Let my heart go to Love
And to those lovely eyes
Where she sits in the shade.
If my grief is allayed
By pouring out in tears or mournful sighs,
One thing hurts me, and one
The other; skill is gone.

O gentle rhymes and sweet
That in the first assault
Of Love I used, having no other arms,
Who shall ever defeat
My heart's enamel vault,
That I may at least mourn my endless harms?
Someone describes the charms
Of my lady inside
My heart and speaks of her:
To paint her portrait there
I am not able: I have lost my pride.
Alas! like this is gone
My consolation.

As a child who begins
To move and turn its tongue,
Who cannot speak and yet hates to be dumb,
So desire spurs and wins
Me, and I speak and long
For her to hear me before death will come.
If her pleasures' whole sum
Is only her own sight,
Nothing else any more,
Hear it, o you green shore,
And give to my lament such a wide flight,
That you until the end
May be known as my friend.

Ben sai che sí bel piede
Non toccò terra unquanco
Come quel dí che giá segnata fosti:
Onde 'l cor lasso riede,
Col tormentoso fianco,
A partir teco i lor pensier nascosti.
Cosí avestú riposti
De' be' vestigi sparsi
Ancor tra fiori e l'erba,
Che la mia vita acerba,
Lagrimando, trovasse ove acquetarsi!
Ma come pò s'appaga
L'alma dubbiosa e vaga.

Ovunque gli occhi volgo
Trovo un dolce sereno
Pensando: qui percosse il vago lume.
Qualunque erba o fior colgo
Credo che nel terreno
Aggia radice, ov'ella ebbe in costume
Gir fra le piagge e 'l fiume,
E talor farsi un seggio
Fresco, fiorito e verde.
Cosí nulla sen perde;
E piú certezza averne fôra il peggio.
Spirto beato, quale
Se', quando altrui fai tale?

O poverella mia, come se' rozza!
Credo che tel conoschi:
Rimanti in questi boschi.

CXXVI

Chiare, fresche, e dolci acque,
Ove le belle membra
Pose colei che sola a me par **donna**;
Gentil ramo, ove piacque

You know that such fair foot
Had never touched the earth
Before the day that you were pressed by her:
And my heart finds the fruit
Of its tormenting dearth
By telling you the thoughts it could not share.
Had you given repair
To her scattered remains
Between flower and grass,
So that my life, alas,
In weeping found a comfort to its pains!
But the soul full of doubt
Enjoys what is about.

Wheresoever I gaze,
I find a limpid sky,
And think:—Once here was seen the lovely light.—
Whatever grass I graze,
I think that in the dry
Ground it has roots where she had some delight,
On rivers, on a height,
Sometimes making a seat
With green, flowers and moss,
And so there is no loss;
And to be sure perhaps would be less sweet.
Dear soul, what is your bliss,
If you soothe me like this?

My little song, how crude
You are! I think you know it:
Better stay in this wood.

CXXVI

Clear, cool, and lovely brook
Where the fair body lies
Of one who seems the only woman here;
Sweet branch that once she took

(con sospir mi rimembra)
A lei di fare al bel fianco colonna;
Erba e fior, che la gonna
Leggiadria ricoverse
Co l'angelico seno;
Aere sacro, sereno,
Ove Amor co' begli occhi il cor m'aperse;
Date udienzia insieme
A le dolenti mie parole estreme.

S'egli è pur mio destíno
(E 'l cielo in ciò s'adopra)
Ch'Amor quest'occhi lagrimando chiuda,
Qualche grazia il meschino
Corpo fra voi ricopra,
E torni l'alma al proprio albergo ignuda.
La morte fia men cruda
Se questa spene porto
A quel dubbioso passo;
Ché lo spirito lasso
Non poría mai in piú riposato porto
Né in piú tranquilla fossa
Fuggir la carne travagliata e l'ossa.

Tempo verrá ancor forse
Ch'a l'usato soggiorno
Torni la fera bella e mansueta,
E lá 'v'ella mi scòrse
Nel benedetto giorno,
Volga la vista disiosa e lieta,
Cercandomi; et, o pièta!,
Giá terra in fra le pietre
Vedendo, Amor l'inspiri
In guisa che sospiri
Sí dolcemente che mercé m'impetre,
E faccia forza al cielo,
Asciugandosi gli occhi col bel velo.

Da' be' rami scendea
(dolce ne la memoria)

(I think of it with sighs)
As a column to lean on, sitting near;
Grass and flower that her dear
Gown surrounded and starred,
With her angelic breast;
Limpid air, holy rest,
Where Love with her fair eyes opened my heart;
O hear you, all at once,
The mournful parting words that I pronounce.

If it must be my fate
(Such task heaven assays)
That Love close up my eyes with their last tear,
Let my poor body's weight
Be covered by your grace,
And let my soul come home naked and bare.
Death would be less to fear
If I could bring this hope
Unto that dubious goal;
For the exhausted soul
Could never in a more secluded scope
Or in a quieter zone
Retire and flee from aching flesh and bone.

Perhaps the time will come
That to the well-known way
The lovely and tame animal regress;
Then where I once stood numb,
Upon a blessed day
She will seek me with hope and happiness,
And, ah! all in distress
Before my earth and stone,
Perhaps Love will inspire
Her, and she will suspire
So sweetly that some mercy will be shown.
And she will force the skies
Wiping with her fair veil her weeping eyes.

From all the branches fair
(Sweet in my memory)

Una pioggia di fior sovra 'l suo grembo;
Et ella si sedea
Umíle in tanta gloria,
Coverta giá de l'amoroso nembo:
Qual fior cadea sul lembo,
Qual su le treccie bionde,
Ch'oro forbito e perle
Eran quel dí a vederle;
Qual si posava in terra, e qual su l'onde;
Qual con un vago errore
Girando parea dir—qui regna Amore.—

Quante volte diss'io
Allor pien di spavento:
—Costei per fermo nacque in paradiso!—
Cosí carco d'oblio
Il divin portamento,
E 'l vólto, e le parole, e 'l dolce riso,
M'aveano e sí diviso
Da l'imagine vera,
Ch'i' dicea sospirando:
—Qui come venn'io, o quando?—
Credendo esser in ciel, non lá dov'era.
Da indi in qua mi piace
Questa erba sí, ch'altrove non ho pace.

Se tu avessi ornamenti, quant'hai voglia,
Poresti arditamente
Uscir del bosco, e gir in fra la gente.

CXXVII

In quella parte dove Amor mi sprona
Conven ch'io volga le dogliose rime,
Che son seguaci de la mente afflitta.
Quai fíen ultime, lasso!, e qua' fíen prime?
Collui che del mio mal meco ragiona

A rain of flowers on her lap fell down;
And she was sitting there,
Humble in such glory,
Already covered with a loving crown;
One flower fell on her gown,
One on her golden locks,
Which were like pearl and gold
On that day to behold;
Some lay upon the earth and waves and rocks,
Some strayed around, above,
In a sweet error, saying:—Here rules Love.

How often did I say,
At such time, full of dread:
—She certainly was born in paradise!—
Such forgetful delay
On her figure was spread,
And her words and her laughter and her eyes
So veiled like a disguise
Whatever came to pass,
That I said sighing then:
—How did I come here, when?—
Thinking that it was heaven where I was.
And since that time I care
So for this grass, I find no peace elsewhere.

Had you as many gifts as you have wishes,
You could with a brave mind
Part from this wood and go among mankind.

CXXVII

Toward the side where I am led by Love
I must direct my discontented rhyme
That ever follows the long-suffering mind.
Which is the last and which the first in time?
He who talks of my ill as if to prove

Mi lascia in dubbio, sí confuso ditta.
Ma pur quanto l'istoria trovo scritta
In mezzo 'l cor, che sí spesso rincorro,
Co la sua propria man, de' miei martíri,
Dirò; perché i sospiri
Parlando han triegua, et al dolor soccorro.
Dico che, perch'io miri
Mille cose diverse attento e fiso,
Sol una donna veggio, e 'l suo bel viso.

Poi che la dispietata mia ventura
M'ha dilungato dal maggior mio bene,
Noiosa, inesorabile e superba,
Amor col rimembrar sol mi mantene:
Onde s'io veggio in giovenil figura
Incominciarsi il mondo a vestir d'erba,
Parmi vedere in quella etate acerba
La bella giovenetta, ch'ora è donna;
Poi che sormonta riscaldando il sole,
Parmi qual esser sòle,
Fiamma d'amor che 'n cor alto s'endonna;
Ma quando il dí si dole
Di lui che passo passo a dietro torni,
Veggio lei giunta a' suoi perfetti giorni.

In ramo fronde, o ver viole in terra
Mirando a la stagion che 'l freddo perde,
E le stelle miglior acquistan forza,
Ne gli occhi ho pur le violette e 'l verde
Di ch'era nel principio de mia guerra
Amor armato, sí, ch'ancor mi sforza,
E quella dolce leggiadretta scorza
Che ricopria le pargolette membra
Dove oggi alberga l'anima gentile
Ch'ogni altro piacer vile
Sembiar mi fa; sí forte mi rimembra
Del portamento umíle
Ch'allor fioriva, e poi crebbe anzi a gli anni,
Cagion sola e riposo de' miei affanni.

It, leaves me doubtful, nothing is defined.
But I will tell the tale I find designed
Within my heart, which I always pursue,
By Love's own hand, with all the pain I bear;
For my sighs and despair
Have their relief in speech, so has my rue.
I say that, though I stare
At thousand things in many earnest ways,
I see only one lady and her face.

Since my merciless fortune separates
Me from my only consolation,
Inexorable, troublesome and grim,
Love by remembering makes me live on:
Hence when I see the world's juvenile traits
Beginning to dress up, and the grass trim,
I recognize in that unripe and dim
Sight the beautiful girl that was my lady;
When the sun mounts and spreads warmth everywhere,
It seems as if it were
A flame of love in a heart pure and steady;
When the day sighs with care
For one who slowly sinks back to his place,
I see her come and reach her perfect days.

Leaves on a bough or violets in the soil
During the season that dispels the cold,
When the great stars have all their shining power,
Violets and green still in my eyes I hold,
With which at the beginning of my toil
Love was armed in such way that at this hour
He curbs me, and that sweet delicate bower
Which covered in childhood each little member
Where today dwells the much-beloved soul
That banishes the goal
Of other joys; so strongly I remember
Her gait's humble control
Blossoming then and growing with the years,
Only cause, only solace of my tears.

Qualor tenera neve per li colli
Dal sol percossa veggio di lontano,
Come 'l sol neve mi governa Amore,
Pensando nel bel viso piú che umano
Che pò da lunge gli occhi miei far molli,
Ma da presso gli abbaglia, e vince il core;
Ove, fra 'l bianco e l'aureo colore,
Sempre si mostra quel che mai non vide
Occhio mortal, ch'io creda, altro che 'l mio;
E del caldo desio,
Ch'è quando sospirando ella sorride,
M'infiamma sí che oblio
Niente aprezza, ma diventa eterno;
Né state il cangia, né lo spegne il verno.

Non vidi mai dopo notturna pioggia
Gir per l'aere sereno stelle erranti,
E fiammeggiar fra la rugiada e 'l gielo,
Ch'i' non avesse i begli occhi davanti,
Ove la stanca mia vita s'appoggia,
Quali io gli vidi a l'ombra d'un bel velo;
E sí come di lor bellezze il cielo
Splendea quel dí, cosí bagnati ancóra
Li veggio sfavillare; ond'io sempre ardo.
Se 'l sol levarsi sguardo,
Sento il lume apparir che m'innamora;
Se tramontarsi al tardo,
Parmel veder quando si volge altrove
Lassando tenebroso onde si move.

Se mai candide ròse con vermiglie
In vasel d'oro vider gli occhi miei,
Allor allor da vergine man còlte,
Veder pensaro il viso di colei
Ch'avanza tutte l'altre meraviglie
Con tre belle eccellenzie in lui raccolte:
Le bionde treccie sopra 'l collo sciolto,
Ov'ogni latte perderia sua prova,
E le guancie ch'adorna un dolce foco.
Ma pur che l'òra un poco

As you see the soft snow over the hills
Hit sometimes by the sun from far away,
Like this I am subjected to Love's dart,
And I think of that face's divine ray
That with so many tears my poor eyes fills
From a distance, and when near breaks my heart:
In white or gold such art
Of shade is shown as has never been seen
By mortal eyes, except I think my own;
A wish so overgrown,
When through her sighs her smiles come in between,
Into such flame is blown
That no oblivion its strength can abate,
And neither summer change nor winter sate.

I never watched after nocturnal rain
The erring stars glide in the limpid air
And sparkle through the dew and through the frost,
Without seeing her eyes for which I care,
And which my weary life always sustain,
As I saw them in a veil dimmed and lost;
And from their beauty heaven's light almost
Shining that day, so I see them still wet
And luminous; wherefore I always burn.
If some light I discern,
I feel the dawn arise that is my net;
At the sunset's return
I see it go to sparkle somewhere else,
Leaving the darkness that its glow dispels.

If ever snow-white and vermilion roses
My eyes did see in some vessel of gold,
Just being plucked by a virginal hand,
They thought her own enchantment to behold,
That the greatest of all wonders discloses
By three perfections that united stand:
The locks that wreathe her neck in golden band,
Where any milk would fail if put to test,
And the cheeks all aglow with a sweet fire.
When the breezes inspire

Fior bianchi e gialli per le piaggie mova,
Torna a la mente il loco
E 'l primo dí ch'i' vidi a l'aura sparsi
I capei d'oro, ond'io sí súbito arsi.

Ad una ad una annoverar le stelle,
E 'n picciol vetro chiuder tutte l'acque
Forse credea, quando in sí poca carta
Novo penser di ricontar mi nacque
In quante parti il fior de l'altre belle,
Stando in se stessa, ha la sua luce sparta
A ciò che mai da lei non mi diparta;
Né farò io; e se pur talor fuggo,
In cielo e 'n terra m'ha rachiuso i passi;
Perch'a gli occhi miei lassi
Sempre è presente, ond'io tutto mi struggo;
E cosí meco stassi,
Ch'altra non veggio mai, né veder bramo,
Né 'l nome d'altra ne' sospir miei chiamo.

Ben sai, canzon, che quant'io parlo è nulla
Al celato amoroso mio pensero,
Che dí e notte ne la mente porto;
Solo per cui conforto
In cosí lunga guerra anco non pèro;
Ché ben m'avria giá morto
La lontananza del mio cor piangendo;
Ma quinci da la morte indugio prendo.

CXXVIII

Italia mia, ben che 'l parlar sia indarno
A le piaghe mortali
Che nel bel corpo tuo sí spesse veggio,
Piacemi almen che 'miei sospir sian quali
Spera 'l Tevero e l'Arno,
E 'l Po, dove doglioso e grave or seggio.

The white and yellow flowers to spring and nest,
My mind seems to desire
The place and day that I saw loose and free
The golden hair that sets a fire in me.

To count the constellations one by one
And to pour in a goblet all the seas
Was perhaps my intention when I took
This small sheet to relate such mysteries:
How many sides the flower of the throne
Staying itself can brighten with its light
To retain me forever in its sight!
I will not try; by her I am restrained
When I run through the earth and through the sky,
And to my weary eye
She is visible still until I faint;
For when she is so nigh
I see no other lady nor wish to,
I do not call another in my rue.

You know, my song, that my words are unable
To tell the thoughts concealed so deep and far
That day and night I bear them in my brain;
But this comforting strain
Makes me avoid defeat in such a war;
For I should have been slain
By crying for the absence of my breath;
But here I find a respite from my death.

CXXVIII

My Italy, though words do not avail
To heal the mortal wounds
That in your lovely body I see so dense,
I wish at least to let my sighing sounds
With Arno and Tiber wail,
And Po, where now I sit in deep suspense.

Rettor del cielo, io cheggio
Che la pietá che ti condusse in terra
Ti volga al tuo diletto almo paese:
Vedi, segnor cortese,
Di che lievi cagion che crudel guerra;
E i cor, che 'ndura e serra
Marte superbo e fero,
Apri tu, padre, e 'ntenerisci e snoda;
Ivi fa che 'l tuo vero,
Qual io mi sia, per la mia lingua s'oda.

Voi, cui fortuna ha posto in mano il freno
De le belle contrade,
Di che nulla pietá par che vi stringa,
Che fan qui tante pellegrine spade?
Perché 'l verde terreno
Del barbarico sangue si depinga?
Vano error vi lusinga;
Poco vedete, e parvi veder molto,
Ché 'n cor venale amor cercate o fede.
Qual piú gente possede
Colui è piú da' suoi nemici avolto.
O diluvio raccolto
Di che deserti strani
Per inondar i nostri dolci campi!
Se da le proprie mani
Questo n'avene, or chi fia che ne scampi?

Ben provide natura al nostro stato,
Quando de l'Alpi schermo
Pose fra noi e la tedesca rabbia;
Ma 'l desir cieco, e 'n contr'al suo ben fermo,
S'è poi tanto ingegnato,
Ch'al corpo sano ha procurato scabbia.
Or dentro ad una gabbia
Fiere selvagge e mansuete gregge
S'annidan sí che sempre il miglior geme:
Et è questo del seme,
Per piú dolor, del popol senza legge,
Al qual, come si legge,

O Lord, send thy defence,
Turn the pity which once drew thee to her
On thy beloved and blessed human shore.
Consider, courteous Sir,
From what slight causes what a cruel war;
And the hearts' hardened core
By Mars held in a trance
Open thou, Father, that it may be stirred,
And let thy truth here once
(Whoever I may be) through me be heard.

You in whose hands Fortune has put the rein
Of the beautiful places
For which no pity seems to touch your heart,
What for so many swords of other races?
To let your verdant plain
Be painted by barbaric blood and art?
Flattered by an idle part,
You do not see and think that you can see,
Who in bribed peoples expect love or trust.
He who welcomes more must
Be more surrounded by his enemy.
O flood so fatally
Called from what desert lands
To inundate our sweet and peaceful fields!
If by our very hands
This has been done, who shelters now or shields?

Nature did well provide for our weak state
When she raised like a screen
The Alps to guard us from the German rage.
But blind desire fought against good, blind sin
Managed to adulterate
A healthy body with the tares of age.
Inside a single cage
Now wild beasts mingle with the meekest flocks,
Are nested so that the best are in need;
And this comes from the seed,
For greater grief, of the unlawful stocks
Whose destruction still shocks,

Mario aperse sí 'l fianco,
Che memoria de l'opra anco non langue,
Quando, assetato e stanco,
Non piú bevve del fiume acqua che sangue.

Cesare taccio che per ogni piaggia
Fece l'erbe sanguigne
Di lor véne, ove 'l nostro ferro mise.
Or par, non so per che stelle maligne,
Che 'l cielo in odio n'aggia:
Vostra mercé, cui tanto si commise:
Vostre voglie divise
Guastan del mondo la piú bella parte.
Qual colpa, qual giudicio, o qual destíno
Fastidire il vicino
Povero, e le fortune afflitte e sparte
Perseguire, e 'n disparte
Cercar gente, e gradire,
Che sparga 'l sangue e venda l'alma a prezzo?
Io parlo per ver dire,
Non per odio d'altrui né per disprezzo.

Né v'accorgete ancor per tante prove
Del bavarico inganno
Ch'alzando il dito, colla morte scherza?
Peggio è lo strazio, al mio parer, che 'l danno:
Ma 'l vostro sangue piove
Piú largamente: ch'altr'ira vi sferza.
Da la matina a terza
Di voi pensate, e vederete come
Tien caro altrui chi tien sé cosí vile.
Latin sangue gentile,
Sgombra da te queste dannose some;
Non far idolo un nome
Vano senza soggetto;
Ché 'l furor de lassú, gente ritrosa,
Vincerne d'intelletto,
Peccato è nostro, e non natural cosa.

Non è questo 'l terren ch'i' toccai pria?

Whose sides were opened wide
By Marius, and the memory is still good,
When he, thirsty and tired,
Did not find water in the stream, but blood.

I will not speak of Caesar who all round
Made the grass red as rose
By the veins where our weapons plunged and rusted.
Now, by what evil stars nobody knows,
Hate is sown in our ground,
And thanks to you, to whom so much was trusted,
Your wills by ill infested
Ruin the loveliest country of the earth.
What guilt, what punishment, what destiny
Drives you to scatter death
On your poor neighbour and spread misery
And hunt for amity
Outside and call friends those
Who shed the blood and sell the soul for prize?
I speak the truth; no cause
Have I to hate another or despise.

Are you not yet aware after so long
Of the Bavarian treason
Which like a fool will play the game of death?
And the anguish is far worse than the wrong.
Your blood runs for no reason,
Copiously, and more anger draws your breath.
One moment since your birth
Think of your self: those who misunderstood
Their worth cannot respect another's fame.
O gentle Latin blood,
Throw down this burden, rise up from this shame,
Do not worship a name
Empty of all subject.
To let a Nordic fury, a savage race,
Conquer our intellect,
Is our own sin, no natural disgrace.

Is not this the dear soil for which I pined?

Non è questo il mio nido
Ove nudrito fui sí dolcemente?
Non è questa la patria in ch'io mi fido,
Madre benigna e pia,
Che copre l'un a l'altro mio parente?
Per Dio, questo la mente
Talor vi mova, e con pietá guardate
Le lagrime del popol doloroso,
Che sol da voi riposo
Dopo Dio spera; e pur che voi mostriate
Segno alcun di pietate,
Vertú contra furore
Prenderá l'arme; e fia 'l combatter corto,
Ché l'antiquo valore
Ne l'italici cor non è ancor morto.

Signor, mirate come 'l tempo vola,
E sí come la vita
Fugge, e la morte n'è sovra le spalle:
Voi siete or qui; pensate a la partita;
Ché l'alma ignuda e sola
Conven ch'arrive a quel dubbioso calle.
Al passar questa valle,
Piacciavi porre giú l'odio e lo sdegno,
Vènti contrarî a la vita serena;
E quel che 'n altrui pena
Tempo si spende, in qualche atto piú degno
O di mano o d'ingegno,
In qualche bella lode,
In qualche onesto studio si converta:
Cosí qua giú si gode,
E la strada del ciel si trova aperta.

Canzone, io t'ammonisco
Che tua ragion cortesemente dica;
Perché fra gente altèra ir ti convene
E le voglie son piene
Giá de l'usanza pessima et antica,
Del ver sempre nemica.
Proverai tua ventura

Is not this my own nest
Where I was nourished and was given life?
Is not this the dear land in which we trust,
Mother loving and kind
Who shelters parents, brother, sister, wife?
O God, that in such strife
You may remember this; that you may gaze
With pity on the tears of suffering men
Who in their terror raise
Their hope to you on earth; relieve their pain,
Feed them with pity's grain,
And against cruelty
Virtue will fight and soon the debt be paid:
For the old gallantry
In the Italian hearts is not yet dead.

O my lords, look how time is come and gone,
And how life hurries by,
And how death is already upon us;
You are now here, but you will have to die.
The naked soul alone
Must reach one day that most uncertain pass:
Through valley and morass
Get rid of all your hatred and abuse,
Winds that are contrary to life's content;
And the time that was spent
In harming others put to worthier use,
To hand's or mind's intent,
To some beautiful praise,
Let it by honest studies be fulfilled,
The joy of mortal days:
And the road of the sky will be revealed.

Canzone, I warn you
To tell your reasons with a courteous soul,
For among haughty people you must go,
Whose will can never know
More than the old and worst custom of all,
To truth inimical.
But you must try your art

Fra magnanimi pochi a chi 'l ben piace:
Di' lor:—Chi m'assicura?
I' vo gridando: "Pace, pace, pace!"—

CXXIX

Di pensier in pensier, di monte in monte
Mi guida Amor; ch'ogni segnato calle
Provo contrario a la tranquilla vita.
Se 'n solitaria piaggia, rivo, o fonte,
Se 'n fra duo poggi siede ombrosa valle,
Ivi s'acqueta l'alma sbigottita;
E come Amor l'envita,
Or ride, or piange, or teme, or s'assecura:
E 'l vólto che lei segue ov'ella il mena
Si turba e rasserena,
Et in un esser picciol tempo dura;
Onde a la vista uom di tal vita esperto
Diria:—Questo arde, e di suo stato è incerto.—

Per alti monti e per selve aspre trovo
Qualche riposo; ogni abitato loco
È nemico mortal de gli occhi miei.
A ciascun passo nasce un penser novo
De la mia donna, che sovente in gioco
Gira 'l tormento ch'i' porto per lei;
Et a pena vorrei
Cangiar questo mio viver dolce amaro,
Ch'i' dico:—Forse ancor ti serva Amore
Ad un tempo migliore;
Forse, a te stesso vile, altrui se' caro.—
Et in questa trapasso sospirando:
Or porrebbe esser vero? or come? or quando?

Ove porge ombra un pino alto od un colle
Talor m'arresto, e pur nel primo sasso
Disegno co la mente il suo bel viso.

Among the valiant few who seek release;
Tell them:—Who gives me heart?
I go around and cry for peace, peace, peace.—

CXXIX

From one to other thought, from mount to mount
Love leads me on; and every trodden trail
I find unsuited to a tranquil mood.
If on a lovely shore, river, or fount,
My eyes perceive between two slopes a vale,
The soul finds there a rest from its long feud;
And while Love makes it brood,
It laughs or cries or fears or dares to climb:
And my face that reveals where it has been
Is clouded or serene,
And in each stage remains a little time;
Hence, seeing it, whoever knows such fate
Would say:—He burns and does not know his state.—

In the high mountains and wild woods I find
Some comfort; any inhabited nest
Seems to my eyes a mortal enemy.
At each step a new thought comes to my mind
Of my lady who often turns to jest
The ills I suffer and my agony;
But if I want to flee
And change this life of mine bitter and fair,
I say at once:—Perhaps Love will content
You in the next event,
You hate yourself, but may be dear to her.—
And in such thought I lose my strength and sigh:
Could it be true? and how or when or why?

Where a tall pine or a hill throws a shade
Sometimes I halt, and on the first-met stone
I draw within my mind her lovely face.

Poi ch'a me torno, trovo il petto molle
De la pietate; et alor dico:—Ahi, lasso,
Dove se' giunto! et onde se' diviso!—
Ma mentre tener fiso
Posso al primo pensier la mente vaga,
E mirar lei, et obliar me stesso,
Sento Amor sí da presso
Che del suo proprio error l'alma s'appaga:
In tante parti e sí bella la veggio,
Che se l'error durasse, altro non cheggio.

I' l'ho piú volte (or chi fia che m'il creda?)
Ne l'acqua chiara, e sopra l'erba verde
Veduto viva, e nel troncon d'un faggio,
E 'n bianca nube sí fatta che Leda
Avria ben detto che sua figlia perde,
Come stella che 'l sol copre col raggio;
E quanto in piú selvaggio
Loco mi trovo e 'n piú deserto lido,
Tanto piú bella il mio pensier l'adombra.
Poi quando il vero sgombra
Quel dolce error, pur lí medesmo assido
Me freddo, pietra morta, in pietra viva,
In guisa d'uom che pensi e pianga e scriva.

Ove d'altra montagna ombra non tócchi
Verso 'l maggiore e 'l piú espedito giogo
Tirar mi suol un desiderio intenso.
Indi i miei danni a misurar con gli occhi
Comincio, e 'n tanto lagrimando sfogo
Di dolorosa nebbia il cor condenso,
Alor ch'i' miro e penso,
Quanta aria dal bel viso mi diparte,
Che sempre m'è sí presso e sí lontano;
Poscia fra me pian piano:
—Che sai tu, lasso? Forse in quella parte
Or di tua lontananza si sospira—;
Et in questo penser l'alma respira.

When I wake up and find my breast inlaid
With pity, I exclaim:—O wretched one,
Where have you come! and how far from that place!—
But while I fix the trace
Of this thought in my mind for her own sake,
And gaze on her and forget all my woes,
Then I feel Love so close
That my soul is seduced by its mistake:
So pervading, so beautiful her mask,
That if my error lasts I nothing ask.

I saw her many times (who believes this?)
In the clear water, over the green grass,
Alive, and in the trunk of a beech-tree,
And in a cloud whose shape gave such a bliss,
That Leda would have said her daughter was
Beaten as by the sun a star must be;
And as the place I see
Gets wilder and more desert grows the shore,
As much more lovely she seems to my thought.
When the truth turns to nought
My sweet mistake, I still sit as before,
Frozen like a dead stone on living heights,
As a man does who thinks and weeps and writes.

Where falls no shadow of another hill,
Toward the highest and the steepest chain
I am drawn by desire as to a tryst.
Then I measure my sorrow and I fill
Its length with tears, and with my weeping rain
I free the heart condensing in the mist,
And when my eyes persist
To gauge the air that parts me from her face
Which is always so near, always away,
Then to myself I say:
—What can you know, poor fool? Now in that place
Perhaps someone is sighing after you—;
And in this thought my soul can breathe anew.

Canzone, oltra quell'alpe,
Lá dove il ciel è piú sereno e lieto,
Mi rivedrai sovr'un ruscel corrente,
Ove l'aura si sente
D'un fresco et odorifero laureto:
Ivi è 'l mio cor, e quella che 'l m'invola;
Qui veder pòi l'imagine mia sola.

CXXX

Poi che 'l camin m'è chiuso di mercede,
Per desperata via son dilungato
Da gli occhi ov'era (i' non so per qual fato)
Riposto il guidardon d'ogni mia fede.

Pasco 'l cor di sospir, ch'altro non chiede,
E di lagrime vivo, a pianger nato:
Né di ciò duolmi, perché in tale stato
È dolce il pianto piú ch'altri non crede.

E sol ad una imagine m'attegno,
Che fe' non Zeusi, o Prasitele, o Fidia,
Ma miglior mastro, e di piú alto ingegno.

Qual Scizia m'assicura, o qual Numidia,
S'ancor non sazia del mio essilio indegno,
Cosí nascosto mi ritrova invidia?

My song, beyond that Alp,
Where the sky is more limpid and more gay,
You shall see me along a running rill
Where the breezes distil
The aura of a fresh and fragrant bay:
There is my heart, and she who makes me groan;
Here you can only see my ghost alone.

CXXX

The way of mercy being closed to me,
Through a desperate path I fled and swerved
From the eyes where (perhaps by destiny)
The reward of my faith had been preserved.

I feed my heart with sighs, its only bait,
I live on tears, born as it were to grieve,
Nor do I mind, because in such a state
Weeping is sweeter than one may believe.

And only to one image I will drift,
Not in Praxiteles' or Pheidias' style,
But by a master of superior gift.

What Scythia, what Numidia can assure
Me that, not yet appeased by my exile,
Though I am hidden, envy is no more?

CXXXI

Io canterei d'amor sí novamente
Ch'al duro fianco il dí mille sospiri
Trarrei per forza, e mille alti desiri
Raccenderei ne la gelata mente;

E 'l bel viso vedrei cangiar sovente,
E bagnar gli occhi, e piú pietosi giri
Far, come suol chi de gli altrui martíri
E del suo error quando non val si pente;

E le ròse vermiglie in fra le neve
Mover da l'ôra, e discovrir l'avorio
Che fa di marmo chi da presso 'l guarda;

E tutto quel per che nel viver breve
Non rincresco a me stesso, anzi mi glorio
D'esser servato a la stagion piú tarda.

CXXXII

S'amor non è, che dunque è quel ch'io sento?
Ma s'egli è amor, per Dio, che cosa e quale?
Se bona, ond'è l'effetto aspro mortale?
Se ria, ond'è sí dolce ogni tormento?

S'a mia voglia ardo, ond'è 'l pianto e lamento?
S'a mal mio grado, il lamentar che vale?
O viva morte, o dilettoso male,
Come puoi tanto in me, s'io no 'l consento?

E s'io 'l consento, a gran torto mi doglio.
Fra sí contrarî vènti in frale barca
Mi trovo in alto mar, senza governo,

Sí lieve di saver, d'error sí carca,
Ch'i' medesmo non so quel ch'io mi voglio,
E tremo a mezza state, ardendo il verno.

CXXXI

I should sing of my love in such new strain
That would draw out by force a thousand sighs
From her pitiless breast, and thousand cries
Would kindle with desire her frozen brain;

Then her fair face would show a discontent,
I should see her eyes wet, turning about
As those who saddened by another's doubt,
And by their error, much too late repent.

And the vermilion roses in the snow
Would be stirred by the aura and reveal
The ivory that turns to stone our reason,

And all the things that in life make me feel
Less miserable and relieved to know
That I will last until the final season.

CXXXII

If not love, then what is it that I feel?
If it is love, good God, what kind of thing?
If good, why does the effect smite and sting,
If bad, why does the torment sweetly steal?

If I burn at my will, why do I cry?
If in spite of myself, what is the use?
O living death, o delightful abuse,
How can you conquer me if I deny?

And if I yield, my heart must quietly break.
Among such warring winds in a frail boat
Without a helm on the high seas I float,

So light in wisdom, so full of mistake,
That what I want I myself cannot learn,
And freeze in summer and in winter burn.

CXXXIII

Amor m'ha posto come segno a strale,
Come al sol neve, come cera al foco,
E come nebbia al vento; e son giá roco,
Donna, mercé chiamando, e voi non cale.

Da gli occhi vostri uscío 'l colpo mortale,
Contra cui non mi val tempo né loco;
Da voi cola procede, e parvi un gioco,
Il sole, e 'l foco, e 'l vento, ond'io son tale.

I pensier son saette, e 'l viso un sole,
E 'l desir foco; e 'nseme con quest'arme
Mi punge Amor, m'abbaglia, e mi distrugge:

E l'angelico canto, e le parole,
Col dolce spirto, ond'io non posso aitarme,
Son l'aura inanzi a cui mia vita fugge.

CXXXIV

Pace non trovo, e non ho da far guerra;
E temo, e spero; et ardo, e son un ghiaccio;
E volo sopra 'l cielo, e giaccio in terra;
E nulla stringo, e tutto 'l mondo abbraccio.

Tal m'ha in pregion, che non m'apre né serra,
Né per suo mi riten né scioglie il laccio;
E non m'ancide Amore, e non mi sferra,
Né mi vuol vivo né mi trae d'impaccio.

Veggio senza occhi, e non ho lingua, e grido;
E bramo di perir, e cheggio aita;
Et ho in odio me stesso, et amo altrui.

Pascomi di dolor, piangendo rido;
Egualmente mi spiace morte e vita:
In questo stato son, donna, per vui.

CXXXIII

Love set me like a signal to the course
Of arrows, snow to sun, and wax to fire,
Like a mist against wind; and I am hoarse,
Lady, from calling you with my desire.

From your eyes started first the mortal stroke
Against which time or place do not avail;
Only from you it comes, you think a joke
The sun, the fire, the wind that make me fail.

The thoughts are arrows, and the face a sun,
And desire fire; with the sum of these arms
Love pierces me and blinds me and destroys:

And the angelic singing and the voice,
With the sweet mind that wins me with its charms,
Are the aura on which my life is gone.

CXXXIV

I find no peace and I am not at war;
I fear and hope, and I burn and I freeze;
I rise up to the sky, lie on earth's floor;
And I grasp nothing and I hug the trees.

She has jailed me, and nor opens nor shuts,
Nor keeps me for her own, nor tears the noose,
Love does not slay and does not set me loose,
He wants me nor alive nor out of ruts.

I see and have no eyes; no tongue, and cry;
I wish to perish and call help to fly;
And I abhor myself and love another.

I feed on grief, in tears and laugh I smother;
Death and life are the objects of my hate:
Lady, because of you, such is my state.

CXXXV

Qual piú diversa e nova
Cosa fu mai in qualche stranio clima,
Quella, se ben s'estima,
Piú mi rasembra; a tal son giunto, Amore.
Lá, onde il di vèn fòre,
Vola un augel, che sol, senza consorte,
Di volontaria morte
Rinasce, e tutto a viver si rinova.
Cosí sol si ritrova
Lo mio voler, e cosí in su la cima
De' suoi alti pensieri al sol si volve,
E cosí si risolve,
E cosí torna al suo stato di prima;
Arde, e more, e riprende i nervi suoi,
E vive poi con la fenice a prova.

Una petra è sí ardita
Lá per l'índico mar, che da natura
Tragge a sé il ferro, e 'l fura
Dal legno, in guisa che ' navigi affonde.
Questo prov'io fra l'onde
D'amaro pianto; ché quel bello scoglio
Ha col suo duro argoglio
Condutta ove affondar conven mia vita:
Cosí l'alm'ha sfornita
(Furando 'l cor, che fu giá cosa dura
E me tenne un, ch'or son diviso e sparso)
Un sasso a trar piú scarso
Carne che ferro. O cruda mia ventura,
Che 'n carne essendo, veggio trarmi a riva
Ad una viva dolce calamita!

Ne l'estremo occidente
Una fera è soave e queta tanto
Che nulla piú; ma pianto
E doglia, e morte, dentro a gli occhi porta:
Molto convene accorta
Esser qual vista mai vèr' lei si giri;

CXXXV

The most diverse and new
Thing to be found in an outlandish clime,
If one can judge my rhyme,
Is most like me; to this, Love, I have come.
Where the dawn leaves its home
There flies a bird, alone, without a mate,
From voluntary fate
It dies and is reborn and lives anew.
Like this my will is true
To solitude, like this it likes to climb
On top of its high thoughts, watching the sun,
Like this soon it is gone,
Like this it comes back where it knew its prime;
It burns and dies and then regains its nerves,
And its old life like the phoenix preserves.

A stone there is, so bold,
Over the purple sea, that it can draw
Iron and by nature's law
Steal it from wood, so all the ships go down.
This I feel when I drown
In bitter tears; because that handsome rock
By its disdainful shock
Pushes my life where it sinks in the cold:
And thus the soul is mauled
(Robbed of the heart which was of solid weight
And kept me whole, who now am torn and split)
By a stone made to hit
Instead of iron, flesh. O cruel fate,
Though made of flesh I am pulled to the shore
By the sweet living magnet I adore!

In the remotest West
There is a wild beast so gentle and quiet
That nothing more; her sight
However, shows dismay and tears and death:
You must withhold your breath
If ever toward her you want to turn;

Pur che gli occhi non miri,
L'altro puossi veder securamente.
Ma io incauto, dolente,
Corro sempre al mio male; e so ben quanto
N'ho sofferto, e n'aspetto; ma l'engordo
Voler, ch'è cieco e sordo,
Sí mi trasporta, che 'l bel viso santo
E gli occhi vaghi, fíen cagion ch'io pèra,
Di questa fera   angelica innocente.

Surge nel mezzo giorno
Una fontana, e tien nome dal Sole;
Che per natura sòle
Bollir le notti, e 'n sul giorno esser fredda;
E tanto si raffredda
Quanto 'l Sol monta, e quanto è piú da presso.
Cosí aven a me stesso,
Che son fonte di lagrime, e soggiorno:
Quando 'l bel lume adorno,
Ch'è 'l mio sol, s'allontana, e triste e sole
Son le mie luci, e notte oscura è loro,
Ardo allor; ma se l'oro
E i rai veggio apparir del vivo sole,
Tuttot dentro e di fòr sento cangiarme,
E ghiaccio farme;   cosí freddo torno.

Un'altra fonte ha Epiro
Di cui si scrive, ch'essendo fredda ella,
Ogni spenta facella
Accende, e spegne qual trovasse accesa.
L'anima mia, ch'offesa
Ancor non era d'amoroso foco,
Appréssandosi un poco
A quella fredda, ch'io sempre sospiro,
Arse tutta; e martíro
Simil giá mai né Sol vide, né stella,
Ch'un cor di marmo a pietá mosso avrebbe:
Poi che 'nfiammata l'ebbe,
Rispensela vertú gelata e bella.
Cosí piú volte ha 'l cor racceso e spento:

Only if you unlearn
To look into her eyes, you see the rest.
But I, unwise, distressed,
Run to my ruin; and I know my plight,
How much I suffered, feared; but the unkind
Will which is deaf and blind
So pushes me, that the holy delight
Of her face, of her eyes, keeps me beguiled
By this angelic animal and wild.

Where leads the southern way,
A fountain springs that is named from the sun,
Which when the heat is gone
Begins to boil, and in the day is cold,
And gets as much more cold
As the sun rises, as it comes more near.
The same thing happens here
To the fountains of tears that in me spray:
When the beautiful ray,
Which is my sun, departs, and all alone
Are left my lights, in the dark of the night
I burn; but if the bright
Splendour returns of the true living sun,
I feel all changed at once inside, outside,
I become ice; and frozen I abide.

Epirus has a spring
Of which they write that, although it is cold,
It kindles with more gold
Extinguished sparks and quenches those aflame.
My soul that the sad shame
Of love had not yet felt nor knew its price,
Going near to that ice
Which hurts me and which makes me sigh and sing,
Was set on fire: the ring
Of sun and stars never saw such a bold
Torture that would have stirred a heart of stone.
When my soul was undone,
Virtue began to quell it and to scold;
Thus many times she lit and she put out

I 'l so che 'l sento, e spesso me n'adiro.

Fuor tutt'i nostri lidi,
Ne l'isole famose di Fortuna,
Due fonti ha: chi de l'una
Bee, mor ridendo; e chi de l'altra, scampa.
Simil fortuna stampa
Mia vita, che morir poría ridendo,
Del gran piacer, ch'io prendo,
Se no 'l temprassen dolorosi stridi.
Amor, ch'ancor mi guidi
Pur a l'ombra di fama occulta e bruna,
Tacerem questa fonte, ch'ogni or piena,
Ma con piú larga vena
Veggiàm, quando col Tauro il Sol s'aduna:
Cosí gli occhi miei piangon d'ogni tempo,
Ma piú nel tempo che madonna vidi.

Chi spiasse, canzone,
Quel ch'i' fo, tu pòi dir:—Sotto un gran sasso
In una chiusa valle, ond'esce Sorga,
Si sta; né chi lo scorga
V'è, se no Amor, che mai no 'l lascia un passo,
E l'imagine d'una, che lo strugge;
Ch'e' per sé fugge tutt'altre persone.—

My heart, and I feel it, and rage and doubt.

Beyond our horizon,
In Fortune's islands famous among men,
There are two springs, one vein
Kills laughing; who the other drinks, escapes:
Much the same fortune shapes
My life, which also might from laughing die
Through the joy of my eye
When my heart does not feel distraction.
O Love who lead me on
Under the shadow of a hidden fame,
We will not speak of this spring we saw teem
And flow with broader stream
When the sunlight gathers in Taurus' flame:
And so my eyes to weep are always ready,
But more specially when I see my lady.

Canzone, if they watch
My actions, please tell them:—Under a stone
In a closed valley from which Sorga flows
He lies; and no one goes
Near him, save Love, who leaves him not alone,
And the image of one who breaks him down.
He himself flees the people and the town.—

CXXXVI

Fiamma dal ciel su le tue treccie piova,
Malvagia, che dal fiume e da le ghiande
Per l'altrui impoverir se' ricca e grande,
Poi che di mal oprar tanto ti giova:

Nido di tradimenti, in cui si cova
Quanto mal per lo mondo oggi si spande,
De vin serva, di letti e di vivande,
In cui lussuria fa l'ultima prova.

Per le camere tue fanciulle e vecchi
Vanno trescando, e Belzebub in mezzo
Co' mantici, e col foco, e co li specchi.

Giá non fostú nudrita in piume al rezzo,
Ma nuda al vento, e scalza fra gli stecchi:
Or vivi sí ch'a Dio ne venga il lezzo.

CXXXVII

L'avara Babilonia ha colmo il sacco
D'ira di Dio, e di vizii empii e rei,
Tanto che scoppia, ed ha fatti suoi dèi,
Non Giove e Palla, ma Venere e Bacco.

Aspettando ragion mi struggo e fiacco;
Ma pur novo soldan veggio per lei,
Lo qual fará, non giá quand'io vorrei,
Sol una sède; e quella fia in Baldacco.

Gl'idoli suoi sarranno in terra sparsi,
E le tórre superbe, al ciel nemiche,
E i suoi torrer di fòr come dentro arsi.

Anime belle, e di virtute amiche,
Terranno il mondo; e poi vedrem lui farsi
Aureo tutto, e pien de l'opre antiche.

CXXXVI

May a flame from the sky fall on your braid,
Impious, who thanks to river and acorn
By starving others feed your mighty scorn,
While your foul deeds to your own profit spread:

Nest of betrayals where conspires and broods
Whatever evil through the world is blown,
The slave of wine, of beds, of various foods,
Where lecherousness comes into its own.

Within your chambers young girls and old men
Are flirting, and the devil in the middle
With bellows, mirrors, fire, prepares his riddle.

You were not nursed with feathers in the breeze,
But naked in the wind among dry trees;
Now your life sends to God your stinking stain.

CXXXVII

The greedy Babylon has filled her bag
With the anger of God and her foul vices,
So that it bursts, and in gods' place entices
Not Pallas, Jove, but Venus,' Bacchus' tag.

Waiting for reason, I despair and brood;
But I see a new sultan come to her,
Who shall make, not as early as I would,
One single see, in Baldacco the chair.

Her idols shall be shattered in the earth,
And the arrogant towers fighting our creeds,
And their keepers, shall burn outside, inside.

The noble souls with virtue on their side
Shall fill the world; we shall see its rebirth
Figured with gold and with the ancient deeds.

CXXXVIII

Fontana di dolore, albergo d'ira,
Scola d'errori, e templo d'eresia,
Giá Roma, or Babilonia falsa e ria,
Per cui tanto si piange e si sospira;

O fucina d'inganni, o pregion dira,
Ove 'l ben more, e 'l mal si nutre e cria,
Di vivi inferno, un gran miracol fia
Se Cristo teco al fine non s'adira.

Fondata in casta et umil povertate,
Contr'a' tuoi fondatori alzi le corna,
Putta sfacciata: e dove hai posto spene?

Ne gli adúlteri tuoi? Ne le mal nate
Richezze tante? Or Constantin non torna;
Ma tolga il mondo tristo che 'l sostene.

CXXXIX

Quanto piú disiose l'ali spando
Verso di voi, o dolce schiera amica,
Tanto Fortuna con piú visco intrica
Il mio volare, e gir mi face errando.

Il cor, che mal suo grado a torno mando,
È con voi sempre in quella valle aprica,
Ove 'l mar nostro piú la terra implíca;
L'altr'ier da lui partimmi lagrimando.

I' da man manca, e' tenne il camin dritto;
I 'tratto a forza, et e' d'Amore scorto;
Egli in Ierusalem, et io in Egitto.

Ma sofferenza è nel dolor conforto;
Ché per lungo uso, giá fra noi prescritto,
Il nostro esser insieme è raro e corto.

CXXXVIII

Fountain of sorrow, dwelling of revolts,
The school of errors, place of heresy,
Once Rome, now Babylon wicked and false,
For which the world suffers in infamy;

O forge of treacheries, o cruel jail
Where the good die, the bad prosper and scream,
Hell of the living, a wonder it will seem
If in the end Christ's wrath does not prevail.

Founded on chaste and humble poverty,
Against your founders you lift up your horn,
Shameless strumpet: your hope, where can it be?

In your adulteries? In the ill-born
Measureless wealth? Constantine will not come,
But let him take away his guilty home.

CXXXIX

The more full of desire I spread my wings
Toward you, gentle troop of friends and true,
The more Fortune ensnares within her glue
My flight, and to my erring journey clings.

The heart that to his grief I send around,
Is forever with you in that clear vale
Where our own sea embraces more the ground;
The other day I left him there to wail.

I go to left and he goes to the right;
I follow force and he is led by Love;
He in Jerusalem, I in Egypt.

But suffering brings comfort to my plight;
For by an ancient custom of our script
Our company is brief and we must move.

CXL

Amor, che nel penser mio vive e regna
E 'l suo seggio maggior nel mio cor tène,
Talor armato ne la fronte vène,
Ivi si loca, et ivi pon sua insegna.

Quella ch'amare e sofferir ne 'nsegna
E vòl che 'l gran desio, l'accesa spene,
Ragion, vergogna e reverenza affrene,
Di nostro ardir fra se stessa si sdegna.

Onde Amor paventoso fugge al core,
Lasciando ogni sua impresa, e piange, e trema;
Ivi s'asconde, e non appar piú fòre.

Che poss'io far, temendo il mio signore,
Se non star seco in fin a l'ora estrema?
Ché bel fin fa chi ben amando more.

CXLI

Come talora al caldo tempo sòle
Semplicetta farfalla al lume avezza
Volar ne gli occhi altrui per sua vaghezza,
Onde aven ch'ella more, altri si dole;

Cosí sempre io corro al fatal mio sole
De gli occhi onde mi vèn tanta dolcezza
Che 'l fren de la ragion Amor non prezza,
E chi discerne è vinto da chi vòle.

E veggio ben quant'elli a schivo m'hanno,
E so ch'i' ne morrò veracemente,
Ché mia vertú non pò contra l'affanno;

Ma si m'abbaglia Amor soavemente
Ch'i' piango l'altrui noia, e no 'l mio danno;
E, cieca, al suo morir l'alma consente.

CXL

Love who within my thought does live and reign,
Who keeps his favoured seat inside my heart,
Sometimes likes on my forehead to remain,
And there in arms displays his bow and dart.

She who taught us to love and suffer pain,
Who demands that desire and ardent hope
Be bound by reason, within worship's scope,
Feels for our daring an inner disdain.

Hence Love in fright again to the heart flies,
Abandoning all tasks, and tries to hide,
Trembles and weeps and comes no more outside.

What can I do, who fear my master's power,
But stay with him until the final hour?
Because he ends well who well loving dies.

CXLI

As oftentimes a foolish butterfly,
Used to the light, in the hot weather will
Fly into people's eyes his joy to fill,
Whence comes that others weep and he will die,

Like this I turn toward the fatal rills
Of the eyes from which comes a ray so bright
That Love tears reason's fetters in despite,
And who discerns is conquered by who wills.

And I see well how great is their disdain,
I know that this will mean true death to me,
My valour being lesser than my pain;

But Love dazzles my sight so pleasantly,
That I mourn others' wrongs and not my breath,
And my blind soul consents to its own death.

CXLII

A la dolce ombra de le belle frondi
Corsi fuggendo un dispietato lume
Che 'n fin qua giú m'ardea dal terzo cielo;
E disgombrava giá di neve i poggi
L'aura amorosa che rinova il tempo,
E fiorian per le piagge l'erbe e i rami.

Non vide il mondo sí leggiadri rami,
Né mosse il vento mai sí verdi frondi,
Come a me si mostrâr quel primo tempo;
Tal che temendo de l'ardente lume,
Non volsi al mio refugio ombra di poggi,
Ma de la pianta piú gradita in cielo.

Un lauro mi difese allor dal cielo;
Onde piú volte, vago de' bei rami,
Da po' son gito per selve e per poggi;
Né giá mai ritrovai tronco né frondi
Tanto onorate dal superno lume,
Che non mutasser qualitate a tempo.

Però piú fermo ogni or di tempo in tempo,
Seguendo ove chiamar m'udia dal cielo,
E scorto d'un soave e chiaro lume,
Tornai sempre devoto a i primi rami
E quando a terra son sparte le frondi
E quando il sol fa verdeggiar i poggi.

Selve, sassi, campagne, fiumi, e poggi,
Quanto è creato, vince e cangia il tempo;
Ond'io cheggio perdóno a queste frondi,
Se, rivolgendo poi molt'anni il cielo,
Fuggir disposi gl'invescati rami
Tosto ch'incominciai di veder lume.

Tanto mi piacque prima il dolce lume
Ch'i' passai con diletto assai gran poggi
Per poter appressar gli amati rami;
Ora la vita breve, e 'l loco, e 'l tempo

CXLII

In the sweet shadow of the lovely leaves
I ran away, fleeing a ruthless lamp
That came to burn me here from the third heaven;
The snow was being melted on the hills
By the air that renews weather and time,
And on the meadows sprang up grass and branches.

The world has never seen such pretty branches,
Nor has the wind ever stirred such green leaves
As those I saw appear in that first time;
So that in dread of the resplendent lamp
I did not seek the shadow of the hills,
But only of the plant preferred by heaven.

A laurel was my shelter against heaven;
And many times, yearning for those fair branches,
I strolled among the woods, along the hills;
Nor did I ever find or trunk or leaves
So honoured by the greatness of that lamp,
That their qualities did not change with time.

Therefore more firmly I from time to time
Followed there where I heard the call of heaven,
And guided by the sweet luminous lamp
I returned full of love to the first branches
When the earth was all covered with dead leaves
And when the sun again made green the hills.

Woods, stones and countryside, rivers and hills,
All things created are transformed by time;
So I will ask forgiveness from these leaves
If after many years of changing heaven
I decided to flee the snaring branches
As soon as I began to see the lamp.

So pleased was I at first by the sweet lamp,
That I walked with delight through craggy hills
To come a little nearer to those branches;
Now life is short, and the place and the time

Mostranmi altro sentier di gire al cielo,
E di far frutto non pur fior e frondi.

Altr'amor, altre frondi, et altro lume,
Altro salir al ciel per altri poggi
Cerco, ché n'è ben tempo, et altri rami.

CXLIII

Quand'io v'odo parlar sí dolcemente
Com'Amor proprio a' suoi seguaci instilla,
L'acceso mio desir tutto sfavilla,
Tal che 'nfiammar devria l'anime spente.

Trovo la bella donna allor presente,
Ovunque mi fu mai dolce o tranquilla,
Ne l'abito ch'al suon, non d'altra squilla,
Ma di sospir mi fa destar sovente.

Le chiome a l'aura sparse, e lei conversa
In dietro veggio; e cosí bella riede,
Nel cor, come colei che tien la chiave.

Ma 'l soverchio piacer, che s'atraversa
A la mia lingua, qual dentro ella siede
Di mostrarla in palese ardir non have.

Show me another path to climb to heaven
And to bear fruit, not only flowers and leaves.

Other love, other leaves, another lamp,
Another way to heaven, other hills
I seek, it is high time, and other branches.

CXLIII

When I hear you speak as sweetly as Love
Himself speaks to his pupils in his role,
My desire is inflamed as if to prove
That it could set on fire a lifeless soul.

Then I find my fair lady present there
Where she was sweet and calm addressing me,
And with the sound of all the sighs I bear,
And not of bells, she wakes me suddenly.

Her hair spread in the aura, she is turned
Backward; and then she comes into my heart
As fair as is the one who holds its key.

But the excessive pleasure that I earned
Obstructs my tongue; and as she is, apart,
It does not dare to show her outwardly.

CXLIV

Né cosí bello il sol giá mai levarsi
Quando 'l ciel fosse piú de nebbia scarco,
Né dopo pioggia vidi 'l celeste arco
Per l'aere in color tanti variarsi,

In quanti fiammeggiando trasformarsi,
Nel dí ch'io presi l'amoroso incarco,
Quel viso al quale (e son nel mio dir parco)
Nulla cosa mortal pòte aguagliarsi

I' vidi Amor che 'begli occhi volgea
Soave sí ch'ogni altra vista oscura
Da indi in qua m'incominciò apparere.

Sennuccio, i' 'l vidi, e l'arco che tendea,
Tal che mia vita poi non fu secura,
Et è sí vaga ancor del rivedere.

CXLV

Pommi ove 'l sole occide i fiori e l'erba,
O dove vince lui il ghiaccio e la neve;
Pommi ov'è 'l carro suo temprato e leve,
Et ov'è chi cel rende, o chi cel serba;

Pommi in umil fortuna, od in superba,
Al dolce aere sereno, al fosco e greve;
Pommi a la notte, al dí lungo ed al breve,
A la matura etate od a l'acerba;

Pommi in cielo, od in terra, od in abisso,
In alto poggio, in valle ima e palustre,
Libero spirto, od a' suoi membri affisso;

Pommi con fama oscura, o con illustre:
Sarò qual fui, vivrò com'io son visso,
Continuando il mio sospir trilustre.

CXLIV

I did not see the sun sparkle so fair
When the sky was unloaded of the mist,
Nor after rain the rainbow paint the air
And in so many colours turn and twist,

As her face changed in glowing before me
The day that I assumed my loving share,
A face to which, and I speak cautiously,
No other mortal thing one can compare.

I saw Love turn around her lovely eyes
So sweetly, that since then all other sight
Seems to me gloomy, without any light.

Sennuccio, I saw him, I saw his bow,
And my life from then on became unwise
And is still eager to see the same show.

CXLV

Lay me where the sun kills the flowers and grass,
And where it is destroyed by ice and snow;
Lay me where its more temperate wheels pass,
And where somebody stores and sheds its glow;

Lay me in humble or in proud estate,
In the thick gloomy air, or sweet and bright,
In the day, long or short, or in the night,
In the early green season, in the late;

Lay me in heaven, earth, in the abyss,
In a damp valley, on a high hill heaved,
A spirit free, or to the body bent;

Lay me with great renown, or without this:
I will be what I was, live as I lived,
Pursuing my three-lusters-old lament.

CXLVI

O d'ardente vertute ornata e calda
Alma gentil, cui tante carte vergo;
O sol giá d'onestate intero albergo,
Tórre in alto valor fondata e salda;

O fiamma, o ròse sparse in dolce falda
Di viva neve, in ch'io mi specchio e tergo;
O piacer, onde l'ali al bel viso ergo,
Che luce sovra quanti il sol ne scalda;

Del vostro nome, se mie rime intese
Fossin sí lunge, avrei pien Tile e Battro,
La Tana e 'l Nilo, Atlante, Olimpo e Calpe.

Poi che portar no 'l posso in tutte e quattro
Parti del mondo, udrallo il bel paese
Ch'Appennin parte, e 'l mar circonda e l'Alpe.

CXLVII

Quando 'l voler che con duo sproni ardenti,
E con un duro fren, mi mena e regge,
Trapassa ad or ad or l'usata legge
Per far in parte i miei spiriti contenti,

Trova chi le paure e gli ardimenti
Del cor profondo ne la fronte legge,
E vede Amor che sue imprese corregge,
Folgorar ne' turbati occhi pungenti.

Onde, come collui che 'l colpo teme
Di Giove irato, si ritragge in dietro;
Ché gran temenza gran desire affrena.

Ma freddo foco, e paventosa speme
De l'alma che traluce come un vetro,
Talor sua dolce vista rasserena.

CXLVI

Warmed and adorned by virtue's brilliancy,
Ravishing soul of which I always write,
The only perfect home of honesty,
Tower that are founded on valour and right;

O flame, o roses scattered in a fold
Of living snow where I wash and reflect,
O pleasure of my wings when I behold
The face that is the sun's favoured object;

I would fill with your name Tana and Nile,
If my rhymes were heard there, Battro and Thyle,
Atlas, Olympus, Calpe. I cannot

Take it to the four corners of our plot;
Then in the lovely land it shall resound
That Apennine and Alp and sea surround.

CXLVII

When the dear will that with two burning spurs
And with a fastened rein leads me to right,
From time to time the accustomed law reverts
To give my spirit a partial delight,

It finds the terrors and the audacities
Of the deep heart writ in my countenance,
Sees Love, who rules his own vivacities,
Glare in the troubled pungency of my glance;

Then like to one who dreads the furious pace
Of angry Jove, it instantly draws back,
For a great fear will check desire's attack:

But a cool fire, an amorous suspense
Of the soul, as transparent as a lens,
Sometimes will fill with clarity her fair face.

CXLVIII

Non Tesin, Po, Varo, Arno, Adige, e Tebro,
Eufrate, Tigre, Nilo, Ermo, Indo, e Gange,
Tana, Istro, Alfeo, Garona, e 'l mar che frange,
Rodano, Ibero, Ren, Sena, Albia, Era, Ebro,

Non edra, abete, pin, faggio, o genebro,
Poría 'l foco allentar che 'l cor tristo ange,
Quant'un bel rio ch'ad ogni or meco piange,
Co l'arboscel che 'n rime orno e celèbro.

Questo un soccorso trovo tra gli assalti
D'Amore, ove conven ch'armato viva
La vita che trapassa a sí gran salti.

Cosí cresca il bel lauro in fresca riva,
E chi 'l piantò pensier leggiadri et alti
Ne la dolce ombra al suon de l'acque scriva.

CXLIX

Di tempo in tempo mi si fa men dura
L'angelica figura, e 'l dolce riso,
E l'aria del bel viso
E de gli occhi leggiadri meno oscura.
Che fanno meco omai questi sospiri,
Che nascean di dolore,
E mostravan di fòre
La mia angosciosa e desperata vita?
S'aven che 'l vólto in quella parte giri
Per acquetare il core,
Parmi vedere Amore
Mantener mia ragion e darmi aita.
Né però trovo ancor guerra finita,
Né tranquillo ogni stato del cor mio;
Chó piú m'arde 'l desio,
Quanto piú la speranza m'assicura.

CXLVIII

Not Tessin, Po, Varo, Adige, Tebro,
Euphrates, Tigris, Nile, Ermo, Indo, Ganges,
Tana, Ister, Alpheus, Garonne, and the sea-ranges,
Rhone, Iber, Rhine, Seine, Albia, Era, Ebro,

Not ivy, cedar, beech or juniper
Could soothe the fire that in my sad heart leaps,
As a fair stream that in me always weeps,
And the small tree that with my rhymes I stir.

This is a comfort against the assaults
Of Love, where I am bound to live in arms
A life that runs away by jumps and jolts.

Then may the laurel grow on a fresh ground,
And he who planted it write of its charms
In the sweet shadow where the waters sound.

CXLIX

With the passing of time they seem less hard,
That angelic regard and that sweet smile,
And the air and the style
Of her countenance less dark and less on guard.

What do they want to do with me, these sighs
That were born out of woe,
And did so clearly show
My distressful and miserable life?
If to that side I sometimes turn my eyes
Where my heart wants to go,
I seem to see Love glow
And mould my reason and protect my strife.
But still I always find that war is rife,
And no state of my heart knows any peace;
For my desires increase
As my hopes are more sure of a reward.

CL

—Che fai, alma? Che pensi? avrem mai pace?
Avrem mai tregua? od avrem guerra eterna?—
—Che fia di noi, non so; ma, in quel ch'io scerna,
A' suoi begli occhi il mal nostro non piace.—

—Che pro, se con quelli occhi ella ne face
Di state un ghiaccio, un foco quando iverna?—
—Ella non, ma colui che gli governa.—
—Questo ch'è a noi, s'ella sel vede, e tace?—

—Talor tace la lingua, e 'l cor si lagna
Ad alta voce, e 'n vista asciutta e lieta
Piange dove mirando altri no 'l vede.—

—Per tutto ciò la mente non s'acqueta,
Rompendo il duol che 'n lei s'accoglie e stagna;
Ch'a gran speranza uom misero non crede.—

CLI

Non d'atra e tempestosa onda marina
Fuggío in porto giá mai stanco nocchiero,
Com'io dal fosco e torbido pensero
Fuggo ove 'l gran desio mi sprona e 'nchina.

Né mortal vista mai luce divina
Vinse, come la mia quel raggio altèro
Del bel dolce soave bianco e nero,
In che i suoi strali Amor dora et affina.

Cieco non giá, ma faretrato il veggo;
Nudo, se non quanto vergogna il vela;
Garzon con ali; non pinto, ma vivo.

Indi mi mostra quel ch'a molti cela;
Ch'a parte a parte entro a' begli occhi leggo
Quant'io parlo d'Amore, e quant'io scrivo.

CL

—What do you think, my soul? Shall we have peace?
Shall we have respite, or eternal war?—
—What will become of us I cannot score,
But our ill in her eyes finds no release.—

—What is the use, if with those eyes she makes
A frost in summer, in winter a flame?—
—Not she, but he who rules our passion's stakes.—
—What do we care? she sees it without shame!—

—Sometimes the tongue is silent and the heart
Loudly laments, and looking glad and dry
It weeps where those who watch it cannot spy.—

—In spite of that the mind can never start
To break the sorrows that amass and rust;
For a great hope no wretched man can trust.—

CLI

No weary pilot ever fled a dark
And stormy ocean in the port he sought,
As I flee from the gloomy, troubled thought
Where this mighty desire propels my bark.

No divine light ever conquered our sight
As mine was smitten by that haughty ray
Of the sweet and enchanting black and white
Where Love gilds and refines his arrows' play.

Not blind, with quiver I see him arrive;
Naked, except what shame does not reveal;
A boy with wings; not painted, but alive.

Then he shows me what he likes to conceal;
Because in her fair eyes each word I read
Of what I say of Love and write and plead.

CLII

Questa umil fera, un cor di tigre o d'orsa,
Che 'n vista umana, e 'n forma d'angel vène,
In riso e 'n pianto, fra paura e spene
Mi rota sí ch'ogni mio stato inforsa.

Se 'n breve non m'accoglie o non mi smorsa,
Ma pur, come suol far, tra due mi tène,
Per quel ch'io sento al cor gir fra le vène
Dolce veneno, Amor, mia vita è corsa.

Non pò piú la vertú fragile e stanca
Tante varietati omai soffrire;
Che 'n un punto arde, agghiaccia, arrossa e 'nbianca.

Fuggendo spera i suoi dolor finire,
Come colei che d'ora in ora manca;
Ché ben pò nulla chi non pò morire.

CLIII

Ite, caldi sospiri, al freddo core;
Rompete il ghiaccio che pietá contende,
E se prego mortale al ciel s'intende,
Morte, o mercé sia fine al mio dolore.

Ite, dolci penser, parlando fòre
Di quello ove 'l bel guardo non se stende:
Se pur sua asprezza, o mia stella n'offende,
Sarem fuor di speranza e fuor d'errore.

Dir se pò ben per voi, non forse a pieno,
Che 'l nostro stato è inquieto e fosco,
Sí come 'l suo pacifico e sereno.

Gite securi omai, ch'Amor vèn vosco;
E ria fortuna pò ben venir meno,
S'a i segni del mio sol l'aere conosco.

CLII

This humble beast, heart of tiger or bear,
Who comes in human shape, angelic form,
With tears and laughter, between hope and fear,
Reels around me and shakes me like a storm.

If she will not take me or break my chains,
But still continues to keep me enslaved,
From the sweet poison running through my veins
I feel, Love, that my life will not be saved.

No longer can my valour, tired and frail,
So many changing attitudes endure;
It freezes, burns at once, is red or pale.

It hopes to end its woes seeking to fly,
Like a woman whose strength fails more and more;
For you can nothing if you cannot die.

CLIII

Go, burning sighs, into that frozen heart;
Shatter the ice that now with pity vies,
And if a mortal prayer can reach the skies,
Let death or mercy end at last this smart.

Go, loving thoughts, and speak aloud and show
What hides where her fair glance is not extended:
If her contempt or my star is offended
We shall be out of hope and out of woe.

You certainly can say, though not quite well,
That our condition is as dark as hell,
While her own is serene, peaceful and fair.

Go, you are safe, because Love comes with us;
And wicked fortune may decline and pass,
If the signs of my sun predict the air.

CLIV

Le stelle, il cielo, e gli elementi a prova
Tutte lor arti, et ogni estrema cura
Poser nel vivo lume, in cui Natura
Si specchia, e 'l Sol ch'altrove par non trova.

L'opra è sí altèra, sí leggiadra e nova,
Che mortal guardo in lei non s'assecura;
Tanta ne gli occhi bei fòr di misura
Par ch'Amore e dolcezza e grazia piova.

L'aere percosso da' lor dolci rai
S'infiamma d'onestate, e tal diventa,
Che 'l dir nostro e 'l penser vince d'assai.

Basso desir non è ch'ivi si senta,
Ma d'onor, di vertute. Or quando mai
Fu per somma beltá vil voglia spenta?

CLV

Non fûr ma' Giove e Cesare sí mossi
A folminar collui, questo a ferire
Che pietá non avesse spente l'ire,
E lor de l'usate arme ambeduo scossi.

Piangea madonna, e 'l mio signor ch'i' fossi
Volse a vederla, e suoi lamenti a udire,
Per colmarmi di doglia e di desire
E ricercarmi le medolle e gli ossi.

Quel dolce pianto mi depinse Amore,
Anzi scolpio, e que' detti soavi
Mi scrisse entro un diamante in mezzo 'l core;

Ove con salde ed ingegnose chiavi
Ancor torna sovente a trarne fòre
Lagrime rare e sospir lunghi e gravi.

CLIV

The stars, the sky, the elements directed
All their arts, and devoted all their care
To the bright lamp where Nature is reflected,
And the sun too, that finds nothing so fair.

The work is so supreme, charming and new,
That mortal look in her is not secure;
So strange in her fair eyes, so hardly true,
Love and sweetness and grace together pour.

The air struck by their beam is set aflame
With honesty and is transformed by duty
In what surpasses all we think or say.

No low desire can come in it and stay,
Only virtue and honour. When did beauty
So great extinguish all unworthy claim?

CLV

Never was Jove or Caesar so inflamed
By lightnings or by wounds to cause alarms,
That pity did not make him feel ashamed
Of wrath, and shake his weapons from his arms.

My lady wept, and my lord wanted me
To see her grief, to hear her plaintive moans,
In order to fill me with agony
And rummage in my marrow and my bones.

That sweet weeping was painted by Love's art
Or rather sculptured, and those tender cries
Were written with a diamond in my heart;

Where with ingenious keys and solid ties
He still returns and often draws apart
My hidden tears and my long, heavy sighs.

CLVI

I' vidi in terra angelici costumi
E celesti bellezze al mondo sole;
Tal che di rimembrar mi giova e dole,
Ché quant'io miro par sogni, ombre, e fumi.

E vidi lagrimar que' duo bei lumi,
C'han fatto mille volte invidia al sole;
Et udí' sospirando dir parole
Che farian gire i monti e stare i fiumi.

Amor, senno, valor, pietate, e doglia
Facean piangendo un piú dolce concento
D'ogni altro che nel mondo udir si soglia:

Ed era il cielo a l'armonia sí intento
Che non se vedea in ramo mover foglia,
Tanta dolcezza avea pien l'aere e 'l vento.

CLVII

Quel sempre acerbo et onorato giorno
Mandá sí al cor l'imagine sua viva
Che 'ngegno o stil non fia mai che 'l descriva,
Ma spesso a lui co la memoria torno.

L'atto d'ogni gentil pietate adorno,
E 'l dolce amaro lamentar ch'i' udiva,
Facean dubbiar se mortal donna o diva
Fosse che 'l ciel rasserenava intorno.

La testa òr fino, e calda neve il vólto,
Ebeno i cigli, e gli occhi eran due stelle,
Onde Amor l'arco non tendeva in fallo;

Perle, e ròse vermiglie, ove l'accolto
Dolor formava ardenti voci e belle;
Fiamma i sospir, le lagrime cristallo.

CLVI

I saw on earth angelic manners show;
Heavenly beauties, in the world, alone,
So that recalling them is joy and woe,
For it seems shadow, smoke or dream that shone.

And I saw those two lights with tears abound,
That thousand times were envied by the sun;
And I heard between sighs some words resound
That make hills move and rivers stop to run.

Love, wisdom, valour, pity and distress
Made in weeping a sweeter symphony
Than any to be heard here in this world;

The sky was so entranced by the harmony,
That no leaf on the branch was being curled:
The air and wind were filled with such sweetness.

CLVII

That ever-cruel, ever-honoured day
Laid so deep in my heart her image true,
That neither style nor talent can convey
What my memory often brings me to.

The act adorned with pity's gentleness
And the sweet bitter moaning that I heard,
Made one doubt whether woman or goddess
Cleared the air around us that had been blurred.

Fine gold the hair, warm snow the face appears,
Lashes of ebony, eyes like coupled stars
From where Love bent the bow that made our scars;

Pearls and vermilion roses where the hive
Of sorrow found a voice pure and alive;
Her sighs like flame, and like crystal her tears.

CLVIII

Ove ch'i' posi gli occhi lassi o giri
Per quetar la vaghezza che gli spinge,
Trovo chi bella donna ivi depinge
Per far sempre mai verdi i miei desiri.

Con leggiadro dolor par ch'ella spiri
Alta pietá che gentil core stringe:
Oltr'a la vista, a gli orecchi orna e 'nfinge
Sue voci vive, e suoi santi sospiri.

Amor e 'l ver fûr meco a dir che quelle
Ch'i' vidi, eran bellezze al mondo sole,
Mai non vedute piú sotto le stelle.

Né sí pietose e sí dolci parole
S'udiron mai, né lagrime sí belle
Di sí belli occhi uscir mai vide 'l sole.

CLIX

In qual parte del ciel in quale idea
Era l'essempio, onde Natura tolse
Quel bel viso leggiadro, in ch'ella volse
Mostrar qua giú quanto lassú potea?

Qual ninfa in fonti, in selve mai qual dea,
Chiome d'oro sí fino a l'aura sciolse?
Quando un cor tante in sé vertuti accolse?
Ben che la somma è di mia morte rea.

Per divina bellezza indarno mira
Chi gli occhi de costei giá mai non vide
Come soavemente ella gli gira;

Non sa come Amor sana, e come ancide,
Chi non sa come dolce ella sospira,
E come dolce parla, e dolce ride.

CLVIII

Wheresoever I turn my tired eyes' stare
To subdue the seduction that inspires
Them, I find a fair lady painted there
By someone who makes green all my desires.

With charming sorrow she seems to surmise
A lofty pity that contracts her heart;
After my sight my ears by the same art
Figure her living voice and holy sighs.

Love and Truth said with me that what I saw
Were beauties that this world shows only once,
They do not come again under its law.

Such pitiful, sweet words nobody hears,
And the sun never saw such lovely tears
As were shed then by such a lovely glance.

CLIX

In what part of the sky, in what idea
Was the example from which Nature wrought
That charming lovely face wherein she sought
To show her power in the upper sphere?

What nymph in fountain, what goddess in mead
Shook in the air such a fine hair of gold?
When did a heart so many virtues hold?
Although their sum is the cause why I bleed.

He looks in vain for beauty's divine lights
Who never saw the loveliness of her eyes,
And how softly she moves them all the while.

He knows not how Love heals and how he smites
Who does not know the sweetness of her sighs,
And how sweet is her speech, how sweet her smile.

CLX

Amor et io sí pien di meraviglia
Come chi mai cosa incredibil vide,
Miriam costei quand'ella parla o ride
Che sol se stessa e nulla altra simiglia.

Dal bel seren de le tranquille ciglia,
Sfavillan sí le mie due stelle fide,
Ch'altro lume non è ch'infiammi e guide
Chi d'amar altamente si consiglia.

Qual miracolo è quel, quando tra l'erba
Quasi un fior siede, o ver quand'ella preme
Col suo candido seno un verde cespo!

Qual dolcezza è ne la stagione acerba
Vederla ir sola 'co i pensier suoi inseme,
Tessendo un cerchio a l'oro terso e crespo!

CLXI

O passi sparsi! o pensier vaghi e pronti!
O tenace memoria! o fero ardore!
O possente desire! o debil core!
Oi occhi miei, occhi non giá, ma fonti!

O fronde, onor de le famose fronti,
O sola insegna al gemino valore!
O faticosa vita, o dolce errore,
Che mi fate ir cercando piagge e monti!

O bel viso, ove Amor inseme pose
Gli sproni e 'l fren, ond'el mi punge e volve,
Come a lui piace, e calcitrar non vale!

O anime gentili et amorose,
S'alcuna ha 'l mondo, e voi nude ombre e polve,
Deh, ristate a veder quale è 'l mio male.

CLX

Love and myself, as overcome by wonder
As those whom the incredible beguiles,
Gaze on her when she speaks and when she smiles,
Whose semblance from all others we must sunder.

From the clear heaven of her tranquil brows
So limpid my two stars sparkle and move,
That there is left no other light to rouse
And guide those who are learning a true love.

What miracle when she among the grass
Sits like a flower, or when I see her brush
With her white breast the green of a small bush!

What sweetness to see her during the cold
Season walk lonely with her thoughts and pass,
Weaving a band for the clear curly gold!

CLXI

O scattered steps, o thoughts charming and neat!
O tenacious remembrance, o wild fire!
O feeble heart, o powerful desire!
O my eyes, no more eyes, but streaming sheet!

O branches, honour of the glorious brow,
O single sign of what valour instils!
O weary life, o sweet error that now
Make me wander and look for shores and hills!

O handsome face where Love together thrust
The spurs and bridles with which he can rein
Me as he likes, and it is vain to balk!

O gentle souls who know how Love can talk,
If some can still be found, o shades and dust,
I beg you, stay, and see what is my pain.

CLXII

Lieti fiori e felici, e ben nate erbe
Che madonna pensando premer sòle;
Piaggia ch'ascolti sue dolci parole,
E del bel piede alcun vestigio serbe;

Schietti arboscelli, e verdi frondi acerbe,
Amorosette e pallide viole;
Ombrose selve, ove percote il sole
Che vi fa co' suoi raggi alte e superbe;

O soave contrada, o puro fiume
Che bagni il suo bel viso e gli occhi chiari,
E prendi qualitá dal vivo lume;

Quanto v'invidio gli atti onesti e cari!
Non fia in voi scoglio omai che per costume
D'arder co la mia fiamma non impari.

CLXIII

Amor, che vedi ogni pensero aperto
E i duri passi onde tu sol mi scorgi,
Nel fondo del mio cor gli occhi tuoi porgi,
A te palese, a tutt'altri coverto.

Sai quel che per seguirte ho giá sofferto;
E tu pur via di poggio in poggio sorgi,
Di giorno in giorno, e di me non t'accorgi
Che son sí stanco, e 'l sentir m'è troppo erto.

Ben veggio io di lontano il dolce lume,
Ove per aspre vie mi sproni e giri;
Ma non ho come tu da volar piume.

Assai contenti lasci i miei desiri,
Pur che ben desiando i' mi consume,
Né le dispiaccia che per lei sospiri.

CLXII

Glad, happy flowers, and you, well-born grass,
That my lady in musing likes to tread;
Sea-shore that listen to the words she said,
And keep some vestige of her feet that pass;

Straight-growing trees and green branches still young,
Little violets in love, of a pale hue,
And shady woods that the sun, breaking through,
With his radiance makes tall and proud and strong.

O lovely countryside, o limpid stream
That wet her charming visage and her clear
Eyes and take splendour from that living beam!

How much I envy you her actions dear!
There is no cliff in you that by long use
Has not learned how to take fire from my fuse.

CLXIII

Love, who see all my thoughts down to the root,
And the rough spots where you lead me alone,
In the depths of my heart you come to loot,
Open to you and closed to everyone.

You know what I have stood to follow you;
And yet from hill to hill you push and goad
Day after day, and never bother to
Notice how tired I am, how steep the road.

I see indeed from far the lovely light
Where you spur and draw me aiming so high;
But I have not, like you, feathers to fly.

You leave my wish contented with its plight
As long as I with passion pine away,
And she is not displeased with my dismay.

CLXIV

Or che 'l ciel e la terra e 'l vento tace
E le fere e gli augelli il sonno affrena,
Notte il carro stellato in giro mena,
E nel suo letto il mar senz'onda giace,

Vegghio, penso, ardo, piango; e chi mi sface
Sempre m'è inanzi per mia dolce pena:
Guerra è 'l mio stato, d'ira e di duol piena;
E sol di lei pensando ho qualche pace.

Cosí sol d'una chiara fonte viva
Move 'l dolce e l'amaro, ond'io mi pasco;
Una man sola mi risana e punge.

E perché 'l mio martír non giunga a riva
Mille volte il dí moro e mille nasco;
Tanto da la salute mia son lunge.

CLXV

Come 'l candido pie' per l'erba fresca
I dolci passi onestamente move,
Vertú che 'ntorno i fiori apra e rinove
De le tenere piante sue par ch'èsca.

Amor, che solo i cor leggiadri invesca
Né degna di provar sua forza altrove,
Da' begli occhi un piacer sí caldo piove,
Ch'i' non curo altro ben né bramo altr'èsca.

E co l'andar e col soave sguardo
S'accordan le dolcissime parole,
E l'atto mansueto, umíle e tardo.

Di tai quattro faville, e non giá sole,
Nasce 'l gran foco, di ch'io vivo et ardo,
Che son fatto un augel notturno al sole.

CLXIV

Now that the sky, the earth, the wind, are still,
And all the beasts and birds are caught by sleep,
The night carries about her starry wheel,
And in his bed untroubled lies the deep,

I watch, I burn, I weep, and she who tears
My heart is always here for my sweet grief;
War is my state, full of anger and cares,
And only in her thought I find relief.

Only from that one clear and lovely spring
Flows the sweet bitter food by which I am torn,
Only one hand, the same, can heal and sting.

And that my wreck may never reach the strand,
A thousand times I die and am reborn,
So far I drift from my heavenly land.

CLXV

When over the cool grass her white foot goes,
All full of sweetness, at a gentle pace,
The flowers are opened and receive new grace
From the delicate footprints of her toes.

Love who only ensnares the longing hearts
And never stoops to show his strength elsewhere,
Such a warm pleasure from her eyes imparts
That for no other good or bait I care.

And with her gait and with her charming glance
Is blended all the sweetness of her word
And the meek gesture humble and deferred.

From those four sparks, and not from them alone,
Leaps the great fire that makes me live in trance
Till I become a nightbird in the sun.

CLXVI

S'i' fussi stato fermo a la spelunca
Lá dove Apollo diventò profeta,
Fiorenza avria forse oggi il suo poeta,
Non pur Verona e Mantoa et Arunca;

Ma perché 'l mio terren piú non s'ingiunca
De l'umor di quel sasso, altro pianeta
Conven ch'i' segua, e del mio campo mieta
Lappole e stecchi co la falce adunca.

L'oliva è secca, et è rivolta altrove
L'acqua che di Parnaso si deriva,
Per cui in alcun tempo ella fioriva.

Cosí sventura o ver colpa mi priva
D'ogni buon frutto, se l'etterno Giove
De la sua grazia sopra me non piove.

CLXVII

Quando Amor i belli occhi a terra inchina
E i vaghi spirti in un sospiro accoglie
Co le sue mani, e poi in voce gli scioglie,
Chiara, soave, angelica, divina,

Sento far del mio cor dolce rapina,
E sí dentro cangiar penseri e voglie,
Ch'i' dico:—Or fíen di me l'ultime spoglie,
Se 'l ciel sí onesta morte mi destina.—

Ma 'l suon che di dolcezza i sensi lega
Col gran desir d'udendo esser beata
L'anima al dipartir presta raffrena.

Cosí mi vivo, e cosí avolge e spiega
Lo stame de la vita che m'è data,
Questa sola fra noi del ciel sirena.

CLXVI

If I had remained firmly in the cave
Of which Apollo was prophet and owner,
Florence today her own poet would have,
Not only Arunca, Mantua, Verona;

But since my earthly loam no longer yields
Or raises rushes out of stone, I must
Follow another star, and from my fields
Mow sticks and burrs with my hooked scythe, and dust.

The olive tree is dry, gone from the grove
The stream that from Parnassus is derived,
Which made it blossom in the bygone days.

Thus mischance or my own guilt has deprived
Me of every good fruit, unless great Jove
Pour over me the shower of his grace.

CLXVII

When Love bends her fair eyes toward the ground
And makes her spirits in a sigh combine
With his own hands, and then loosens their sound
In a voice clear, angelic and divine,

I feel a sweet kidnapping of my heart,
And thoughts and wants are so changed inside me
That I say:—Here I drop my living part
If heaven lets me die so honestly.—

But the sound that with sweetness binds my sense,
With the desire of achieving the bliss
Of hearing, holds the soul eager to pass.

So I live, and she folds, unfolds, like this,
The woof of life that was given me thence,
This siren of the sky lone among us.

CLXVIII

Amor mi manda quel dolce pensero
Che secretario antico è fra noi due,
E mi conforta, e dice che non fue
Mai come or presto a quel ch'io bramo e spero.

Io che talor menzogna e talor vero
Ho ritrovato le parole sue,
Non so s'i' 'l creda, e vivomi intra due,
Né sí né no nel cor mi sona intero.

In questa passa 'l tempo, e ne lo specchio
Mi veggio andar vèr' la stagion contraria
A sua impromessa, et a la mia speranza.

Or sia che pò: giá sol io non invecchio;
Giá per etate il mio desir non varia:
Ben temo il viver breve che n'avanza.

CLXIX

Pien d'un vago penser, che me desvia
Da tutti gli altri, e fammi al mondo ir solo,
Ad or ad ora a me stesso m'involo
Pur lei cercando che fuggir devria;

E veggiola passar sí dolce e ria
Che l'alma trema per levarsi a volo,
Tal d'armati sospir conduce stuolo
Questa bella d'Amor nemica, e mia.

Ben, s'i' non erro, di pietate un raggio
Scorgo fra 'l nubiloso, altèro ciglio,
Che 'n parte rasserena il cor doglioso:

Allor raccolgo l'alma, e poi ch'i' aggio
Di scovrirle il mio mal preso consiglio,
Tanto gli ho a dir che 'ncominciar non oso.

CLXVIII

Love sends to me that pleasurable thought
Which has been an old courier through the air
Between us two, and says that he has brought
More promptness than before to serve my prayer.

I, who have found his words to be a lie
At times, at other times true to desire,
Know not what to believe, what to deny,
Nor yes nor no sounds in my heart entire.

And seasons run, and in the looking-glass
I see myself go to the time contrary
To what Love pledges and my hopes believe.

Let it be so: not I alone shall pass,
Neither does my desire with my age vary:
I rather fear the rest I have to live.

CLXIX

Full of a gentle thought that divides me
From all the others and makes me go alone,
Now and again from my own self I flee,
Always pursuing one I ought to shun.

And I see her go by, my darling dove,
So cruel that my heart shudders and flies:
She leads such armies of assaulting sighs,
This handsome adversary of my love.

I seem at times to catch a pitying ray
Between those cloudy, haughty brows and mien,
Which partly takes my agony away:

Then I gather my soul, I tell my mind
To reveal all its suffering; and I find
So much to say, that I cannot begin.

CLXX

Piú volte giá dal bel sembiante umano
Ho preso ardir co le mie fide scorte
D'assalir con parole oneste accorte
La mia nemica in atto umíle e piano;

Fanno poi gli occhi suoi mio penser vano,
Per ch'ogni mia fortuna, ogni mia sorte,
Mio ben, mio male, e mia vita, e mia morte
Quei che solo il pò far, l'ha posto in mano.

Ond'io non poté' mai formar parola
Ch'altro che da me stesso fosse intesa;
Cosí m'ha fatto Amor tremante e fioco.

E veggi' or ben che caritate accesa
Lega la lingua altrui, gli spirti invola:
Chi pò dir com'egli arde, è 'n picciol foco.

CLXXI

Giunto m'ha Amor fra belle e crude braccia,
Che m'ancidono a torto; e s'io mi doglio,
Doppia 'l martír; onde pur, com'io soglio,
Il meglio è ch'io mi mora amando, e taccia:

Ché poría questa il Ren qualor piú agghiaccia
Arder con gli occhi, e rompre ogni aspro scoglio;
Et ha sí egual a le bellezze orgoglio,
Che di piacer altrui par che le spiaccia.

Nulla posso levar io per mi' 'ngegno
Del bel diamante ond'ell'ha il cor sí duro;
L'altro è d'un marmo che si mova e spiri:

Ned ella a me per tutto 'l suo disdegno
Torrá giá mai, né per sembiante oscuro,
Le mie speranze, e i mei dolci sospiri.

CLXX

Several times from her fair human face
I took the courage with my faithful guide
To assault with wise words and honest ways
My enemy, looking meek, without pride;

Then her eyes make all thought of mine disband,
Because every fate or fortune's trend,
My good, my evil, my life and my end,
Are only one thing, which is in her hand.

Therefore I never could utter a word
That from others besides me might be heard;
Like this, trembling and faint, Love has made me.

And now I see that glowing charity
Fastens the tongue of men, stills their desire:
Who can say how he burns, feeds a small fire.

CLXXI

Love has caught me between two cruel arms
That unjustly slay me; if I protest,
The torture doubles; then I think the best
Is to die loving and without alarms;

This lady with her eyes could kindle, stir,
Rhine when it freezes, break a rugged rock;
And so matched to her beauty is her stock
Of pride, that pleasing others injures her.

I can draw nothing with my intellect
Out of the diamond that hardens her heart;
The rest is marble that can breathe by art:

Nor shall she ever with her disrespect
Take out of me in such a somber guise
My sweetest hopes and my long-suffering sighs.

CLXXII

O invidia nimica di vertute,
Ch'a' bei principii volentier contrasti,
Per qual sentier cosí tacita intrasti
In quel bel petto, e con qual arti il mute?

Da radici n'hai svelta mia salute:
Troppo felice amante mi mostrasti
A quella che miei preghi umíli e casti
Gradi alcun tempo, or par ch'odi' e refute.

Né, però che con atti acerbi e rei
Del mio ben pianga e del mio pianger rida,
Poría cangiar sol un de' pensier mei.

Non, perché mille volte il dí m'ancida,
Fia ch'io non l'ami, e ch'i' non speri in lei;
Che s'ella mi spaventa, Amor m'affida.

CLXXIII

Mirando 'l sol de' begli occhi sereno,
Ove è chi spesso i miei depinge e bagna,
Dal cor l'anima stanca si scompagna
Per gir nel paradiso suo terreno.

Poi, trovandol di dolce e d'amar pieno,
Quant'al mondo si tesse, opra d'aragna
Vede: onde seco e con Amor si lagna,
C'ha sí caldi gli spron, sí duro 'l freno.

Per questi estremi duo contrarî e misti,
Or con voglie gelate, or con accese,
Stassi cosí fra misera e felice.

Ma pochi lieti, e molti penser tristi;
E 'l piú si pente de l'ardite imprese:
Tal frutto nasce di cotal radice.

CLXXII

O Envy, of all virtue enemy,
That gladly break every noble rule,
By what path could you go so silently
In that fair breast and change it, by what school?

By the root you did pull out my salvation:
As a too happy lover you showed me
To her who once enjoyed my adoration
And now seems to refuse it and to flee.

Yet, though by actions cruel and unkind
She mourns my fortune, laughs at my despair,
She shall not change one thought within my mind.

Nor, though she kill me thousand times a day,
Shall I cease to love her, to hope in her;
For if she frightens me, I trust Love's way.

CLXXIII

Watching the sun of the fair eyes, serene,
Where is someone who paints and wets my own,
My weary soul has left my heart alone
To seek her paradise on earthly scene.

Then finding it of sweet and bitter full,
What in the world is woven, spider-wise,
She sees: and with herself and Love she sighs,
Who has such heated spurs, such frozen pull.

In these two opposite and mingled plots,
And now with chilly wishes, now with warm,
She stays like this, now peaceful, now in storm.

Few are the glad and many the sad thoughts;
More often she repents of her bold deeds;
Such is the fruit that is born of such seeds.

CLXXIV

Fera stella (se 'l cielo ha forza in noi
Quant'alcun crede) fu sotto ch'io nacqui,
E fera cuna, dove nato giacqui,
E fera terra, ove' pie' mossi poi;

E fera donna, che con gli occhi suoi,
E con l'arco, a cui sol per segno piacqui,
Fe' la piaga, onde, Amor, teco non tacqui,
Che con quell'arme risaldar la pòi.

Ma tu prendi a diletto i dolor miei;
Ella non giá, perché non son piú duri,
E 'l colpo è di saetta, e non di spiedo.

Pur mi consola che languir per lei
Meglio è che gioir d'altra; e tu mel giuri
Per l'orato tuo strale, et io tel credo.

CLXXV

Quando mi vène inanzi il tempo e 'l loco
Ov'i' perdei me stesso, e 'l caro nodo
Ond'Amor di sua man m'avinse in modo
Che l'amar mi fe' dolce, e 'l pianger gioco,

Solfo et ésca son tutto, e 'l cor un foco,
Da quei soavi spirti, i quai sempre odo,
Acceso dentro sí, ch'ardendo godo,
E di ciò vivo, e d'altro mi cal poco.

Quel sol, che solo a gli occhi mei resplende,
Co i vaghi raggi ancor indi mi scalda,
A vespro tal qual era oggi per tempo;

E cosí di lontan m'alluma e 'ncende,
Che la memoria ad ogni or fresca e salda
Pur quel nodo mi mostra e 'l loco e 'l tempo.

CLXXIV

A savage star (if heaven has such might
Over us as some say) shone on my birth,
A savage cradle where I lay all quiet,
And where I moved my feet, a savage earth;

Savage the woman who with her own eyes
And with the bow that wants me for a goal
Opened the wound whence, Love, you hear my cries,
Who by those arms could again make it whole.

But you play with my pain as with a toy;
Not she, because it is not more severe,
And the shot is of arrow, not of spear.

Yet I am soothed by this, to grieve for her
Is better than another to enjoy;
I believe in your dart by which you swear.

CLXXV

When I call to my mind the time and place
In which I lost myself, and the dear knot
Which Love himself in such a way has wrought
That makes my bitter sweet, my tears like plays,

I am sulphur and flint, my heart a fire,
From those sweet sighs that I forever hear,
So kindled inside me, that I desire
To burn like this, and live without a fear.

That sun which on my eyes alone has power,
From there can warm me now with its delight
At vesper as it did at matin time;

From the distance it burns me so with light
That my memory, quick at any hour,
Shows me the same knot, the same place and time.

CLXXVI

Per mezz'i boschi inospiti e selvaggi,
Onde vanno a gran rischio uomini et arme,
Vo securo io; ché non pò spaventarme
Altri che 'l sol c'ha d'Amor vivo i raggi.

E vo cantando (o penser miei non saggi!)
Lei che 'l ciel non poría lontana farme;
Ch'i' l'ho ne gli occhi; e veder seco parme
Donne e donzelle, e sono abeti e faggi.

Parme d'udirla, udendo i rami e l'ôre,
E le frondi, e gli augei lagnarsi, e l'acque
Mormorando fuggir per l'erba verde.

Raro un silenzio, un solitario orrore
D'ombrosa selva mai tanto mi piacque;
Se non che dal mio sol troppo si perde.

CLXXVII

Mille piagge in un giorno e mille rivi
Mostrato m'ha per la famosa Ardenna
Amor, ch'a' suoi le piante e i cori impenna
Per fargli al terzo ciel volando ir vivi.

Dolce m'è sol senz'arme esser stato ivi,
Dove armato fièr Marte, e non acenna,
Quasi senza governo, e senza antenna,
Legno in mar, pien di penser gravi e schivi.

Pur giunto al fin de la giornata oscura,
Rimembrando ond'io vegno e con quai piume,
Sento di troppo ardir nascer paura.

Ma 'l bel paese, e 'l dilettoso fiume
Con serena accoglienza rassecura
Il cor giá vòlto ov'abita il suo lume.

CLXXVI

Across inhospitable woods and drear,
Where men and arms at a great peril move,
I go secure; because I nothing fear,
But the sun with the rays of living love.

And I go singing (o my thoughts perverse!)
Of her whom heaven cannot part from me;
For she is in my eyes; with her I see
Women and girls, though these are beeches, firs.

I seem to hear her, hearing boughs and air,
And foliage, and birds singing, and the streams
Murmur in running through the verdant grass.

Never the lonely dread, the silence rare
Of shady forests were so full of dreams;
Only too distant from my sun, alas!

CLXXVII

A thousand shores a day, a thousand rills
Were shown to me on the famous Ardenne
By Love who hearts and feet with pinions fills
To make them fly alive to the third heaven.

'Tis sweet unarmed and lonely to have passed
Where rages armoured Mars and tells not why,
Almost without a helm, without a mast,
Wood in the sea, full of thoughts grave and shy.

And yet when comes the end of the dark day,
Recalling where I come from, with what feather,
I feel of too much boldness some dismay.

But the fair country, the delightful streams
Do reassure with an unclouded weather
My heart already turned where its lamp beams.

CLXXVIII

Amor mi sprona in un tempo et affrena,
Assecura e spaventa, arde et agghiaccia,
Gradisce e sdegna, a sè mi chiama e scaccia,
Or mi tène in speranza et or in pena,

Or alto or basso il meo cor lasso mena;
Onde 'l vago desir perde la traccia
E 'l suo sommo piacer par che li spiaccia;
D'error sí novo la mia mente è piena!

Un amico penser le mostra il vado,
Non d'acqua che per gli occhi si resolva,
Da gir tosto ove spera esser contenta;

Poi, quasi maggior forza indi la svolva,
Conven ch'altra via segua, e mal suo grado
A la sua lunga, e mia, morte consenta.

CLXXIX

Geri, quando talor meco s'adira
La mia dolce nemica, ch'è sí altèra,
Un conforto m'è dato ch'i' non pera,
Solo per cui vertú l'alma respira.

Ovunque ella sdegnando li occhi gira
(Che di luce privar mia vita spera?)
Le mostro i miei pien d'umiltá sí vera,
Ch'a forza ogni suo sdegno in dietro tira.

E cciò non fusse, andrei non altramente
A veder lei, che 'l vólto di Medusa,
Che facea marmo diventar la gente.

Cosí dunque fa tu; ch'i' veggio esclusa
Ogni altra aita; e 'l fuggir val niente
Dinanzi a l'ali che 'l signor nostro usa.

CLXXVIII

Love at the same time goads me and restrains,
Confirms and frightens me, inflames and freezes,
Accepts and spurns, holds me close and releases,
Now he nurses my hopes and now my pains,

Now high, now low, he leads my weary heart;
And so my dear desire loses its road,
And its high pleasure seems more like a smart;
Of such new error my mind bears the load!

A friendly thought teaches it how to ford,
But not the water that the eyes have stored,
And go soon where it may find its delight;

Then, as if overwhelmed by greater might,
It thinks it fit to take another way,
And against us consents to our decay.

CLXXIX

Geri, when she appears angry at me,
My sweetest enemy who is so hard,
One hope I have to survive misery,
Whose single virtue is all my reward.

Wherever she lets roam her scornful eyes
(Does she hope to deprive my life of light?)
I show her mine so humble and so wise
That she is forced to draw back her despite.

And if it were not so, I should have gone
To see her in the way they saw Medusa
Who transmuted all people into stone.

Then do the same; there are no other ways
Left that may help; he who flees is a loser
Before the wings on which our master sways.

CLXXX

Po, ben puo' tu portartene la scorza
Di me con tue possenti e rapide onde,
Ma lo spirto ch'iv'entro si nasconde
Non cura né di tua né d'altrui forza;

Lo qual, senz'alterar poggia con orza,
Dritto per l'aure al suo desir seconde,
Battendo l'ali verso l'aurea fronde,
L'aqua, e 'l vento, e la vela e i remi sforza.

Re de gli altri, superbo, altèro fiume,
Che 'ncontro 'l sol, quando e' ne mena 'l giorno,
E 'n ponente abandoni un piú bel lume,

Tu te ne vai col mio mortal sul corno;
L'altro, coverto d'amoroso piume,
Torna volando al suo dolce soggiorno.

CLXXXI

Amor fra l'erbe una leggiadra rete
D'oro e di perle tese sott'un ramo
Dell'arbor sempre verde ch'i' tant'amo,
Ben che n'abbia ombre piú triste che liete.

L'ésca fu 'l seme ch'egli sparge e miete,
Dolce et acerbo, ch'i' pavento e bramo;
Le note non fûr mai, dal dí ch'Adamo
Aperse gli occhi, sí soavi e quete.

E 'l chiaro lume che sparir fa 'l sole
Folgorava d'intorno; e 'l fune avolto
Era a la man ch'avorio e neve avanza.

Cosí caddi a la rete, e qui m'han còlto
Gli atti vaghi, e l'angeliche parole,
E 'l piacer, e 'l desire, e la speranza.

CLXXX

Po, you can drag away with you my rind
In your powerful waves' unbroken course,
But what remains concealed in it, my mind,
Cares not for yours nor for another's force;

This, without changing windward for lee side,
Straight through the breezes seeks for its relief,
Beating its wings to reach the golden leaf,
And water, wind, and sail, and oars, will ride.

King of the others, proud and haughty stream,
Who meet the sun when the day brings its beam
And in the west leave fairer lights forlorn,

You run away with my flesh on your horn;
The spirit, covered with its feathered load,
Returns in flying to its sweet abode.

CLXXXI

Love laid amid the grass a lovely net
Of gold and pearls, under the branches of
The evergreen bay-tree that I so love,
Though in its shade I do not breathe but fret.

And the bait was the seed he spreads and mows,
Acid and sweet, that I desire and fear;
The notes, since Adam's eyes did first disclose
To him the day, have never been so clear.

And the bright lamp that effaces the sun
Was shining over me; I saw the rope
Coiled in the hand of ivory and snow.

Then I fell in the net and was caught so
By the angelic words and action,
By pleasure and desire and by my hope.

CLXXXII

Amor, che 'ncende il cor d'ardente zelo,
Di gelata paura il tèn constretto,
E qual sia piú, fa dubbio a l'intelletto,
La speranza o 'l temor, la fiamma o 'l gielo.

Trem'al piú caldo, ard'al piú freddo cielo,
Sempre pien di desire e di sospetto,
Pur come donna in un vestire schietto
Celi un uom vivo, o sotto un picciol velo.

Di queste pene è mia propia la prima,
Arder di e notte; e quanto è 'l dolce male
Nè 'n penser cape, non che 'n versi o 'n rima:

L'altra non giá; ché 'l mio bel foco è tale
Ch'ogni uom pareggia; e del suo lume in cima
Chi volar pensa, indarno spiega l'ale.

CLXXXIII

Se 'l dolce sguardo di costei m'ancide,
E le soavi parolette accorte,
E s'Amor sopra me la fa sí forte,
Sol quando parla, o ver quando sorride,

Lasso!, che fia, se forse ella divide,
O per mia colpa o per malvagia sorte,
Gli occhi suoi da mercé, sí che di morte
Lá dove or m'assicura, allor mi sfide?

Però s' i ' tremo, e vo col cor gelato,
Qualor veggio cangiata sua figura,
Questo temer d'antiche prove è nato.

Femina è cosa mobil per natura;
Ond'io so ben ch'un amoroso stato
In cor di donna picciol tempo dura.

CLXXXII

Love, who inflames my heart with ardent zeal,
With frozen terror holds it to its post,
And which is more intense my doubts conceal,
Whether the fear, the hope, the flame, the frost.

It trembles in the heat, burns in the cold,
Always full of suspicion and desire,
Like to a woman who in her attire
Hides a live man, or in a small veil's fold.

Of these two punishments, the first is mine,
Burning by day and night; this pain so fine
Cannot be grasped by thought or poems' strings:

But not the other; for my fire is such
That it equals all men; who dreams to touch
Its top by flight, in vain spreads out his wings.

CLXXXIII

If the sweet gaze of this lady beguiles
Me, and the cunning small words of her tongue,
And if Love above me makes her so strong
Simply when she is speaking, when she smiles,

What will become of me if she divides,
Because of my own guilt, or else my doom,
Her eyes from mercy, and while now she sides
With me, what if she challenges my gloom?

Thus if I tremble in a frozen clime
Of feeling, when her manners alternate,
This fear from ancient trials gets the spring.

A woman is by nature a frail thing;
And I know well that an amorous state
Within a woman's heart lasts little time.

CLXXXIV

Amor, Natura, e la bella alma umíle,
Ov'ogn'alta vertute alberga e regna,
Contra me son giurati: Amor s'ingegna
Ch'i' mora a fatto, e 'n ciò segue suo stile;

Natura tèn costei d'un sí gentile
Laccio, che nullo sforzo è che sostegna;
Ella è sí schiva, ch'abitar non degna
Piú ne la vita faticosa, e vile.

Cosí lo spirto d'or in or vèn meno
A quelle belle care membra oneste,
Che specchio eran di vera leggiadria;

E s'a morte pietá non stringe 'l freno,
Lasso!, ben veggio in che stato son queste
Vane speranze, ond'io viver solía.

CLXXXV

Questa fenice, de l'aurata piuma
Al suo bel collo, candido, gentile,
Forma, senz'arte, un sí caro monile,
Ch'ogni cor addolcisce, e 'l mio consuma:

Forma un diadema natural ch'alluma
L'aere d'intorno; e 'l tacito focile
D'Amor tragge indi un liquido sottile
Foco che m'arde a la piú algente bruma.

Purpurea vesta, d'un ceruleo lembo
Sparso di ròse i belli omeri vela;
Novo abito, e bellezza unica e sola.

Fama ne l'odorato e ricco grembo
D'arabi monti lei ripone, e cela,
Che per lo nostro ciel sí altèra vola.

CLXXXIV

Love, Nature, and the beautiful meek soul
Where every other virtue dwells and sways,
Are all sworn against me; and Love assays
To make me die, according to his role;

Nature holds her by such a gentle brace
That she has not to bear any constraint,
She is so shy that she does not consent
To lodge in this fatiguing life and base.

Therefore the spirit hour by hour grows less
In those dear limbs full of honour and faith,
That were a mirror of true loveliness;

And unless mercy pulls the reins of death,
Alas! I see in what a plight are these
Vain hopes in which I used to find release.

CLXXXV

This phoenix forges with her golden plumes,
Without the help of art, a jewel bright
For her beautiful neck so smooth and white
That it soothes every heart and mine consumes:

She forges nature's diadem to inspire
The air around with light; Love's silent spear
Draws out of it a liquid subtle fire
That burns me even in the chilliest air.

In purple gown and with an azure stole
Full of roses her fair shoulders she veils;
A new attire, a beauty single, sole.

She stores and hides in her sweet lap the leaven
And the rich legends of Arabian tales,
This stately bird that flies across our heaven.

CLXXXVI

Se Virgilio et Omero avessin visto
Quel sole il qual vegg'io con gli occhi miei,
Tutte lor forze in dar fama a costei
Avrian posto, e l'un stil coll'altro misto:

Di che sarebbe Enea turbato e tristo,
Achille, Ulisse, e gli altri semidei,
E quel che resse anni cinquantasei
Sí bene il mondo, e quel ch'ancise Egisto.

Quel fiore antico di vertuti e d'arme
Come sembiante stella ebbe con questo
Novo fior d'onestate e di bellezze!

Ennio di quel cantò ruvido carme,
Di quest'altro io: et oh pur non molesto
Gli sia il mio ingegno, e 'l mio lodar non sprezze!

CLXXXVII

Giunto Alessandro a la famosa tomba
Del fero Achille, sospirando disse:
—O fortunato, che sí chiara tromba
Trovasti, e chi di te sí alto scrisse!—

Ma questa pura e candida colomba,
A cui non so s'al mondo mai par visse,
Nel mio stil frale assai poco rimbomba;
Cosí son le sue sorti a ciascun fisse.

Ché, d'Omero dignissima, e d'Orfeo,
O del pastor ch'ancor Mantova onora,
Ch'andassen sempre lei sola cantando,

Stella difforme, e fato sol qui reo
Commise a tal che 'l suo bel nome adora,
Ma forse scema sue lode parlando.

CLXXXVI

If both Virgil and Homer could have seen
The sun that I behold with my own eye,
They would have given all their force to vie,
And mixed each other's style to praise this queen:

Which would have made Aeneas troubled and sad,
Achilles and Ulysses and their peers,
And he who ruled the world fifty-six years
So well, and he whom Aegisthus struck dead.

That ancient flower of arms and gallantry
How similar a star it had to this
New flower of beauties and of honesty!

Ennius sang of the first in rugged lays,
I of the second; may she not dismiss
My talent, may she not disdain my praise!

CLXXXVII

When Alexander came to the great tomb
Of fierce Achilles, sighing he declared:
—O lucky man who found such clarion-room
And one who told so nobly what you dared!—

But this immaculate and pure-white dove,
The like of which has never touched this ground,
In my frail style makes such a little sound!
Each of us has his fate sent from above.

Worthy of Homer and of Orpheus,
And of the bard that Mantua still reveres,
Who should have always sung only her story,

An ugly star and a dark fate, alas,
Gave her to one who worships and endears,
But by his speech perhaps lessens her glory.

CLXXXVIII

Almo Sol, quella fronde ch'io sola amo
Tu prima amasti: or sola al bel soggiorno
Verdeggia, e senza par, poi che l'addorno
Suo male e nostro vide in prima Adamo.

Stiamo a mirarla: i' ti pur prego e chiamo,
O Sole; e tu pur fuggi, e fai d'intorno
Ombrare i poggi, e te ne porti il giorno,
E fuggendo mi tôi quel ch'i' piú bramo.

L'ombra che cade da quel umil colle,
Ove favilla il mio soave foco,
Ove 'l gran lauro fu picciola verga,

Crescendo mentr'io parlo, a gli occhi tolle
La dolce vista del beato loco,
Ove 'l mio cor co la sua donna alberga.

CLXXXIX

Passa la nave mia colma d'oblio
Per aspro mare, a mezza notte il verno,
Enfra Scilla e Caribdi; et al governo
Siede 'l signore, anzi 'l nimico mio;

A ciascun remo un penser pronto e rio
Che la tempesta e 'l fin par ch'abbi a scherno;
La vela rompe un vento umido, eterno,
Di sospir, di speranze, e di desio;

Pioggia di lagrimar, nebbia di sdegni
Bagna e rallenta le giá stanche sarte,
Che son d'error con ignoranzia attorto.

Celansi i duo mei dolci usati segni;
Morta fra l'onde è la ragion e l'arte,
Tal ch'i' 'ncomincio a desperar del porto.

CLXXXVIII

O glorious Sun, the leaf I love alone
You did love first; now in her charming home
It grows more green, unequalled since the groan
Of our fair illness did to Adam come.

We look at it: but still I call and pray
You, Sun; and you still flee and make the hills
Full of shade all around, and loot the day,
And fleeing steal from me what my heart wills.

The shadow falling from that humble slope
Where shines and sparkles my inflaming hope,
Where the great laurel once had a small size,

Increasing while I speak, deprives my eyes
Of the sweet vision of the blessed dell
Where my heart with my lady used to dwell.

CLXXXIX

My ship is sailing, full of mindless woe,
Through the rough sea, in winter-midnight drear,
Between Scylla and Charybdis; there to steer
Stands my master, or rather stands my foe.

At each oar sits a rapid wicked thought
Which seems to scoff at storms and at their end;
The sail, by wet eternal winds distraught,
With hopes, desires and sighs is made to rend.

A rain of tears, a fog of scornful lines,
Washes and tugs at the too sluggish cords
Which by error with ignorance are wound.

Vanished are my two old beloved signs,
Dead in the waves are all reason and words,
And I despair ever to reach the ground.

CXC

Una candida cerva sopra l'erba
Verde m'apparve, con duo corna d'oro,
Fra due riviere, all'ombra d'un alloro,
Levando 'l sole, a la stagione acerba.

Era sua vista sí dolce superba,
Ch'i' lasciai per seguirla ogni lavoro;
Come l'avaro, che 'n cercar tesoro,
Con diletto l'affanno disacerba.

"Nessun mi tócchi—al bel collo d'intorno
Scritto avea di diamanti e di topazî—
Libera farmi al mio Cesare parve".

Et era 'l sol giá vòlto al mezzo giorno;
Gli occhi miei stanchi di mirar non sazî,
Quand'io caddi ne l'acqua, et ella sparve.

CXCI

Sí come eterna vita è veder Dio,
Né piú si brama, né bramar piú lice,
Cosí me, donna, il voi veder felice
Fa in questo breve e fraile viver mio.

Né voi stessa com'or bella vid'io,
Giá mai, se vero al cor l'occhio ridice;
Dolce del mio penser ora beatrice,
Che vince ogni alta speme, ogni desio.

E se non fusse il suo fuggir sí ratto,
Piú non demanderei: che s'alcun vive
Sol d'odore, e tal fama fede acquista,

Alcun d'acqua, o di foco, e 'l gusto e 'l tatto
Acquetan cose d'ogni dolzor prive,
I' per che non de la vostra alma vista?

CXC

A pure-white doe in an emerald glade
Appeared to me, with two antlers of gold,
Between two streams, under a laurel's shade,
At sunrise, in the season's bitter cold.

Her sight was so suavely merciless
That I left work to follow her at leisure,
Like the miser who looking for his treasure
Sweetens with that delight his bitterness.

Around her lovely neck "Do not touch me"
Was written with topaz and diamond stone,
"My Caesar's will has been to make me free."

Already toward noon had climbed the sun,
My weary eyes were not sated to see,
When I fell in the stream and she was gone.

CXCI

As it is life eternal to see God,
Nor do we wish, nor may, for more than this,
So to see you, my Lady, is my bliss
In my frail life that the days ride and prod.

I have never seen you as fair as now,
If my heart to my eyes confides the truth;
O lovely hour that blesses every vow
Of mine, and passes wishes, hopes and youth!

And if its flight were not made in such haste,
I should not ask for more; for if some live
Only by scent, and such talks we believe,

Some by water and fire, and touch and taste
Can soften things devoid of any grace,
Why should I not be calmed by your dear face?

CXCII

Stiamo, Amor, a veder la gloria nostra,
Cose sopra natura altère e nove:
Vedi ben quanta in lei dolcezza piove;
Vedi lume ch 'l cielo in terra mostra;

Vedi quant'arte dora e 'mperla e 'nostra
L'abito eletto, e mai non visto altrove,
Che dolcemente i piedi e gli occhi move
Per questa di bei colli ombrosa chiostra.

L'erbetta verde e i fior di color mille
Sparsi sotto quel elce antiqua e negra,
Pregan pur che 'l bel pe' li prema o tócchi;

E 'l ciel di vaghe e lucide faville
S'accende intorno, e 'n vista si rallegra
D'esser fatto seren da sí belli occhi.

CXCIII

Pasco la mente d'un sí nobil cibo,
Ch'ambrosia e nectar non invidio a Giove;
Ché sol mirando, oblio ne l'alma piove
D'ogni altro dolce, e Lete al fondo bibo.

Talor ch'odo dir cose, e 'n cor describo,
Per che da sospirar sempre ritrove,
Rapto per man d'Amor, né so ben dove,
Doppia dolcezza in un vólto delibo:

Ché quella voce in fin al ciel gradita,
Suona in parole sí leggiadre, e care,
Che penser no 'l poría, chi non l'ha udita.

Allor inseme, in men d'un palmo, appare
Visibilmente, quanto in questa vita
Arte, ingegno, e natura, e 'l ciel pò fare.

CXCII

Let us look, Love, and wonder at our glory,
At objects beyond nature great and new:
You see what sweetness falls on her like dew,
You see what light spreads heaven's allegory.

You see what art to gold and pearl allies,
And to purple, her form nowhere else made,
And how sweetly she moves her feet, her eyes,
In this enclosure of fine hills and shade.

The small green grass and the many-hued flowers
Under that dark and ancient ilex-tree
Beg her light foot to press them where they rise;

And in the sky are kindled shining showers
Of pretty sparks, and it looks full of glee
To be made limpid by such lovely eyes.

CXCIII

I feed my mind on such a divine food,
That nectar or ambrosia I despise,
For, if I look, it pours into my eyes
Like Lethe's source, the loss of other good.

Then I hear something said and then I think
Of it again to find reasons to sigh;
Kidnapped by Love I know not where or why,
A double sweetness from one face I drink,

Because that voice which to the sky brings mirth
Resounds in words so gentle and so dear,
That no one can conceive who does not hear.

Then suddenly at once it becomes clear
And visible to what wonders on earth
Art, genius, nature, heaven can give birth.

CXCIV

L'aura gentil, che rasserena i poggi
Destando i fior per questo ombroso bosco,
Al soave suo spirto, riconosco,
Per cui conven che 'n pena e 'n fama poggi.

Per ritrovar ove 'l cor lasso appoggi,
Fuggo dal mi' natío dolce aere tósco;
Per far lume al penser torbido e fosco,
Cerco 'l mio sole e spero vederlo oggi.

Nel qual provo dolcezze tante e tali
Ch'Amor per forza a lui mi riconduce;
Poi sí m'abbaglia che 'l fuggir m'è tardo.

I' chiedrei a scampar, non arme, anzi ali;
Ma perir mi dá 'l ciel per questa luce,
Ché da lunge mi struggo e da presso ardo.

CXCV

Di dí in dí vo cangiando il viso e 'l pelo;
Né però smorso i dolce inescati ami,
Né sbranco i verdi et invescati rami
De l'arbor che né sol cura né gielo.

Senz'acqua il mare e senza stelle il cielo
Fia inanzi ch'io non sempre téma, e brami,
La sua bell'ombra, e ch'i' non odi', et ami,
L'alta piaga amorosa, che mal celo.

Non spero del mio affanno aver mai posa,
In fin ch'i' mi disosso, e snervo, e spolpo,
O la nemica mia pietá n'avesse.

Esser pò in prima ogni impossibil cosa,
Ch'altri che morte, od ella, sani 'l colpo,
Ch'Amor co' suoi belli occhi al cor m'impresse.

CXCIV

The gentle aura that clears up the hills
Waking the flowers throughout the shady wood
I recognize by its enchanting mood,
And I must lean on fame and on my ills.

To find again a place that will support
My heart, I leave my own sweet Tuscan air;
To give to my dark thought the light's resort,
I seek my sun, and hope to see it there.

So great a sweetness from it in me springs,
That Love by force directs and pushes me;
Then it dazzles me so that I must flee.

I would beg, to be safe, not arms but wings;
But heaven wants me from this light to die,
For when absent I fail, and burn near by.

CXCV

Day after day I change my face, my hair,
But do not drop the bit of hook and bait,
Nor do I shake the green ensnaring weight
Of the bay-leaves that for no climate care.

Without water the sea, starless the sky
Shall be seen when I cease to love and chide
Its pleasant shade, or to hate, and to sigh
For the amorous wound I cannot hide.

I do not hope to rest from this ordeal
Until my bones and nerves and flesh succumb,
Or till my enemy pities me once.

Any strange thing can happen before some
Other beings than Death or herself heal
The blow that Love dealt me with her fair glance.

CXCVI

L'aura serena che fra verdi fronde
Mormorando a ferir nel vólto viemme,
Fammi risovenir quand'Amor diemme
Le prime piaghe, sí dolci profonde;

E 'l bel viso veder, ch'altri m'asconde,
Che sdegno, o gelosia, celato tiemme;
E le chiome or avolte in perle e 'n gemme,
Allora sciolte e sovra òr terso bionde;

Le quali ella spargea sí dolcemente,
E raccogliea con sí leggiadri modi,
Che ripensando ancor trema la mente;

Torsele il tempo poi in piú saldi nodi,
E strinse 'l cor d'un laccio sí possente
Che Morte sola fia ch'indi lo snodi.

CXCVII

L'aura celeste che 'n quel verde lauro
Spira, ov'Amor ferí nel fianco Apollo,
Et a me pose un dolce giogo al collo,
Tal che mia libertá tardi restauro,

Pò quello in me che nel gran vecchio mauro
Medusa, quando in selce transformollo;
Né posso dal bel nodo omai dar crollo,
Lá 've il sol perde, non pur l'ambra, o l'auro;

Dico le chiome bionde e 'l crespo laccio,
Che sí soavemente lega, e stringe,
L'alma che d'umiltate e non d'altr'armo.

L'ombra sua sola fa 'l mio cor un ghiaccio,
E di bianca paura il viso tinge;
Ma li occhi hanno vertú di farne un marmo.

CXCVI

The serene aura that among green boughs
Murmuring came to strike me in the face,
Makes me remember when Love did arouse
My heart with the first wounds so sweet to trace;

It makes me see the face that now condemns
Me, and scorn and jealousy withhold;
And the hair all entwined with pearls and gems,
Then scattered, and more blond than limpid gold;

And she spread it so sweetly in the light,
And gathered up again in such soft ways,
That in thinking of it my mind still sways;

Time has entwisted it in knots so tight,
And tied my heart with such a potent noose,
That Death alone can make it free and loose.

CXCVII

The divine aura that in breathing broke
Through the bay where Love pierced Apollo's side,
And imposed on my neck a gentle yoke
So that too late my liberty I chide,

Can do to me what on another wrought
Medusa, when she turned him into stone,
Nor can I toss and pull in that fair knot
Which defeats amber, gold, and even sun.

I mean the yellow hair and curly snare
Which so sweetly can tie, so sweetly tear
My soul that with humility I arm.

Her very shadow makes my heart of ice,
And paints my countenance with pale alarm;
But I am turned to marble by her eyes.

CXCVIII

L'aura soave al sole spiega e vibra
L'auro ch'Amor di sua man fila e tesse
Lá da' belli occhi, e de le chiome stesse
Lega 'l cor lasso, e i lievi spirti cribra.

Non ho medolla in osso, o sangue in fibra,
Ch'i' non senta tremar, pur ch'i' m'apresse
Dove è chi morte e vita inseme, spesse
Volte, in frale bilancia, appende e libra.

Vedendo ardere i lumi, ond'io m'accendo,
E folgarare i nodi, ond'io son preso,
Or su l'omero destro et or sul manco,

I' no 'l posso ridir, ché no 'l comprendo;
Da ta' due luci è l'intelletto offeso,
E di tanta dolcezza oppresso e stanco.

CXCIX

O bella man, che mi destringi 'l core,
E' n poco spazio la mia vita chiudi;
Man, ov'ogni arte e tutti loro studî
Poser Natura e 'l Ciel per farsi onore;

Di cinque perle oriental colore,
E sol ne le mie piaghe acerbi e crudi,
Diti schietti soavi, a tempo ignudi
Consente or voi, per arricchirme, Amore.

Candido, leggiadretto e caro guanto,
Che copria netto avorio e fresche ròse,
Chi vide al mondo mai sí dolci spoglie?

Cosí avess'io del bel velo altrettanto!
O inconstanzia de l'umane cose!
Pur questo è furto, e vien chi me ne spoglie.

CXCVIII

The mellow aura in the sun displays
The gold that Love himself both spins and weaves
From the fair eyes, and with the same hair preys
On my sad heart and my frail spirit cleaves.

No marrow in my bones, blood in my veins
That does not tremble when I reach the trail
Where she suspends and poises and retains
My death and life upon a flimsy scale.

Seeing those lights that set on fire my brand,
And the knots kindle that fasten me tight
On the left shoulder now, now on the right,

I cannot say, I do not understand;
By such two lights my intellect is torn,
And by so great a sweetness weighed and worn.

CXCIX

O lovely hand that clasp and hold my heart
And in a tiny space enclose my days;
Hand where was spent every care and art
Of nature and of heaven for its praise,

With your five pearls of oriental make,
Only inside my wounds cruel and rough,
Fingers delicate, neat, that sometimes Love
Allows to be uncovered for my sake;

Charming and spotless glove that I adore,
Used to wrap ivory, roses of spring,
Who ever saw on earth such sweet telltale?

Could I have the same token of her veil!
O instability of every thing!
This is a theft they ask me to restore.

CC

Non pur quell'una bella ignuda mano,
Che con grave mio danno si riveste,
Ma l'altra, e le duo braccia accorte e preste
Son a stringere il cor timido e piano.

Lacci Amor mille, e nesun tende in vano
Fra quelle vaghe nove forme oneste,
Ch'adornan sí l'alto abito celeste,
Ch'agiunger no 'l pò stil né 'ngegno umano.

Li occhi sereni e le stellanti ciglia,
La bella bocca, angelica, di perle
Piena e di ròse e di dolci parole,

Che fanno altrui tremar di meraviglia,
E la fronte, e le chiome, ch'a vederle
Di state, a mezzo dí, vincono il sole.

CCI

Mia ventura, et Amor, m'avean sí adorno
D'un bello aurato e serico trapunto,
Ch'al sommo del mio ben quasi era aggiunto,
Pensando meco a chi fu quest'intorno.

Né mi riede a la mente mai quel giorno,
Che mi fe' ricco, e povero, in un punto,
Ch'i' non sia d'ira, e di dolor, compunto,
Pien di vergogna, e d'amoroso scorno;

Ché la mia nobil preda non piú stretta
Tenni al bisogno, e non fui piú constante
Contra lo sforzo sol d'un'angioletta;

O, fugendo, ale non giunsi a le piante,
Per far almen di quella man vendetta,
Che de li occhi mi trae lagrime tante.

CC

Not just one single hand naked and fair
That, to my sorrow, is covered anew,
But both, and her arms quick and cunning, too,
Are grasping my poor heart that does not dare.

A thousand snares Love lays, and not one sign
Is vain among those new, dear, honest forms
Which so adorn her attitude divine
That they dispense with human skill and norms:

The serene eyes, the lashes' starry curls,
The lovely mouth of angel, full of pearls
And of roses and sweet words, and the voice,

That make all others tremble and rejoice,
And the forehead, the hair, that if someone
Sees in summer, at noon, glows more than sun.

CCI

Love and my fortune had so flattered me
With a beautiful golden silken stuff,
That I had almost touched heaven above
Thinking of her on whom it used to be.

And I never remember that past day
Which made me rich and poor in the same point,
Without being by wrath and anguish joined,
Distressed by shame and amorous dismay,

Because I did not hold faster my grand
Prey as I wished, and put not more constraint
Against the effort of a little saint,

And because flying I did not add wings
To my feet, and take vengeance on that hand
Which draws so many tears from my eyes' springs.

CCII

D'un bel, chiaro, polito e vivo ghiaccio
Move la fiamma che m'incende e strugge,
E sí le véne e 'l cor m'asciuga e sugge
Che 'nvisibilemente i' mi disfaccio.

Morte, giá per ferire alzato 'l braccio,
Come irato ciel tona o leon rugge,
Va perseguendo mia vita che fugge;
Et io, pien di paura, tremo, e taccio.

Ben poría ancor pietá con amor mista,
Per sostegno di me, doppia colonna
Porsi fra l'alma stanca e 'l mortal colpo;

Ma io no 'l credo, né 'l conosco in vista
Di quella dolce mia nemica, e donna:
Né di ciò lei, ma mia ventura incolpo.

CCIII

Lasso!, ch'i' ardo, et altri non mel crede;
Sí crede ogni uom, se non sola colei
Che sovr'ogni altra, e ch'i' sola vorrei:
Ella non par che 'l creda, e sí sel vede.

Infinita bellezza, e poca fede,
Non vedete voi 'l cor nelli occhi mei?
Se non fusse mia stella, i' pur devrei
Al fonte di pietá trovar mercede.

Quest'arder mio, di che vi cal sí poco,
E i vostri onori, in mie rime diffusi,
Ne porían infiammar fors'ancor mille;

Ch'i' veggio nel penser, dolce mio foco,
Fredda una lingua, e duo belli occhi chiusi
Rimaner, dopo noi, pien di faville.

CCII

From a beautiful, clear, polished, live ice
Flows the flame that ignites me and devours,
And heart and veins it so squeezes and dries,
That in a hidden way I lose my powers.

Having already raised his arm to wound,
As wrath makes lions roar and the sky thunder,
Death persecutes my life that fleeing swooned,
And I, silent, in terror, tremble, ponder.

Pity mingled with love could even now
For my support place itself like a double
Column between the soul and the last blow;

But I do not believe, I do not glean
This from the sight of my foe and my queen:
I blame not her but fortune for my trouble.

CCIII

Alas! I burn and one does not trust me:
Everyone believes it save that one
Whom above others I desire, alone:
She seems not to believe, yet she must see.

O endless beauty and little belief,
Do you not see my eyes showing my mind?
It may not be my star, still I should find
At the fountain of pity some relief.

This fire of mine, for which you do not care,
And your honours exalted by my verse,
Would set aflame perhaps a thousand more;

But I see in my thought, my sweetest glare,
A frozen tongue and two eyes' darkened door
Remain after us bright, lucid, and terse.

CCIV

Anima, che diverse cose tante
Vedi, odi, e leggi, e parli, e scrivi, e pensi;
Occhi miei vaghi, e tu, fra li altri sensi,
Che scorgi al cor l'alte parole sante;

Per quanto non vorreste o poscia od ante
Esser giunti al camin che sí mal tiensi,
Per non trovarvi i duo bei lumi accensi,
Né l'orme impresse de l'amate piante?

Or con sí chiara luce, e con tai segni
Errar non dêsi in quel breve viaggio
Che ne pò far d'etterno albergo degni.

Sfòrzati al cielo, o mio stanco coraggio,
Per la nebbia entro de' suoi dolci sdegni
Seguendo i passi onesti, e 'l divo raggio.

CCV

Dolci ire, dolci sdegni e dolci paci,
Dolce mal, dolce affanno, e dolce peso
Dolce parlare, e dolcemente inteso,
Or di dolce ôra, or pien di dolci faci;

Alma, non ti lagnar, ma soffra e taci,
E tempra il dolce amaro, che n'ha offeso,
Col dolce onor che d'amar quella hai preso
A cui io dissi:—Tu sola mi piaci.—

Forse ancor fia chi sospirando dica,
Tinto di dolce invidia:—Assai sostenne,
Per bellissimo amor, quest'al suo tempo.—

Altri:—O fortuna a gli occhi miei nemica!
Perché non la vid'io? perché non venne
Ella piú tardi, o ver io piú per tempo?—

CCIV

Soul that so many diverse times and tenses
See, hear and read, speak and think and record;
My longing eyes, and you, among the senses,
That bring into my heart the holy word,

What would you give to be, now or before,
Upon the path that we so badly meet,
Not finding there the two fires we adore
Nor the imprints of her beloved feet?

Now, with such a clear light and with such signs,
He cannot err, who that journey designs
Which may allow him an eternal stay.

Strive for the sky, o my courage forlorn,
Following through the mist of her sweet scorn
Those graceful steps and that heavenly ray.

CCV

Sweet quarrels, sweet resentments and sweet peaces,
Sweet illness, sweet distress, sweet tribulation,
Sweet speech that understood sweetly releases
Now a sweet air, now a sweet conflagration;

My soul, do not complain but suffer more,
And temper the sweet bitter of your shame
With the sweet honour of loving the same
To whom I said one time:—You I adore.—

There may be some who between sighs will say,
Flushing with a sweet envy:—He bore much
For a beautiful love in his own time.—

Others:—O fortune hostile to my day!
Why did I not see her? Why did not such
Woman come later, or I in her time?—

CCVI

S'i' 'l dissi mai, ch'i' vegna in odio a quella
Del cui amor vivo, e senza 'l qual morrei;
S'i' 'l dissi, che 'miei dí sian pochi, e rei,
E di vil signoria l'anima ancella;
S'i' 'l dissi, contra me s'arme ogni stella,
E dal mio lato sia
Paura e gelosia,
E la nemica mia
Piú feroce vèr' me sempre e piú bella.

S'i' 'l dissi, Amor l'aurate sue quadrella
Spenda in me tutte, e l'impiombate in lei;
S'i' 'l dissi, cielo e terra, uomini e dèi
Mi sian contrarî, et essa ogni or piú fella;
S'i' 'l dissi, chi con sua cieca facella
Dritto a morte m'invia,
Pur come suol si stia,
Né mai piú dolce o pia
Vèr' me si mostri, in atto od in favella.

S'i' 'l dissi mai, di quel ch'i' men vorrei,
Piena trovi quest'aspra e breve via;
S'i' 'l dissi, il fero ardor, che mi desvia,
Cresca in me, quanto il fier ghiaccio in costei;
S'i' 'l dissi, unqua non veggian li occhi mei
Sol chiaro, o sua sorella,
Né donna, né donzella,
Ma terribil procella,
Qual Faraone in perseguir li ebrei.

S'i' 'l dissi, co i sospir, quant'io mai fêi,
Sia pietá per me morta, e cortesia;
S'i' 'l dissi, il dir s'innaspri, che s'udia
Sí dolce allor che vinto mi rendrei;
S'i' 'l dissi, io spiaccia a quella ch'i' tôrrei,
Sol, chiuso in fosca cella,
Dal dí che la mamella
Lasciai, fin che si svella
Da me l'alma, adorar: forse e 'l farei.

CCVI

If I ever said so, let her deny
And hate me, for whose love I rise and fall;
If I said so, may my days be dismal
And my soul subject to a tyrant's tie;
If I said so, may every star defy
Me and besiege me here
With jealousy and fear,
And my enemy dear
Become more fair, more fain to make me cry.

If I said so, may Love thrust his sharp die
Of gold in me, the leaden in her hall;
If I said so, may sky and earth and all
Gods and men assault me, she never sigh;
If I said so, may who with blinded eye
Brings me to death so near,
In such way always steer,
And never sweet and clear
Approach me or by action or reply.

If I ever said so, may my life sprawl
Full of whatever is to me more drear;
If I said so, may the flame of this spear
Leap inside me and as her ice grow tall;
If I said so, may I see a black wall,
No sun, no moon, his shy
Sister, no maid go by;
And may I see the high
Tempest that did Pharaoh's soldiers appal.

If I said sighing what I cannot scrawl,
Let pity die and kindness disappear;
If I said so, let the words used to cheer
So sweetly when I failed, now pierce my gall;
If I said so, may I hurt her whose thrall
I am in a cell dry
And dark, since I did lie
In my crib till I die,
To worship with my soul: I should not stall.

Ma s'io no 'l dissi, chi sí dolce apria
Meo cor a speme ne l'etá novella,
Regga 'ncor questa stanca navicella
Col governo di sua pietá natia,
Né diventi altra, ma pur qual solía
Quando piú non potei,
Che me stesso perdei,
Né piú perder devrei.
Mal fa, chi tanta fé sí tosto oblia.

I' no 'l dissi giá mai, né dir poría,
Per oro, o per cittadi, o per castella.
Vinca 'l ver dunque, e si rimanga in sella,
E vinta a terra caggia la bugia.
Tu sai in me il tutto, Amor: s'ella ne spia,
Dinne quel che dir dêi.
I' beato direi,
Tre volte, e quattro, e sei,
Chi, devendo languir, si morí pria.

Per Rachel ho servito, e non per Lia;
Né con altra saprei
Viver; e sosterrei,
Quando 'l ciel ne rappella,
Girmen, con ella, in sul **carro de Elia.**

CCVII

Ben mi credea passar mio tempo omai
Come passato avea quest'anni a dietro,
Senz'altro studio, e senza novi ingegni;
Or poi che da madonna i' non impetro
L'usata aita, a che condutto m'hai,
Tu 'l vedi, Amor, che tal arte m'insegni.
Non so s'i' me ne sdegni;
Ché 'n questa etá mi fai divenir **ladro**
Del bel lume leggiadro,

But if I said not so, may who did rear
Me from my tender youth with hopes so nigh,
Rule for a while this weary boat I ply
With the helm of her pity that does hear;
May she not be another, but her sheer
Self that once used to trawl
Me when I feared the squall
That shall not make me crawl.
It is an evil at such faith to sneer.

I never said so, and I could not veer,
For castles, cities, gold, I could not try;
Let the truth win, let it never comply,
Let falsehood, fallen down, reveal its gear.
You know all of me, Love; if she should peer,
Tell her the big, the small.
Ever blessed I shall—
Three, four and six times—call
Him who condemned to languish chose a bier.

For Rachel I have served, and not for Leah;
With no one else I haul
My life; and dare withal,
When summoned to the sky,
With her to fly on the cart of Elijah.

CCVII

I believed that I should now spend my time
As I spent it so many years before,
Without any new study or new skill;
Since I ask not for pity any more
From my lady, you see, Love, in what clime
You make me live, teaching me what you will.
I know not if this ill
Disturbs me, at my age to be a thief
Of her sweet eyes' relief,

Senza 'l qual non vivrei in tanti affanni.
Cosí avess'io i primi anni
Preso lo stil ch'or prender mi bisogna;
Ché 'n giovenil fallir è men vergogna.

Li occhi soavi, ond'io soglio aver vita,
De le divine lor alte bellezze
Fûrmi in sul cominciar tanto cortesi,
Che 'n guisa d'uom cui non proprie ricchezze,
Ma celato di fòr soccorso aita,
Vissimi; ché né lor né altri offesi.
Or, ben ch'a me ne pesi,
Divento ingiurioso, et importuno;
Ché 'l poverel digiuno
Vèn ad atto talor ch 'n miglior stato
Avria in altrui biasmato.
Se le man di Pietá invidia m'ha chiuse,
Fame amorosa, e 'l non poter, mi scuse.

Ch'i' ho cercate giá vie piú di mille
Per provar senza lor se mortal cosa
Mi potesse tenér in vita un giorno.
L'anima, poi ch'altrove non ha posa,
Corre pur a l'angeliche faville;
Et io, che son di cera, al foco torno.
E pongo mente intorno,
Ove si fa men guardia a quel ch'i' bramo;
E come augel in ramo,
Ove men teme, ivi piú tosto è còlto,
Cosí dal suo bel vólto
L'involo or uno et or un altro sguardo;
E di ciò inseme mi nutrico et ardo.

Di mia morte mi pasco, e vivo in fiamme:
Stranio cibo, e mirabil salamandra!
Ma miracol non è, da tal si vòle.
Felice agnello, a la penosa mandra
Mi giacqui un tempo; or a l'estremo famme
E Fortuna et Amor pur come sòle:
Cosí ròse e viole

Without which I should never know such cares.
Had I from my first years
Chosen the style that now I must reclaim!
For in a youthful sin there is less shame.

The lovely eyes from which I draw my sense
Were so courteous to me of their fair light
In the beginning of my painful quest,
That like a man not helped by riches' might,
But by a hidden outward providence,
I lived; nor them nor others I distressed.
Now, though I am oppressed
By my guilt, I become mean and unpleasant;
For the poor hungry peasant
May commit actions that in better state
Himself would deprecate.
If envy did the hands of Mercy tie,
May love's starvation and my want reply.

For I have trod more than a thousand roads,
To try if outside them a mortal thing
Could keep me living for a single day.
My soul, that to no other place will cling,
Still runs toward those angelic abodes;
And I, who am of wax, burn in their ray.
I spy from every way
Where they keep lesser vigilance on thieves;
And as a bird through leaves,
When it is less afraid falls prey to chance,
So from her countenance
I steal one look, another, through her eye;
And by this I am nourished and I die.

I feed on my own death, I live in flames:
A curious food and an odd salamander!
No miracle, because it comes from there.
A lucky lamb in the flock I did wander
And lie sometime; now to the final shames
Fortune and Love push me for my despair:
Thus roses, violets fair,

Ha primavera, e 'l verno ha neve e ghiaccio.
Però, s'i' mi procaccio
Quinci e quindi alimenti al viver curto.
Se vòl dir che sia furto,
Sí ricca donna deve esser contenta,
S'altri vive del suo, ch'ella no 'l senta.

Chi no 'l sa di ch'io vivo, e vissi sempre,
Dal dí che 'n prima que' belli occhi vidi,
Che mi fecer cangiar vita e costume?
Per cercar terra e mar da tutt'i lidi,
Chi pò saver tutte l'umane tempre?
L'un vive, ecco, d'odor, lá sul gran fiume;
Io qui di foco e lume
Queto i frali e famelici miei spirti.
Amor (e vo' ben dirti),
Disconvensi a signor l'esser sí parco.
Tu hai li strali, e l'arco;
Fa di tua man, non pur bramand'io mora:
Ch'un bel morir tutta la vita onora.

Chiusa fiamma è piú ardente; e se pur cresce,
In alcun modo piú non pò celarsi;
Amor, i' 'l so, che 'l provo a le tue mani.
Vedesti ben, quando sí tacito arsi;
Or de' miei gridi a me medesmo incresce,
Che vo noiando e prossimi e lontani.
O mondo, o penser vani!
O mia forte ventura a che m'adduce!
O di che vaga luce
Al cor mi nacque la tenace speme,
Onde l'annoda e preme,
Quella che con tua forza al fin mi mena!
La colpa è vostra, e mio 'l danno, e la pena.

Cosí di ben amar porto tormento,
E del peccato altrui cheggio perdóno;
Anzi del mio, ché devea torcer li occhi
Dal troppo lume, e di sirene al suono
Chiuder li orecchi; et ancor non men pento,

Come out in spring, in winter snow and ice.
Therefore if I entice
From here and there some substance for my walled
Life, if theft this is called,
Such a rich woman must be satisfied
If some live on her wealth and on her pride.

Who does not know by what I lived and live
Since I first saw those two beautiful eyes,
That made me change my costume to the seam?
Although one may new lands and seas surmise,
Who will discover all the human hive?
One lives by smell, I say, on a great stream;
I here by fire and beam
Appease my ailing, famished need and rue.
Love (I want to tell you),
It becomes not a lord to fall so low.
You own arrows and bow:
Let me by your own hand, not by need fail,
For to die well honours our life's whole tale.

A closed flame is more ardent: if it grows,
In no way one can hide it any more;
Love, I know this, I feel it in your scar.
You saw how silently I burned before;
Now for these groans I suffer other woes,
For I tire who is near, and who is far.
O world, o thoughts at war!
O my crude fortune that have caused my plight!
O by what shining light
She took my heart, by what tenacious hope,
Tying it with a rope,
She who aided by you now has me slain!
The guilt is yours, mine the damage and pain.

And thus of loving well I bear the wrong,
And ask forgiveness for another's sin,
Perhaps my own, because I did not close
My eyes in the great light, and in the din
Of sirens did not shut my ears; my tongue

Che di dolce veleno il cor trabocchi.
Aspett'io pur che scocchi,
L'ultimo colpo chi mi diede 'l primo:
E fia, s'i' dritto estimo,
Un modo di pietate, occider tosto,
Non essendo ei disposto
A far altro di me che quel che soglia;
Ché ben muor chi morendo esce di doglia.

Canzon mia, fermo in campo
Starò, ch'elli è disnor morir fuggendo;
E me stesso reprendo
Di tai lamenti; sí dolce è mia sorte,
Pianto, sospiri e morte!
Servo d'Amor, che queste rime leggi,
Ben non ha 'l mondo che 'l mio mal pareggi.

CCVIII

Rapido fiume, che d'alpestra vena
Rodendo intorno, ond 'l tuo nome prendi,
Notte e dí meco disioso scendi
Ov'Amor me, te sol Natura mena,

Vattene innanzi: il tuo corso non frena
Né stanchezza né sonno; e pria che rendi
Suo dritto al mar, fiso u' si mostri attendi
L'erba piú verde, e l'aria piú serena.

Ivi è quel nostro vivo e dolce sole
Ch'addorna e 'nfiora la tua riva manca:
Forse (oh, che spero?) el mio tardar le dole.

Basciale 'l piede, o la man bella e bianca;
Dille, e 'l basciar sie 'n vece di parole:
—Lo spirto è pronto, ma la carne è stanca.—

Repents not, but the sweet bane overflows.
I wait for the last blows
From the same hand that inflicted the first:
It would not be the worst
Act, but kindness itself to kill me soon;
I can expect no boon
From him, except what he does always give:
For he dies well who out of pain will live.

My song, I will stay firm
In the field; 'tis dishonour to die fleeing;
And I reproach my being
For these complaints; I have such a sweet chance
To cry, sigh for a glance!
Servant of Love, who read this poem's lines,
The world has no one else who like me pines.

CCVIII

Swift river that from vein of Alpine blue
Running around, whence you derive your name,
Night and day carry on your and my claim
There where Love directs me and Nature you,

Go on; your course is not restrained by fear
Of weariness or sleep; before you trace
Its rights back to the sea, observe a place
Where the grass is more green, the air more clear.

There lies that sweet and living sun of ours
Which graces your left bank with many flowers:
She may (what hope!) blame my delay and mourn.

Give a kiss to her foot, to her white hand;
Make her with kisses, not words, understand:
—The soul is ready, but the flesh is worn.—

CCIX

I dolci colli ov'io lasciai me stesso,
Partendo, onde partir giá mai non posso,
Mi vanno innanzi; et èmmi ogni or a dosso
Quel caro peso, ch'Amor m'ha commesso.

Meco di me mi meraviglio spesso,
Ch'i' pur vo sempre, e non son ancor mosso
Dal bel giogo piú volte indarno scosso,
Ma com' piú me n'allungo, e piú m'appresso.

E qual cervo ferito di saetta,
Col ferro avelenato dentr'al fianco,
Fugge, e piú duolsi quanto piú s'affretta,

Tal io, con quello stral dal lato manco,
Che mi consuma, e parte mi diletta,
Di duol mi struggo, e di fuggir mi stanco.

CCX

Non da l'ispano Ibero a l'indo Idaspe
Ricercando del mar ogni pendice,
Né dal lito vermiglio a l'onde caspe,
Né 'n ciel né 'n terra è piú d'una fenice.

Qual destro corvo o qual manca cornice
Canti 'l mio fato? O qual Parca l'innaspe?
Ché sol trovo Pietá sorda com'aspe,
Misero, onde sperava esser felice!

Ch'i' non vo' dir di lei; ma chi la scorge,
Tutto 'l cor di dolcezza e d'amor gli empie;
Tanto n'ha seco, e tant'altrui ne porge.

E per far mie dolcezze amare et empie,
O s'infinge, o non cura, o non s'accorge
Del fiorir queste inanzi tempo tempie.

CCIX

The darling hills where I left my best part,
Parting from them that I can never leave,
Loom before me; and they still weigh my heart
With that dear weight Love wants me to retrieve.

I often marvel at the stubborn way
I still go on, never able to break
The fair yoke that in vain I try to shake;
And the farther I go, the nearer stay.

Like a hart who, when wounded by an arrow,
With the poisonous spear inside his marrow,
Flees on and suffers more, the more he speeds,

So, with this dart in my left side that bleeds,
Which consumes me and yet gives me delight,
I faint with pain and grow tired of this flight.

CCX

From Indian waters to the springs of Spain,
Exploring every secret of the sea,
From the red shores down to the Caspian main,
Only one single phoenix there can be.

What crow from the left side, raven from right
Sings my doom? Or what Fate winds it and clasps?
For I alone find Pity deaf as asps,
Poor wretch, just where I hoped to have delight!

I will not speak of her, but who perceives
Her face, feels in himself sweetness and love;
So much of that she has, so much she gives.

And to make my own sweetness sharp and rough,
She pretends or ignores or cannot see
My temples put forth blooms prematurely.

CCXI

Voglia mi sprona, Amor mi guida e scorge,
Piacer mi tira, usanza mi trasporta,
Speranza mi lusinga e riconforta,
E la man destra al cor giá stanco porge.

E 'l misero la prende, e non s'accorge
Di nostra cieca e disleale scorta;
Regnano i sensi, e la ragion è morta;
De l'un vago desio l'altro risorge.

Vertute, onor, bellezza, atto gentile,
Dolci parole a i be' rami m'han giunto
Ove soavemente il cor s'invesca.

Mille trecento ventisette, a punto
Su l'ora prima, il dí sesto d'aprile
Nel laberinto intrai; né veggio ond'èsca.

CCXII

Beato in sogno e di languir contento,
D'abbracciar l'ombre e seguir l'aura estiva,
Nuoto per mar che non ha fondo o riva,
Solco onde, e 'n rena fondo, e scrivo in vento,

E 'l sol vagheggio sí, ch'elli ha giá spento
Col suo splendor la mia vertú visiva;
Et una cerva errante e fugitiva
Caccio con un bue zoppo e 'nfermo e lento.

Cieco e stanco ad ogni altro ch'al mio danno,
Il qual dí e notte palpitando cerco,
Sol Amor e madonna, e Morte chiamo.

Cosí vénti anni, grave e lungo affanno,
Pur lagrime e sospiri e dolor merco:
In tale stella presi l'èsca e l'amo!

CCXI

My wish spurs me, Love watches and assents,
Pleasure draws me and old habits transport,
Hope flatters me and soothes by her retort,
And to my weary heart her hand presents.

And the wretch takes it, and is not aware
That our leader is treacherous and blind;
Our senses rule, our reason is not there;
With one desire another is aligned.

Virtue and honour, beauty, gentle vows,
Sweet words, have fastened me to the fair boughs
That have ensnared my heart in their sweet tie.

In thirteen hundred twenty-seven, I,
At the first hour, in April's sixth day,
Entered the labyrinth, and lost my way.

CCXII

Blissful in dreams, glad of languishing more,
Of hugging shades and seeking a warm land,
I swim on seas that have no ground nor shore,
I tread waves, write on wind, and plunge in sand,

And court the sun so much, that by its glow
It has extinguished the gift of my sight;
And I hunt a deer wandering in flight
With an ox crippled and ailing and slow.

Blind and dull to all else but to my wrong,
Which day and night in throbbing I pursue,
Only for Love, for Death, for her I look.

Thus twenty years, a grief severe and long,
And tears and sighs and suffering I woo:
From such a star I took my bait and hook!

CCXIII

Grazie ch'a pochi il ciel largo destina:
Rara vertú, non giá d'umana gente,
Sotto biondi capei canuta mente,
E 'n umil donna alta beltá divina;

Leggiadria singulare e pellegrina,
E 'l cantar che ne l'anima si sente,
L'andar celeste, e 'l vago spirto ardente,
Ch'ogni dur rompe, et ogni altezza inchina;

E que' belli occhi che i cor fanno smalti,
Possenti a rischiarar abisso e notti,
E tôrre l'alme a' corpi, e darle altrui;

Col dir pien d'intelletti dolci et alti,
Co i sospiri soavemente rotti:
Da questi magi transformato fui.

CCXIV

Anzi tre dí creata era alma in parte
Da por sua cura in cose altère e nove,
E dispregiar di quel ch'a molti è 'n pregio.
Questa 'ncor dubbia del fatal suo corso,
Sola, pensando, pargoletta, e sciolta,
Intrò di primavera in un bel bosco.

Era un tenero fior nato in quel bosco
Il giorno avanti, e la radice in parte
Ch'appressar no 'l poteva anima sciolta;
Ché v'eran di lacciuo' forme sí nove,
E tal piacer precipitava al corso,
Che perder libertate ivi era in pregio.

Caro, dolce, alto, e faticoso pregio,
Che ratto mi volgesti al verde bosco,
Usato di sviarne a mezzo 'l corso!

CCXIII

Graces that heaven's bounty gives to few:
A rare virtue not found in humankind,
Under blond hair a wise and ripened mind,
And in a humble woman beauty true;

A loveliness unique in excellence,
And the singing that one hears in the heart,
The heavenly gait, the dear and ardent sense
That breaks the hardest, curbs the highest **art**;

The eyes that every heart can petrify,
Puissant to lighten darkness, the abyss,
And to steal souls from bodies where they **stormed**;

And the speech full of reasons pure and high,
With the sighs sweetly broken for my bliss:
By these magicians I have been transformed.

CCXIV

Three days before a soul rose in a part
Where she should care for lofty things and new,
And despise what to many is a prize.
This soul, still doubtful of her fatal course,
Alone and thoughtful, innocent and loose,
Entered in the springtime a lovely wood.

There was a tender flower, born in that wood
The day before, its root was in a part
That could not be approached if you were loose,
For there were little snares of shapes so new,
And such a pleasure driving to that course,
That to lose freedom there was deemed a prize.

Dear, darling, noble and wearisome prize,
That quickly turned my steps to the green **wood**,
Used to confound in the mid of the course!

Et ho cerco poi 'l mondo a parte a parte,
Se versi, o petre, o suco d'erbe nove,
Mi rendesser un dí la mente sciolta.

Ma, lasso!, or veggio che la carne sciolta
Fia di quel nodo, ond'è 'l suo maggior pregio,
Prima che medicine, antiche o nove,
Saldin le piaghe ch'i' presi in quel bosco,
Folto di spine; ond'i' ho ben tal parte,
Che zoppo n'esco, e 'ntrâvi a sí gran corso.

Pien di lacci e di stecchi un duro corso
Aggio a fornire, ove leggera e sciolta
Pianta avrebbe uopo, e sana d'ogni parte.
Ma tu, Signor, c'hai di pietate il pregio,
Porgimi la man destra, in questo bosco;
Vinca 'l tuo sol le mie tenebre nove.

Guarda 'l mio stato, a le vaghezze nove,
Che 'nterrompendo di mia vita il corso,
M'han fatto abitator d'ombroso bosco;
Rendimi, s'esser pò, libera e sciolta
L'errante mia consorte; e fia tuo 'l pregio,
S'ancor teco la trovo in miglior parte.

Or ecco in parte le question mie nove:
S'alcun pregio in me vive, o 'n tutto è corso,
O l'alma sciolta, o ritenuta al bosco.

I have explored the world from part to part,
To see if rhymes or stones or juices new
Would give me back one day a spirit loose.

Alas! I see that my flesh will be loose
From that knot whence derives its greatest prize,
Before some medicines, ancient or new,
Heal the wounds that I suffered in that wood
All thick with thorns; and thus I gained my part
Coming out lame where I ran at full course.

Filled with nooses and sticks, a rugged course
I must pursue, where we need light and loose
Feet that can walk, and sound in every part.
But you, good Lord, whose mercy is our prize,
Give me your right hand in this threatening wood;
Let your sun vanquish this deep darkness new.

Look to my state, to the attractions new
That, interrupting my life's usual course,
Made me a dweller of a shady wood;
Give me back, if it please you, free and loose,
My erring comrade; let it be your prize
If I should find her in a better part.

Here are in part my arguments anew:
Whether my value lives, or spent its course,
Whether my soul is loose, or in the wood.

CCXV

In nobil sangue vita umile e queta,
Et in alto intelletto un puro core,
Frutto senile in sul giovenil fiore,
E 'n aspetto pensoso anima lieta,

Raccolto ha 'n questa donna il suo pianeta,
Anzi 'l re de le stelle; e 'l vero onore,
Le degne lode, e 'l gran pregio, e 'l valore,
Ch'è da stancar ogni divin poeta.

Amor s'è in lei con onestate aggiunto,
Con beltá naturale abito adorno,
Et un atto che parla con silenzio,

E non so che 'nelli occhi, che 'n un punto
Pò far chiara la notte, oscuro il giorno,
E 'l mèl amaro, et adolcir l'assenzio.

CCXVI

Tutto 'l dí piango; e poi la notte, quando
Prendon riposo i miseri mortali,
Trovomi in pianto e raddopiarsi i mali:
Cosí spendo 'l mio tempo lagrimando.

In tristo umor vo li occhi consumando,
E 'l cor in doglia; e son fra li animali
L'ultimo sí, che li amorosi strali
Mi tengon ad ogni or di pace in bando.

Lasso!, che pur da l'un a l'altro sole,
E da l'una ombra a l'altra, ho giá 'l piú corso
Di questa morte che si chiama vita.

Piú l'altrui fallo che 'l mi' mal mi dole;
Ché Pietá viva e 'l mio fido soccorso
Vedem'arder nel foco, e non m'aita.

CCXV

In noble blood a life humble and quiet,
In a high spirit a heart pure and whole,
A mature fruit in a flower young and bright,
And in a pensive face a merry soul,

In my lady her planet did comprise,
The king of all the stars; the true reward,
The worthy praise, the valour and the prize
That would exhaust every divine bard.

Love has been joined to honesty in her,
To genuine beauty an apparel neat,
And an action that speaks in silent trance,

And I know not what thing, that in her glance
At once brightens the night, darkens the air,
Makes honey bitter and makes absinth sweet.

CCXVI

I weep all day; and at night, when the poor
Mortals can take a rest after their fears,
My ills are doubled and I weep still more;
Like this I spend my time in shedding tears.

With this grim humour I consume my sight,
My heart with sorrow; among animals
I am so much the last, that Love appals
Me at all hours and exiles me from quiet.

Alas! going from one to other sun,
From one to other shade, I have now run
Most of the course of this death known as life.

I grieve for others' fault, not for my strife;
Because she sees me, Pity, torn by doubt,
Burn in this fire, yet does not help me out.

CCXVII

Giá desiai con sí giusta querela
E 'n sí fervide rime farmi udire,
Ch'un foco di pietá fêssi sentire
Al duro cor ch'a mezza state gela;

E l'empia nube, che 'l rafredda e vela,
Rompesse a l'aura del mi' ardente dire,
O fêssi quella 'ltrui in odio venire
Che ' belli, onde mi strugge, occhi mi cela.

Or non, odio per lei, per me pietate,
Cerco; ché quel non vo', questo non posso;
Tal fu mia stella, e tal mia cruda sorte!

Ma canto la divina sua beltate;
Ché, quand'i' sia di questa carne scosso,
Sappia 'l mondo che dolce è la mia morte.

CCXVIII

Tra quantunque leggiadre donne e belle
Giunga costei, ch'al mondo non ha pare,
Col suo bel viso suol dell'altre fare
Quel che fa 'l dí de le minori stelle.

Amor par ch'a l'orecchie mi favelle,
Dicendo:—Quanto questa in terra appare,
Fia 'l viver bello; e poi 'l vedrem turbare,
Perir vertuti, e 'l mio regno con elle.

Come natura al ciel la luna e 'l sole,
A l'aere i vènti, a la terra erbe e fronde,
A l'uomo e l'intelletto e le parole,

Et al mar ritollesse i pesci e l'onde;
Tanto e piú fíen le cose oscure e sole,
Se morte li occhi suoi chiude et asconde.—

CCXVII

I once desired by such a righteous plaint
And by such fervent rhymes to find release,
So that a fire of pity might be sent
To the stiff heart that does in summer freeze;

That the bad cloud which makes it chill and dull
Might break in the warm aura of my words,
And of hatred for her all might be full,
Who hides from me the eyes that are my lords.

Hatred for her no longer do I stress,
Nor pity for myself; that I will not,
This I cannot; such is my star and lot!

But I do sing her divine loveliness,
So when I flee the flesh and its decoy,
The world may know that my death is a joy.

CCXVIII

Among whatever ladies sweet and rare
She find herself, who this earth's visions mars,
With her beautiful face she makes of their
Sight what the daylight makes of lesser stars.

Love seems to whisper to me in my ears
And says:—All that she offers to the earth
Makes living lovely; when she disappears
The virtues fall and my kingdom and mirth.—

As if nature had stolen moon and sun
From heaven, grass from earth, and wind from air,
From man the spirit, the words, and the brain,

As if from sea, fishes and waves were gone,
So much more dark and lonely will remain
All things, if death obscures her eyes so fair.

CCXIX

Il cantar novo e 'l pianger delli augelli
In sul dí fanno retentir le valli,
E 'l mormorar de' liquidi cristalli
Giú per lucidi, freschi rivi, e snelli.

Quella c'ha neve il vólto, oro i capelli,
Nel cui amor non fûr mai inganni né falli,
Destami al suon delli amorosi balli,
Pettinando al suo vecchio i bianchi velli.

Cosí mi sveglio a salutar l'Aurora
E 'l Sol ch'è seco, e piú l'altro ond'io fui
Ne' primi anni abagliato, e son ancóra.

I' gli ho veduti alcun giorno ambedui
Levarsi inseme, e 'n un punto e 'n un'ora
Quel far le stelle, e questo sparir lui.

CCXX

Onde tolse Amor l'oro, e di qual vena,
Per far due treccie bionde? e 'n quali spine
Colse le ròse, e 'n qual piaggia le brine
Tènere e fresche, e die' lor polso e lena?

Onde le perle, in ch'ei frange et affrena
Dolci parole, oneste e pellegrine?
Onde tante bellezze, e sí divine,
Di quella fronte, piú che 'l ciel serena?

Da quali angeli mosse, e di qual spera,
Quel celeste cantar che mi disface
Sí che m'avanza omai da disfar poco?

Di qual sol nacque l'alma luce altèra
Di que' belli occhi ond'io ho guerra e pace,
Che mi cuocono il cor in ghiaccio e 'n foco?

CCXIX

The early singing and the weeping birds
In the valleys at dawn resound so tender,
And the murmur of crystal water-words
On brooks lucid and liquid, fresh and slender.

She, whose face is of snow, whose hair of gold,
In whose love never were deceits or chances,
Awakes me with the sound of loving dances
Combing the white fleece of her lover old.

Then I wake up and I salute the Dawn
And her Sun, and the other I love more,
Who dazzled me and does it as before.

I saw them both sometime shine on the lawn
In the same moment, the same point and hour;
One extinguished the stars, one the sun's power.

CCXX

Whence did Love get the gold, and from what ore,
To make two yellow braids? And in what bower
Of thorns did he pluck roses, in what shore
The fresh and fragile hoar, and give it power?

Whence come the pearls in which he breaks and ties
Sweet honest words, incomparably fine?
Whence all the beauties that are so divine
Of that forehead serener than the skies?

From what angels derives and from what sphere,
The holy singing by which I am slain,
So that little is left to give me pain?

From what sun came the lofty light and clear
That declares peace and war to my desire,
And scalds my heart with ice as well as fire?

CCXXI

Qual mio destín, qual forza, o qual inganno,
Mi riconduce disarmato al campo,
Lá 've sempre son vinto? e s'io ne scampo,
Meraviglia n'avrò; s'i' moro, il danno.

Danno non giá, ma pro; sí dolci stanno
Nel mio cor le faville e 'l chiaro lampo,
Che l'abbaglia e lo strugge, e 'n ch'io m'avampo;
E son giá ardendo nel vigesimo anno.

Sento i messi di morte, ove apparire
Veggio i belli occhi e folgorar da lunge;
Poi, s'aven ch'appressando a me li gire

Amor, con tal dolcezza m'unge e punge
Ch'i' no 'l so ripensar, non che ridire;
Ché né 'ngegno né lingua al vero agiunge.

CCXXII

—Liete, e pensose, accompagnate, e sole,
Donne, che ragionando ite per via,
Ove è la vita, ove la morte mia?
Perché non è con voi, com'ella sòle?—

—Liete siam per memoria di quel sole;
Dogliose per sua dolce compagnia,
La qual ne toglie invidia e gelosia,
Che d'altrui ben, quasi suo mal, si dole.—

—Chi pon freno a li amanti, o dá lor legge?—
—Nesun a l'alma; al corpo ira et asprezza:
Questo or in lei, tal or si prova in noi.

Ma spesso ne la fronte il cor si legge:
Sí vedemmo oscurar l'alta bellezza,
E tutti rugiadosi li occhi suoi.—

CCXXI

What destiny, what force or what deceit
Leads me again disarmed to the same field
Where I am always beaten? If I meet
Life I shall marvel, death is my bad yield.

Not really bad, but good; they are so sweet
Those pure sparks in my heart and their deep glares
That dazzle and consume it with their heat:
I have been burning now for twenty years.

I feel Death's messengers when I see them
Appear and sparkle like a distant gem;
Then if by chance Love turns them to my sight,

With such a sweetness he anoints, disjoints,
That I cannot recall it or recite:
Neither talent nor tongue add to truth's points.

CCXXII

—Merry and thoughtful, escorted, alone,
Ladies who in conversing go about,
Where is my life, my death, where is she gone?
Why is she not with you when you are out?—

—We are happy remembering her sun;
And lonely for her lovely company
Taken from us by envy, jealousy,
Which make some loathe the others' good, and shun.—

—Who restrains lovers, who gives them a law?—
—No one, the soul; the body, wrath and rue:
It is in us at times, is in her now.

But the heart often is read in the brow:
Thus all her beauty overcast we saw,
And her eyes wet as the grass in the dew.—

CCXXIII

Quando 'l Sol bagna in mar l'aurato carro,
E l'aere nostro, e la mia mente imbruna,
Col cielo, e co le stelle, e co la luna,
Un'angosciosa e dura notte innarro.

Poi, lasso!, a tal che non m'ascolta narro
Tutte le mie fatiche, ad una ad una,
E col mondo, e con mia cieca fortuna,
Con Amor, con madonna, e meco garro.

Il sonno è 'n bando, e del riposo è nulla;
Ma sospiri, e lamenti in fin a l'alba,
E lagrime che l'alma e li occhi invia.

Vien poi l'aurora, e l'aura fosca inalba,
Me no; ma 'l sol che 'l cor m'arde e trastulla,
Quel pò solo adolcir la doglia mia.

CCXXIV

S'una fede amorosa, un cor non finto,
Un languir dolce, un desiar cortese;
S'oneste voglie in gentil foco accese,
Un lungo error in cieco laberinto;

Se ne la fronte ogni penser depinto,
Od in voci interrotte a pena intese,
Or da paura, or da vergogna offese;
S'un pallor di viola e d'amor tinto;

S'aver altrui piú caro che se stesso;
Se sospirare e lagrimar mai sempre,
Pascendosi di duol, d'ira e d'affanno;

S'arder da lunge et agghiacciar da presso,
Son le cagion ch'amando i' mi distempre,
Vostro, donna, 'l peccato, e mio fia 'l danno.

CCXXIII

When the sun dips its chariot in the sea,
And our horizon and my mind grow dark,
With sky and stars and moon for company,
Upon a hard, cruel night I embark.

To one who does not listen I narrate
One by one all my trials, this and that,
And with the world and with my blinded fate,
With Love, my lady and myself I chat.

Sleep has been banished, all rest is withdrawn,
But sighs and lamentations until dawn,
And tears that the soul sends up to the eyes.

Then comes the dawn, and then the gloomy air
Brightens, not I; but my sun does entice,
The only one that softens my despair.

CCXXIV

If a loving belief, an artless heart,
A soft abandon, a courteous desire,
If honest wishes which a pure fire start,
An endless erring through a blind empire,

If on my forehead every thought revealed,
Or in some words broken as soon as heard,
And now by fear and now by shame repealed,
If in violet and love my face interred,

If holding someone else more than self dear,
Ever weeping and sighing without rest,
Feeding on grief, on anger and torment,

If burning when away and freezing near,
Are the causes why loving I am distressed,
Yours the sin, Lady, mine the punishment.

CCXXV

Dodici donne onestamente lasse,
Anzi dodici stelle, e 'n mezzo un sole
Vidi in una barchetta allegre e sole,
Qual non so s'altra mai onde solcasse.

Simil non credo che Iason portasse
Al vello onde oggi ogni uom vestir si vòle,
Né 'l pastor di ch'ancor Troia si dole;
De' qua' duo tal romor al mondo fasse.

Poi le vidi in un carro triumfale,
Laurea mia con suoi santi atti schifi
Sedersi in parte, e cantar dolcemente.

Non cose umane, o vision mortale:
Felice Autumedon, felice Tifi,
Che conduceste sí leggiadra gente!

CCXXVI

Passer mai solitario in alcun tetto
Non fu quant'io, né fera in alcun bosco;
Ch'i' non veggio 'l bel viso, e non conosco
Altro sol, né quest'occhi hann'altro obietto.

Lagrimar sempre è 'l mio sommo diletto,
Il rider doglia, il cibo assenzio e tòsco;
La notte affanno, e 'l ciel seren m'è fosco,
E duro campo di battaglia il letto.

Il sonno è veramente, qual uom dice,
Parente de la morte, e 'l cor sottragge
A quel dolce penser che 'n vita il tène.

Solo al mondo paese almo, felice,
Verdi rive fiorite, ombrose piagge
Voi possedete, et io piango il mio bene.

CCXXV

I saw twelve women lying gracefully,
Twelve stars indeed, and among them a sun,
In a small boat, full of mirth and alone,
Like to no other boat that furrowed sea.

It was not such that gave Jason the joy
Of the fleece with which now are made our clothes,
Not such that brought the shepherd mourned by Troy,
Of both of which such a great fame arose.

Then I saw them in a triumphal cart,
My Laura with her shyness full of bliss
Sitting aside and singing with sweet art.

No human things they were, no mortal vision;
Happy Automedon, happy Tiphys,
Who were the drivers of such lovely legion!

CCXXVI

Never was sparrow lonely on a roof
As I am now, nor beast in shady nook;
I see not the dear face, I do not look
For other sun, I seek no other proof.

To weep for ever is my greatest pleasure,
To laugh is pain, food is poison, absinth;
The night distress, the clear sky my displeasure,
And like a battlefield my bed is rent.

Sleep is indeed, as men say, a relation
Of death, and steals the heart till it ignores
The gentle thought that makes it live and move.

You alone in the world, land of salvation,
Green, blooming meadows, shadow-covered shores,
You alone own, and I lament, my love.

CCXXVII

Aura che quelle chiome bionde e crespe
Cercondi e movi, e se' mossa da loro
Soavemente, e spargi quel dolce oro,
E poi 'l raccogli e 'n bei nodi il rincrespe,

Tu stai nelli occhi ond'amorose vespe
Mi pungon sí, che 'n fin qua il sento e ploro,
E vacillando cerco il mio tesoro,
Come animal che spesso adombre e 'ncespe;

Ch'or mel par ritrovar, et or m'accorgo
Ch'i' ne son lunge, or mi sollievo or caggio,
Ch'or quel ch'i' bramo, or quel ch'è vero scorgo.

Aer felice, col bel vivo raggio
Rimanti. E tu, corrente e chiaro gorgo,
Ché non poss'io cangiar teco viaggio?

CCXXVIII

Amor co la man destra il lato manco
M'aperse, e piantòvi entro in mezzo 'l core
Un lauro verde, sí che di colore
Ogni smeraldo avria ben vinto e stanco.

Vomer di penna, con sospir del fianco,
E 'l piover giú dalli occhi un dolce umore
L'addornâr sí, ch'al ciel n'andò l'odore,
Qual non so giá se d'altre frondi unquanco.

Fama, onor, e vertute, e leggiadria,
Casta bellezza in abito celeste
Son le radici de la nobil pianta.

Tal la mi trovo al petto, ove ch'i' sia,
Felice incarco; e con preghiere oneste
L'adoro, e 'nchino come cosa santa.

CCXXVII

Aura that fold her blond and curly hair,
And move it softly and are moved by it,
And scatter that sweet gold as you think fit,
Then gather it and bind in knots so fair,

You fill her eyes from where some loving wasp
Stings me so that I feel it here, and grumble,
And, wavering, my treasure seek to clasp,
Like animals that often shy and stumble.

I think I have it, and I realize
That I am far from it, and fall and rise
Seeing now what I wish, now what is true.

Happy air, stay with the ray of her look,
Life-giving, fair. And you, clear running brook,
Why can I not change my journey with you?

CCXXVIII

Love with his right hand opened my left side
And planted in the middle of my heart
A laurel green that by its colour's art
Would cause every emerald to hide.

Ploughshare of pen with sighing of the breast,
And the pouring of sweet rain from the eyes,
Adorned it so that a scent reached the skies
Such as no other leaves ever expressed.

Fame, honour, virtue and enchantment,
A chaste beauty in heavenly array,
Are the roots from which rises the great bay.

Such I find it in me, no matter where
I am, my lovely load; and with deep prayer
I worship and revere it as a saint.

CCXXIX

Cantai, or piango, e non men di dolcezza
Del pianger prendo che del canto presi;
Ch'a la cagion, non a l'affetto intesi
Son i miei sensi vaghi pur d'altezza.

Indi e mansuetudine e durezza
Et atti feri, et umili, e cortesi,
Porto egualmente; né me gravan pesi,
Né l'arme mie punta di sdegni spezza.

Tengan dunque vèr' me l'usato stile
Amor, madonna, il mondo, e mia fortuna;
Ch'i' non penso esser mai se non felice.

Viva o mora, o languisca, un piú gentile
Stato del mio non è sotto la Luna;
Sí dolce è del mio amaro la radice.

CCXXX

I' piansi, or canto; ché 'l celeste lume
Quel vivo sole alli occhi mei non cela,
Nel qual onesto Amor chiaro revela
Sua dolce forza, e suo santo costume:

Onde e' suol trar di lagrime tal fiume,
Per accorciar del mio viver la tela,
Che non pur ponte o guado, o remi o vela,
Ma scampar non potiemmi ale né piume.

Sí profondo era, e di sí larga vena
Il pianger mio, e sí lunge la riva,
Ch'i' v'aggiungeva col penser a pena.

Non lauro o palma, ma tranquilla oliva
Pietá mi manda, e 'l tempo rasserena,
E 'l pianto asciuga, e vuol ancor ch'i' viva.

CCXXIX

I sang, and now I weep, and not less rich
Than a song is to me a weeping sigh;
For to the cause, not the effect, I hitch
My senses ever loving what is high.

Therefore, meekness as well as cruelty,
A fierce appearance, humble or polite,
I bear alike; the weight does not crush me,
Nor are my weapons split by point of spite.

Let them wear toward me their usual stance,
Love and my lady, the world and my chance;
Nothing can come to me but happiness.

Whether I live or die or languish soon,
There is no sweeter state under the moon;
So pleasant is the root of my distress.

CCXXX

I wept, and now I sing; for heaven's light
Does not hide from my eyes that living sun
From which a gracious Love has clearly won
His gentle power and his hallowed rite:

Thence he is wont to draw such stream of wails,
To shorten what is woven in my loom,
That not a bridge or ford or oars or sails
Can help me to escape, nor wing or plume.

So profound was my weeping, of such broad
Vein, and so distant was from me the shore,
That I could hardly reach it with my load.

Not bay or palm tree, but calm olive groves,
Pity sends me, and the weather improves,
And dries my tears and bids me live some more.

CCXXXI

I' mi vivea di mia sorte contento,
Senza lagrime, e senza invidia alcuna;
Che s'altro amante ha piú destra fortuna,
Mille piacer non vaglion un tormento.

Or quei belli occhi, ond'io mai non mi pento
De le mie pene, e men non ne voglio una,
Tal nebbia copre, sí gravosa e bruna,
Che 'l sol de la mia vita quasi spento.

O Natura, pietosa e fera madre,
Onde tal possa, e sí contrarie voglie
Di far cose e disfar tanto leggiadre?

D'un vivo fonte ogni poder s'accoglie:
Ma tu come 'l consenti, o sommo Padre,
Che del tuo caro dono altri ne spoglie?

CCXXXII

Vincitore Alessandro l'ira vinse,
E fe' 'l minore in parte che Filippo:
Che li val se Pirgotile e Lisippo
L'intagliâr, solo, et Appelle il depinse?

L'ira Tideo a tal rabbia sospinse,
Che, morendo ei, si róse Menalippo:
L'ira cieco del tutto, non pur lippo
Fatto avea Silla; a l'ultimo l'estinse.

Sal Valentinian, ch'a simil pena
Ira conduce; e sal quei che ne more,
Aiace, in molti e poi in se stesso forte.

Ira è breve furore e, chi no 'l frena,
È furor lungo, che 'l suo possessore
Spesso a vergogna, e talor mena a morte.

CCXXXI

I lived contented on my fate to hang
Without a tear and without envy's glance,
For if another lover has more chance,
A thousand pleasures are not worth a pang.

Now those fair eyes that make me never hark
To my sorrows, I would not cancel one,
Are covered with a mist so thick and dark,
That it has almost blotted my life's sun.

O Nature, generous and cruel mother,
Whence such a might and such contrasting wills
To do and to undo many a joy?

A single living source each act fulfills,
But how can you allow, o supreme Father,
That others dare your dear gift to destroy?

CCXXXII

Anger victorious Alexander swayed,
And made him somewhat lesser than Philippus:
What gains he if Pyrgoteles, Lysippus,
Carved him alone, and Apelles portrayed?

Anger worked in Tydeus such aberration,
That he gnawed Menalippus when he died:
Anger made wholly blind, not just blear-eyed,
Sylla until he reached his consummation.

Valentinianus knows to what disaster
Anger will bring; Ajax, who from it fell,
Against the others, then his own self strong.

Anger is a brief fury, and a long
Fury when not controlled, that leads a master
Often to shame, some other times to hell.

CCXXXIII

Qual ventura mi fu, quando da l'uno
De' duo i piú belli occhi che mai fûro,
Mirandol di dolor turbato e scuro,
Mosse vertú che fe' 'l mio infermo e bruno!

Send'io tornato a solver il digiuno
Di veder lei che sola al mondo curo,
Fummi il Ciel et Amor men che mai duro,
Se tutte altre mie grazie inseme aduno.

Ché dal destr'occhio, anzi dal destro sole
De la mia donna, al mio destr'occhio venne
Il mal che mi diletta, e non mi dole;

E pur com'intelletto avesse, e penne,
Passò quasi una stella che 'n ciel vóle;
E natura e pietate il corso tenne.

CCXXXIV

O cameretta, che giá fosti un porto
A le gravi tempeste mie diurne,
Fonte se' or di lagrime notturne,
Che 'l dí celate per vergogna porto!

O letticciuol, che requie eri e conforto
In tanti affanni, di che dogliose urne
Ti bagna Amor, con quelle mani eburne,
Solo vèr' me crudeli a sí gran torto!

Né pur il mio secreto, e 'l mio riposo,
Fuggo, ma piú me stesso, e 'l mio pensero,
Che, seguendol talor, levommi a volo;

E 'l vulgo, a me nemico, et odioso
(Chi 'l pensò mai?), per mio refugio chero:
Tal paura ho di ritrovarmi solo.

CCXXXIII

What luck was mine when one of the twain
Handsomest eyes that ever were created,
While I was watching it darkened by pain,
Sent out a virtue that mine obfuscated!

When I returned, delivered from the fast
Of not seeing the only one I love,
Heaven and Love toward me were less rough,
If I count all the graces of my past.

From her right eye, rather from the right sun
Of my lady to my right eye did spring
The ill that delights me without remorse;

And as if it had reason or a wing,
Flew like a star on the horizon,
And nature and compassion led its course.

CCXXXIV

O little room that used to be a harbour
In the severest tempests of my day,
You are now the source of my nocturnal terror
Which from the light for shame I hide away.

O little bed, once a comforting land
After so many woes, from what cruel urn
Love waters you with that ivory hand
Only to me unkind, unjustly stern!

Not only do I flee my place, my peace,
As I did once, but more myself, my thought,
Which when I followed raised me to the sun:

And the vulgar, to me such alien lot,
(Who would believe it?) I seek for release:
Such dread have I to find myself alone.

CCXXXV

Lasso,! Amor mi trasporta, ov'io non voglio;
E ben m'accorgo che 'l dever si varca,
Onde, a chi nel mio cor siede monarca,
Sono importuno assai piú ch'i' non soglio.

Né mai saggio nocchier guardò da scoglio
Nave di merci preziose carca,
Quant'io sempre la debile mia barca
Da le percosse del suo duro orgoglio.

Ma lagrimosa pioggia, e fieri vènti
D'infiniti sospiri or l'hanno spinta,
Ch'è nel mio mare orribil notte e verno,

Ov'altrui noie, a sé doglie e tormenti
Porta, e non altro, giá da l'onde vinta,
Disarmata di vele e di governo.

CCXXXVI

Amor, io fallo, e veggio il mio fallire,
Ma fo sí com'uom ch'arde e 'l foco ha 'n seno,
Ché 'l duol pur cresce, e la ragion vèn meno
Et è giá quasi vinta dal martíre.

Solea frenare il mio caldo desire,
Per non turbare il bel viso sereno:
Non posso piú; di man m'hai tolto il freno,
E l'alma desperando ha preso ardire.

Però, s'oltra suo stile ella s'aventa,
Tu 'l fai, che sí l'accendi, e sí la sproni,
Ch'ogni aspra via per sua salute tenta;

E piú 'l fanno i celesti e rari doni,
C'ha in sé madonna. Or fa almen ch'ella il senta,
E le mie colpe a se stessa perdoni.

CCXXXV

Love drags me where I will not go, alas;
And I know well that I trespass the part
Where to her who holds sway over my heart
I become more annoying than I was.

Never a pilot guarded from a cliff
A ship full of a precious merchandise,
As I survey and guard my fragile skiff
From the attacks of her contempt's surprise.

But now a tearful rain and the rough gales
Of endless sighs have pushed it where it goes,
For in my sea it is winter and night;

There it harms others and brings pain and woes
To itself, nothing else, tossed by the spite
Of waves, and shorn of rudder and of sails.

CCXXXVI

Love, I do err, and I perceive my error,
And I act like a man who feeds his fire,
For the pain grows, and reason will expire,
Being already vanquished by this terror.

I used to check my turbulent desire
Not to disturb the clear face I behold;
I can no more; you made my check retire,
And my soul in despair has grown more bold.

Then if against its style it dares and shifts,
It is your doing, who burn it and goad,
For it tries, to be saved, the roughest road,

And more the doing of the heavenly gifts
Of my lady. Let her at least feel this,
And forgive her own self for what I miss.

CCXXXVII

Non ha tanti animali il mar fra l'onde,
Né lassú sopra 'l cerchio de la Luna
Vide mai tante stelle alcuna notte,
Né tanti augelli albergan per li boschi,
Né tant'erbe ebbe mai campo né piaggia,
Quant'ha 'l mio cor pensier ciascuna sera.

Di dí in dí spero omai l'ultima sera,
Che scevri in me dal vivo terren l'onde,
E mi lasci dormire in qualche piaggia:
Ché tanti affanni uom mai sotto la Luna
Non sofferse quant'io; sannolsi i boschi
Che sol vo ricercando giorno e notte.

Io non ebbi giá mai tranquilla notte,
Ma sospirando andai matino e sera,
Poi ch'Amor fêmmi un cittadin de' boschi.
Ben fia, prima ch'i' posi, il mar senz'onde,
E la sua luce avrá 'l Sol da la Luna,
E i fior d'april morranno in ogni piaggia.

Consumando mi vo di piaggia in piaggia,
El dí pensoso, poi piango la notte;
Né stato ho mai, se non quanto la Luna.
Ratto, come imbrunir veggio la sera,
Sospir del petto, e di li occhi escono onde,
Da bagnar l'erbe, e da crollare i boschi.

Le cittá son nemiche, amici i boschi,
A' miei pensier, che per quest'alta piaggia
Sfogando vo col mormorar de l'onde
Per lo dolce silenzio de la notte:
Tal ch'io aspetto tutto 'l dí la sera,
Che 'l Sol si parta, e dia luogo a la Luna.

Deh, or foss'io col vago de la Luna
Adormentato in qua' che verdi boschi;
E questa ch'anzi vespro a me fa sera,
Con essa e con Amor in quella piaggia

CCXXXVII

The sea has not so much fish in the waves,
Nor above, in the circle of the moon,
Ever did see so many stars the night,
And not so many birds dwell in the woods,
Not so much grass there is on field or shore,
As many thoughts my heart has in the evening.

From day to day I hope for the last evening
To part in me the live earth from the waves,
And let me find some sleep on any shore:
As many trials none under the moon
Has borne as I: they know it well, the woods
That I visit alone and day and night.

I never had the calmness of a night,
But I have always sighed, morning and evening,
Since Love made me a dweller of the woods.
Before I rest, the sea shall have no waves,
The sun shall receive splendour from the moon,
The April flowers shall die on every shore.

I go pining away from shore to shore,
Pensive in the daytime, weeping at night;
Nor am I stable more than is the moon.
Quickly, when I see darkness bring the evening,
Deep sighs come from my breast, from eyes flow waves
To wet the grass and inundate the woods.

The towns are foes, but friendly are the woods
To my thoughts, which along this lofty shore
I pour out with the murmur of the waves
Amid the gentle silence of the night:
So that the whole day I wait for the evening
When the sun leaves and gives room to the moon.

I would I were with the charm of the moon
Asleep somewhere in the green of the woods;
And she who before vesper makes my evening,
Came with it and with Love toward the shore,

Sola venisse a starsi ivi una notte;
E 'l dí si stesse e 'l Sol sempre ne l'onde.

Sovra dure onde, al lume de la Luna,
Canzon, nata di notte in mezzo i boschi,
Ricca piaggia vedrai deman da sera.

CCXXXVIII

Real natura, angelico intelletto,
Chiara alma, pronta vista, occhio cerviero,
Providenzia veloce, alto pensero,
E veramente degno di quel petto:

Sendo di donne un bel numero eletto,
Per adornar il dí festo et altèro,
Súbito scorse il buon giudicio intero
Fra tanti, e sí bei vólti, il piú perfetto.

L'altre maggior di tempo, o di fortuna,
Trarsi in disparte comandò con mano,
E caramente acolse a sé quell'una.

Li occhi e la fronte con sembiante umano
Basciolle sí che rallegrò ciascuna;
Me empié d'invidia l'atto dolce e strano.

CCXXXIX

Lá vèr' l'aurora, che sí dolce l'aura
Al tempo novo suol movere i fiori
E li augelletti incominciar lor versi,
Sí dolcemente i pensier dentro a l'alma
Mover mi sento a chi li ha tutti in forza,
Che ritornar convemmi a le mie note.

Alone, and remained there during one night;
And the day hid with the sun in the waves.

Over rough waves, in the light of the moon,
Canzone born at night among the woods,
You will see a rich shore tomorrow evening.

CCXXXVIII

A royal nature, an angelic mind,
A clear soul, a quick sight, a faultless eye,
A swift foresight, an intellect refined
And truly worthy in that breast to lie,

Finding there ladies in selected guise
To celebrate the festive day and blest,
Did at once with keen judgment recognize
Among many fair visages the best.

Others greater in fortune, time or place,
With a sign of the hand he asked to move,
And called to him only that one with love.

He kissed her eyes and forehead with a face
So human, that the others seemed to cheer;
And I envied his action sweet and queer.

CCXXXIX

When comes the dawn, and so sweetly the aura
At the first break of day flatters the flowers,
And the small birds begin to sing their verses,
With so much sweetness the thoughts in my soul
Are moved by her who holds them by her force,
That I return again to my old notes.

Temprar potess'io in sí soavi note
I miei sospiri, ch'addolcissen Laura,
Faccendo a lei ragion ch'a me fa forza!
Ma pria fia 'l verno la stagion de' fiori,
Ch'amor fiorisca in quella nobil alma,
Che non curò giá mai rime né versi.

Quante lagrime, lasso!, e quanti versi
Ho giá sparti al mio tempo, e 'n quante note
Ho riprovato umiliar quell'alma!
Ella si sta pur com'aspr'alpe a l'aura
Dolce, la qual ben move frondi e fiori,
Ma nulla pò se'n contr'ha maggior forza.

Omini e dèi solea vincer per forza
Amor, come si legge in prose e 'n versi:
Et io 'l provai in sul primo aprir de' fiori.
Ora né 'l mio signor, né le sue note,
Né 'l pianger mio, né i preghi pôn far Laura
Trarre o di vita o di martír quest'alma.

A l'ultimo bisogno, o misera alma,
Accampa ogni tuo ingegno, ogni tua forza,
Mentre fra noi di vita alberga l'aura.
Nulla al mondo è che non possano i versi;
E li aspidi incantar sanno in lor note,
Non che 'l gielo adornar di novi fiori.

Ridon or per le piagge erbette e fiori:
Esser non pò che quella angelica alma
Non senta il suon de l'amorose note.
Se nostra ria fortuna è di piú forza,
Lagrimando e cantando i nostri versi
E col bue zoppo andrem cacciando l'aura.

In rete accolgo l'aura, e 'n ghiaccio i fiori,
E 'n versi tento sorda e rigida alma,
Che né forza d'Amor prezza, né note.

Could I temper with such melodious notes
My sighs until they mollified my Laura,
Using reason on her who uses force!
But winter shall become the time of flowers
Before Love thrives in that obdurate soul
Which does not care for poems or for verses.

How many tears, alas, how many verses
I scattered in my time, how many notes
I attempted, to make humble that soul!
She stands like a rough Alp in the sweet aura
Which does indeed caress the leaves and flowers,
But can do nothing against greater force.

Love used to conquer men and gods by force,
As it is read in many tales and verses;
And this I felt when first blossomed the flowers.
But neither my dear lord nor his dear notes,
Nor my weeping, or praying, can make Laura
Pull out of life or martyrdom my soul.

In your last need, o miserable soul,
You must set up every skill and force
Till among us will dwell the living aura.
Nothing there is that is not wrought by verses;
They can charm even serpents with their notes,
And can adorn the frost with newborn flowers.

Now on the shore small grasses laugh, and flowers:
It cannot be that her angelic soul
Hear not the sound of these amorous notes.
If our bad fortune has a greater force,
We shall go weeping and singing our verses,
And with a lame ox we shall hunt the aura.

I lay nets for the aura, ice for flowers,
And with verses I try a deaf, stiff soul
Who respects neither force of love, nor notes.

CCXL

I' ho pregato Amor, e 'l ne riprego,
Che mi scusi appo voi, dolce mia pena,
Amaro mio diletto, se, con piena
Fede, dal dritto mio sentier mi piego.

I' no 'l posso negar, donna, e no 'l nego,
Che la ragion, ch'ogni bona alma affrena,
Non sia dal voler vinta; ond'ei mi mena
Talor in parte ov'io per forza il sego.

Voi, con quel cor, che di sí chiaro ingegno,
Di sí alta vertute il cielo alluma,
Quanto mai piovve da benigna stella,

Devete dir, pietosa, e senza sdegno:
—Che pò questi altro? il mio vólto il consuma:
Ei perché ingordo, et io perché sí bella?—

CCXLI

L'alto signor dinanzi a cui non vale
Nasconder, né fuggir, né far difesa,
Di bel piacer m'avea la mente accesa,
Con un ardente et amoroso strale;

E ben che 'l primo colpo aspro e mortale
Fossi da sé, per avanzar sua impresa,
Una saetta di pietate ha presa,
E quinci e quindi il cor punge et assale.

L'una piaga arde, e versa foco e fiamma;
Lagrime l'altra che 'l dolor distilla,
Per li occhi mei, del vostro stato rio.

Né, per duo fonti, sol una favilla
Rallenta de l'incendio che m'infiamma;
Anzi, per la pietá, cresce 'l desio.

CCXL

I have prayed Love, and I pray him again
To excuse me before you, my sweet death
And my bitter delight, if with full faith
I drift away from my rightful terrain.

I cannot, Lady, I do not deny
That reason, which restrains every good soul,
Is not beaten by will; this leads me nigh
A part where I must cut it and control.

You, with a heart that by such intellect
And by such virtue enlightens the air,
As much as ever poured from any star,

Ought to say, merciful, ceasing from war:
—What can he do? By my face he is wrecked:
Why is he greedy, and why am I fair?—

CCXLI

The noble lord before whom it is vain
To hide or run away or raise defences,
With a fair pleasure had inflamed my brain
And with an ardent dart my loving senses;

And although his first blow brought death's distress
In itself, to advance his enterprise,
He takes an arrow of mercifulness
And from here and from there my heart defies.

One wound is burning and pours flames and fire,
The other tears distilled by misery
Through my eyes, for your cruel malady.

Yet, with those springs, not a spark is entombed
Of the ardour by which I am consumed;
Rather pity increases my desire.

CCXLII

Mira quel colle, o stanco mio cor vago:
Ivi lasciammo ier lei, ch'alcun tempo ebbe
Qualche cura di noi, e le ne 'ncrebbe,
Or vorria trar de li occhi nostri un lago.

Torna tu in lá, ch'io d'esser sol m'appago;
Tenta se forse ancor tempo sarebbe
Da scemar nostro duol, che 'n fin qui crebbe,
O del mio mal participe, e presago.

—Or tu c'hai posto te stesso in oblio,
E parli al cor pur come e' fusse or teco,
Miser, e pien di pensier vani e sciocchi!

Ch'al dipartir dal tuo sommo desio,
Tu te n'andasti, e' si rimase seco;
E si nascose dentro a' suoi belli occhi.—

CCXLIII

Fresco, ombroso, fiorito e verde colle,
Ov'or pensando et or cantando siede,
E fa qui de' celesti spirti fede
Quella ch'a tutto 'l mondo fama tolle,

Il mio cor che per lei lasciar mi volle,
E fe' gran senno, e piú se mai non riede,
Va or cantando ove da quel bel piede
Segnata è l'erba, e da quest'occhi è molle.

Seco si stringe, e dice a ciascun passo:
—Deh fusse or qui, quel miser, pur un poco,
Ch'è giá di pianger, e di viver, lasso!—

Ella sel ride; e non è pari il gioco:
Tu paradiso, i' senza cor un sasso,
O sacro, aventuroso, e dolce loco!

CCXLII

Look at that hill, o heart, my weary fool:
We left there yesterday one who had once
Some sympathy for us, then blamed her glance,
And now would draw out of our eyes a pool.

You return there, for I love solitude,
Try if the time at last has come to still
Our anguish that with time has grown more crude,
O companion and prophet of my ill.

—Now you, forgetting your own soul's welfare,
Talk to your heart as if it were with you,
Poor wretch, and full of vain and silly sighs!

For, in departing from what you must woo,
You went away and it remained with her
And hid itself within her beauteous eyes.—

CCXLIII

Cool, shady, flowered hill, blooming green field,
Where now musing, now singing, she sits down
Like a witness of some celestial town,
She, before whom all worldly fame must yield,

My heart that wanted to leave me for her,
And showed great wisdom not to feel regret,
Now tries to tell where the grass by her fair
Foot has been trodden, and my eyes are wet.

It comes near her and says at every trace:
—Oh, that the wretch were here a little time,
Who is worn out by crying and by living!—

She laughs at it; and the game is deceiving:
You paradise, a heartless stone I climb,
O delectable, holy, and sweet place!

CCXLIV

Il mal mi preme, e mi spaventa il peggio,
Al qual veggio sí larga e piana via,
Ch'i' son intrato in simil frenesia,
E con duro penser teco vaneggio;

Né so se guerra o pace a Dio mi cheggio,
Ché 'l danno è grave, e la vergogna è ria.
Ma per che piú languir? di noi pur fia
Quel ch'ordinato è giá nel sommo seggio.

Ben ch'i' non sia di quel grand'onor degno
Che tu mi fai, ché te n'ingana Amore,
Che spesso occhio ben san fa veder torto,

Pur d'alzar l'alma a quel celeste regno
È il mio consiglio, e di spronare il core;
Perché 'l camin è lungo, e 'l tempo è corto.

CCXLV

Due ròse fresche, e còlte in paradiso
L'altr'ier, nascendo il dí primo di maggio,
Bel dono, e d'un amante antiquo e saggio,
Tra duo minori egualmente diviso,

Con sí dolce parlar e con un riso
Da far innamorare un uom selvaggio,
Di sfavillante et amoroso raggio
E l'un e l'altro fe' cangiare il viso.

—Non vede un simil par d'amanti il Sole—
Dicea, ridendo e sospirando inseme;
E stringendo ambedue, volgeasi a torno.

Cosí partía le ròse e le parole;
Onde 'l cor lasso ancor s'allegra e teme:
O felice eloquenzia! o lieto giorno!

CCXLIV

I am crushed by the ill, scared by the worse
To which I see the way opened so broad,
That I have entered the same frantic road
And with difficult thoughts with you converse;

I know not if I pray for peace or war,
Because the harm is deep and the shame hot.
But why languish still more? Our human lot
Has been decreed above by supreme law.

Although indeed I am not worthy of
The honour you do me, deceived by Love,
Who often makes a healthy eye see wrong,

Yet my advice is to lift up your soul
To that celestial kingdom, your heart's goal,
Because the time is short, the way is long.

CCXLV

Two fragrant roses plucked in paradise
The other day, being the first of May,
A fair gift from a lover old and wise,
Between two younger ones were shared and lay,

With such sweet talking and such smiling gleam,
That would make any savage fall in love,
With their radiating and amorous beam
Causing the one and other heart to move.

—Two such lovers the sun never discloses—
He said in laughing and sighing at once;
And holding both of them he turned around.

Thus he divided the words and the roses;
Whence the tired heart rejoices in a trance:
O happy eloquence! O blessed ground!

CCXLVI

L'aura, che 'l verde lauro e l'aureo crine
Soavemente sospirando move,
Fa con sue viste leggiadrette e nove
L'anime da' lor corpi pellegrine.

Candida ròsa nata in dure spine,
Quando fia chi sua pari al mondo trove?
Gloria di nostra etate! O vivo Giove,
Manda, prego, il mio in prima che 'l suo fine;

Sí ch'io non veggia il gran publico danno
E 'l mondo remaner senza 'l suo sole,
Né li occhi miei, che luce altra non hanno,

Né l'alma, che pensar d'altro non vòle,
Né l'orecchie, ch'udir altro non sanno,
Senza l'oneste sue dolci parole.

CCXLVII

Parrà forse ad alcun che 'n lodar quella
Ch'i' adoro in terra, errante sia 'l mio stile,
Faccendo lei sovr'ogni altra gentile,
Santa, saggia, leggiadra, onesta, e bella.

A me par il contrario; e temo ch'ella
Non abbia a schifo il mio dir troppo umíle,
Degna d'assai piú alto e piú sottile:
E chi no 'l crede, venga egli a vedella.

Sí dirá ben:—Quello ove questi aspira
È cosa da stancare Atene, Arpino,
Mantova, e Smirna, e l'una e l'altra lira.—

Lingua mortale al suo stato divino
Giunger non pòte: Amor la spinge e tira,
Non per elezion, ma per distíno.

CCXLVI

The aura's sighings that so sweetly move
The verdant laurel and the golden hair,
Make with their aspects delightful and rare
The souls like pilgrims free from bodies rove.

Whiteness of rose that ugly thorns did bear,
When shall someone her like here apprehend?
Glory of our age! O living Jupiter,
I beg you to send mine before her end;

So that I may not see the public blight
And the world being left without its sun,
Also my eyes that have no other light,

And my soul too, that thinks of nothing else,
My ears, unable to hear anyone
Without her honest words' enchanting spells.

CCXLVII

It may seem to someone that praising her
Whom I adore on earth, my style is wrong
To make her above others in my song
Holy, wise, charming, distinguished and fair.

I think the opposite; and fear that she
May disdain my appraisal all too tame,
Deserving a much higher, subtler fame:
Who does not trust me, let him come and see.

It will be said:—The thing for which he strives
Is such that would Athens, Arpino tire,
Mantua, Smyrna, one and the other lyre.—

Mortal tongue cannot touch her divine state,
For it is Love who pushes her and drives,
Not by his own election, but by fate.

CCXLVIII

Chi vuol veder quantunque pò Natura
E 'l Ciel tra noi, venga a mirar costei,
Ch'è sola un sol, non pur a li occhi mei,
Ma al mondo cieco, che vertú non cura;

E venga tosto, perché Morte fura
Prima i migliori, e lascia star i rei:
Questa, aspettata al regno delli dèi,
Cosa bella mortal, passa e non dura.

Vedrá, s'arriva a tempo, ogni vertute,
Ogni bellezza, ogni real costume
Giunti in un corpo con mirabil tempre.

Allor dirá che mie rime son mute,
L'ingegno offeso dal soverchio lume:
Ma se piú tarda, avrá da pianger sempre.

CCXLIX

Qual paura ho, quando mi torna a mente
Quel giorno ch'i' lasciai grave e pensosa
Madonna, e 'l mio cor seco! e non è cosa
Che sí volentier pensi, e sí sovente.

I' la riveggio starsi umilemente,
Tra belle donne, a guisa d'una ròsa
Tra minor fior; né lieta né dogliosa,
Come chi teme, et altro mal non sente.

Deposta avea l'usata leggiadria,
Le perle, e le ghirlande, e i panni allegri,
E 'l riso, e 'l canto, e 'l parlar dolce umano.

Cosí in dubbio lasciai la vita mia:
Or tristi augurî, e sogni, e penser negri
Mi dánno assalto; e piaccia a Dio che 'n vano.

CCXLVIII

Who wants to see what nature and the sky
Can among us, let him gaze upon her
Who is a sun not only to my eye
But to the world, which for good does not care;

Let him come soon, because Death steals away
Early the best, to the bad only nods:
This, waited in the kingdom of the gods,
Beautiful mortal thing will pass, not stay.

He shall see every virtue if he come
In time, every beauty, royal rule,
Joined in one body by a tempered tool.

Then he will say that my verses are dumb;
My talent overwhelmed by light too deep:
If he is late he shall forever weep.

CCXLIX

What fear I feel when I call to my mind
The day I left my lady grave and quiet
And my own heart with her! I do not find
Another thought in me with more delight.

Again I see her humbly sitting down
Among fair ladies, looking like a rose
Among small flowers; she does not smile or frown,
As one who dreads, and feels no other woes.

She had discarded all her loveliness,
Her pearls, her garlands and her merry dress,
Her laughing, singing, and sweet talking strain.

Thus full of doubts I abandoned my life:
Now dreary omens, dreams, my dark thoughts' strife,
Assault me; and may God prove them all vain.

CCL

Solea lontana in sonno consolarme
Con quella dolce angelica sua vista
Madonna; or mi spaventa e mi contrista,
Né di duol né di téma posso aitarme;

Ché spesso nel suo vólto veder parme
Vera pietá con grave dolor mista,
Et udir cose, onde 'l cor fede acquista,
Che di gioia e di speme si disarme.

—Non ti soven di quella ultima sera
—Dice ella—ch'i' lasciai li occhi tuoi molli
E sforzata dal tempo me n'andai?

I' non tel potei dir, allor, né volli;
Or tel dico per cosa esperta e vera:
Non sperar di vedermi in terra mai.—

CCLI

O misera et orribil visione!
È dunque ver che 'nnanzi tempo spenta
Sia l'alma luce che suol far contenta
Mia vita in pene et in speranze bone?

Ma come è che sí gran romor non sone,
Per altri messi, e per lei stessa il senta?
Or giá Dio e Natura no 'l consenta,
E falsa sia mia trista opinione.

A me pur giova di sperare ancóra
La dolce vista del bel viso adorno,
Che me mantene e 'l secol nostro onora.

Se per salir a l'eterno soggiorno
Uscita è pur del bel albergo fòra,
Prego non tardi il mio ultimo giorno.

CCL

She used from far away to soothe my sleep,
With her angelic and beautiful face,
My lady; now she scares me, makes me weep,
Neither sorrow nor fear can be my grace;

For often in her look I seem to see
True pity with a serious suffering knit,
And I hear things that the heart must admit,
Till joy and hope desert its company.

—And do you not remember that last night—
She says—when I left you in tears of pain
And forced by the late hour I went away?

I could not tell you then, I dared not quite,
Now as a proved, true thing, to you I say:
—Hope not to see me ever here again.—

CCLI

O horrible and miserable dream!
Is it true that the holy light went out
Before its time, whose comfort had made stout
My life in grief, shedding its hopeful beam?

But why does not such mighty rumour run
By other couriers, or from herself sent?
May God and Nature forbid such event
And prove untrue my wretched vision.

Because I must still hope to see again
The sweet adornment of her lovely face
That gives me life, and honour to our day.

If to ascend to the eternal domain
She is departed from her dwelling-place,
I beg that my last hour may not delay.

CCLII

In dubbio di mio stato, or piango or canto,
E temo e spero; et in sospiri e 'n rime
Sfogo il mio incarco: Amor tutte sue lime
Usa sopra 'l mio core afflitto tanto.

Or fia giá mai che quel bel viso santo
Renda a quest'occhi le lor luci prime?
(Lasso!, non so che di me stesso estime)
O li condanni a sempiterno pianto?

E per prendere il ciel, debito a lui,
Non curi che si sia di loro in terra,
Di ch'egli è 'l sole, e non veggiono altrui?

In tal paura e 'n sí perpetua guerra
Vivo, ch'i' non son piú quel che giá fui;
Qual chi per via dubbiosa teme et erra.

CCLIII

O dolci sguardi, o parolette accorte,
Or fia mai il dí ch'i' vi riveggia et oda?
O chiome bionde, di che 'l cor m'annoda
Amor, e cosí preso il mena a morte;

O bel viso a me dato in dura sorte,
Di ch'io sempre pur pianga, e mai non goda;
O chiuso inganno et amorosa froda,
Darmi un piacer che sol pena m'apporte!

E se talor da' belli occhi soavi,
Ove mia vita, e 'l mio pensero alberga,
Forse mi vèn qualche dolcezza onesta,

Súbito, a ciò ch'ogni mio ben disperga
E m'allontane, or fa cavalli or navi
Fortuna, ch'al mio mal sempre è sí presta.

CCLII

Doubtful of my own state I sing and weep,
And fear and hope; in sighs and verses' guiles
I pour my burden; Love uses his files
Upon my heart torn by a grief so deep.

Will ever once the holy, handsome face
Give back their primal vision to my eyes?
(Alas! I do not know what I surmise)
Or will it doom them to their tears' disgrace?

And the sky, taking back what has to go,
Will not care what becomes of us below,
Whose sun she is, who have no other one?

In such a fright, in such continuous wrath
I live, from my old self very far gone,
As one who fears and errs on dubious path.

CCLIII

O sweet glances, o little cunning words,
Shall I ever again see you and hear?
O golden hair that Love fastens with fear
Around my heart to drag it to death's swards;

O lovely face by hard Luck given me
That I may always weep, never rejoice;
O closed betrayal, o deceitful choice,
To bring a pleasure which is agony!

And if at times from the sweet darling eyes
Where my life and my thought have found a nest
Does come to me some honest, happy rest,

At once, in order to destroy my gain,
And banish me, horses and ships arise,
Sent by Luck always quick to cause me pain.

CCLIV

I' pur ascolto, e non odo novella,
De la dolce et amata mia nemica,
Né so ch'i' me ne pensi o ch'i' mi dica,
Sí 'l cor téma e speranza mi puntella.

Nocque ad alcuna giá l'esser sí bella:
Questa piú d'altra è bella e piú pudica:
Forse vuol Dio tal di vertute amica
Tôrre a la terra, e 'n ciel farne una stella,

Anzi un sole; e se questo è, la mia vita,
I miei corti riposi e i lunghi affanni
Son giunti al fine. O dura dipartita,

Perché lontan m'hai fatto da' miei danni?
La mia favola breve è giá compita,
E fornito il mio tempo a mezzo gli anni.

CCLV

La sera desiare, odiar l'aurora
Soglion questi tranquilli e lieti amanti;
A me doppia la sera e doglia e pianti,
La matina è per me piú felice ora:

Ché spesso in un momento apron allora
L'un sole e l'altro quasi duo levanti,
Di beltate e di lume sí sembianti,
Ch'anco il ciel de la terra s'innamora;

Come giá fece, allor che 'primi rami
Verdeggiâr, che nel cor radice m'hanno,
Per cui sempre altrui piú che me stesso ami.

Cosí di me contrarie ore fanno;
E chi m'acqueta è ben ragion ch'i' brami,
E téma et odi' chi m'adduce affanno.

CCLIV

I listen and I hear not any news
Of my sweet enemy, my love and fay,
I know not what to think or what to say,
So great the fear and hope that my heart bruise.

Some others have been harmed by being fair:
She more than any other is, and chaste:
Perhaps God wants this virtue's friend to tear
From earth and give the sky a star to taste,

Better, a sun; if it is so, my life,
My brief respites and my protracted strife,
Have come to end. Cruel division,

Why do you separate me from my cares?
My little fable is already done,
And my time over in my middle years.

CCLV

To long for evening and to hate the dawn
Is the custom of tranquil, happy lovers;
To me the night a double grief discovers,
The morning shows to me a fresher lawn:

For often at the same moment they strike
Together, the two suns, as from two easts,
In their beauty and their shining so alike,
That heaven falls in love with earthly feasts,

As it did when the first rays made the bole
Don green boughs, that is rooted in my soul,
Making me scorn myself to seek my dove.

The two contrary hours do this to me:
And it is right that what calms me I love,
And fear and hate what brings me misery.

CCLVI

Far potess'io vendetta di colei
Che guardando, e parlando, mi distrugge,
E per piú doglia poi s'asconde e fugge,
Celando li occhi, a me sí dolci e rei.

Cosí li afflitti e stanchi spirti mei
A poco a poco consumando sugge;
E 'n sul cor, quasi fiero leon, rugge
La notte allor quand'io posar devrei.

L'alma, cui Morte del suo albergo caccia,
Da me si parte; e di tal nodo sciolta,
Vassene pur a lei che la minaccia.

Meravigliomi ben, s'alcuna volta,
Mentre le parla, e piange, e poi l'abbraccia,
Non rompe il sonno suo, s'ella l'ascolta.

CCLVII

In quel bel viso ch'i' sospiro e bramo,
Fermi eran li occhi desiosi e 'ntensi,
Quando Amor porse (quasi a dir:—che pensi?—)
Quella onorata man che second'amo.

Il cor preso ivi come pesce a l'amo,
Onde a ben far per vivo essempio viensi,
Al ver non volse li occupati sensi,
O come novo augello al visco in ramo;

Ma la vista privata del suo obietto,
Quasi sognando si facea far via,
Senza la qual è 'l suo bene imperfetto:

L'alma, tra l'una e l'altra gloria mia,
Qual celeste, non so, novo diletto
E qual strania dolcezza si sentia.

CCLVI

I would I could take vengeance against her
Who by looking and speaking has me slain,
Who, to increase my grief, hides and flees where
I am put out of her sweet eyes' disdain.

She consumes hour by hour my weary soul,
Sucking my hard existence clean away,
Roaring upon my heart with a lion's call:
At night, when I should rest, I am her prey.

The spirit that death chases from its home
Departs from me, and of that bondage free,
Rushes to meet her threat, there to succumb.

It would indeed be a surprise to me
If weeping, talking, embracing its dear,
It should not break her sleep; if she will hear.

CCLVII

In that fair face for which I sigh and long,
The eyes seemed stunned, full of wishes, intense,
When Love stretched (as if saying:—What is wrong?—)
Her honoured hand, second joy of my sense.

My heart caught there, like a fish on the hook,
Whence we come having learned how to do well,
Did not turn its absorption to truth's book,
Like a small bird ensnared in gluey spell;

But my eyes that had been robbed of their sight,
As in a dream were looking for a guide
To see what makes their good not illusory;

And my soul, taken between either glory,
Some celestial, who knows, some new delight,
Some utterly new sweetness felt inside.

CCLVIII

Vive faville uscian de' duo bei lumi
Vèr' me sí dolcemente folgorando,
E parte d'un cor saggio sospirando,
D'alta eloquenzia sí soavi fiumi,

Che pur il rimembrar par mi consumi
Qualor a quel dí torno, ripensando
Come venieno i miei spirti mancando
Al variar de' suoi duri costumi.

L'alma nudrita sempre in doglia e 'n pene,
(Quanto è 'l poder d'una prescritta usanza!)
Contra 'l doppio piacer sí 'nferma fue,

Ch'al gusto sol del disusato bene,
Tremando or di paura or di speranza,
D'abandonarme fu spesso en tra due.

CCLIX

Cercato ho sempre solitaria vita
(Le rive il sanno, e le campagne e i boschi)
Per fuggir questi ingegni sordi e loschi,
Che la strada del cielo hanno smarrita:

E se mia voglia in ciò fusse compita,
Fuor del dolce aere de' paesi tóschi
Ancor m'avria tra 'suoi bei colli foschi
Sorga, ch'a pianger e cantar m'aita.

Ma mia fortuna, a me sempre nemica,
Mi risospigne al loco ov'io mi sdegno
Veder nel fango il bel tesoro mio.

A la man, ond'io scrivo, è fatta amica
A questa volta; e non è forse indegno:
Amor sel vide, e sal madonna et io.

CCLVIII

A living radiance shone out of the beam
Of two eyes scintillating toward me,
And a wise heart lamented destiny
With the high eloquence of such sweet stream,

That memory itself makes me break down
When I come back to that day and recall
How all my spirits then began to fall
Under the change of her habitual frown.

The soul nourished in continuous pain and grief,
(How great the power of a strict routine!)
Struck by the double pleasure felt so ill,

That in tasting the unusual relief,
Now from hope, now from terror trembling still,
Was about to desert me in between.

CCLIX

I always sought a solitary place
(The shores can tell, the forests and the plains)
To run away from the deaf, devious brains
That have betrayed the sky and lost its trace.

And if my wish in this were satisfied
Out of the gentle Tuscan country air,
Sorga would still have me along the side
Of its dark hills, weeping and singing there.

But Fortune, always hostile to my measure,
Pushes me back where I disdain and hate
To see in the mud my sweet and precious treasure.

To the hand which I praise she will keep faith
Going on this road; it may not be amiss:
Love saw to it, my lady and I know this.

CCLX

In tale stella duo belli occhi vidi,
Tutti pien d'onestate e di dolcezza,
Che presso a quei d'Amor leggiadri nidi
Il mio cor lasso ogni altra vista sprezza.

Non si pareggi a lei qual piú s'aprezza,
In qual ch'etade, in quai che strani lidi:
Non chi recò con sua vaga bellezza
In Grecia affanni, in Troia ultimi stridi;

No la bella romana che col ferro
Apre il suo casto e disdegnoso petto;
Non Polissena, Isifile et Argia.

Questa eccellenzia è gloria, s'i' non erro,
Grande a natura, a me sommo diletto,
Ma che vèn tardo, e súbito va via.

CCLXI

Qual donna attende a gloriosa fama,
Di senno, di valor, di cortesia,
Miri fiso nelli occhi a quella mia
Nemica, che mia donna il mondo chiama.

Come s'acquista onor, come Dio s'ama,
Come è giunta onestá con leggiadria,
Ivi s'impara, e qual è dritta via
Di gir al ciel, che lei aspetta e brama;

Ivi 'l parlar che nullo stile aguaglia,
E 'l bel tacere, e quei cari costumi,
Che 'ngegno uman non pò spiegar in carte.

L'infinita bellezza, ch'altrui abbaglia,
Non vi s'impara; ché quei dolci lumi
S'acquistan per ventura e non per arte.

CCLX

In such a star did I see two fair eyes
Overflowing with beauty, honesty,
That near to those two nests of harmony
My heart all kinds of life seemed to despise.

Let no one who is valued be compared
To her in any age, on any shore:
Not she who by her loveliness brought sore
Trials to Greece and in Troy's ruin shared;

Not the beautiful Roman who with iron
Opened her chaste and contemptuous breast;
Not Polyxena, Isifile, Argia.

This excellence brings glory, I will say,
To Nature, and to me delight and rest,
But it comes late and quickly goes away.

CCLXI

Let any lady who wants glorious fame,
Wisdom, valour, and courtesy's renown,
Intently gaze in the eyes of my own
Foe, that my lady the world likes to name.

How we can acquire honour and love God,
How honesty is joined to loveliness,
Shall be learned there, and the right road and rod
To climb the sky that awaits her to bless;

There the speaking unlike to any sound,
And the fair silence and the darling ways
That human talent cannot dare expound.

The boundless beauty that dazzles the heart
Is not learned there; for its enchanting rays
One can acquire by fortune, not by art.

CCLXII

—Cara la vita, e dopo lei mi pare
Vera onestá, che 'n bella donna sia.—
—L'ordine volgi: e' non fûr, madre mia,
Senza onestá mai cose belle o care.

E qual si lascia di suo onor privare,
Né donna è piú, né viva; e se qual pria
Appare in vista, è tal vita aspra e ria
Via piú che morte, e di piú pene amare.

Né di Lucrezia mi meravigliai,
Se non come a morir le bisognasse
Ferro, e non le bastasse il dolor solo.—

Vengan quanti filosofi fûr mai
A dir di ciò: tutte lor vie fíen basse;
E quest'una vedremo alzarsi a volo.

CCLXIII

Arbor vittoriosa triumfale,
Onor d'imperadori e di poeti,
Quanti m'hai fatto dí dogliosi e lieti
In questa breve mia vita mortale!

Vera donna, et a cui di nulla cale,
Se non d'onor, che sovr'ogni altra mieti,
Né d'Amor visco témi o lacci o reti,
Né 'ngano altrui contr'al tuo senno vale.

Gentilezza di sangue, e l'altre care
Cose tra noi, perle e robini et oro,
Quasi vil soma egualmente dispregi.

L'alta beltá, ch'al mondo non ha pare,
Noia t'è, se non quanto il bel tesoro
Di castitá par ch'ella adorni e fregi.

CCLXII

—Life is most dear, and after it, I guess,
In a fair lady will come honesty.—
—You shift the order; no fair things, unless
Honesty is with them, can ever be.

And who permits to her honour a stain,
Is not alive or lady; if some seem
Such in appearance, their life is more grim
Than death, and full of bitterness and pain.

I did not marvel at Lucretia's story,
Who in order to die needed a knife,
For grief was not enough to stop her life.—

Let all philosophers who attained glory
Come to say this: their systems will stay low,
And we shall see this one to heaven go.

CCLXIII

Victorious, noble, and triumphal tree,
Honour of poet, emperor and king,
How many doleful days you made to sing
In this short life of my mortality!

True woman who on nothing set your care,
Save honour that above others you mow,
Nor do you fear Love's viscous glue or snare,
Nor can others' deceits in your mind grow.

Gentility of blood and all the dear
Things that we prize, like pearls, rubies and gold,
As a base load you neglect and disdain.

The beauty that among us has no peer
Is wearisome to you, unless it hold
Chastity's treasure like a precious chain.

SECOND PART
AFTER LAURA'S DEATH

CCLXIV

I' vo pensando, e nel penser m'assale
Una pietá sí forte di me stesso,
Che mi conduce spesso
Ad altro lagrimar ch'i' non soleva;
Ché, vedendo ogni giorno il fin piú presso,
Mille fiate ho chieste a Dio quell'ale
Co le quai del mortale
Carcer nostro intelletto al ciel si leva;
Ma in fin a qui niente mi releva
Prego, o sospiro, o lagrimar ch'io faccia;
E cosí per ragion conven che sia,
Ché chi possendo star, cadde tra via,
Degno è che mal suo grado a terra giaccia.
Quelle pietose braccia,
In ch'io mi fido, veggio aperte ancóra;
Ma temenza m'accora
Per gli altrui essempli, e del mio stato tremo;
Ch'altri mi sprona, e son forse a l'estremo.

L'un penser parla co la mente, e dice:
—Che pur agogni? onde soccorso attendi?
Misera, non intendi
Con quanto tuo disnore il tempo passa?
Prendi partito accortamente, prendi;
E del cor tuo divelli ogni radice
Del piacer, che felice
No 'l pò mai fare, e respirar no 'l lassa.
Se giá è gran tempo fastidita e lassa
Se' di quel falso dolce fugitivo
Che 'l mondo traditor può dare altrui,
A che ripon piú la speranza in lui,
Che d'ogni pace e di fermezza è privo?
Mentre che 'l corpo è vivo,
Hai tu 'l freno in bailía de' penser tuoi.
Deh, stringilo or che pòi,
Ché dubbioso è 'l tardar, come tu sai,
E 'l cominciar non fia per tempo omai.

CCLXIV

I go thinking, and thinking I am caught
By such a pity of my destiny,
That often it leads me
To other grief than when I used to cry;
For since each day the end I nearer see,
A thousand times I begged from God and sought
Those wings with which our thought
Flies from its mortal prison to the sky;
But until now there has come no reply,
Though I pray, sigh, or shed many a tear;
And it is just that this price we should pay,
For who standing upright fell on his way
Deserves to find over the ground his bier.
Those arms merciful, dear,
In which I trust, are open to me still;
But sad examples fill
Me with anxiety and I dread my state:
For I am spurred, and it may be too late.

One thought speaks to the mind in these astute
Words:—What do you long for? What help, what hope?
Don't you see while you grope
With what dishonour time passes away?
Decide with wisdom, determine your scope;
And pull out of your heart every root
Of pleasure, which no fruit
Brings to your kind, and makes your breath decay.
For a long time you felt too tired to play
With that lovely deceitful fleeting good
Which the treacherous world gives to some men;
Why do you lay your hope on it again,
Which is devoid of peace and fortitude?
While life is in your blood
You are given the rein of your thoughts' race:
O hold them in their place
Now that you can, to be late is evasion,
And to start now is not your first occasion.

Giá sai tu ben quanta dolcezza porse
A gli occhi tuoi la vista di colei
La qual anco vorrei
Ch'a nascer fosse per piú nostra pace.
Ben ti ricordi (e ricordar ten dêi)
De l'imagine sua, quand'ella corse
Al cor, lá dove forse
Non potea fiamma intrar per altrui face:
Ella l'accese; e se l'ardor fallace
Durò molt'anni in aspettando un giorno,
Che per nostra salute unqua non vène,
Or ti solleva a piú beata spene,
Mirando 'l ciel, che ti si volve intorno
Immortal et addorno:
Ché dove, del mal suo qua giú sí lieta,
Vostra vaghezza acqueta
Un mover d'occhi, un ragionar, un canto,
Quanto fia quel piacer, se questo è tanto?—

Da l'altra parte un pensier dolce et agro,
Con faticosa, e dilettevol, salma
Sedendosi entro l'alma,
Preme 'l cor di desio, di speme il pasce;
Che sol per fama gloriosa et alma
Non sente quand'io agghiaccio, o quand'io flagro,
S'i' son pallido o magro;
E s'io l'occido, piú forte rinasce.
Questo d'allor ch'i' m'addormiva in fasce
Venuto è di dí in dí crescendo meco;
E temo ch'un sepolcro ambeduo chiuda.
Poi che fia l'alma de le membra ignuda,
Non pò questo desio piú venir seco.
Ma se 'l latino e 'l greco
Parlan di me dopo la morte, è un vento;
Ond'io, perché pavento
Adunar sempre quel ch'un'ora sgombre,
Vorre' 'l ver abbracciar, lassando l'ombre.

Ma quell'altro voler, di ch'i' son pieno,
Quanti press'a lui nascon par ch'adugge;

You know too well how much sweetness was stored
Into your eyes by the sight of your dear,
Who I wish were not here,
And were still to be born, for our own peace.
You well remember (if you are sincere)
Her image when she rushed at once and poured
In your heart that adored
Her, a flame that no others could release.
She kindled it; if the heat did not cease
For many years, aspiring to one day
Which for our soul's salvation does not come,
Now rise and think of a more blessed home,
Gaze at the sky that revolves around you
In its immortal blue:
Because if here you are pleased with your ill
And two quick eyes can still
Your passion, or a spoken word, a song,
What will be that, if this joy is so strong?—

Another thought, sweet, sour, then takes its turn
With weary and agreeable countenance;
Sits in my soul at once,
Fills my heart with desire and with hope feeds;
Only caring for fame and glory's glance,
It feels not how I freeze and how I burn,
If I decline or yearn;
And if I kill it, it sows stronger seeds.
This, since I slept the sleep a baby needs,
Has been growing with me day after day,
And I fear that one grave shall have us both.
When the soul leaves the body's living cloth
This desire shall with it no longer stay.
But if scholars display
My merits after death, 'tis but a wind;
Thus, fearing in my mind
To hoard and hoard what in one moment dies,
I would embrace the truth, leaving the lies.

But the desire that wants there to remain
Seems to dislike all those that soar and climb;

E parte il tempo fugge,
Che scrivendo d'altrui, di me non calme;
E 'l lume de' begli occhi che mi strugge
Soavemente al suo caldo sereno,
Mi ritien con un freno
Contra cui nullo ingegno o forza valme.
Che giova dunque perché tutta spalme
La mia barchetta, poi che 'n fra li scogli
È ritenuta ancor da ta' duo nodi?
Tu che da gli altri, che 'n diversi modi
Legano 'l mondo, in tutto mi disciogli,
Signor mio, ché non togli
Omai dal vólto mio questa vergogna?
Ché 'n guisa d'uom che sogna,
Aver la morte inanzi gli occhi parme;
E vorrei far difesa, e non ho l'arme.

Quel ch'i' fo, veggio, e non m'inganna il vero
Mal conosciuto, anzi mi sforza Amore,
Che la strada d'onore
Mai no 'l lassa seguir chi troppo il crede;
E sento ad ora ad or venirmi al core
Un leggiadro disdegno, aspro e severo,
Ch'ogni occulto pensero
Tira in mezzo la fronte, ov'altri 'l vede;
Ché mortal cosa amar con tanta fede,
Quanta a Dio sol per debito convensi,
Piú si disdice a chi piú pregio brama.
E questo al alta voce anco richiama
La ragione sviata dietro a i sensi:
Ma perch'ell'oda, e pensi
Tornare, il mal costume oltre la spigne,
Et a gli occhi depigne
Quella che sol per farmi morir nacque,
Perch'a me troppo, et a se stessa, piacque.

Né so che spazio mi si désse il cielo
Quando novellamente io venni in terra
A soffrir l'aspra guerra
Che 'n contr'a me medesmo seppi ordire,

And nearly gone the time
I spent, lost to myself, writing some tales;
And the light of those eyes that stole my prime
So gently in a warm unclouded plain,
Holds me back with a rein
Against which neither mind nor might avails.
What is the use of trimming my boat's sails,
When it is still confined between two rocks
And still fastened and tied by those two knots?
You who, from those that with different thoughts
Enslave the world, free me breaking their locks,
O Lord, relieve the shocks
Of shame upon my face, see how it streams!
For like a man who dreams
I seem to see before me Death's alarms;
And I would fight for life, and have no arms.

I see what happens, nor am I deceived
By a mistaken truth, but pushed by Love,
Who closes the road of
Honour to those who toward him have been
Too faithful, and at each hour comes to move
My heart a gentle scorn severe and grieved
Which brings my thoughts above,
On my forehead where my secrets are seen:
To love a mortal thing beyond the mean,
With a faith that to God only pertains,
Is less becoming when praise we desire.
And this does with loud voice also require
That reason cease to bear the senses' chains;
But although it does mean
To return, the bad custom drives it on,
And paints to it like sun
One who was born only to make me die,
Because she pleased to mine and to her eye.

Nor do I know what space gave me to fill
The sky, when first I came upon the earth
To suffer from my birth
That war I liked against myself to wage,

Né posso il giorno che la vita serra
Antiveder per lo corporeo velo;
Ma variarsi il pelo
Veggio, e dentro cangiarsi ogni desire.
Or ch'i' mi credo al tempo del partire
Esser vicino, o non molto da lunge,
Come chi 'l perder face accorto e saggio,
Vo ripensando ov'io lassai 'l viaggio
Da la man destra, ch'a buon porto aggiunge;
E da l'un lato punge
Vergogna e duol, che 'n dietro mi rivolve;
Dall'altro non m'assolve
Un piacer per usanza in me sí forte
Ch'a patteggiar n'ardisce co la morte.

Canzon, qui sono; ed ho 'l cor via piú freddo
De la paura che gelata neve,
Sentendomi perir senz'alcun dubbio;
Ché pur deliberando ho vòlto al subbio
Gran parte omai de la mia tela breve;
Né mai peso fu greve
Quanto quel ch'i' sostengo in tale stato;
Ché co la morte a lato
Cerco del viver mio novo consiglio,
E veggio 'l meglio et al peggior m'appiglio.

Nor can I see the day that ends our mirth,
Or foresee it, bound by the body's ill;
But I see my hair still
Change and inside me all my longings age.
Now that I feel near me the parting-stage,
Or not too far away, as he who heeds
Experience and is made wise by his loss,
I think of when I did not care to cross
To the right way which to salvation leads;
On one side my sad needs
Are pierced by shame and grief, bid to retire;
The other is on fire
By a pleasure with time grown so intense,
That it bargains with Death and Providence.

Song, I am here; and my heart is more cold
With terror than the ice of frozen snow,
Feeling lost in the night, without a gleam;
For in musing I have rolled on the beam
Most of my woven cloth that soon must go;
No burden do I know
Hard as the one I bear in such a state,
For, with Death as my mate,
I seek a way of life, another thing,
And see the best and to the worst I cling.

CCLXV

Aspro core e selvaggio, e cruda voglia
In dolce, umile, angelica figura,
Se l'impreso rigor gran tempo dura,
Avran di me poco onorata spoglia;

Ché quando nasce e mor fior, erba e foglia,
Quando è 'l dí chiaro, e quando è notte oscura,
Piango ad ogni or. Ben ho di mia ventura,
Di madonna, e d'Amore, onde mi doglia.

Vivo sol di speranza, rimembrando
Che poco umor giá per continua prova
Consumar vidi marmi e pietre salde.

Non è sí duro cor che lagrimando,
Pregando, amando, talor non si smova,
Né sí freddo voler che non si scalde.

CCLXVI

Signor mio caro, ogni pensier mi tira
Devoto a veder voi, cui sempre veggio;
La mia fortuna (or che mi pò far peggio?)
Mi tène a freno, e mi travolve e gira.

Poi quel dolce desio ch'Amor mi spira
Menami a morte, ch'i' non me n'aveggio;
E mentre i miei duo lumi indarno cheggio,
Dovunque io son, dí e notte si sospira.

Caritá di signore, amor di donna
Son le catene ove con molti affanni
Legato son, perch'io stesso mi strinsi.

Un lauro verde, una gentil colonna,
Quindici l'una, e l'altra diciotto anni
Portato ho in seno, e giá mai non mi scinsi.

CCLXV

A fierce and savage heart, a cruel will
In a sweet, humble, and angelic sight,
If this harshness persists and threatens still,
Shall have my spoils with an unhonoured rite:

When flowers are born and die, or grass or leaf,
When the day shines, when it is dark or shady,
I always weep. And with good cause my grief
Complains of Fortune and Love and my lady.

I live only by hope, remembering
That a small drop continually formed
Can wear away, I know, marble and stone.

There is no heart so hard, that, if you sing
Your love, and pray and weep, cannot be won,
Nor will so cold that it cannot be warmed.

CCLXVI

My dearest lord, every thought draws me
Devoutly to see you, toward you goes;
My fortune (how could it more hostile be?)
Holds me in check, and turns me, overthrows.

Then the dear wish that Love in me inspires
Leads me to death while I am unaware;
And in myself, looking for two lights' glare,
Wherever I may be, always suspires.

Charity of a lord, love of a lady,
Are the fetters by which with fear and spleen
I am fastened, that I myself made ready.

A green bay tree, a gentle column I
Kept within me, one fifteen years, eighteen
The other, and I never broke the tie.

CCLXVII

Oimè il bel viso, oimè il soave sguardo,
Oimè il leggiadro portamento altèro!
Oimè il parlar ch'ogni aspro ingegno e fero
Facevi umíle, ed ogni uom vil gagliardo!

Et oimè il dolce riso onde uscío 'l dardo
Di che morte, altro bene omai non spero!
Alma real, dignissima d'impero,
Se non fossi fra noi scesa sí tardo!

Per voi conven ch'io arda e 'n voi respire;
Ch'i' pur fui vostro; e se di voi son privo,
Via men d'ogni sventura altra mi dole.

Di speranza m'empieste, e di desire,
Quand'io partí' dal sommo piacer vivo;
Ma 'l vento ne portava le parole.

CCLXVIII

Che debb'io far? che mi consigli, Amore?
Tempo è ben di morire,
Et ho tardato piú ch'i' non vorrei.
Madonna è morta, et ha seco il mio core;
E volendol seguire,
Interromper conven quest'anni rei;
Perché mai veder lei
Di qua non spero, e l'aspettar m'è noia;
Poscia ch'ogni mia gioia,
Per lo suo dipartire, in pianto è volta,
Ogni dolcezza di mia vita è tolta.

Amor, tu 'l senti, ond'io teco mi doglio,
Quant'è 'l danno aspro e grave;
E so che del mio mal ti pesa e dole,
Anzi del nostro; perch'ad uno scoglio

CCLXVII

Alas! the lovely face, the eyes that save,
Alas! the charming countenance and proud!
And the speech that could tame each fierce and loud
Intellect, and make cowardly men brave!

And alas! the sweet laugh whence came the dire
Arrow of Death, which is now all my hope:
Royal soul, more than worthy of empire,
Only looming too late within our scope!

To you I must aspire, in you suspire;
For I was yours; and now, bereft of you,
I suffer less for all my other pains.

You filled me once with hope and with desire,
When I departed from a joy most true;
But the wind spread our words across the plains.

CCLXVIII

What shall I do? What do you counsel, Love?
It is now time to die,
And I have waited longer than I would.
My lady died and did my heart remove;
To follow it and fly,
I must disrupt my years' long servitude;
To see her where she stood
I cannot hope, and to wait is distress;
Now every happiness
Is turned by her departure into tears,
Every joy of my life disappears.

Love, you feel this, therefore with you I groan
In my pain deep and dark;
I know that for my suffering you grieve,
Our suffering; because against a stone

Avem rotto la nave,
Et in un punto n'è scurato il sole.
Qual ingegno a parole
Poria aguagliare il mio doglioso stato?
Ahi orbo mondo, ingrato!
Gran cagion hai di dever pianger meco;
Ché quel bel ch'era in te, perduto hai seco.

Caduta è la tua gloria, e tu no 'l vedi;
Né degno eri, mentr'ella
Visse qua giú, d'aver sua conoscenza,
Né d'esser tócco da' suoi santi piedi;
Perché cosa sí bella
Devea 'l ciel adornar di sua presenza.
Ma io, lasso!, che senza
Lei, né vita mortal, né me stesso amo,
Piangendo la richiamo:
Questo m'avanza di cotanta spene,
E questo solo ancor qui mi mantene.

Oimè!, terra è fatto il suo bel viso,
Che solea far del cielo
E del ben di lassú fede fra noi;
L'invisibil sua forma è in paradiso,
Disciolta di quel velo
Che qui fece ombra al fior de gli anni suoi,
Per rivestirsen poi
Un'altra volta, e mai piú non spogliarsi,
Quando alma e bella farsi
Tanto piú le vedrem, quanto piú vale
Sempiterna bellezza che mortale.

Piú che mai bella e piú leggiadra donna
Tornami inanzi, come
Lá dove piú gradir sua vista sente.
Questa è del viver mio l'una colonna,
L'altra è 'l suo chiaro nome,
Che sona nel mio cor sí dolcemente.
Ma tornandomi a mente
Che pur morta è la mia speranza, viva
Allor ch'ella fioriva,

We did shatter our bark,
And then we saw our sun darken and leave.
What talent could relieve
With words, or equal my unrest of mind?
Ah, orphan world, unkind!
How right it is that you should weep with me;
For all the good you had, with her did flee.

Fallen your glory, though you do not know;
You were not worthy, while
She lived below, to have knowledge of her,
Or to be touched by her angelic toe;
Because her beauty's smile
Was to adorn the sky by going there.
But I, who do not care
For myself or my life in such a pain,
Crying call her again:
This is what is left me of a great hope,
And this alone makes me stay here and grope.

Woe! unto earth is turned her lovely face
That did witness the sky
And the goodness of angels among us;
Her invisible form is in that Place,
Untrammeled by the tie
Of a veil that threw shadows where she was,
And which will encompass
Her self again and never more will fall,
When we shall see her tall
And great become, of as much nobler use
As grace eternal passes mortal views.

More fair than ever, a more lovely maid,
She looks, as she is there
Where her beauty is properly admired.
This is one of the columns that are laid
In me, the other her
Name that so sweetly my heart has inspired.
But my hope is expired:
When I remember this, and that it lived
As long as she received

Sa ben Amor qual io divento, e, spero,
Vedel colei ch'è or sí presso al vero.

Donne, voi che miraste sua beltate,
E l'angelica vita,
Con quel celeste portamento in terra,
Di me vi doglia, e vincavi pietate,
Non di lei ch'è salita
A tanta pace, e m'ha lassato in guerra;
Tal che s'altri mi serra
Lungo tempo il camin da seguitarla,
Quel ch'Amor meco parla
Sol mi riten ch'io non recida il nodo;
Ma e' ragiona dentro in cotal modo:

—Pon freno al gran dolor che ti trasporta;
Ché per soverchie voglie
Si perde 'l cielo, ove 'l tuo core aspira,
Dove è viva colei, ch'altrui par morta,
E di sue belle spoglie
Seco sorride, e sol di te sospira;
E sua fama che spira
In molte parti ancor per la tua lingua,
Prega che non estingua,
Anzi la voce al suo nome rischiari,
Se gli occhi suoi ti fûr dolci né cari.—

Fuggi 'l sereno e 'l verde,
Non t'appressare ove sia riso o canto,
Canzon mia, no, ma pianto:
Non fa per te di star fra gente allegra,
Vedova, sconsolata, in vesta negra.

Blooms, I become as Love knows me, I pray
To see her who is now near the true ray.

Women, who saw her beauty and the fashion
Of holy life she chose,
With her bearing that came from higher star,
Suffer with me, be vanquished by compassion,
Not for her who arose
To so much peace, for me who am at war;
Because if some will bar
To me for long the path I must pursue,
What Love tells me to do
Alone can keep me from breaking this knot;
But he reasons in me with such a thought:

—Restrain the great affliction that is spread
In you; your wishes' coils
Make you forego the sky your heart desires,
Where she lives now, who to others seems dead;
And she laughs at her spoils
Of loveliness, only for you suspires;
Her fame that has lit fires
In many places, because of your tongue,
She asks you to keep young,
And that your voice may be cleared by her name
If you once found her eyes sweet, as you claim.—

Flee the clearness, the green,
Do not go near where there is song and laughter,
Canzone, follow after
Weeping: you are not fit for merry folk,
A widow, without comfort, in black cloak.

CCLXIX

Rotta è l'alta colonna, e 'l verde lauro,
Che facean ombra al mio stanco pensero;
Perduto ho quel che ritrovar non spero
Dal borrea a l'austro, o dal mar indo al mauro.

Tolto m'hai, Morte, il mio doppio tesauro,
Che mi fea viver lieto, e gire altèro;
E ristorar no 'l pò terra né impero,
Né gemma oriental, né forza d'auro.

Ma se consentimento è di destíno,
Che posso io piú, se no aver l'alma trista,
Umidi gli occhi sempre, e 'l viso chino?

O nostra vita, ch'è sí bella in vista,
Com' perde agevolmente in un matino
Quel che 'n molti anni a gran pena s'acquista!

CCLXX

Amor, se vuo' ch'i' torni al giogo antico,
Come par che tu mostri, un'altra prova
Meravigliosa e nova,
Per domar me, convènti vincer pria.
Il mio amato tesoro in terra trova,
Che m'è nascosto, ond'io son sí mendico,
E 'l cor saggio pudico,
Ove suol albergar la vita mia:
E s'egli è ver che tua potenzia sia
Nel ciel sí grande, come si ragiona,
E ne l'abisso (perché qui fra noi
Quel che tu val e puoi,
Credo che 'l sente ogni gentil persona),
Ritogli a Morte quel ch'ella n'ha tolto,
E ripon le tue insegne nel bel vólto.

Riponi entro 'l bel viso il vivo lume

CCLXIX

Broken the column and the green bay tree
That lent a shade to my exhausted thought;
And I have lost what can nowhere be sought
In any distant wind or distant sea.

You took away from me my double treasure,
Death, which had made my life proud and secure;
What neither earth nor kingdom can allure,
Nor oriental gem, nor golden measure.

But if to accept this is destiny,
What can I do but wear eyes wet with tears,
A sad soul and a face shut to all views?

O life that are so beautiful to see,
How quickly in one morning do we lose
What we gained with great pain in many years!

CCLXX

Love, if you offer me the ancient yoke,
As you seem to propose, you need a test
Astonishing, the best,
To conquer me, before you can proceed.
Find in the earth the treasure of my breast
That is denied to me, that I invoke,
And the chaste heart that spoke
To my life and is now its home and creed:
If it is true that your might is indeed
Puissant in heaven, as many men recall,
And in the pit (because over the earth
What your power is worth
I think is felt by every gentle soul),
Take back from Death what he stole, and replace
The colours of your signs upon her face.

Replace on the fair visage the live beam

Ch'era mia scorta, e la soave fiamma
Ch'ancor, lasso!, m'infiamma,
Essendo spenta; or che fea dunque ardendo?
E' non si vide mai cervo né damma
Con tal desio cercar fonte né fiume,
Qual io il dolce costume
Onde ho giá molto amaro, e piú n'attendo,
Se ben me stesso e mia vaghezza intendo,
Che mi fa vaneggiar sol del pensero,
E gire in parte ove la strada manca,
E co la mente stanca
Cosa seguir che mai giugner non spero.
Or al tuo richiamar venir non degno,
Ché segnoria non hai fuor del tuo regno.

Fammi sentir de quell'aura gentile
Di fòr, sí come dentro ancor si sente;
La qual era possente,
Cantando, d'acquetar li sdegni e l'ire,
Di serenar la tempestosa mente,
E sgombrar d'ogni nebbia oscura e vile,
Ed alzava il mio stile
Sovra di sé, dove or non poría gire.
Aguaglia la speranza col desire;
E poi che l'alma è in sua ragion piú forte,
Rendi a gli occhi, a gli orecchi il proprio obgetto,
Senza qual, imperfetto
È lor oprare, e 'l mio vivere è morte.
Indarno or sovra me tua forza adopre,
Mentre 'l mio primo amor terra ricopre.

Fa ch'io riveggía il bel guardo, ch'un sole
Fu sopra 'l ghiaccio ond'io solea gir carco;
Fa ch'i' ti trovi al varco,
Onde senza tornar passò 'l mio core;
Prendi i dorati strali, e prendi l'arco,
E facciamisi udir, sí come sòle,
Col suon de le parole,
Ne le quali io imparai che cosa è amore;
Movi la lingua, ov'erano a tutt'ore

That was my guide, and the endearing flame
Which, alas! can inflame
Now, being dead; what was it when it burned?
One never saw a deer or hart acclaim
With such desire a fountain or a stream,
As I do my old dream
That gave me so much pain, from which I learned
To expect more, if some knowledge I earned
Of the feeling that makes my reason rave
And go and seek the pathway that is gone,
And with a mind undone
Follow a thing I do not hope to have.
Now when you call I do not care to come,
For your empire is dead out of your home.

Let me feel around me that gentle air,
Just as inside me I can feel it still,
Which was able to fill
With peace, by singing, all disdain and woe,
And to clear up my tempest-shaken will,
And free it from the mist and from despair,
And lift my style up there,
Above itself, where now it could not go.
Make hope equal desire and with it grow;
And since the soul gets from reason more breath,
Give back to eyes and ears their proper thing
Without which their working
Is imperfect and my life is a death.
In vain now toward me you ply your trade,
While my first love inside a tomb is laid.

Let me see the fair glance that the sun stirred
Upon the ice which used to be my load;
Wait for me on the road
Where, never coming back, my heart did move;
Take the arrows of gold and take the goad
And bow, that I may hear as once I heard
The sounding of a word
From which I learned what thing it is to love;
Move the tongue where were placed more than enough

Disposti gli ami ov'io fui preso, e l'ésca
Ch'i' bramo sempre; e i tuoi lacci nascondi
Fra i capei crespi e biondi,
Ché 'l mio volere altrove non s'invesca;
Spargi co le tue man le chiome al vento,
Ivi mi lega, e puomi far contento.

Dal laccio d'òr non sia mai chi me scioglia,
Negletto ad arte, e 'nnanellato et irto,
Né de l'ardente spirto
De la sua vista dolcemente acerba,
La qual dí e notte piú che lauro o mirto
Tenea in me verde l'amorosa voglia,
Quando si veste e spoglia
Di fronde il bosco e la campagna d'erba.
Ma poi che Morte è stata sí superba
Che spezzò il nodo, ond'io temea scampare,
Né trovar pôi, quantunque gira il mondo,
Di che ordischi 'l secondo,
Che giova, Amor tuoi ingegni ritentare?
Passata è la stagion, perduto hai l'arme,
Di ch'io tremava: ormai che puoi tu farme?

L'arme tue furon gli occhi, onde l'accese
Saette uscivan d'invisibil foco,
E ragion temean poco,
Ché 'n contr'al ciel non val difesa umana;
Il pensar, e 'l tacer, il riso, e 'l gioco,
L'abito onesto, e 'l ragionar cortese,
Le parole, che 'ntese
Avrian fatto gentil d'alma villana,
L'angelica sembianza, umile e piana,
Ch'or quinci or quindi udía tanto lodarsi,
E 'l sedere e lo star, che spesso altrui
Poser in dubbio a cui
Devesse il pregio di piú laude darsi:
Con quest'armi vincevi ogni cor duro;
Or se' tu disarmato, i' son securo.

Gli animi ch'al tuo regno il cielo inchina

Hooks to catch me, and where was placed the bait
That I long for; and hide away your snare
In the blond curly hair,
Because my longings nothing else await;
Spread her hair with your hands upon the wind,
And tie me there, and so delight my mind.

No one shall free me from the golden wire
Artfully careless, in a crisp rings' row,
Or from the ghostly glow
Of her countenance hostile as a glass,
That more than myrtle, laurel, helped to grow
Green in my heart this amorous desire,
When woods don the attire
Of leaves and doff it, and the earth of grass.
But because Death has wanted to trespass
And break the knot that could my wish fulfill,
Nor can you find, though you may search the world,
Another one so curled,
What avails, Love, to try again your skill?
The time is passed, and you have lost the arms
That made me tremble; where are your alarms?

Your arms were once those eyes from which was shot
Out of a fire invisible the spear
That reason did not fear,
For against heaven human strength is vain;
The speech, the silence, the laughter and cheer,
The honest habit and the courteous thought,
The words that would have brought
A savage soul into grace's domain,
The angelic appearance, humble, plain,
That from all sides was used to hear its praise,
And the sitting and standing that made some
Doubt to which did become
The greater prize to bestow on her ways;
With these arms you could tame every heart;
Now I am safe, you cannot find a dart.

The spirits the sky bends to your control,

Leghi ora in uno et ora in altro modo;
Ma me sol ad un nodo
Legar potêi, ché 'l ciel di piú non volse.
Quel uno è rotto; e 'n libertá non godo,
Ma piango, e grido:—Ahi, nobil pellegrina,
Qual sentenzia divina
Me legò inanzi, e te prima disciolse?
Dio, che sí tosto al mondo ti ritolse,
Ne mostrò tanta e sí alta virtute
Solo per infiammar nostro desio.—
Certo omai non tem'io,
Amor, de la tua man nove ferute:
Indarno tendi l'arco, a voito scocchi;
Sua virtú cadde al chiuder de' begli occhi.

Morte m'ha sciolto, Amor, d'ogni tua legge:
Quella che fu mia donna, al ciel è gita,
Lasciando trista e libera mia vita.

CCLXXI

L'ardente nodo ov'io fui d'ora in ora,
Contando anni ventuno interi preso,
Morte disciolse; né giá mai tal peso
Provai, né credo ch'uom di dolor mora.

Non volendomi Amor perdere ancóra,
Ebbe un altro lacciuol fra l'erba teso,
E di nova ésca un altro foco acceso,
Tal ch'a gran pena indi scampato fôra.

E se non fosse esperienzia molta
De' primi affanni, i' sarei preso, et arso,
Tanto piú quanto son men verde legno.

Morte m'ha liberato un'altra volta,
E rotto 'l nodo, e 'l foco ha spento e sparso;
Contra la qual non val forza, né 'ngegno.

You bind with one or with another lace;
But me just in one place
You bound, because the sky asks for no more.
Broken the knot; freedom is not my grace,
I weep and cry:—Ah, noble, pilgrim soul,
What divine judgment's goal
Tied me first and delivered you before?
God, who so soon took you far from our shore,
Showed us such lofty full virtue's command
Only to set on fire our inward need.—
I fear no more to bleed,
Love, from another wound made by your hand:
In vain you bend the bow, your shot is void,
Its power fell when her eyes were destroyed.

Death has loosened me, Love, from all your laws,
She, who was once my lady, went above,
And left me sad and free to live and rove.

CCLXXI

The ardent knot in which hour after hour
I was caught, it is now twenty-one years,
Was cut by Death; I never felt the power
Of such a weight, man does not die from cares.

Love, yet unwilling to lose me, did hint,
Laying another noose amid the grass,
And lit another fire from a new flint
So that with a great struggle I should pass.

And were it not the long experience
Of my first ills, I should be trapped and burned,
As much more as my wood less green is turned.

Death has delivered me another time—
The knot is split, scattered the fiery lime—
Against whom neither force nor skill defends.

CCLXXII

La vita fugge, e non s'arresta una ora,
E la morte vien dietro a gran giornate,
E le cose presenti, e le passate
Mi dánno guerra, e le future ancóra

E 'l rimembrare e l'aspettar m'accora
Or quinci or quindi, sí che 'n veritate,
Se non ch'i' ho di me stesso pietate,
I' sarei giá di questi pensier fòra.

Tornami avanti s'alcun dolce mai
Ebbe 'l cor tristo; e poi da l'altra parte
Veggio al mio navigar turbati i vènti;

Veggio fortuna in porto, e stanco omai
Il mio nocchier, e rotte arbore e sarte,
E i lumi bei, che mirar soglio, spenti.

CCLXXIII

Che fai? che pensi? che pur dietro guardi?
Nel tempo, che tornar non pòte omai?
Anima sconsolata, che pur vai
Giugnendo legne al foco ove tu ardi?

Le soavi parole e i dolci sguardi
Ch'ad un ad un descritti e depinti hai
Son leváti de terra; et è, ben sai,
Qui ricercarli, intempestivo, e tardi.

Deh, non rinovellar quel che n'ancide;
Non seguir piú penser vago, fallace,
Ma saldo e certo, ch'a buon fin ne guide.

Cerchiamo 'l ciel, se qui nulla ne piace;
Ché mal per noi quella beltá si vide,
Se viva e morta ne devea tôr pace.

CCLXXII

Life runs away and the hours do not last,
And Death comes after us with mighty stride,
And the things of the present and the past
And the future wage war against my side;

And to remember and to wait torments
Me, whether here or there, so, honestly,
If I did not have pity of my sense,
I should by now from these worries be free.

Whatever sweetness my sad heart did move
Comes before me; then I see winds and clouds
Rush from the other side around my sail;

I see fortune in port, and faint and frail
My pilot, and destroyed the masts and shrouds,
And the fair lights extinguished that I love.

CCLXXIII

What do you do or think? Why do you turn
To look at what is past and comes no more?
Unhappy soul, why do you heap and store
More lumber for the fire that makes you burn?

The loving words and the enchanting glance,
Which one by one you did describe and praise,
Have been taken from earth; this is no chance
To look for them, these are untimely days.

Do not call back again what tortures us;
Do not go after thoughts that err and pass,
Seek a firm one leading to your release.

Let us long for the sky, if nothing here
Pleases; alas, we saw a grace appear,
That would, alive or dead, dispel our peace.

CCLXXIV

Datemi pace, o duri miei pensieri:
Non basta ben ch'Amor, Fortuna, e Morte
Mi fanno guerra intorno, e 'n su le porte,
Senza trovarmi dentro altri guerreri?

E tu, mio cor, ancor se' pur qual eri?
Disleal a me sol, ché fere scorte
Vai ricettando, e se' fatto consorte
De' miei nemici sí pronti e leggieri.

In te i secreti suoi messaggi Amore,
In te spiega Fortuna ogni sua pompa,
E Morte la memoria di quel colpo

Che l'avanzo di me conven che rompa;
In te i vaghi pensier s'arman d'errore:
Per che d'ogni mio mal te solo incolpo.

CCLXXV

Occhi miei, oscurato è 'l nostro sole,
Anzi è salito al cielo, et ivi splende;
Ivi il vedremo ancóra, ivi n'attende,
E di nostro tardar forse li dole.

Orecchie mie, l'angeliche parole
Sonano in parte, ove è chi meglio intende.
Pie' miei, vostra ragion lá non si stende,
Ov'è colei ch'esercitar vi sòle.

Dunque perché mi date questa guerra?
Giá di perdere a voi cagion non fui
Vederla, udirla, e ritrovarla in terra:

Morte biasmate; anzi laudate lui
Che lega e scioglie, e 'n un punto apre e serra,
E dopo 'l pianto sa far lieto altrui.

CCLXXIV

Give me relief, o my hard thoughts and woes,
Around me wage a war, Death, Fortune, Love,
And at my doors; should not this be enough
Without facing inside my other foes?

And you, my heart, are you still as you were?
Disloyal to me only, for you send
And gather here rough guides, and are a friend
Of my opponents quick and light as air.

In you Love does his secret letters show,
In you Fortune displays her pomps and frills,
And Death the recollection of that blow

Which shall break up what remains of my song:
In you my gentle thoughts are armed with wrong;
And this is why I blame you for my ills.

CCLXXV

My eyes, our sun is faded in the dark,
Nay, it climbed heaven to shine there and wait;
We shall see it again when we embark,
Perhaps it mourns because we are too late.

My ears, now her angelic words resound
In a place where is One able to hear.
My feet, your reason cannot there rebound
Where she is gone, who used to call you near.

Then why do you assault me with such war?
I have not been the cause why you are doomed
Not to see, hear, or follow her on earth:

Blame Death; or rather praise the divine law
That binds and frees, has opened and entombed,
And after sorrow will restore our mirth.

CCLXXVI

Poi che la vista angelica, serena,
Per súbita partenza, in gran dolore
Lasciato ha l'alma e 'n tenebroso orrore,
Cerco parlando d'allentar mia pena.

Giusto duol certo a lamentar mi mena;
Sassel chi n'è cagione, e sallo Amore;
Ch'altro rimedio non avea 'l mio core
Contra i fastidî, onde la vita è piena.

Questo un, Morte, m'ha tolto la tua mano:
E tu che copri, e guardi, et hai or teco,
Felice terra, quel bel viso umano,

Me dove lasci, sconsolato e cieco,
Poscia che 'l dolce et amoroso e piano
Lume de gli occhi miei non è piú meco?

CCLXXVII

S'Amor novo consiglio non n'apporta,
Per forza converrá che 'l viver cange:
Tanta paura e duol l'alma trista ange,
Che 'l desir vive, e la speranza è morta:

Onde si sbigottisce, e si sconforta
Mia vita in tutto, e notte e giorno piange,
Stanca, senza governo in mar che frange,
E 'n dubbia via senza fidata scorta.

Imaginata guida la conduce;
Ché la vera è sotterra, anzi è nel cielo,
Onde piú che mai chiara al cor traluce;

A gli occhi no, ch'un doloroso velo
Contende lor la disiata luce,
E me fa sí per tempo cangiar pelo.

CCLXXVI

Now that her sight angelic, clear, and calm,
By its sudden departure left my soul
In anguish, in a horror black as coal,
I try in speaking to allay my qualm.

A just suffering drives me to lament;
She knows, who caused it, and Love also knows;
No other remedy to me was sent
Against the trials that our fate bestows.

This one, Death, you have stolen with your hand:
And you that cover, watch, and keep with you,
Fortunate Earth, that fair face of our kind,

Where do you leave me, comfortless and blind,
Now that the sweet and amorous and true
Lamp of my eyes is no more in my land?

CCLXXVII

If Love does not bring me a new device,
I am compelled to change the life I led:
So great a terror in my sad soul lies,
That desire lives and every hope is dead:

Hence my life is bewildered, mortified
In every thing, and day and night it weeps,
Weary, without a helm, on angry deeps,
And in a dubious course without a guide.

An illusory leader drives it on,
The true is underground, nay, to heaven gone,
Whence she shines to my heart even more hale;

Not to my eyes, because a woeful veil
Forbids them to behold a thing so fair,
And much too early turns to white my hair.

CCLXXVIII

Ne l'etá sua piú bella e piú fiorita,
Quando aver suol Amor in noi piú forza,
Lasciando in terra la terrena scorza,
È l'aura mia vital da me partita,

E viva e bella e nuda al ciel salita:
Indi mi signoreggia, indi mi sforza.
Deh, perché me del mio mortal non scorza
L'ultimo dí, ch'è primo a l'altra vita?

Ché, come i miei pensier dietro a lei vanno,
Cosí lève, espedita, e lieta l'alma
La segua, et io sia fuor di tanto affanno.

Ciò che s'indugia è proprio per mio danno,
Per far me stesso a me piú grave salma.
Oh, che bel morir era, oggi, è terzo anno!

CCLXXIX

Se lamentar augelli, o verdi fronde
Mover soavemente a l'aura estiva,
O ròco mormorar di lucide onde
S'ode d'una fiorita e fresca riva,

Lá 'v'io seggia d'amor pensoso, e scriva,
Lei che 'l ciel ne mostrò, terra n'asconde,
Veggio, et odo, et intendo ch'ancor viva,
Di sí lontano, a' sospir miei risponde.

—Deh, perché inanzi 'l tempo ti consume?
—Mi dice con pietate—a che pur versi
De gli occhi tristi un doloroso fiume?

Di me non pianger tu; ché ' miei dí fêrsi
Morendo eterni, e ne l'interno lume,
Quando mostrai de chiuder, gli occhi apersi.—

CCLXXVIII

In her loveliest age, most full of bloom,
When Love has upon us the greatest force,
Leaving her earthly rind in earthly tomb,
My living aura deserted my course,

And alive, fair, and nude, mounted the sky:
From there she masters me, I bend and kneel;
Why from my mortal fruit does she not peel
The last day, which will be the first I fly?

Then, as my thoughts are going after her,
So, light and speedy and happy, my soul
Would follow her and I be out of woe.

What is delayed is my unhappy dole,
To make my corpse a heavier load to bear.
O how sweet to have died three years ago!

CCLXXIX

If a moaning of birds or of green leaves
Placidly rustled by the summer air,
Or a hoarse murmur of transparent waves
Is heard from a shore blossoming and fair,

Where I sit down and think of love and write,
I see, I hear, I feel her, she abides,
Whom heaven showed to us and the earth hides;
From far away she answers to my plight.

—O why before your time pining away?—
She tells me softly.—Why do you pour down
From your sad eyes such an impassioned stream?

Do not weep over me; because my day
Was made eternal, and their inner beam
Opened my eyes when, closed, they seemed to drown.—

CCLXXX

Mai non fui in parte ove sí chiar vedessi
Quel che veder vorrei, poi ch'io no 'l vidi,
Né dove in tanta libertá mi stessi,
Né ' mpiessi il ciel de sí amorosi stridi;

Né giá mai vidi valle aver sí spessi
Luoghi da sospirar risposti e fidi;
Né credo giá ch'Amore in Cipro avessi,
O in altra riva, sí soavi nidi.

L'acque parlan d'amore, e l'ôra, e i rami,
E gli augelletti, e i pesci, e i fiori, e l'erba,
Tutti inseme pregando ch'i' sempre ami.

Ma tu, ben nata, che dal ciel mi chiami,
Per la memoria di tua morte acerba
Preghi ch'i' sprezzi 'l mondo e i suoi dolci ami.

CCLXXXI

Quante fiate al mio dolce ricetto,
Fuggendo altrui, e, s'esser pò, me stesso,
Vo con gli occhi bagnando l'erba e 'l petto,
Rompendo co' sospir l'aere da presso!

Quante fiate sol, pien di sospetto,
Per luoghi ombrosi e foschi mi son messo,
Cercando col penser l'alto diletto,
Che Morte ha tolto, ond'io la chiamo spesso!

Or in forma di ninfa, o d'altra diva,
Che del piú chiaro fondo di Sorga èsca,
E pongasi a sedere in su la riva;

Or l'ho veduto su per l'erba fresca
Calcare i fior com'una donna viva,
Mostrando in vista che di me le 'ncresca.

CCLXXX

I never saw a place where did arise
So clear what I would see and could not see,
Nor where I was at such a liberty,
Or filled the sky with such amorous cries;

Nor did I ever see valley display
Such thick recesses made for sighs, for rest,
Nor do I think Love did in Cyprus stay,
Or on another shore, for sweeter nest.

The waters speak of love, the boughs, the bowers,
And the small birds, the fishes, grass and flowers,
All together beseeching me to look.

But you, who from above now stir my breath,
For the remembrance of your cruel death,
Beg me to scorn the world and its sweet hook.

CCLXXXI

How many times I go to my sweet nest,
Fleeing all, and myself, if I am wise,
And I wet with my eyes the grass, my breast,
Breaking the air around me with my sighs!

How many times, alone, full of suspicion,
In gloomy, shady places I did crawl,
Pursuing with my thought my dear fruition
That Death has snatched and that I often call!

As a goddess or nymph of fairy lore
That might from the clear depth of Sorga whirl,
And then come to sit down along the shore;

I saw her now walking on the green grass,
Pressing the flowers like a living girl,
And her look seemed to say to me:—Alas!—

CCLXXXII

Alma felice, che sovente torni
A consolar le mie notti dolenti
Con gli occhi tuoi, che Morte non ha spenti,
Ma sovra 'l mortal modo fatti adorni,

Quanto gradisco che ' miei tristi giorni
A rallegrar de tua vista consenti!
Cosí comincio a ritrovar presenti
Le tue bellezze a' suoi usati soggiorni.

Lá 've cantando andai di te molt'anni,
Or, come vedi, vo di te piangendo;
Di te piangendo, no, ma de' miei danni.

Sol un riposo trovo in molti affanni,
Che, quando torni, te conosco, e 'ntendo,
A l'andar, a la voce, al vólto, a' panni.

CCLXXXIII

Discolorato hai, Morte, il piú bel vólto
Che mai si vide, e i piú begli occhi spenti;
Spirto piú acceso di vertuti ardenti,
Del piú leggiadro e piú bel nodo hai sciolto.

In un momento ogni mio ben m'hai tolto;
Post'hai silenzio a' piú soavi accenti
Che mai s'udíro, e me pien di lamenti:
Quant'io veggio m'è noia, e quant'io ascolto.

Ben torna a consolar tanto dolore
Madonna, ove pietá la riconduce;
Né trovo in questa vita altro soccorso.

E se come ella parla, e come luce,
Ridir potessi, accenderei d'amore,
Non dirò d'uom, un cor di tigre o d'orso.

CCLXXXII

O blissful soul that repeatedly come
To soothe my nights by sorrow pierced and torn,
Bringing your eyes that Death did not make numb,
But above mortal aspects did adorn,

How I thank you for cheering my dark days
Allowing me your image to behold!
I can again find present in each place
Your many beauties, as they were of old.

There, where I sang of you for many years,
Now, as you see, I go weeping for you;
Not for you, no indeed, but for my woes.

Only one joy I find in many cares,
That when you come I know that you are true
From your walking, your voice, your face, your clothes.

CCLXXXIII

Death, you discoloured the most lovely face
We ever saw, quenched the most lovely look,
The spirit gleaming with the noblest grace
From the most charming knot you snatched and shook.

In one moment you robbed me of all good,
You put to silence the accents most dear
That have been heard, and left me here to brood:
What I see is a pain, and what I hear.

She does indeed come back to soothe this grief,
My lady, where compassion pushes her:
I do not find any other relief.

And if I could describe what she speaks of,
And how she shines, I should inflame with love
The heart not of a man but of a bear.

CCLXXXIV

Sí breve è 'l tempo e 'l penser sí veloce
Che mi rendon madonna cosí morta,
Ch'al gran dolor la medicina è corta:
Pur, mentr'io veggio lei, nulla mi nòce.

Amor, che m'ha legato e tiemmi in croce,
Trema quando la vede in su la porta
De l'alma ove m'ancide, ancor sí scorta,
Sí dolce in vista, e sí soave in voce.

Come donna in suo albergo altèra vène,
Scacciando de l'oscuro e grave core
Co la fronte serena i pensier tristi.

L'alma, che tanta luce non sostene,
Sospira e dice:—O benedette l'ore
Del dí che questa via con li occhi apristi!—

CCLXXXV

Né mai pietosa madre al caro figlio,
Né donna accesa al suo sposo diletto
Die' con tanti sospir, con tal sospetto
In dubbio stato sí fedel consiglio,

Come a me quella che 'l mio grave essiglio
Mirando dal suo eterno alto ricetto,
Spesso a me torna co l'usato affetto,
E di doppia pietate ornata il ciglio;

Or di madre, or d'amante, or teme, or arde
D'onesto foco; e nel parlar mi mostra
Quel che 'n questo viaggio fugga o segua,

Contando i casi de la vita nostra,
Pregando ch'a levar l'alma non tarde:
E sol quant'ella parla ho pace o tregua.

CCLXXXIV

So brief the time, and the thought is so quick,
Which gives me back my lady who is dead,
That medicines are short for one so sick;
Still, while I see her, I am not afraid.

Love who tied me and keeps me on this cross,
Trembles when he sees her in the doorway
Of the soul where, so strong, she comes to slay,
So sweet her sight, her voice that is my loss.

As a mistress she comes to her own home,
Chasing from an oppressed and gloomy heart,
With her forehead serene, the thoughts that smart.

The soul that is by such light overcome,
Draws sighs and says:—Blessed be every hour
Since you opened this way with your eyes' power!—

CCLXXXV

Never did tender mother her dear son,
Or ardent woman her husband entice,
And with such sadness, such suspicion,
Give in a doubtful state such kind advice,

As she who watching my heavy exile
From her eternal and superior city,
Often returns to me with her love's guile,
Her lashes shining with a double pity;

Now mother and now mistress, now she fears,
Now she burns with pure fire; and shows me by
Her words the way that must be shunned or pressed;

Recounting the events of our past years,
Begging my soul not to be late to fly;
And only when she speaks I find some rest.

CCLXXXVI

Se quell'aura soave de' sospiri
Ch'i' odo di colei che qui fu mia
Donna, or è in cielo, et ancor par qui sia,
E viva, e senta, e vada, et ami, e spiri,

Ritrar potessi, or che caldi desiri
Movrei parlando! sí gelosa e pia
Torna ov'io son, temendo non fra via
Mi stanchi, o 'n dietro o da man manca giri.

Ir dritto, alto, m'insegna; et io che 'ntendo
Le sue caste lusinghe, e i giusti preghi
Col dolce mormorar pietoso e basso,

Secondo lei conven mi regga e pieghi,
Per la dolcezza che del suo dir prendo,
Ch'avria vertú di far piangere un sasso.

CCLXXXVII

Sennuccio mio, ben che doglioso e solo
M'abbi lasciato, i' pur mi riconforto,
Perché del corpo, ov'eri preso e morto,
Alteramente se' levato a volo.

Or vedi inseme l'un e l'altro polo,
Le stelle vaghe, e lor viaggio torto,
E vedi il veder nostro quanto è corto:
Onde col tuo gioir tempro 'l mio duolo.

Ma ben ti prego che 'n la terza spera
Guitton saluti, e messer Cino, e Dante,
Franceschin nostro, e tutta quella schiera.

A la mia donna puoi ben dire in quante
Lagrime io vivo; e son fatt'una fera,
Membrando il suo bel viso, e l'opre sante.

CCLXXXVI

If I could mirror the sweet aura's sighs
That are coming from her who here was mine,
My lady, now in heaven, though my eyes
See her still live and feel, walk, love and shine,

If I could do it, what desires would burn
Excited by my talk! so pure and shy
She comes back where I am, fearing that I
May tire along the way, renounce or turn.

She teaches me to go straight and ascend:
I, knowing her chaste favours that beseech,
With that sweet whispering gentle and deep,

To second her, must hold myself and bend,
Out of the sweetness I get from her speech
That has the virtue to make marble weep.

CCLXXXVII

Sennuccio, though you left me all alone
And mournful, I still comfort my sad plight,
Since from the body where you were undone
You spread your pinions in a lofty flight.

Now you can see the one and other pole,
The moving stars and their revolving light,
And you can see how short is our eyesight:
With your rejoicing I solace my soul.

But I pray you to greet in the third sphere
Guittone, Dante, Cino, and our dear
Little Francis, and all that company.

You can tell to my lady about me
How many are my tears; I become wild
Recalling her fair face and gestures mild.

CCLXXXVIII

I' ho pien di sospir quest'aere tutto,
D'aspri colli mirando il dolce piano,
Ove nacque colei ch'avendo in mano
Meo cor, in sul fiorire e 'n sul far frutto,

È gita al cielo, ed hammi a tal condutto,
Col súbito partir, che di lontano
Gli occhi miei stanchi, lei cercando in vano,
Presso di sé non lassan loco asciutto.

Non è sterpo, né sasso in questi monti,
Non ramo, o fronda verde in queste piagge,
Non fiore in queste valli, o foglia d'erba,

Stilla d'acqua non vèn di queste fonti,
Né fiere han questi boschi sí selvagge,
Che non sappian quanto è mia pena acerba.

CCLXXXIX

L'alma mia fiamma oltra le belle bella,
Ch'ebbe qui 'l ciel sí amico e sí cortese,
Anzi tempo per me nel suo paese
È ritornata, et a la par sua stella.

Or comincio a svegliarmi, e veggio ch'ella
Per lo migliore al mio desir contese,
E quelle voglie giovenili accese
Temprò con una vista dolce e fella.

Lei ne ringrazio, e 'l suo alto consiglio,
Che col bel viso, e co' soavi sdegni,
Fecemi, ardendo, pensar mia salute.

O leggiadre arti, e lor effetti degni,
L'un co la lingua oprar, l'altra col ciglio,
Io gloria in lei et ella in me virtute!

CCLXXXVIII

I have filled all the air with my sighs' bruit
Gazing from rugged hills on the sweet land
Where she was born, who, my heart in her hand,
In its blossoming time and in its fruit,

Went to the sky, plunging me in such mood
By her sudden departure, that from here
My weary eyes seeking in vain their dear,
Leave not a dry spot in this neighbourhood.

There is no stick or stone among these mountains,
Not a branch or green leaf along these shores,
Not a flower in these valleys, blade of grass,

No drop of water trickles from these fountains,
No savage beasts are seen these woods to pass,
That do not know how cruel are my sores.

CCLXXXIX

My lofty flame, more than the fairest fair,
That here had heaven as a courteous friend,
Before her time has reached her journey's end,
And returns to her land her star to share.

Now I begin to wake, I understand
That she for our own good fought my desire,
And made my youthful wishes to retire
Tempering them with a look hard and bland.

I thank her soul and her holy device
That with her face and her sweet anger's bolts
Bid me in burning think of my salvation.

O lovely arts bringing worthy results,
One working with the tongue, one with the eyes,
I for her glory, she for my vocation!

CCXC

Come va 'l mondo! or mi diletta e piace
Quel che piú mi dispiacque; or veggio e sento
Che, per aver salute, ebbi tormento,
E breve guerra per eterna pace.

O speranza, o desir sempre fallace,
E de gli amanti piú ben per un cento!
O quant'era il peggior farmi contento
Quella ch'or siede in cielo, e 'n terra giace!

Ma 'l ceco Amor, e la mia sorda mente
Mi traviavan sí, ch'andar per viva
Forza mi convenia, dove morte era.

Benedetta colei ch'a miglior riva
Volse il mio corso, e l'empia voglia ardente,
Lusingando, affrenò, perch'io non pèra.

CCXCI

Quand'io veggio dal ciel scender l'Aurora
Co la fronte di ròse e co' crin d'oro,
Amor m'assale; ond'io mi discoloro,
E dico sospirando:—Ivi è l'aura ora.

O felice Titon! tu sai ben l'ora
Da ricovrare il tuo caro tesoro;
Ma io che debbo far del dolce alloro?
Che se 'l vo' riveder, conven ch'io mora.

I vostri dipartir non son sí duri;
Ch'almen di notte suol tornar colei
Che non ha schifo le tue bianche chiome:

Le mie notti fa triste, e i giorni oscuri,
Quella che n'ha portato i penser miei,
Né di sé m'ha lasciato altro che 'l nome.—

CCXC

What is the world! Now I am charmed and pleased
By what displeased me most; I see and feel
That to be saved I was tormented, teased,
Given short war for an eternal weal.

O hopes, o wishes treacherous and mad,
The greatest price that all lovers are worth,
How much worse had it been to make me glad,
Of her who sits in heaven, sleeps in earth!

But the blind Love and my own deafened mind
Had me so stranded, that led by sheer force
I had to go where Death wants us to lie.

Blessed be she who to the better shores
Turned my direction and flattered my blind
Hot will and checked it, so I may not die.

CCXCI

When I see from the sky descend the dawn
With her forehead of roses, golden hair,
Love assails me; my colours are withdrawn,
And I say sighing:—The aura is there.—

Glad Tithonus! You know the time of day
When you can hold again your precious treasure;
But I, what can I do with the sweet bay,
Since, to go where she is, death is the measure?

Your departures are not as hard as ours;
Because at night she comes back all the same
And she does not despise your hoary head:

My nights she makes forlorn and my days dread,
She who keeps all my thoughts chained by her powers,
And of herself left me only her name.

CCXCII

Gli occhi di ch'io parlai sí caldamente,
E le braccia, e le mani, e i piedi, e 'l viso,
Che m'avean sí da me stesso diviso,
E fatto singular da l'altra gente;

Le crespe chiome d'òr puro lucente,
E 'l lampeggiar de l'angelico riso
Che solean fare in terra un paradiso,
Poca polvere son, che nulla sente.

Et io pur vivo; onde mi doglio e sdegno,
Rimaso senza 'l lume ch'amai tanto,
In gran fortuna, e 'n disarmato legno.

Or sia qui fine al mio amoroso canto:
Secca è la vena de l'usato ingegno,
E la cetera mia rivolta in pianto.

CCXCIII

S'io avesse pensato che sí care
Fossin le voci dè' sospir miei in rima,
Fatte l'avrei, dal sospirar mio prima,
In numero piú spesse, in stil piú rare.

Morta colei che mi facea parlare,
E che si stava de' pensier miei in cima,
Non posso, e non ho piú sí dolce lima,
Rime aspre e fosche far soavi e chiare.

E certo ogni mio studio in quel tempo era
Pur di sfogare il doloroso core
In qualche modo, non d'acquistar fama.

Pianger cercai, non giá del pianto onore:
Or vorrei ben piacer; ma quella altèra,
Tacito, stanco, dopo sé mi chiama.

CCXCII

The eyes of which I spoke with such emotion,
And the arms and the hands, the face, the feet,
That had divided me from my self-notion,
And made me all unlike the ones I meet;

The frizzled hair of pure, luminous gold,
The lightning flashes of her smile and eyes
That used to make of earth a paradise,
Are a few ashes that now nothing hold.

And I still live; hence I lament and brood,
Left here without the lamp I loved so long,
In a great tempest, in a battered wood.

Then let this be the end of my love song:
Dried is the vein of my habitual skill,
And my zither can only weep my ill.

CCXCIII

If I had ever thought that my sighs' voice,
Expressed in verses, would be found so dear,
I should have made them since my earliest tear
More numerous in bulk, more rare in choice.

She being dead, who used to make me speak
And who sat on the summit of my mind,
I cannot, since my file I do not find,
Make clear and sweet rhymes that are wild and weak.

Certainly at that time my only care
Was to pour forth my heart's dejection
In this or in that way, not to gain fame.

I tried to weep, not to honour my name;
Now I would gladly please, but that proud one,
Calls me, silent and weary, after her.

CCXCIV

Soleasi nel mio cor star bella e viva,
Com'alta donna in loco umile e basso;
Or son fatto io per l'ultimo suo passo,
Non pur mortal, ma morto, et ella è diva.

L'alma d'ogni suo ben spogliata e priva,
Amor de la sua luce ignudo e casso
Devrian de la pietá romper un sasso;
Ma non è chi lor duol riconti, o scriva:

Ché piangon dentro, ov'ogni orecchia è sorda,
Se non la mia, cui tanta doglia ingombra,
Ch'altro che sospirar nulla m'avanza.

Veramente siam noi polvere et ombra;
Veramente la voglia cieca e 'ngorda;
Veramente fallace è la speranza.

CCXCV

Soleano i miei penser soavemente
Di lor obgetto ragionare inseme:
—Pietá s'appressa, e del tardar si pente:
Forse or parla di noi, o spera, o teme.—

Poi che l'ultimo giorno, e l'ore estreme
Spogliâr di lei questa vita presente,
Nostro stato dal ciel vede, ode, e sente:
Altra di lei non è rimaso speme.

O miracol gentile! o felice alma!
O beltá senza essempio altèra e rara,
Che tosto è ritornata ond'ella uscío!

Ivi ha del suo ben far corona e palma
Quella ch'al mondo sí famosa e chiara
Fe' la sua gran vertute, e 'l furor mio.

CCXCIV

She used, fair and alive, my heart to plumb,
As a great lady in a humble place;
Now, because of her death, I have become
Not just mortal but dead, and she my grace.

My soul despoiled, deprived of good, alone,
Love destitute and barren of its light,
Should out of pity break a heart of stone;
But no one can describe their grief, or write:

They weep inside where ears are deaf with rust,
Save mine, who am encumbered by such pain
That there are only sighs which still remain.

Verily we are only shades and dust;
Verily our desires are blind and grope;
Verily treacherous is all our hope.

CCXCV

My thoughts used to converse and talk about
Their object and exchange their sweet debate:
—Pity approaches, regrets to be late,
Perhaps she speaks of us, in hope or doubt.—

After the final day, the extreme hours,
Deprived of her this present life and lair,
She sees from heaven, hears, feels what is ours:
No other hope has remained here of her.

O gentle miracle! O happy soul!
O beauty above others high and rare
That soon returned to your abandoned goal!

There of her good she gets the crown and palm,
She who was made on earth famous and clear
By her high virtue and my furious qualm.

CCXCVI

I' mi soglio accusare, et or mi scuso,
Anzi me pregio, e tengo assai piú caro
De l'onesta pregion, del dolce amaro
Colpo, ch'i' portai giá molt'anni chiuso.

Invide Parche, sí repente il fuso
Troncaste, ch'attorcea soave e chiaro
Stame al mio laccio, e quello aurato e raro
Strale, onde morte piacque oltra nostro uso!

Ché non fu d'allegrezza a' suoi dí mai,
Di libertá, di vita alma sí vaga,
Che non cangiasse 'l suo natural modo,

Togliendo anzi per lei sempre trar guai,
Che cantar per qualunque, e di tal piaga
Morir contenta, e vivere in tal nodo.

CCXCVII

Due gran nemiche inseme erano agiunte,
Bellezza et Onestá, con pace tanta
Che mai rebellion l'anima santa
Non sentí poi ch'a star seco fûr giunte.

Et or per morte son sparse e disgiunte:
L'una è nel ciel, che se ne gloria, e vanta;
L'altra sotterra, che ' begli occhi amanta,
Onde uscîr giá tant'amorose punte.

L'atto soave, e 'l parlar saggio umíle
Che movea d'alto loco, e 'l dolce sguardo
Che piagava il mio core (ancor l'acenna),

Sono spariti; e s'al seguir son tardo,
Forse averrá che 'l bel nome gentile
Consecrerò con questa stanca penna.

CCXCVI

I always scold myself, now I defend,
Nay, I respect myself and hold more dear
For the glad prison, the sweet-bitter blend
Of the blow I endured many a year.

Envious Fates, so suddenly you broke
The spindle that entwined a sweet and clear
Wool in my string, and that rare golden spear
That made us change our mood, and death invoke!

Never a soul did so love happiness
Or freedom, or rich life on pleasant ground,
That did not swerve from its natural lot,

Choosing rather for her to reap distress
Than to sing for another, from such wound
To die content and live in such a knot.

CCXCVII

Two great rivals together had been joined,
Beauty and Honesty, with so much peace,
That in her soul rebellion had to cease
Ever since they were lodged in the same point.

And now Death separates them and disjoins:
One is in heaven to exult in glory;
One in the earth that closes her eyes' story
From where used to come out amorous points.

The gentle act, the speech prudent and tame,
That came from a high place—into her ken
And pierced my heart (and still can make it hollow),

Are vanished; and if I am late to follow,
Perhaps it will be seen that her dear name
I shall make sacred with this weary pen.

CCXCVIII

Quand'io mi volgo in dietro a mirar gli anni
C'hanno fuggendo i miei penseri sparsi,
E spento 'l foco, ove agghiacciando io arsi,
E finito il riposo pien d'affanni,

Rotta la fé de gli amorosi inganni,
E sol due parti d'ogni mio ben farsi,
L'una nel cielo, e l'altra in terra starsi,
E perduto il guadagno de' miei danni,

I' mi riscuoto, e trovomi sí nudo,
Ch'i' porto invidia ad ogni estrema sorte:
Tal cordoglio e paura ho di me stesso.

O mia stella, o fortuna, o fato, o morte,
O per me sempre dolce giorno e crudo,
Come m'avete in basso stato messo!

CCXCIX

Ov'è la fronte, che con picciol cenno
Volgea il mio core in questa parte e 'n quella?
Ov'è 'l bel ciglio, e l'una e l'altra stella
Ch'al corso del mio viver lume dênno?

Ov'è 'l valor, la conoscenza, e 'l senno?
L'accorta, onesta, umil, dolce favella?
Ove son le bellezze accolte in ella,
Che gran tempo di me lor voglia fênno?

Ov'è l'ombra gentil del viso umano,
Ch'ôra e riposo dava a l'alma stanca,
E lá 've i miei pensier scritti eran tutti?

Ov'è colei che mia vita ebbe in mano?
Quanto al misero mondo, e quanto manca
A gli occhi miei che mai non fíen asciutti!

CCXCVIII

When I turn backward to look at the years
That running have dispersed my thoughts and throes,
And quenched the fire in which I burned and froze,
And banished my repose oppressed with cares,

Broken the faith of the amorous lies
And in two parts divided all my good,
One staying in the earth, one in the skies,
And lost what I had gained from my pains' feud,

I am all stirred, I find myself so void,
That I envy the most pitiless fate:
Such torment and affright gives me my state.

O my star, o my chance, Death, Destiny,
O to me always sweet day that destroyed,
In what a low condition you lay me!

CCXCIX

Where is the brow that with a little nod
Turned my heart toward this, toward that side?
And the fine lashes where two stars did glide
To give a light to the life-path I trod?

Where is the valour, the knowledge, the wit,
The prudent, honest, humble, lovely tongue?
Where are the beauties come in her to sit
That made of me their subject for so long?

Where is the gentle shadow of a face
That gave to my tired soul relief and grace,
And where my thoughts were all written and told?

And where is she, who had me in her hold?
How does the sad world miss her, how do I
Miss her with eyes that never will be dry!

CCC

Quanta invidia io ti porto, avara terra,
Ch'abbracci quella, cui veder m'è tolto,
E mi contendi l'aria del bel vólto,
Dove pace trovai d'ogni mia guerra!

Quanta ne porto al ciel, che chiude e serra,
E sí cupidamente ha in sé raccolto
Lo spirto da le belle membra sciolto,
E per altrui sí rado si diserra!

Quanta invidia a quell'anime che 'n sorte
Hanno or sua santa e dolce compagnia,
La qual io cercai sempre con tal brama!

Quant'a la dispietata e dura morte,
Ch'avendo spento in lei la vita mia,
Stassi ne' suoi begli occhi, e me non chiama!

CCCI

Valle che de' lamenti miei se' piena,
Fiume che spesso del mio pianger cresci,
Fere selvestre, vaghi augelli, e pesci
Che l'una e l'altra verde riva affrena,

Aria de' miei sospir calda e serena,
Dolce sentier che sí amaro riesci,
Colle che mi piacesti, or mi rincresci,
Ov'ancor per usanza Amor mi mena,

Ben riconosco in voi l'usate forme,
Non, lasso!, in me, che da sí lieta vita
Son fatto albergo d'infinita doglia.

Quinci vedea 'l mio bene; e per queste orme
Torno a vedere ond'al ciel nudo è gita,
Lasciando in terra la sua bella spoglia.

CCC

How much I envy you, Earth, who embrace
Stingily her, whose vision I have lost,
And grudge to me the air of her fair face
Where I found peace from all the storms I crossed!

How I envy the sky that wants to hold
And greedily has gathered on its side
The spirit taken from her fair limbs' mould,
While to some others seldom it replied!

How I envy the souls who in their choir
Enjoy her sweet and holy company
That I always longed for with such desire!

How I envy the cruel, unfeeling Death,
Who having snatched with her my living breath,
Stays in her eyes and does not summon me!

CCCI

Vale that are filled with my lamenting words,
River that swell with all the tears I pour,
Beasts of the woods, fishes, and pretty birds
That are contained between either green shore,

Warm, serene air exhaling from my sighs,
Sweet lane that all too bitter have become,
Hill that pleased me and that now leave me numb,
Where my old custom Love can still entice,

I recognize in you the usual traces,
But not in me, who from that happy soil
Have been set in a dwelling of despair.

From here I used to see her; in these places
I come to see whence she ascended, bare,
Leaving inside the earth her lovely spoil.

CCCII

Levommi il mio penser in parte ov'era
Quella ch'io cerco, e non ritrovo in terra:
Ivi, fra lor che 'l terzo cerchio serra,
La rividi piú bella, e meno altèra.

Per man mi prese, e disse:—In questa spera
Sarai ancor meco, se 'l desir non erra;
I' so' colei che ti die' tanta guerra,
E compié' mia giornata inanzi sera.

Mio ben non cape in intelletto umano:
Te solo aspetto, e quel che tanto amasti
E lá giuso è rimaso, il mio bel velo.—

Deh, perché tacque, et allargò la mano?
Ch'al suon de' detti sí pietosi e casti
Poco mancò ch'io non rimasi in cielo.

CCCIII

Amor, che meco al buon tempo ti stavi
Fra queste rive, a' pensier nostri amiche,
E per saldar le ragion nostre antiche
Meco e col fiume ragionando andavi;

Fior, frondi, erbe, ombre, antri, onde, aure soavi,
Valli chiuse, alti colli e piagge apriche,
Porto de l'amorose mie fatiche,
De le fortune mie tante, e sí gravi;

O vaghi abitator de' verdi boschi,
O ninfe, e voi che 'l fresco erboso fondo
Del liquido cristallo alberga e pasce;

I dí miei fûr sí chiari, or son sí foschi,
Come Morte che 'l fa. Cosí nel mondo
Sua ventura ha ciascun dal dí che nasce.

CCCII

My thought lifted me up to the place where
Was she I seek and cannot find on earth:
There, among those within the third sphere's mirth,
I beheld her again, less proud, more fair.

She took me by the hand and said:—My friend,
You shall be here with me, if wish is law;
I am the one who made you such a war
And completed my day before the end.

My good does not conform to human brand,
I only wait for you, and what you loved
So much, and I left there, my pretty veil.—

Why did she pause? Why did she drop her hand?
Because in hearing words so chaste and moved,
I was about to stay in heaven's dale.

CCCIII

Love, who would dwell with me in that sweet season,
Within those borders, our thoughts' friendly source,
And in order to seal our ancient reason
With me and with the river would discourse,

Flowers, leaves and grass, shady caves and soft air,
Closed valleys, hills, open, delightful plains,
Haven of all my amorous despair,
Of my so many fortunes and constraints,

Lovely inmates of green wood and park,
O nymphs, and you, in the cool grassy bed
Of liquid crystal harboured and well fed,

So clear were once my days! Now they are dark
As Death, who knows it: in this way on earth
Each of us has his destiny with birth.

CCCIV

Mentre che 'l cor da gli amorosi vermi
Fu consumato, e 'n fiamma amorosa arse,
Di vaga fera le vestigia sparse
Cercai per poggi solitarii et ermi;

Et ebbi ardir cantando di dolermi
D'Amor, di lei che sí dura m'apparse:
Ma l'ingegno e le rime erano scarse
In quella etate a i pensier novi e 'nfermi.

Quel foco è morto, e 'l copre un picciol marmo:
Che se col tempo fossi ito avanzando,
Come giá in altri, in fino a la vecchiezza,

Di rime armato, ond'oggi mi disarmo,
Con stil canuto avrei fatto parlando
Romper le pietre, e pianger di dolcezza.

CCCV

Anima bella, da quel nodo sciolta
Che piú bel mai non seppe ordir Natura,
Pon dal ciel mente a la mia vita oscura,
Da sí lieti pensieri a pianger volta.

La falsa opinion dal cor s'è tolta,
Che mi fece alcun tempo acerba e dura
Tua dolce vista; omai tutta secura
Volgi a me gli occhi, e i miei sospiri ascolta.

Mira 'l gran sasso, donde Sorga nasce,
E vedra'vi un che sol tra l'erbe e l'acque
Di tua memoria, e di dolor si pasce.

Ove giace il tuo albergo, e dove nacque
Il nostro amor, vo' ch'abbandoni e lasce,
Per non veder ne' tuoi quel ch'a te spiacque.

CCCIV

When my heart was the amorous worms' meat
And did in amorous consumption rave,
I sought the scattered footsteps of a sweet
Wild animal through wood and hill and cave;

And I dared in my singing to complain
Of Love, of her, who seemed to scorn my pain.
But my genius and rhymes were much too weak
In that new age for thoughts so young and sick.

That fire is dead, in a small marble press.
Ah, if with time it had increased in rage
As in the past, until my oldest age,

Armed with my rhymes that now I leave alone,
My gray-haired style would have broken a stone
With words, and made it weep from tenderness.

CCCV

Beautiful soul, delivered from that knot
Which was the loveliest Nature could prepare,
Consider from the sky my darkened lot,
Leave your glad thoughts, my suffering to share.

My heart has given up the false device
Which in the past had made cruel and sore
Your sweet appearance: now you can, secure,
Turn toward me your eyes, o hear my sighs.

Look at the rock where Sorga comes to leap,
You will see one, amid water and grass,
Who feeds on memory and pain, forlorn.

Where your house stands and where our love was born,
I want you to ignore and leave and pass,
Not to see in your own what made you weep.

CCCVI

Quel sol che mi mostrava il camin destro
Di gire al ciel con gloriosi passi,
Tornando al sommo sole, in pochi sassi
Chiuse 'l mio lume, e 'l suo carcer terrestro;

Ond'io son fatto un animal silvestro,
Che co' pie' vaghi solitarii e lassi
Porto 'l cor grave, e gli occhi umidi e bassi
Al mondo, ch'è per me un deserto alpestro.

Cosí vo ricercando ogni contrada
Ov'io la vidi; e sol tu che m'affligi,
Amor, vien meco, e mostrimi ondio vada.

Lei non trov'io; ma suoi santi vestigi
Tutti rivolti a la superna strada
Veggio, lunge da' laghi averni e stigi.

CCCVII

I' pensava assai destro esser su l'ale,
Non per lor forza, ma di chi le spiega,
Per gir cantando a quel bel nodo eguale,
Onde Morte m'assolve, Amor mi lega.

Trovaimi a l'opra via piú lento e frale
D'un picciol ramo cui gran fascio piega;
E dissi:—A cader va chi troppo sale;
Né si fa ben per uom quel che 'l ciel nega.—

Mai non poría volar penna d'ingegno,
Non che stil grave o lingua, ove Natura
Volò tessendo il mio dolce ritegno.

Seguilla Amor con sí mirabil cura
In adornarlo, ch'i' non era degno
Pur de la vista; ma fu mia ventura.

CCCVI

The sun that showed to me the rightful zones
That bring us to the sky on glory's stamp,
Returned to the high sun and closed my lamp
And its terrestrial cage in a few stones;

I have become like a beast of these woods
That with tired feet, and lonely and stiff,
Carries a heavy heart, low eyes, and broods
In a world like a desert on a cliff.

Thus I go visiting every region
Where I saw her; and you, cause of my sins,
Love, come along and lead my step and vision.

I find her not; but her holy footprints
All set toward the high spiritual stakes
Can be seen, far from hellish Stygian lakes.

CCCVII

I thought that I was skilful with my wings,
Not by their strength, but by whose hands they are
    wrought,
By singing equal to that gentle knot
In which Death pardons me and Love still clings.

I found myself in this more slow and small
Than a frail branch which a great burden bends,
And I said:—Who will fly too high will fall,
Nor can a man do well what God defends.—

Never could an ingenious feather venture,
Nor a grave style or tongue, where did go Nature
Weaving the pattern of my sweet restraint;

Love followed her with such wondrous intent
Adorning it, that made me unfit to look:
But this was my salvation and good luck.

CCCVIII

Quella per cui con Sorga ho cangiato Arno,
Con franca povertá serve richezze,
Volse in amaro sue sante dolcezze,
Ond'io giá vissi, or me ne struggo e scarno.

Da poi piú volte ho riprovato indarno
Al secol che verrá l'alte bellezze
Pinger cantando, a ciò che l'ame e prezze;
Né col mio stile il suo bel viso incarno.

Le lode mai non d'altra, e proprie sue,
Che 'n lei fûr come stelle in cielo sparte,
Pur ardisco ombreggiare, or una, or due;

Ma poi ch'i' giungo a la divina parte,
Ch'un chiaro e breve sole al mondo fue,
Ivi manca l'ardir, l'ingegno e l'arte.

CCCIX

L'alto e novo miracol ch'a' dí nostri
Apparve al mondo, e star seco non volse,
Che sol ne mostrò 'l ciel, poi sel ritolse,
Per adornarne i suoi stellanti chiostri,

Vuol ch'i' depinga a chi no 'l vide, e 'l mostri,
Amor, che 'n prima la mia lingua sciolse,
Poi mille volte indarno a l'opra volse
Ingegno, tempo, penne, carte, enchiostri.

Non son al sommo ancor giunte le rime:
In me il conosco; e proval ben chiunque
È 'n fin a qui, che d'amor parli o scriva.

Chi sa pensare, il ver tacito estime,
Ch'ogni stil vince, e poi sospire:—Adunque
Beati gli occhi che la vider viva!—

CCCVIII

She for whom I exchanged Sorga for Arno,
And for a servile wealth free poverty,
Turned into bitter the sweet melody
By which I lived, by which I now decline.

After that, many times I did desire
And vainly try to sing her lofty grace
For the next age to love her and admire,
But my style cannot make alive her face.

Not any other's praises, but her own
That were scattered on her like stars from birth
I dared to paint, one or two I have shown.

But when I come to touch the divine part
That was a clear and fleeting sun on earth,
There fails my courage, my talent, my art.

CCCIX

The high, new miracle that in our time
Appeared within our world and did not stay,
That the sky showed to us and took away
And made it to adorn its starry clime,

Love, after causing my tongue to be free,
And thousand times then threatening to sink
Talent and time, pen and paper and ink,
Wants me to paint to those who did not see.

My rhymes have not yet reached their high object:
I know it well myself; and every poet
Who spoke or wrote of love till now, can show it.

Who is able to think, let him reflect
Silently on the truth that defeats style,
And sigh:—Blest be the eyes that saw her smile!—

CCCX

Zefiro torna, e 'l bel tempo rimena,
E i fiori e l'erbe, sua dolce famiglia,
E garrir Progne, e pianger Filomena,
E primavera candida e vermiglia.

Ridono i prati, e 'l ciel si rasserena;
Giove s'allegra di mirar sua figlia;
L'aria, e l'acqua, e la terra è d'amor piena;
Ogni animal d'amar si riconsiglia.

Ma per me, lasso!, tornano i piú gravi
Sospiri, che del cor profondo tragge
Quella ch'al ciel se ne portò le chiavi;

E cantar augelletti, e fiorir piagge,
E 'n belle donne oneste atti soavi
Sono un deserto, e fere aspre e selvagge.

CCCXI

Quel rosigniuol che sí soave piagne,
Forse suoi figli, o sua cara consorte,
Di dolcezza empie il cielo e le campagne
Con tante note sí pietose e scorte;

E tutta notte par che m'accompagne,
E mi rammente la mia dura sorte;
Ch'altri che me non ho di ch'i' mi lagne;
Ché 'n dee non credev'io regnasse Morte.

O che lieve è inganar chi s'assecura!
Que' duo bei lumi assai piú che 'l sol chiari
Chi pensò mai veder far terra oscura?

Or cognosco io che mia fera ventura
Vuol che vivendo e lagrimando impari
Come nulla qua giú diletta, e dura.

CCCX

Zephyr comes back and brings the lovely weather,
Flowers and grass, its sweet family ties,
And Philomela warbles, Procne cries,
And spring returns, the white and the pink feather;

The meadows laugh and the sky is serene;
Jupiter gladly gazes on his daughter;
Love fills the air and the earth and the water;
And all the creatures' instincts on love lean.

But to me only come the heaviest sighs
That from my heart she will draw out and pull,
Who flew away with its keys to the skies;

And small birds singing, and blossoms so full,
And lovely women, their acts fair and mild,
Are a desert to me, beasts rough and wild.

CCCXI

That nightingale who so tenderly weeps
Perhaps his children or his loving mate,
With sweetness fills the sky, and his song sweeps
The earth with many notes that mourn and wait,

And all the night seems to repeat the same
Lament, following me, saying that I
No other than myself have cause to blame
For thinking that an angel does not die.

How easy to deceive him who is sure!
Those two fair eyes, clearer than sun their spark,
Who ever thought would make the earth so dark?

Now I know that this fate I must endure,
And live and weep and learn from all my past
That nothing here below can please and last.

CCCXII

Né per sereno ciel ir vaghe stelle,
Né per tranquillo mar legni spalmati,
Né per campagne cavalieri armati,
Né per bei boschi allegre fere e snelle;

Né d'aspettato ben fresche novelle,
Né dir d'amore in stili alti et ornati,
Né tra chiare fontane e verdi prati
Dolce cantare oneste donne e belle;

Né altro sará mai ch'al cor m'aggiunga,
Sí seco il seppe quella sepellire
Che sola a gli occhi miei fu lume e speglio.

Noia m'è 'l viver sí gravosa e lunga,
Ch'i' chiamo il fine, per lo gran desire
Di riveder cui non veder fu 'l meglio.

CCCXIII

Passato è 'l tempo omai, lasso!, che tanto
Con refrigerio in mezzo 'l foco vissi;
Passato è quella di ch'io piansi e scrissi,
Ma lasciato m'ha ben la penna e 'l pianto.

Passato è 'l viso sí leggiadro e santo,
Ma, passando, i dolci occhi al cor m'ha fissi,
Al cor giá mio, che seguendo partissi
Lei ch'avolto l'avea nel suo bel manto.

Ella 'l se ne portò sotterra, e 'n cielo,
Ove or triumfa, ornata de l'alloro
Che meritò la sua invitta onestate.

Cosí, disciolto dal mortal mio velo
Ch'a forza mi tien qui, foss'io con loro
Fuor de' sospir fra l'anime beate!

CCCXII

No erring stars in the sky's limpid sites,
No well-tarred ships upon a tranquil sea,
No country background around armoured knights,
No merry beasts in the woods' liberty,

No recent news of an expected joy,
No speech of love adorned by noble skills,
No sweet singing of ladies fair and coy
Among the lucid fountains and green hills;

Nor any other thing will touch my heart
That she buried in her with such an art,
Who was my only mirror and my creed.

My life is such a tiresome thing and mean,
That I call for the end, so much I need
To see her whom I should never have seen.

CCCXIII

Gone is the time, alas! that I once spent
With so much solace in the midst of fire;
And she is gone, of whom spoke my lament,
But she still leaves with me pen and desire.

Gone is the face enchanting that I bless,
But in going she nailed unto my heart
Her eyes, it was my heart that did depart
With her who had enwrapped it in her dress.

She took it under earth and in the sky
Where now she triumphs with the laurel leaf
That deserved her unconquered honesty.

Could I, free from this veil, my mortal tie,
That holds me here by force, go there and flee
Toward the blessed souls, out of my grief!

CCCXIV

Mente mia, che presaga de' tuoi danni,
Al tempo lieto giá pensosa e trista,
Sí 'ntentamente ne l'amata vista
Requie cercavi de' futuri affanni,

A gli atti, a le parole, al viso, a i panni,
A la nova pietá con dolor mista,
Potêi ben dir, se del tutto eri avista:
—Questo è l'ultimo dí de' miei dolci anni.—

Qual dolcezza fu quella, o misera alma!
Come ardavamo in quel punto ch'i' vidi
Gli occhi, i quai non devea riveder mai,

Quando a lor, come a' duo amici piú fidi,
Partendo, in guardia la piú nobil salma,
I miei cari penseri e 'l cor lasciai!

CCCXV

Tutta la mia fiorita e verde etade
Passava; e 'ntepidir sentía giá 'l foco
Ch'arse il mio core; et era giunto al loco
Ove scende la vita, ch'al fin cade.

Giá incomminciava a prender securtade
La mia cara nemica a poco a poco
De' suoi sospetti, e rivolgeva in gioco
Mie pene acerbe sua dolce onestade.

Presso era 'l tempo dove Amor si scontra
Con Castitate, et a gli amanti è dato
Sedersi inseme, e dir che lor incontra.

Morte ebbe invidia al mio felice stato,
Anzi a la speme; e fêglisi a l'incontra
A mezza via, come nemico armato.

CCCXIV

O my mind that foreseeing your sad plight,
Already worried in the happiest years,
Intently sought in the beloved sight
A consolation of the future cares,

From her gestures, her words, her face, her guise,
From the new pity mingled with her pain,
You could have said if you had been more wise:
—This is the last link of my loving chain.—

What sweetness you felt then, o tortured soul,
How much we burned the time I did implore
Those eyes I would not see here any more,

When to them, to the truest friends of all,
In leaving I entrusted my best part
And my dear thoughts and my devoted heart!

CCCXV

All my blossoming spring and my green years
Were passing, and less ardent was the fire
That burned my heart, and soon I would retire
To the place where life falls when the end appears.

Already, slowly, my dear enemy
Was beginning to feel sure, to remove
Her first suspicions, she would tease with love
My cruel grief, and with sweet honesty:

The time was near when Love meets Chastity
And when lovers are given liberty
To sit together and talk of their fate.

But jealous Death envied my blissful state,
A hope! and rushed to meet it full of hate,
Halfway, like a strong-armoured enemy.

CCCXVI

Tempo era omai da trovar pace o tregua
Di tanta guerra, et erane in via forse;
Se non che ' lieti passi in dietro torse
Chi le disaguaglianze nostre adegua.

Ché, come nebbia al vento si dilegua,
Cosí sua vita súbito trascorse
Quella che giá co' begli occhi mi scòrse,
Et or conven che col penser la segua.

Poco avev' a 'ndugiar, ché gli anni e 'l pelo
Cangiavano i costumi; onde sospetto
Non fôra il ragionar del mio mal seco.

Con che onesti sospiri l'avrei detto
Le mie lunghe fatiche, ch'or dal cielo
Vede, son certo, e duolsene ancor meco!

CCCXVII

Tranquillo porto avea mostrato Amore
A la mia lunga e torbida tempesta
Fra gli anni de la etá matura onesta,
Che i vizii spoglia, e vertú veste e onore.

Giá traluceva a' begli occhi il mio core,
E l'alta fede non piú lor molesta.
Ahi, Morte ria, come a schíantar se' presta
Il frutto de molt'anni in sí poche ore!

Pur, vivendo, veniasi ove deposto
In quelle caste orecchie avrei, parlando,
De' miei dolci pensier l'antiqua soma;

Et ella avrebbe a me forse resposto
Qualche santa parola sospirando,
Cangiáti i vólti, e l'una e l'altra coma.

CCCXVI

It was now time to find peace or release
From such a war, and perhaps it was near;
But our gay steps were sent back to the rear
By one who levels our diversities.

For as the mist is scattered in the wind,
So she ran through her lifetime suddenly,
She who once with her eyes directed me,
Whom I now follow only with my mind.

There was little to wait, for years and hair
Changed me; and it would not have been a sin
To reason of my agony with her.

With what spontaneous sighs I should have told
Her my long trials, who now does behold
Me, I am sure, and mourns for what has been.

CCCXVII

Love had shown a calm haven to the rage
Of my long-lasting and turbulent storm,
Within the years of the ripe, honest age
That bares vices, and clothes virtues with form.

My heart was now reflected in her eyes
That my pure faith no longer did annoy.
Ah, wicked Death, how quick is your surprise
That tears in a few hours many years' joy!

Had she lived, very soon I could afford
In talking to entrust to her dear care
The ancient load of my passionate thought;

And she perhaps would have answered and brought
To me her sighing and her holy word,
Our faces altered and altered our hair.

CCCXVIII

Al cader d'una pianta che si svelse
Come quella che ferro o vento sterpe,
Spargendo a terra le sue spoglie eccelse,
Mostrando al sol la sua squalida sterpe,

Vidi un'altra ch'Amor obietto scelse,
Subietto in me Calliope et Euterpe;
Che 'l cor m'avinse, e proprio albergo fêlse,
Qual per trunco o per muro edera serpe.

Quel vivo lauro, ove solean far nido
Li alti penseri e i miei sospiri ardenti,
Che de' bei rami mai non mossen fronda,

Al ciel translato, in quel suo albergo fido
Lasciò radici, onde con gravi accenti
È ancor chi chiami, e non è chi responda.

CCCXIX

I dí miei, piú leggier che nesun cervo,
Fuggîr come ombra; e non vider piú bene
Ch'un batter d'occhio, e poche ore serene,
Ch'amare e dolci ne la mente servo.

Misero mondo, instabile e protervo,
Del tutto è cieco chi 'n te pon sua spene:
Ché 'n te mi fu 'l cor tolto; et or sel tène
Tal ch'è giá terra, e non giunge osso a nervo.

Ma la forma miglior, che vive ancóra,
E vivrá sempre su ne l'alto cielo,
Di sue bellezze ogni or piú m'innamora;

E vo, sol in pensar, cangiando il pelo,
Qual ella è oggi, e 'n qual parte dimora,
Qual a vedere il suo leggiadro velo.

CCCXVIII

When a plant crashed that was torn from the soil,
As those pulled out by iron or by wind,
Scattering on the ground its noble spoil
And showing to the sun its stump and rind,

I saw another that Love chose as goal
And Euterpe and Calliope as my aim;
Which tied my heart and found on me her frame
Like an ivy wound up on trunk or wall.

That living laurel where once used to rest
My lofty thoughts, my ardour and my sighs
That never moved a leaf of the fair boughs,

Borne to the sky, left in its faithful nest
Its roots, and there with serious voice and vows
Somebody calls and nobody replies.

CCCXIX

My days, more nimble-footed than a hart,
Fled like a shadow, with no greater good
Than blinking eyes and some hours of calm mood
Whose sweet and bitter I keep in my heart.

O vile world, path unstable, overgrown,
He must be blind who puts his hope in you:
In you my heart was caught and given to
One who is dust, no more nerve joined to bone.

But her best form, which is alive and hale,
And always shall be such in heaven's light,
Makes me worship her beauties even more;

And in thinking of this my hair turns white,
What she is like today, where she did soar,
As when I looked at her enchanting veil.

CCCXX

Sento l'aura mia antica, e i dolci colli
Veggio apparire, onde 'l bel lume nacque
Che tenne gli occhi mei mentr'al ciel piacque
Bramosi e lieti, or li tèn tristi e molli.

O caduche speranze! o penser folli!
Vedove l'erbe, e torbide son l'acque,
E vòto e freddo 'l nido in ch'ella giacque,
Nel qual io vivo, e morto giacer volli,

Sperando al fin de le soavi piante
E da' belli occhi suoi, che 'l cor m'hann'arso,
Riposo alcun de le fatiche tante.

Ho servito a signor crudele e scarso;
Ch'arsi quanto 'l mio foco ebbi davante,
Or vo piangendo il suo cenere sparso.

CCCXXI

È questo 'l nido, in che la mia fenice
Mise l'aurate e le purpuree penne?
Che sotto le sue ali il mio cor tenne,
E parole e sospiri anco ne elice?

O del dolce mio mal prima radice,
Ov'è il bel viso, onde quel lume venne
Che vivo e lieto, ardendo, mi mantenne?
Sol' eri in terra; or se' nel ciel felice.

E m'hai lasciato qui misero, e solo,
Tal che pien di duol sempre al loco torno,
Che per te consecrato onoro e colo;

Veggendo a' colli oscura notte intorno,
Onde prendesti al ciel l'ultimo volo,
E dove li occhi tuoi solean far giorno.

CCCXX

I feel my dear old aura, that sweet hill
Appears to me where the fair lamp was born
That kept my eyes, when it was heaven's will,
Longing and gay, and now wet and forlorn.

O short-lived hopes! o follies of our thought!
Widowed the grass and turbid is the water,
And void and cold her nest that used to flatter
Me, where I live, and where my death I sought,

Hoping at last from her light, gentle feet,
And from her eyes that have smouldered my heart,
A little rest after the burning smart.

I served a lord full of a cruel spite;
For I burned when her fire was in my sight,
And now I weep her ashes' scattered sheet.

CCCXXI

Is this the nest in which my phoenix wore
Her feathers made of purple and of gold?
Who held and hid my heart in her wings' fold
And still draws out of me the sighs I store?

O you, of my sweet illness primal root,
Where is the face whence came the lovely light
Which made me, while I burned, bring forth gay fruit?
A sun on earth, now you make heaven bright.

And you have left me here alone and dry,
So that in torment I always go back
To the place that I honour for your sake;

But now around the hills the night is black,
From where you took your last flight to the sky,
And where your eyes used to bring the daybreak.

CCCXXII

Mai non vedranno le mie luci asciutte
Con le parti de l'animo tranquille
Quelle note, ov'Amor par che sfaville,
E Pietá di sua man l'abbia construtte.

Spirto giá invitto a le terrene lutte,
Ch'or su dal ciel tanta dolcezza stille,
Ch'a lo stil, onde Morte dipartille,
Le disviate rime hai ricondutte,

Di mie tènere frondi altro lavoro
Credea mostrarte. E qual fero pianeta
Ne 'nvidiò inseme, o mio nobil tesoro?

Chi 'nnanzi tempo mi t'asconde e vieta,
Che col cor veggio, e co la lingua onoro,
E 'n te, dolce sospir, l'alma s'acqueta?

CCCXXIII

Standomi un giorno solo a la fenestra,
Onde cose vedea tante, e sí nove,
Ch'era sol di mirar quasi giá stanco,
Una fera m'apparve da man destra,
Con fronte umana, da far arder Giove,
Cacciata da duo veltri, un nero, un bianco,
Che l'un e l'altro fianco
De la fera gentil mordean sí forte,
Che 'n poco tempo la menaro al passo
Ove chiusa in un sasso
Vinse molta bellezza acerba morte;
E mi fe' sospirar sua dura sorte.

Indi per alto mar vidi una nave,
Con le sarte di seta, e d'òr la vela,
Tutta d'avorio e d'ebeno contesta;
E 'l mar tranquillo, e l'aura era soave,

CCCXXII

My eyes shall never see in a dry state,
Nor the parts of my soul tranquil and bland,
Those notes that Love had seemed to radiate
And Pity to have built with her own hand.

Spirit unvanquished by the earthly pain,
Who now distil so much sweet from the skies,
Who to my talent which Death petrifies
The unattended rhymes present again,

I thought I would show you other results
Of my frail branches. What star's evil ray
Hated us both, o my excellent treasure,

That much too early hides and takes away
You whom my heart still sees, my tongue exalts,
And in whom, o sweet sigh, my soul finds leisure?

CCCXXIII

One day out of my window I espied,
Being alone, so many things and new,
That I became almost tired with their sight:
A beast appeared to me from the right side
With a semblance that Jove would love to woo,
Hunted down by two hounds, one black, one white,
That did either side bite
Of the sweet beast, with such a savage breath,
That in an instant they had pushed her on
Where, trapped into a stone,
Her great beauty was slain by cruel death;
And her fate was lamented by my faith.

Then on the deep sea I sighted a boat
With silken shrouds and with a golden sail,
All with ivory and ebony wrought;
The sea was calm and sweet the aura's note,

E 'l ciel qual è se nulla nube il vela;
Ella carca di ricca merce onesta:
Poi repente tempesta
Oriental turbò sí l'aere e l'onde,
Che la nave percosse ad uno scoglio.
O che grave cordoglio!
Breve ora oppresse, e poco spazio asconde,
L'alte ricchezze a nul'altre seconde.

In un boschetto novo i rami santi
Fiorian d'un lauro giovenetto e schietto,
Ch'un delli arbor parea di paradiso;
E di sua ombra uscían sí dolci canti,
Di varî augelli, e tant'altro diletto,
Che dal mondo m'avean tutto diviso:
E mirandol io fiso,
Cangiossi 'l cielo intorno, e tinto in vista,
Folgorando 'l percosse, e da radice
Quella pianta felice
Súbito svelse: onde mia vita è trista,
Ché simile ombra mai non si racquista.

Chiara fontana, in quel medesmo bosco,
Sorgea d'un sasso, et acque fresche e dolci
Spargea, soavemente mormorando:
Al bel seggio, riposto, ombroso, e fosco,
Né pastori appressavan né bifolci,
Ma ninfe e muse, a quel tenor cantando:
Ivi m'assisi; e quando
Piú dolcezza prendea di tal concento,
E di tal vista, aprir vidi uno speco,
E portarsene seco
La fonte, e 'l loco: ond'ancor doglia sento,
E sol de la memoria mi sgomento.

Una strania fenice, ambedue l'ale
Di porpora vestita, e 'l capo d'oro,
Vedendo per la selva altèra e sola,
Veder forma celeste et immortale
Prima pensai, fin ch'a lo svelto alloro

And the sky without clouds and without veil.
She was with honest, rich merchandise fraught:
Then a sudden storm, brought
There from the east, so swelled the waves and grounds,
That it shattered the ship against a rock.
O what a painful shock!
A short hour crushed and a small space surrounds
The noble riches that had known no bounds.

In a new grove the boughs were growing strong
Of a youthful and slender laurel tree
That seemed to have been born in paradise;
And from her shade issued such a sweet song
Of various birds with other kinds of glee,
That they had cut me off from the world's ties:
And while I fixed my eyes
On her, the sky with strange colours was laid,
The lightning struck and pulled out of her root
The plant and her dear fruit
All of a sudden: hence I am afraid,
For men will find no longer the same shade.

A sparkling fountain in that selfsame wood
Sprang from a rock and sprayed her waters sweet
And cool with murmurs of a soft refrain.
In that fair place of shady solitude
Neither shepherds nor churlish boors would meet,
But nymphs and muses singing to her strain:
I sat near her, and when
I was getting more sweetness from that air
And from that sight, I saw open a cave
And take away the brave
Fountain and its surroundings; and from there
Comes my grief; the remembrance brings despair.

When I saw a strange phoenix, with her wings
Covered with purple and her head with gold,
Appear over the forest, proud, alone,
I thought she was one of the holy things
Immortal, till the tree she did behold

Giunse, et al fonte che la terra invola:
Ogni cosa al fin vola;
Ché mirando le frondi a terra sparse,
E 'l troncon rotto, e quel vivo umor secco,
Volse in se stessa il becco,
Quasi sdegnando, e 'n un punto disparse:
Onde 'l cor di pietate, e d'amor m'arse.

Al fin vid'io, per entro i fiori e l'erba,
Pensosa ir sí leggiadra e bella donna,
Che mai no 'l penso ch'i' non arda e treme,
Umile in sé, ma 'n contra Amor superba;
Et avea in dosso sí candida gonna,
Sí testa, ch'oro e neve parea inseme;
Ma le parti supreme
Eran avolte d'una nebbia oscura:
Punta pio nel tallon d'un picciol angue,
Come fior còlto langue,
Lieta si dipartío, non che secura:
Ahi, nulla, altro che pianto, al mondo dura!

Canzon, tu puoi ben dire:
—Queste sei visioni al signor mio
Han fatto un dolce di morir desio.—

And the fountain, which underground was gone:
All things to their end run;
For, gazing on the branches in the grove
Dispersed, the broken trunk, the live sap dry,
She did her beak apply
To herself in disdain and vanished above;
Hence my heart burned with pity and with love.

At last I saw among many a flower
A pensive lady so charming and fair,
That if I think of her I am hot and cold,
Humble within herself, against love sour;
And she was dressed with a gown white and rare,
So woven that it seemed of snow and gold,
But I could not unfold
The upper part shrouded in a dark lure:
And when her heel was stung by a small snake,
As a plucked flower may break,
Happily she dropped down, and quite secure:
Ah, nothing, save our weeping, will endure!

Canzone, you may say:
—These six visions have given to my lord
A sweet desire to die, as a reward.—

CCCXXIV

Amor, quando fioría
Mia spene, e 'l guidardon di tanta fede,
Tolta m'è quella ond'attendea mercede.

Ahi, dispietata morte! ahi, crudel vita!
L'una m'ha posto in doglia,
E mie speranze acerbamente ha spente;
L'altra mi tèn qua giú contra mia voglia,
E lei, che se n'è gita,
Seguir non posso, ch'ella no 'l consente:
Ma pur ogni or presente
Nel mezzo del meo cor madonna siede,
E qual è la mia vita ella sel vede.

CCCXXV

Tacer non posso, e temo non adopre
Contrario effetto la mia lingua al core,
Che vorria far onore
A la sua donna, che dal ciel n'ascolta.
Come poss'io, se non m'insegni, Amore,
Con parole mortali aguagliar l'opre
Divine, e quel che copre
Alta umiltate, in se stessa raccolta?
Ne la bella pregione, onde or è sciolta,
Poco era stato ancor l'alma gentile,
Al tempo che di lei prima m'accorsi;
Onde súbito corsi
(Ch'era de l'anno e di mi' etate aprile)
A coglier fiori, in quei prati d'intorno,
Sperando a li occhi suoi piacer sí addorno.

Muri eran d'alabastro, e 'l tetto d'oro,
D'avorio uscio, e fenestre di zaffiro,
Onde 'l primo sospiro
Mi giunse al cor, e giugnerá l'estremo.

CCCXXIV

Love, when my hope did thrive
And the reward of such a lasting faith,
They took away from me my saving breath.

Alas! Merciless Death! Life's cruel fray!
One gives me pain and shame,
And brutally extinguished all my dreams,
The other keeps me here against my aim,
And one who went away
I may not follow, otherwise she deems;
But still my lady seems
Always to sit in the core of my heart,
And she knows how I live and how I smart.

CCCXXV

I cannot remain silent, and I fear
That my language may not second my heart
Which would like to impart
Honour to her who listens from the sky.
How can I, Love, unless I learn your art,
Equal with mortal words what is so near
God, what does not appear,
Wrapped in the humbleness where it does lie?
In the fair jail she left just now to fly,
Her soul had dwelled as in a landing-stage,
When first I was aware of her appeal;
Then away I did steal
(The year was in the middle, and my age)
To pluck some flowers all around those fields,
Hoping to please her by their beauteous shields.

Alabaster the walls, and the roof gold,
The door of ivory, and of sapphire
The windows whence desire
Came to my heart, and whence my end will come.

Inde i messi d'Amor armati usciro
Di saette e di foco; ond'io di loro,
Coronati d'alloro,
Pur come or fusse, ripensando tremo.
D'un bel diamante, quadro, e mai non scemo,
Vi si vedea, nel mezzo, un seggio altèro,
Ove, sola, sedea la bella donna;
Dinanzi, una colonna,
Cristallina, et iv'entro ogni pensero,
Scritto, e fòr tralucea sí chiaramente,
Che mi fea lieto, e sospirar sovente.

A le pungenti, ardenti, e lucide arme,
A la vittoriosa insegna verde,
Contra cui in campo perde
Giove, et Apollo, e Polifemo, e Marte,
Ov'è 'l pianto ogni or fresco, e si rinverde,
Giunto mi vidi: e non possendo aitarme,
Preso lassai menarme,
Ond'or non so d'uscir la via, né l'arte.
Ma sí com'uom talor che piange, e parte
Vede cosa, che li occhi, e 'l cor alletta,
Cosí colei per ch'io son in pregione,
Standosi ad un balcone,
Che fu sola a' suoi dí cosa perfetta,
Cominciai a mirar con tal desio,
Che me stesso, e 'l mio mal posi in oblio.

I' era in terra, e 'l cor in paradiso,
Dolcemente obliando ogni altra cura;
E mia viva figura
Far sentía un marmo, e 'mpier di meraviglia;
Quando una donna assai pronta e secura,
Di tempo antica, e giovene del viso,
Vedendomi sí fiso,
A l'atto de la fronte, e de le ciglia:
—Meco—mi disse—meco ti consiglia,
Ch'i' son d'altro poder che tu non credi;
E so far lieti e tristi in un momento,
Piú leggiera che 'l vento;

From there rushed out, armed with arrows and fire,
Love's messengers; and thinking of those bold
Ones that my bay did hold,
As if it happened now, I become numb.
Made of square diamond that will not succumb,
In the middle appeared a stately seat
Where the fair lady was sitting alone;
A column of glass stone
Was before it, all thoughts written so neat
And reflected so limpidly outside,
That I felt happy and I often sighed.

I had come to the piercing, blazing arms,
To the victorious, green sign of the grove
That has defeated Jove,
And Mars and Polyphemus and Apollo,
Where tears are always fresh, renewed by Love:
And since I found no help from its alarms,
I fell into its charms
And was led where I saw no way to follow
That would free me. As one who sees with hollow
And weeping face what lures his heart and eyes,
I beheld her, who keeps me in this jail,
At a balcony's rail,
Her who alone was here a perfect prize,
And beheld her with such a deep desire,
That my self and my ill seemed to expire.

I was on earth, my heart in paradise,
Sweetly forgetting any other care;
And all my feelings were
Becoming marble in a wonder-trance;
When a firm woman that seemed used to dare,
Ancient in time, youthful in face and eyes,
Seeing my fixed surprise
In the expression of my brow and glance:
—To me—she said—to me, reveal your wants,
I am another power than you think;
And at once can make sad or gay your mind,
More airy than the wind;

E reggo, e volvo quanto al mondo vedi.
Tien pur li occhi come aquila in quel sole;
Parte dá orecchi a queste mie parole.

Il dí che costei nacque, eran le stelle
Che producon fra voi felici effetti,
In luoghi alti, et eletti,
L'una vèr' l'altra, con amor, converse;
Venere, e 'l padre con benigni aspetti
Tenean le parti signorili e belle;
E le luci impie e felle
Quasi in tutto del ciel eran disperse.
Il sol mai sí bel giorno non aperse;
L'aere, e la terra s'allegrava, e l'acque,
Per lo mar, avean pace, e per il fiumi.
Fra tanti amici lumi,
Una nube lontana mi dispiacque;
La qual temo che 'n pianto si resolve,
Se pietate altramente il ciel non volve.

Com'ella venne in questo viver basso,
Ch'a dir il ver, non fu degno d'averla,
Cosa nova a vederla,
Giá santissima e dolce, ancor acerba,
Parea chiusa in òr fin candida perla;
Et or carpone, or con tremante passo,
Legno, acqua, terra, o sasso,
Verde facea, chiara, soave, e l'erba
Con le palme o co i pie' fresca e superba;
E fiorir co i belli occhi le campagne,
Et acquetar i vènti, e le tempeste,
Con voci ancor non preste
Di lingua che dal latte si scompagne;
Chiaro mostrando al mondo sordo e cieco
Quanto lume del ciel fusse giá seco.

Poi che crescendo in tempo, et in virtute,
Giunse a la terza sua fiorita etate,
Leggiadria, né beltate,
Tanta non vide 'l sol, credo, giá mai:
Li occhi pien di letizia e d'onestate,

I rule and turn the things at which you blink.
Go on looking, as eagles watch the sun;
But partly listen to my words that run.

The day that she was born, those stars did rise,
That produce among you a glad effect,
To places most elect,
One turned toward the other in sweet play;
Venus and Jove with a kindly aspect
Held all the beautiful places and wise;
The lights that you despise
Were from the sky almost vanished away.
The sun never revealed such a fair day;
The air, the earth rejoiced, and all the water
Had found peace in the sea and in the streams.
Among such friendly beams
A distant cloud was a displeasing matter,
Which I still dread to see melt into tears,
If pity does not alter heaven's spheres.

When she descended in this lowly place
That, to be frank, was not worthy of her,
A novel thing and fair
To see, holy and sweet, unripe, she was,
All set in gold like a pearl very rare;
And now crawling, now with a trembling pace,
She made all earthly ways,
Mellow and clear; wherever she did pass
With palms or feet, there grew more proud the grass;
And her eyes called forth blossoms in the land
And calmed the winds and brought peace to the storms
With the uncertain forms
Of a tongue that till then milk had made bland;
Clearly showing to a world deaf and blind
What holy light to her had been assigned.

When, by growing in time and ornament,
She arrived in her third and blooming season,
Such lovely, charming prison
I think the sun never saw till that day:
Her eyes were full of happiness and reason,

E 'l parlar di dolcezza, e di salute.
Tutte lingue son mute,
A dir di lei quel che tu sol ne sai.
Sí chiaro ha 'l vólto di celesti rai,
Che vostra vista in lui non pò fermarse;
E da quel suo bel carcere terreno
Di tal foco hai 'l cor pieno,
Ch'altro piú dolcemente mai non arse.
Ma parmi che sua súbita partita
Tosto ti fia cagion d'amara vita.—

Detto questo, a la sua volubil rota
Si volse, in ch'ella fila il nostro stame,
Trista, e certa indivina de' miei danni;
Ché dopo non molt'anni,
Quella, per ch'io ho di morir tal fame,
Canzon mia, spense Morte, acerba, e rea,
Che piú bel corpo occider non potea.

CCCXXVI

Or hai fatto l'estremo di tua possa,
O crudel Morte; or hai 'l regno d'Amore
Impoverito; or di bellezza il fiore,
E 'l lume, hai spento, e chiuso in poca fossa;

Or hai spogliata nostra vita, e scossa,
D'ogni ornamento, e del sovran suo onore:
Ma la fama e 'l valor, che mai non more,
Non è in tua forza: abbiti ignude l'ossa;

Ché l'altro ha 'l cielo, di sua chiaritate,
Quasi d'un piú bel sol, s'allegra e gloria;
E fi' al mondo de' buon sempre in memoria.

Vinca 'l cor vostro, in sua tanta vittoria,
Angel novo, lassú, di me pietate,
Come vinse qui 'l mio vostra beltate.

Her speech of sweetness and enchantment.
All tongues are impotent
To tell of her what you alone can say.
Her face is full of such celestial ray,
That your sight cannot rest when on her turned;
And from her lovely jail of earthly mire
Your heart caught such a fire,
That no one with such sweetness ever burned.
But I think that her sudden, early leave,
Will be the cause why you will always grieve.—

And then she turned to her voluble wheel
In which she spins our miserable thread,
Mournful, surely a prophet of my cares;
For after a few years
She, for whom I am yearning to be dead,
My song, was slain by Death cruel and bare,
Who could not have destroyed body more fair.

CCCXXVI

Now you have done the utmost of your power,
Merciless Death; now you have ruined the rich
Kingdom of love and ravished beauty's flower,
Put out its light and flung it in a ditch;

Now you have raped our life and you have thrown
Every charm away, our honoured tie;
But fame and valour that shall never die
Are not in your domain. Have the bare bone,

For heaven has the rest; its clarity
Is like a fairer sun in which it thrives,
Its memory will stay in good men's lives.

Let your heart there, in such great victory,
O new-found angel, be vanquished by pity,
As here my own was vanquished by your beauty.

CCCXXVII

L'aura, e l'odore, e 'l refrigerio, e l'ombra
Del dolce lauro, e sua vista fiorita,
Lume e riposo di mia stanca vita,
Tolt'ha colei che tutto 'l mondo sgombra.

Come a noi il sol se sua soror l'adombra,
Cosí l'alta mia luce a me sparita,
I' cheggio a Morte in contr'a Morte aita:
Di sí scuri penseri Amor m'ingombra.

Dormit'hai, bella donna, un breve sonno;
Or se' svegliata fra li spirti eletti,
Ove nel suo Fattor l'alma s'interna:

E se mie rime alcuna cosa ponno,
Consecrata fra i nobili intelletti,
Fia del tuo nome, qui, memoria eterna.

CCCXXVIII

L'ultimo, lasso!, de' miei giorni allegri,
Che pochi ho visto in questo viver breve,
Giunto era, e fatto 'l cor tepida neve,
Forse presago de' dí tristi e negri.

Qual ha giá i nervi e i polsi e i penser egri
Cui domestica febbre assalir deve,
Tal mi sentía, non sappiend'io che lève
Venisse 'l fin de' miei ben non intègri.

Li occhi belli, or in ciel chiari e felici
Del lume onde salute e vita piove,
Lasciando i miei qui miseri e mendici,

Dicean lor con faville oneste e nove:
—Rimanetevi in pace, o cari amici;
Qui mai piú, no, ma rivedrenne altrove.—

CCCXXVII

The aura and the odour, coolness, shade,
Of the sweet laurel, its blossoming sight
That gave to my tired life repose and light,
By Death who removes all have been unmade.

As the sun does behind its sister fade,
So now that my pure lamp vanished above,
I ask from Death against himself some aid,
With such dark thoughts I am besieged by Love.

You slept here, lovely Lady, a brief sleep;
Now you awake among the blessed spirits
Where the soul in its Maker plunges deep:

And if my rhymes are good for any aim,
They shall inscribe among the holy merits
The eternal remembrance of your name.

CCCXXVIII

The last, alas! of my light-hearted days
That I have seldom had in this short life
Had come, and my heart was a snowy maze
Perhaps foreseeing its approaching strife.

As he whose pulse and nerves and thoughts are ill,
Whom a continuous fever will destroy,
The same was I, being ignorant still
Of the near end of my imperfect joy.

Her fair eyes now in heaven shining gay
With the clear light in which life pours and dwells,
Leaving my own down here in such dismay,

Were telling them with a pure, candid glance:
—Farewell and be at peace, my dearest ones,
We shall not meet on earth, but somewhere else.—

CCCXXIX

O giorno, o ora, o ultimo momento,
O stelle congiurate a 'mpoverirme!
O fido sguardo, or che volei tu dirme,
Partend'io per non esser mai contento?

Or conosco i miei danni, or mi risento:
Ch'i' credeva (ahi, credenze vane e 'nfirme!)
Perder parte, non tutto, al dipartirme:
Quante speranze se ne porta il vento!

Ché giá 'l contrario era ordinato in cielo:
Spegner l'almo mio lume ond'io vivea;
E scritto era in sua dolce amara vista.

Ma 'nnanzi a gli occhi m'era post'un velo,
Che mi fea non veder quel ch'i' vedea,
Per far mia vita súbito piú trista.

CCCXXX

Quel vago, dolce, caro, onesto sguardo
Dir parea:—To' di me quel che tu pòi,
Ché mai piú qui non mi vedrai da poi
Ch'avrai quinci il pe' mosso, a mover tardo.—

Intelletto veloce piú che pardo,
Pigro in antivedere i dolor tuoi,
Come non vedestú nelli occhi suoi
Quel che ved'ora, ond'io mi struggo et ardo?

Taciti sfavillando oltra lor modo,
Dicean:—O lumi amici, che gran tempo,
Con tal dolcezza fêste di noi specchi,

Il ciel n'aspetta: a voi parrá per tempo;
Ma chi ne strinse qui, dissolve il nodo,
E 'l vostro, per farv'ira, vuol che 'nvecchi.—

CCCXXIX

O day, o hour, o last moment to come!
O stars that have conspired to my decay!
O faithful look, what did you want to say
When I left you never to find my home?

Now I know the misfortunes that I bear,
For I thought (ah, beliefs vain and unsound!)
To lose a part, not all, leaving her ground:
How many hopes are scattered by the air!

Another thing had been decreed above:
To extinguish the lamp that was my love;
And it was writ in her melancholy.

But before me was interposed a veil
That caused me not to see what I did see,
To make my life at once more sad and frail.

CCCXXX

Her sweet, dear, honest look where lodges Love,
Seemed to say:—Take of me what you desire,
For you shall not see me when you retire
From here your foot that is lazy to move.—

O intellect, more fleet than any leopard,
Slow in guessing the blow that would be dealt,
Why did you not perceive in her regard
What I see now, what makes me burn and melt?

Her eyes, silently sparking, and more strong
Than ever, said:—O lights that for so long
With so much sweetness were our looking-glass,

Heaven is waiting; you shall see it pass;
He who fastened our knot wants it unrolled,
And bids yours, to your anger, to grow old.—

CCCXXXI

Solea da la fontana di mia vita
Allontanarme, e cercar terre e mari,
Non mio voler, ma mia stella seguendo;
E sempre andai, tal Amor diemmi aita,
In quelli essilii, quanto e' vide, amari,
Di memoria e di speme il cor pascendo.
Or, lasso!, alzo la mano, e l'arme rendo
A l'empia e violenta mia fortuna,
Che privo m'ha di sí dolce speranza.
Sol memoria m'avanza,
E pasco 'l gran desir sol di quest'una;
Onde l'alma vien men, frale e digiuna.

Come a corrier tra via, se 'l cibo manca,
Conven per forza rallentare il corso,
Scemando la vertú che 'l fea gir presto,
Cosí, mancando a la mia vita stanca
Quel caro nutrimento, in che di morso
Die' chi 'l mondo fa nudo, e 'l mio cor mesto,
Il dolce acerbo, e 'l bel piacer molesto
Mi si fa d'ora in ora; onde 'l camino
Sí breve non fornir spero e pavento.
Nebbia o polvere al vento,
Fuggo per piú non esser pellegrino:
E cosí vada, s'è pur mio destíno.

Mai questa mortal vita a me non piacque
(Sassel Amor, con cui spesso ne parlo)
Se non per lei che fu 'l suo lume, e 'l mio:
Poi che 'n terra morendo, al ciel rinacque,
Quello spirto, ond'io vissi, a seguitarlo
(Licito fusse!) è 'l mi' sommo desio.
Ma da dolermi ho ben sempre, per ch'io
Fui mal accorto, a proveder mio stato,
Ch'Amor mostrommi sotto quel bel ciglio,
Per darmi altro consiglio:
Ché tal morí giá tristo e sconsolato,
Cui poco inanzi era 'l morir beato.

CCCXXXI

I used to leave the fountain of my life
And go away and look for lands and seas,
Following not my will, only my star;
And I did always, Love so helped my strife,
In those exiles so full of miseries
Feed my heart with remembrance from afar.
Now I lift up my hand, the arms of war
I surrender to wicked, violent Chance
That has deprived me of my sweetest hope.
In memory I grope
And nourish my desire with its last glance;
Hence my soul starves and loses its balance.

As when a courier, if left without food,
Must of necessity retard his course,
The virtue growing less that made him run,
So when lacked in my life the livelihood
That was its essence, bitten by the force
Of one who is the world's perdition,
Hour by hour all my sweetness was undone:
Pleasure is bitter; the remaining road
I hope, and yet I dread, not to complete;
Fog, dust in a wind's sheet
I flee, not to endure the pilgrim's load;
Let it be so, if this is my fate's goad.

This mortal life I always found forlorn
(Love knows it well, with whom I often speak)
Save for her sake, by whom light we received:
When she died in the earth and was reborn
Above, my greatest wish (were I less weak!)
Is to follow her ghost by which I lived.
But I regret and I have always grieved
That I lacked wisdom to help my unrest,
As Love showed it to me in her fair eyes
Giving better advice:
For some have died unhappy and distressed
Who until then their own death would have blessed.

Nelli occhi ov'abitar solea 'l mio core
Fin che mia dura sorte invidia n'ebbe,
Che di sí ricco albergo il pose in bando,
Di sua man propria avea descritto Amore
Con lettre di pietá, quel ch'averrebbe
Tosto del mio sí lungo ir desiando.
Bello e dolce morire era allor quando,
Morend'io, non moría mia vita inseme,
Anzi vivea di me l'ottima parte:
Or mie speranze sparte
Ha morte, e poca terra il mio ben preme;
E vivo; e mai no 'l penso ch'i' non treme.

Se stato fusse il mio poco intelletto
Meco al bisogno, e non altra vaghezza
L'avesse disviando altrove vòlto,
Ne la fronte a madonna avrei ben letto:
—Al fin se' giunto d'ogni tua dolcezza
Et al principio del tuo amaro molto.—
Questo intendono, dolcemente sciolto
In sua presenzia del mortal mio velo
E di questa noiosa e grave carne,
Potea inanzi lei andarne,
A veder preparar sua sedia in cielo;
Or l'andrò dietro, omai, con altro pelo.

Canzon, s'uom trovi in suo amor viver queto,
Di':—Muor, mentre se' lieto;
Ché morte, al tempo, è, non duol, ma refugio;
E chi ben pò morir, non cerchi indugio.—

CCCXXXII

Mia benigna fortuna, e 'l viver lieto,
I chiari giorni, e le tranquille notti,
E i soavi sospiri, e 'l dolce stile
Che solea resonare in versi e 'n rime,

In the eyes where my heart was wont to dwell
Until merciless Chance envied my joy,
Who banished it from such a precious home,
Love with his hand had written the sad spell
In pity's letters, all that would destroy
My long desire, all that was bound to come.
Sweet it had been to die when the whole sum
Of my life with my death would not be dead,
Nay, its best part would still be left alive:
Now all my hopes connive
With death, a little earth on her is spread;
And I live; and I think of this with dread.

If my scant intellect had always stayed
With me in time of need, and if no toy
Had made it stray and turn to other things,
I should have read in my lady's forehead:
—You have come to the end of all your joy,
To the beginning of your sufferings.—
Grasping this truth and feeling loose the strings,
In her presence, that do my spirit tie
And my burdensome flesh, tiresome and slow,
I could have tried to go
Before, to see her chair placed in the sky;
Now I must wait till of old age I die.

Song, if you find a man who loves in quiet,
Say:—Die during delight;
Death to time is no harm, but a safe gate,
And who can die in bliss, let him not wait.—

CCCXXXII

My benign luck and a life that was gay,
The days unclouded and the peaceful nights,
And the delicate sighs and the sweet style
That resounded in poems and in rhymes,

Vòlti subitamente in doglia e 'n pianto,
Odiar vita mi fanno e bramar morte.

Crudele, acerba, inesorabil Morte,
Cagion mi dái di mai non esser lieto,
Ma di menar tutta mia vita in pianto,
E i giorni oscuri e le dogliose notti.
I mei gravi sospir non vanno in rime,
E 'l mio duro martír vince ogni stile.

Ove è condutto il mio amoroso stile?
A parlar d'ira, a ragionar di morte.
U' sono i versi, u' son giunte le rime,
Che gentil cor udia pensoso, e lieto?
Ov'è 'l favoleggiar d'amor le notti?
Or non parl'io, né penso altro che pianto.

Giá mi fu col desir sí dolce il pianto,
Che condía di dolcezza ogni agro stile,
E vegghiar mi facea tutte le notti;
Or m'è 'l pianger amaro piú che morte,
Non sperando mai 'l guardo onesto e lieto,
Alto sogetto a le mie basse rime.

Chiaro segno Amor pose a le mie rime
Dentro a' belli occhi; et or l'ha posto in pianto,
Con dolor rimembrando il tempo lieto:
Ond'io vo col penser cangiando stile,
E ripregando te, pallida Morte,
Che mi sottragghi a sí penose notti.

Fuggito è 'l sonno a le mie crude notti,
E 'l suono usato a le mie roche rime,
Che non sanno trattar altro che morte:
Cosí è 'l mio cantar converso in pianto.
Non ha 'l regno d'Amor sí vario stile,
Ch'è tanto or tristo, quanto mai fu lieto.

Nesun visse giá mai piú di me lieto,
Nesun vive piú tristo a giorni e notti;
E doppiando 'l dolor, doppia lo stile,
Che trae del cor sí lacrimose rime.

Being suddenly turned to grief and tears,
Cause me to detest life and desire death.

Cruel, harsh and inexorable Death,
You give me reason to be never gay
But to spend all my life in shedding tears,
And the dark days and the sorrowful nights.
My heavy sighs cannot be put in rhymes
And my crude martyrdom defeats all style.

Where is carried away my loving style?
To speak of anger, to reason of death.
Where are the lines, where have now come the rhymes
That every gentle heart heard grave and gay?
Where are the loves and legends of my nights?
Now I can only speak and think of tears.

So sweet were once with my desire my tears,
That they seasoned with sweetness a sour style,
And made me sleepless during all my nights;
Now my weeping is more bitter than death,
I cannot hope to see the chaste and gay
Look, lofty subject of my lowly rhymes.

A clear sign Love presented to my rhymes
In her fair eyes; now it is in my tears,
Sadly remembering a time that was gay:
Hence with my thought I am changing my style,
And I pray you again, o pallid Death,
To rescue me from these tormenting nights.

All sleep is gone from my merciless nights
And the old sound from my hoarse-throated rhymes
That cannot deal with anything but death:
Therefore my singing is transformed in tears.
The reign of Love knows not such varied style
That can be now as sad as it was gay.

No one has ever lived who was more gay,
No one has lived more dreary days and nights;
With the doubling of grief doubles the style
That drags out of my heart such plaintive rhymes.

Vissi di speme, or vivo pur di pianto,
Né contra Morte spero altro che Morte.

Morte m'ha morto; e sola pò far Morte
Ch'i' torni a riveder quel viso lieto,
Che piacer mi facea i sospiri e 'l pianto,
L'aura dolce e la pioggia a le mie notti;
Quando i penseri eletti tessea in rime,
Amor alzando il mio debile stile.

Or avess'io un sí pietoso stile
Che Laura mia potesse tôrre a Morte,
Come Euridice Orfeo sua senza rime,
Ch'i' viverei ancor piú che mai lieto!
S'esser non pò, qualcuna d'este notti
Chiuda omai queste due fonti di pianto.

Amor, i' ho molti e molt'anni pianto
Mio grave danno in doloroso stile,
Né da te spero mai men fere notti;
E però mi son mosso a pregar Morte
Che mi tolla di qui, per farme lieto,
Ove è colei ch'i' canto, e piango in rime.

Se sí alto pôn gir mie stanche rime,
Ch'agiungan lei, ch'è fuor d'ira e di pianto,
E fa 'l ciel or di sue bellezze lieto,
Ben riconoscerá 'l mutato stile,
Che giá forse le piacque, anzi che Morte
Chiaro a lei giorno, a me fêsse atre notti.

O voi che sospirate a miglior notti,
Ch'ascoltate d'Amore, o dite in rime,
Pregate non mi sia piú sorda Morte,
Porto de le miserie e fin del pianto;
Muti una volta quel suo antiquo stile,
Ch'ogni uom attrista, e me pò far sí lieto.

Far mi pò lieto in una o 'n poche notti;
E 'n aspro stile, e 'n angosciose rime,
Prego che 'l pianto mio finisca Morte.

I lived on hope, now I must live on tears,
And against Death there is no hope but Death.

Death has me dead; and this could only Death
Perform, that I may see her visage gay
Which made me love my sorrow and my tears,
The sweet air and the rain of all my nights,
When I wove all my longings in my rhymes,
Love ennobling the weakness of my style.

Could I find now such a worshipping style
That would deliver my Laura from Death,
As Orpheus Eurydice, without rhymes,
I should live on and more than ever gay!
If this be not, let any of these nights
Still and dry off these two fountains of tears.

Love, many, many years I have shed tears
For my dark pain in a lamenting style,
Nor do I hope from you less cruel nights;
Therefore I have decided to pray Death
That he may steal me too and make me gay
There where she is, whom I weep in my rhymes.

If to such height can go my weary rhymes
That they reach her, who knows nor wrath nor tears,
And makes the heavens with her beauty gay,
She will surely remember my changed style
Which perhaps flattered her, once, before Death
Made the days clear to her and dark my nights.

O you who always long for better nights,
Who listen to Love's words or sing in rhymes,
Pray that I speak no more to a deaf Death,
Haven of miseries and end of tears;
Let him vary this time his ancient style
That grieves all men and would render me gay.

I could be gay in one or a few nights;
In a wild style and in anguishing rhymes,
I beg these tears of mine be stopped by Death.

CCCXXXIII

Ite, rime dolenti, al duro sasso,
Che 'l mio caro tesoro in terra asconde;
Ivi chiamate chi dal ciel risponde,
Ben che 'l mortal sia in loco oscuro, e basso.

Ditele ch'i' son giá di viver lasso,
Del navigar per queste orribili onde;
Ma ricogliendo le sue sparte fronde,
Dietro le vo pur cosí passo passo,

Sol di lei ragionando viva e morta,
Anzi pur viva, et or fatta immortale,
A ciò che 'l mondo la conosca, et ame.

Piacciale al mio passar esser accorta,
Ch'è presso omai; siami a l'incontro, e quale
Ella è nel cielo, a sé mi tiri e chiame.

CCCXXXIV

S'onesto amor pò meritar mercede,
E se pietá ancor pò, quant'ella suole,
Mercede avrò, ché piú chiara che 'l sole,
A madonna et al mondo, è la mia fede.

Giá di me paventosa, or sa, no 'l crede,
Che quello stesso ch'or per me si vòle,
Sempre si volse; e s'ella udía parole
O vedea 'l vólto, or l'animo, e 'l cor vede.

Ond'i' spero che 'n fin al ciel si doglia
Di miei tanti sospiri; e cosí mostra,
Tornando a me sí piena di pietate.

E spero ch'al por giú di questa spoglia,
Venga per me, con quella gente nostra,
Vera amica di Cristo, e d'onestate.

CCCXXXIII

Go, my sorrowful rhymes, to the hard stone
Where my dear treasure in the earth absconds;
And then call her, who from heaven responds,
Although the mortal in the dark is gone.

Tell her that I am tired of life's false vows
And of sailing across the waves' abyss,
But putting order in her scattered boughs
I follow her, step after step, like this,

Talking only of her, dead or alive,
Rather, alive, made immortal above,
So that the world understand her and love.

Let it please her to take a watchful care
Of my approaching journey, and arrive
Such as she is, meet me, draw me to her.

CCCXXXIV

If honest love deserves a recompense,
And pity still has power in its breath,
I shall have a reward, because my faith
Is more clear than the sun and more intense.

Once suspicious, at last she knows me all,
Does not need to believe that what my word
Asks now is still the same; but when she heard
This, she saw only me, now sees my soul.

Therefore I hope that even in the skies
She may be sorry for my endless sighs;
She shows it when she comes here looking kind.

And I hope that when I drop down this rind
She will meet me with our dear company,
True friend of Christ, true friend of honesty.

CCCXXXV

Vidi fra mille donne una giá tale,
Ch'amorosa paura il cor m'assalse,
Mirandola in imagini non false
A li spirti celesti in vista eguale.

Niente in lei terreno era o mortale,
Sí come a cui del ciel, non d'altro, calse.
L'alma, ch'arse per lei sí spesso et alse,
Vaga d'ir seco, aperse ambedue l'ale.

Ma tropp'era alta al mio peso terrestre;
E poco poi n'uscí in tutto di vista;
Di che pensando, ancor m'aghiaccio e torpo.

O belle et alte e lucide fenestre,
Onde colei che molta gente attrista
Trovò la via d'entrare in sí bel corpo!

CCCXXXVI

Tornami a mente, anzi v'è dentro, quella
Ch'indi per Lete esser non pò sbandita,
Qual io la vidi in su l'etá fiorita,
Tutta accesa de' raggi di sua stella.

Sí nel mio primo occorso onesta e bella,
Veggiola, in sé raccolta, e sí romita,
Ch'i' grido:—Ell'è ben dessa; ancor è in vita—
E 'n don le cheggio sua dolce favella.

Talor risponde, e talor non fa motto.
I' come uom ch'erra, e poi piú dritto estima,
Dico a la mente mia:—Tu se' 'ngannata:

Sai che 'n mille trecento quarantotto,
Il dí sesto d'aprile, in l'ora prima,
Del corpo uscío quell'anima beata.—

CCCXXXV

Among a thousand ladies I saw one
Such that a loving fear assailed my breast,
Seeing her in a truthful vision
Equal in aspect to the spirits blest.

She was unlike the earthly, mortal things,
As one who cared for heaven, nothing else.
My soul that burned and froze under her spells,
Wishing to go with her, opened its wings.

But she was placed too high for my eyesight,
And shortly after she vanished away;
Thinking of this I still shake from that storm.

O windows beautiful and tall and light
Whence Death, who brings to some of us dismay,
Found the way open to that lovely form!

CCCXXXVI

She returns, nay, she is inside my mind,
She, who by Lethe cannot be effaced,
As I saw her with her springtime enshrined,
With the bright beams of her star interlaced.

So fair and honest I see her arrive,
Collected in herself and so remote,
That I cry:—It is she; she is alive.—
And I implore from her her words' sweet note.

And now she answers, now she holds her tongue.
I, like a raving man who gets more strong,
Say to my mind:—You are in fancy's power;

Because in thirteen hundred forty-eight,
On the sixth day of April, the first hour,
That blessed soul left here her mortal weight.—

CCCXXXVII

Quel che d'odore e di color vincea
L'odorifero e lucido oriente,
Frutti, fiori, erbe e frondi, onde 'l ponente
D'ogni rara eccellenzia il pregio avea,

Dolce mio lauro, ove abitar solea
Ogni bellezza, ogni vertute ardente,
Vedeva a la sua ombra onestamente
Il mio signor sedersi a la mia dea.

Ancor io il nido di penseri eletti
Posi in quell'alma pianta; e 'n foco e 'n gielo
Tremando, ardendo, assai felice fui.

Pieno era il mondo de' suoi onor perfetti,
Allor che Dio, per adornarne il cielo,
La si ritolse; e cosa era da lui.

CCCXXXVIII

Lasciato hai, Morte, senza sole il mondo
Oscuro e freddo, Amor cieco et inerme,
Leggiadria ignuda, le bellezze inferme,
Me sconsolato, et a me grave pondo,

Cortesia in bando et onestate in fondo:
Dogliom'io sol, né sol ho da dolerme;
Ché svelt'hai di vertute il chiaro germe:
Spento il primo valor, qual fia il secondo?

Pianger l'aer e la terra e 'l mar devrebbe
L'uman legnaggio, che senz'ella è quasi
Senza fior prato, o senza gemma anello.

Non la conobbe il mondo mentre l'ebbe;
Conobbil'io, ch'a pianger qui rimasi,
E 'l ciel, che del mio pianto or si fa bello.

CCCXXXVII

My tree that whelmed in odour and in shade
The perfume-laden East, its lucid sense,
And the fruits, flowers, branches, grass, that made
The West carry the prize of excellence,

My lovely laurel where once used to dwell
Every beauty, every virtuous gleam,
Saw in its shade, before its branches fell,
My lord sit down and my lady with him.

And I placed in that noble plant the nest
Of my exalted thoughts; in ice and flame
Burning and trembling I found a sweet rest.

The world was full of its honour and fame
When God, to decorate with it the sky,
Called it to him, worthy of being high.

CCCXXXVIII

Death, you have left the world without its sun,
Gloomy and cold, Love blind and without arms,
Loveliness bare, and sick all beauty's charms,
Myself distressed and by this load undone,

Courtesy banished, honesty pretext:
I alone mourn, though not alone I should;
For you uprooted a clear shoot of good.
Torn the first valour, which will be the next?

They ought to weep, the earth, the sea, the air,
The human lineage that without her is
Like a field without flowers, ring without gem.

They did not know her while she was with them;
I did, who am left here and weep for this,
And the sky did, that with my grief grows fair.

CCCXXXIX

Conobbi, quanto il ciel li occhi m'aperse,
Quanto studio et Amor m'alzaron l'ali,
Cose nove e leggiadre, ma mortali,
Che 'n un soggetto ogni stella cosperse.

L'altre tante sí strane e sí diverse
Forme altère, celesti, et immortali,
Perché non fûro a l'intelletto eguali,
La mia debile vista non sofferse.

Onde quant'io di lei parlai né scrissi,
Ch'or per lodi anzi a Dio preghi mi rende,
Fu breve stilla d'infiniti abissi:

Ché stilo oltra l'ingegno non si stende;
E per aver uom li occhi nel sol fissi,
Tanto si vede men quanto piú splende.

CCCXL

Dolce mio caro e prezioso pegno,
Che natura mi tolse, e 'l ciel mi guarda,
Deh, come è tua pietá vèr' me sí tarda,
O usato di mia vita sostegno?

Giá suo' tu far il mio sonno almen degno
De la tua vista, et or sostien ch'i' arda
Senz'alcun refrigerio: e chi 'l retarda?
Pur lassú non alberga ira né sdegno;

Onde quá giuso un ben pietoso core
Talor si pasce delli altrui tormenti,
Sí ch'elli è vinto nel suo regno Amore.

Tu che dentro mi vedi, e 'l mio mal senti,
E sola puoi finir tanto dolore,
Con la tua ombra acqueta i miei lamenti.

CCCXXXIX

I knew, as heaven granted to my eyes,
As high as Love and study raised my wings,
The lovely, rarely seen, but mortal things
That each star in one subject did comprise.

The other many unusual, diverse
And stately forms, celestial and undying,
Because my intellect did not dare flying,
My feeble vision never could rehearse.

Hence all I said and wrote of her who will
Now before God return my praise with prayer,
Was a small drop from an endless abyss:

For style cannot stretch farther than our skill,
And though we fix our eyes in the sun's bliss,
The less we see, the greater is the glare.

CCCXL

My sweet, beloved, my own precious pledge,
That nature stole and the heavens preserve,
O why is your compassion late to swerve,
O you who were my life's support and ledge?

You used at least my sad nights to allay
With your sight; now you let me burn and mourn
Without relief; who causes your delay?
Yet up above there dwells no wrath or scorn;

Even here among us a gentle heart
Sometimes absorbs other people's despair,
So that Love is surpassed in his domain.

You who see me inside and feel my care,
Who alone can appease my cruel smart,
With your shadow bring comfort to my pain.

CCCXLI

Deh, qual pietá, qual angel fu sí presto,
A portar sopra 'l cielo il mio cordoglio?
Ch'ancor sento tornar pur come soglio
Madonna in quel suo atto dolce onesto,

Ad acquetare il cor misero e mesto,
Piena sí d'umiltá, vòta d'argoglio,
E 'n somma tal ch'a morte i' mi ritoglio,
E vivo, e 'l viver piú non m'è molesto.

Beata s'è, che pò beare altrui
Co la sua vista, o ver co le parole
Intellette da noi soli ambedui.

—Fedel mio caro, assai di te mi dole;
Ma pur per nostro ben dura ti fui—
Dice, e cos'altre d'arrestare il sole.

CCCXLII

Del cibo onde 'l signor mio sempre abonda,
Lagrime e doglia, il cor lasso nudrisco;
E spesso tremo e spesso impallidisco,
Pensando a la sua piaga aspra e profonda.

Ma chi né prima simil, né seconda
Ebbe al suo tempo, al letto in ch'io languisco,
Vien tal ch'a pena a rimirarl'ardisco,
E pietosa s'asside in su la sponda.

Con quella man che tanto desiai,
M'asciuga li occhi, e col suo dir m'apporta
Dolcezza ch'uom mortal non sentí mai.

—Che val—dice—a saver, chi si sconforta?
Non pianger piú; non m'hai tu pianto assai?
Ch'or fostú vivo, com'io non son mortal—

CCCXLI

O what good angel was so swift to flee
And bring above to heaven my despair?
For I still feel my lady come to me
As she used to, with that sweet, honest air,

To soothe my heart afflicted, my poor breath,
Full of humility, devoid of pride,
In a word, such that I come back from death
And am alive and take life in my stride.

Blessed is she who can give bliss to one
By her appearance or that special speech
Understood only by the two of us.

—My faithful one, I grieve for you, alas,
But for our good I was out of your reach—
She says, and things that would arrest the sun.

CCCXLII

I feed my heart on the good that my lord
Has in abundance, sorrow and lament;
I tremble, I grow pale with discontent
Thinking of the deep wound made by his sword.

But she who first and second here defied
To be like her, to the bed where I lie
Comes full of pity, and I dare not sigh
Looking at her when she sits on the side.

With the hand that I have so much desired
She wipes my eyes, and with her words she gives
Me all the sweetness that a mortal had.

—What good is knowledge—she says—when one grieves?
Do not weep any more; are you not tired?
Could you be living as I am not dead!—

CCCXLIII

Ripensando a quel, ch'oggi il cielo onora,
Soave sguardo, al chinar l'aurea testa,
Al vólto, a quella angelica modesta
Voce, che m'adolciva, et or m'accora,

Gran meraviglia ho com'io viva ancóra;
Né vivrei giá, se chi tra bella e onesta
Qual fu piú lasciò in dubbio, non sí presta
Fusse al mio scampo, lá verso l'aurora.

O che dolci accoglienze, e caste, e pie!
E come intentamente ascolta, e nota
La lunga istoria dè le pene mie!

Poi che 'l dí chiaro par che la percota,
Tornasi al ciel, ché sa tutte le vie,
Umida li occhi e l'una e l'altra gota.

CCCXLIV

Fu forse un tempo dolce cosa amore,
Non per ch'i' sappia il quando; or è sí amara
Che nulla piú. Ben sa 'l ver chi l'impara
Com'ho fatt'io con mio grave dolore.

Quella che fu del secol nostro onore,
Or è del ciel che tutto orna e rischiara,
Fe' mia requie a' suoi giorni e breve e rara;
Or m'ha d'ogni riposo tratto fòre.

Ogni mio ben crudel Morte m'ha tolto;
Né gran prosperitá il mio stato adverso
Pò consolar di quel bel spirto sciolto.

Piansi e cantai; non so piú mutar verso;
Ma dí e notte il duol ne l'alma accolto,
Per la lingua e per li occhi sfogo e verso.

CCCXLIII

Recalling her sweet look that heaven exalts
Today, the bending of her golden head,
Her face, and that angelic and well-bred
Voice that once softened me and now assaults,

I greatly marvel to be still alive;
Nor should I live if she who made us doubt
What in her was more fair, did not arrive
Quickly to save me when the light comes out.

O what sweet greetings and pious and meek,
And how she listens with grave concentration
To the long tale of my painful probation!

When she seems to be frightened by the day,
She returns to the sky, knowing the way,
Her eyes wet, and the one, the other cheek.

CCCXLIV

There was a time when love was a sweet thing,
Perhaps, I know not when; but now it grows
More bitter than all taste. Who learns this knows
The truth, as I have done by suffering.

She who was once the honour of our clime
Is now the sky's, that gives the light's release:
She made my rest brief and rare in her time,
Now she has banished me from every peace.

Every good of mine Death took away;
Nor could her present bliss soothe my adverse
Condition and relieve me in my loss.

I wept and sang; with rhymes no more I play,
But day and night the pain that is my cross
With my tongue and my eyes I do rehearse.

CCCXLV

Spinse amor e dolor ove ir non debbe,
La mia lingua aviata a lamentarsi,
A dir di lei per ch'io cantai et arsi,
Quel che, se fusse ver, torto sarebbe;

Ch'assai 'l mio stato rio quetar devrebbe
Quella beata, e 'l cor racconsolarsi
Vedendo tanto lei domesticarsi
Con colui che, vivendo, in cor sempre ebbe.

E ben m'acqueto, e me stesso consolo;
Né vorrei riverderla in questo inferno,
Anzi voglio morire, e viver solo:

Ché piú bella che mai con l'occhio interno
Con li angeli la veggio alzata a volo
A' pie' del suo e mio signore eterno.

CCCXLVI

Li angeli eletti, e l'anime beate
Cittadine del cielo, il primo giorno
Che madonna passò, le fûr intorno,
Piene di meraviglia e di pietate.

—Che luce è questa, e qual nova beltate?—
—Dicean tra lor—perch'abito sí adorno
Dal mondo errante a quest'alto soggiorno
Non salí mai in tutta questa etate.—

Ella, contenta aver cangiato albergo,
Si paragona pur co i piú perfetti;
E parte ad or ad or si volge a tergo,

Mirando s'io la seguo, e par ch'aspetti:
Ond'io voglie e pensier tutti al ciel ergo,
Perch'i' l'odo pregar pur ch'i' m'affretti.

CCCXLV

Sorrow and Love have pushed astray my tongue
That to the way of grievances had turned,
Making it tell of her for whom I burned
Things that, if they were true, would be all wrong;

To my unhappy state she should bring quiet,
That blessed one, and my heart should grow firm
Seeing her now on such intimate term
With Him who in her life had her heart's right.

And I do become calm as a reward;
Nor would I like to see her in this hell,
But want to live alone till my farewell:

For fairer than before, my inner eye
Sees her soar up and with the angels fly
At the feet of our own eternal Lord.

CCCXLVI

The lofty angels and the ever-blest
Citizens of the sky, on the first day
That my lady arrived, near her did stay,
Full of wonder and pity in each breast.

—What light is this? What beauty do we see?—
They said among themselves.—No one so sweet
From the unrighteous world to this high seat
Ever mounted in all this century.—

She, happy to have left her dwelling's gate,
Finds herself worthy of the perfect ones;
And at times she turns backward, and her glance

Wonders if I am there, and seems to wait:
Hence I lift up wishes and thoughts above,
Because I hear her pray that I may move.

CCCXLVII

Donna, che lieta col principio nostro,
Ti stai, come tua vita alma rechiede,
Assisa in alta e gloriosa sede,
E d'altra ornata che di perle o d'ostro,

O de le donne altèro e raro mostro,
Or nel vólto di lui che tutto vede,
Vedi 'l mio amore, e quella pura fede,
Per ch'io tante versai lagrime e 'nchiostro,

E senti che vèr' te 'l mio core in terra
Tal fu qual ora è in cielo, e mai non volsi
Altro da te che 'l sol de li occhi tuoi:

Dunque per amendar la lunga guerra,
Per cui dal mondo a te sola mi volsi,
Prega ch'i' venga tosto a star con voi.

CCCXLVIII

Da' piú belli occhi e dal piú chiaro viso
Che mai splendesse, e da' piú bei capelli,
Che facean l'oro e 'l sol parer men belli,
Dal piú dolce parlare, e dolce riso,

Da le man, da le braccia che conquiso,
Senza moversi, avrian quai piú rebelli
Fûr d'Amor mai, da' piú bei piedi snelli,
Da la persona fatta in paradiso,

Prendean vita i miei spirti: or n'ha diletto
Il re celeste, i suoi alati corrieri;
Et io son qui rimaso ignudo e cieco.

Sol un conforto a le mie pene aspetto,
Ch'ella, che vede tutt'i miei penseri,
M'impetre grazia ch'i' possa esser seco.

CCCXLVII

Lady who, happy with our Principle
Remain, as your good life could well request,
Seated in an exalted, glorious nest,
Adorned with more than pearl or purple shell,

O you, of women new and stately wonder,
Now in His face that can see all we think,
You see my love, my faith that does not sunder,
For which I spilled so many tears and ink,

And feel that here toward you every vow
Of mine was as it is, and that I never
Asked anything from you save your eyes' sun;

Therefore to end the war that once did sever
Us, and made me from the world to you run,
Pray that I may come soon where you are now.

CCCXLVIII

From the most beauteous eyes, the clearest face
That ever shone, and from the fairest hair
Which made and sun and gold appear less fair,
From the sweetest discourse and smiling grace,

From the hands, from the arms that bound their ties,
Without moving, on all the foes that meet
The friends of love, from the slenderest feet,
From the form that was shaped in paradise,

My spirit received life; now they delight
The King of heaven and each winged messenger;
And I have been left here, naked and blind.

Only one comfort I ask in my plight,
That she, who sees my thoughts and reads my mind,
Obtain the grace that I may be with her.

CCCXLIX

E' mi par d'or in ora udire il messo
Che madonna mi mande a sé chiamando:
Cosí dentro e di fòr mi vo cangiando,
E sono in non molt'anni sí dimesso,

Ch'a pena riconosco omai me stesso!
Tutto 'l viver usato ho messo in bando:
Sarei contento di sapere il quando,
Ma pur devrebbe il tempo esser da presso.

O felice quel dí, che, del terreno
Carcere uscendo, lasci rotta e sparta
Questa mia grave e frale e mortal gonna,

E da sí folte tenebre mi parta,
Volando tanto su nel bel sereno,
Ch'i' veggia, il mio Signore, e la mia donna.

CCCL

Questo nostro caduco e fragil bene,
Ch'è vento et ombra, et ha nome beltate,
Non fu giá mai se non in questa etate
Tutto in un corpo; e ciò fu per mie pene.

Ché natura non vòl, né si convene,
Per far ricco un, por li altri in povertate:
Or versò in una ogni sua largitate;
Perdonimi qual è bella, o si tène.

Non fu simil bellezza antica o nova,
Né sará, credo; ma fu sí coverta,
Ch'a pena se n'accorse il mondo errante.

Tosto disparve; onde 'l cangiar mi giova
La poca vista a me dal cielo offerta
Sol per piacer a le sue luci sante.

CCCXLIX

I seem to hear each hour the courier ride
That my lady sends me to call me there;
I am changing so much inside, outside,
And in not many years have grown so bare

That I can hardly myself recognize!
All my old life I have banished from here:
I should be glad to know when will arise
That dawn, but now it must be very near.

O how blissful the day when, going out
Of the earth's jail, I leave scattered about
And torn my frail and heavy mortal gown,

And from this gloomy darkness I depart,
Flying toward the light with a glad heart,
And see my lady, my Lord, and his crown.

CCCL

This frail good of our life's unstable stage
That is called beauty, and is shadow, wind,
Has never been, save in our present age,
All in one body; this is why I mind.

For Nature does not wish, nor is it fit,
To make one rich by leaving others poor:
But she did shower her liberal wit
On one; forgive, fair ladies, who are sure.

Such beauty, old or new, was not revealed
And shall not be; but she was so concealed,
That the world could not find her and retrieve.

She disappeared at once; and I must leave
The little sight that granted me the skies,
To please only her own heavenly eyes.

CCCLI

Dolci durezze, e placide repulse,
Piene di casto amore, e di pietate,
Leggiadri sdegni, che le mie infiammate
Voglie tempraro, or me n'accorgo, e 'nsulse;

Gentil parlar, in cui chiaro refulse,
Con somma cortesia, somma onestate,
Fior di vertú, fontana di beltate,
Ch'ogni basso penser del cor m'avulse;

Divino sguardo da far l'uom felice,
Or fiero in affrenar la mente ardita,
A quel che giustamente si disdice,

Or presto a confortar mia frale vita,
Questo bel variar fu la radice
Di mia salute, ch'altramente era ita.

CCCLII

Spirto felice, che sí dolcemente
Volgei quelli occhi, piú chiari che 'l sole,
E formavi i sospiri, e le parole,
Vive ch'ancor mi sonan ne la mente,

Giá ti vid'io, d'onesto foco ardente,
Mover i pie' fra l'erbe e le viole,
Non come donna, ma com'angel sòle,
Di quella ch'or m'è piú che mai presente;

La qual tu poi, tornando al tuo fattore,
Lasciasti in terra, e quel soave velo,
Che per alto destín ti venne in sorte.

Nel tuo partir, partí del mondo Amore
E Cortesia, e 'l Sol cadde del cielo,
E dolce incominciò farsi la Morte.

CCCLI

Sweet unkindness and temperate repulse
Full of chaste love and of loyal devotion,
Charming disdain restraining my emotion
That was inflamed, I see it now, and false;

Gentle speaking in which was clearly brought
To light a supreme courtesy and duty,
Flower of virtue and fountain of beauty
That tore up from my heart every low thought;

Heavenly look that made blessed man's lot,
Now stern in checking the audacious mind
From going after a forbidden fruit,

Now quick to comfort my life frail and blind,
This beautiful variety was the root
Of my salvation that I had forgot.

CCCLII

Blithe spirit that so sweetly turned around
Your eyes which are more limpid than the sun,
And shaped those sighs and words that are not gone,
But still alive within my mind resound,

I did see you, burning with ardent cheer,
Moving those steps among violets and grass,
Not like a woman, but as angels pass,
The steps of one now more than ever near;

Which you, returning to your Maker high,
Left here on earth, with that veil sweet and chaste
Which by a lofty fate was given you.

On your departure Love departed too,
And Courtesy, the sun fell from the sky,
And Death began to have a pleasant taste.

CCCLIII

Vago augelletto, che cantando vai,
O ver piangendo, il tuo tempo passato,
Vedendoti la notte e 'l verno a lato,
E 'l dí dopo le spalle, e i mesi gai,

Se come i tuoi gravosi affanni sai,
Cosí sapessi il mio simile stato,
Verresti in grembo a questo sconsolato,
A partir seco i dolorosi guai.

I' non so se le parti sarian pari,
Ché quella cui tu piangi, è forse in vita,
Di ch'a me morte, e 'l ciel, son tanto avari;

Ma la stagione, e l'ora men gradita,
Col membrar de' dolci anni, e de li amari,
A parlar teco con pietá m'invita.

CCCLIV

Deh, porgi mano a l'affannato ingegno,
Amor, et a lo stile stanco e frale,
Per dir di quella ch'è fatta immortale,
E cittadina del celeste regno;

Dammi, signor, che 'l mio dir giunga al segno
De le sue lode, ove per sé non sale,
Se vertú, se beltá non ebbe eguale
Il mondo, che d'aver lei non fu degno.

Responde:—Quanto 'l ciel et io possiamo,
E i buon consigli, e 'l conversar onesto,
Tutto fu in lei, di che noi morte ha privi;

Forma par non fu mai dal dí ch'Adamo
Aperse li occhi in prima; e basti or questo:
Piangendo il dico; e tu piangendo scrivi.—

CCCLIII

Wandering small bird that go singing away,
Or perhaps weeping the time that is past,
Seeing the night and winter come at last
And behind you the happy month and day,

If, as you know your own affliction,
You knew as well my similar distress,
You would come in the lap of this poor one
To share with him a great unhappiness.

I know not if the portions would be right,
For she, whom you mourn for, perhaps has still
Her life, which Death and heaven envy me;

But the season, the hour of less delight,
The memory of sweetness and of ill,
Drive me to reason with you piteously.

CCCLIV

O lend your hand to my afflicted mind,
Love, to my style exhausted by this weight,
That I may speak of her immortal kind
Become a citizen of heaven's state;

Grant me, lord, that my language hit the mark
Of her praise where alone I cannot rise,
For the world has no virtue's, beauty's spark,
Equal to her, not worthy of her eyes.

He answers:—What the sky and I can bid,
The good counsels, the honest speech of love,
All was in her, of whom Death robs us quite.

Such a form never was, since Adam did
Open his eyes; and let this be enough:
I say it weeping; weeping you must write.—

CCCLV

O tempo, o ciel volubil, che fuggendo
Inganni i ciechi e miseri mortali,
O dí veloci, piú che vento e strali,
Ora ab experto vostre frodi intendo;

Ma scuso voi, e me stesso riprendo,
Ché Natura a volar v'aperse l'ali,
A me diede occhi, et io pur ne' miei mali
Li tenni, onde vergogna e dolor prendo.

E sarebbe ora, et è passata omai,
Di rivoltarli, in piú secura parte,
E poner fine a l'infiniti guai;

Né dal tuo giogo, Amor, l'alma sí parte,
Ma dal suo mal; con che studio tu 'l sai;
Non a caso è vertute, anzi è bell'arte.

CCCLVI

L'aura mia sacra al mio stanco riposo
Spira sí spesso, ch'i' prendo ardimento
Di dirle il mal ch'i' ho sentito, e sento,
Che, vivendo ella, non sarei stat'oso.

I' incomincio da quel guardo amoroso,
Che fu principio a sí lungo tormento,
Poi seguo come misero e contento,
Di dí in dí, d'ora in ora, Amor m'ha róso.

Ella si tace, e di pietá depinta,
Fiso mira pur me; parte sospira,
E di lagrime oneste il viso adorna.

Onde l'anima mia dal dolor vinta,
Mentre piangendo allor seco s'adira,
Sciolta dal sonno a se stessa ritorna.

CCCLV

O time, o turning sky whose motion fleet
Baffles our blind, unhappy humankind,
O days more rapid than arrows and wind,
Now from experience I know your deceit;

But I forgive you, my own self I blame,
For Nature spread your wings to make you fly
And gave me eyes that on my sorrows I
Keep fixed, hence I receive anguish and shame.

Now is the time, it is already past,
To direct them to the places that last,
And make an end of this unending woe;

Still my soul from your yoke does not depart,
But from its grief; how studiously you know:
Virtue is not a chance, it is an art.

CCCLVI

My sacred aura breathes in my tired rest
So often, that I dare to become bold
And tell her how I was and am distressed,
Which in her life I never could have told.

I begin from that first amorous glance
That was the spring of such a long dismay,
Then I go on saying how day by day
I was made sad and glad by Love's keen lance.

She does not speak, and pity holds her eyes
Ever fixed upon me; she partly sighs
And her face is adorned with graceful tears.

And then my soul, all overcome by pain,
While she weeps and rebukes it for its fears,
Loosened from sleep comes to itself again.

CCCLVII

Ogni giorno mi par piú di mill'anni
Ch'i' segua la mia fida e cara duce,
Che mi condusse al mondo, or mi conduce,
Per miglior via, a vita senza affanni;

E non mi posson ritener l'inganni
Del mondo, ch'i' 'l conosco; e tanta luce
Dentro al mio core in fin dal ciel traluce
Ch'i' 'ncomincio a contar il tempo, e i danni.

Né minaccie temer debbo di morte,
Che 'l re sofferse con piú grave pena,
Per farme a seguitar constante e forte;

Et or novellamente in ogni vena
Intrò di lei che m'era data in sorte,
E non turbò la sua fronte serena.

CCCLVIII

Non pò far morte il dolce viso amaro,
Ma 'l dolce viso dolce pò far Morte.
Che bisogn' a morir ben altre scorte?
Quella mi scorge ond'ogni ben imparo.

E quei che del suo sangue non fu avaro,
Che col pe' ruppe le tartaree porte,
Col suo morir par che mi riconforte.
Dunque vien, Morte; il tuo venir m'è caro.

E non tardar, ch'egli è ben tempo omai;
E se non fusse, e' fu 'l tempo in quel punto
Che madonna passò di questa vita.

D'allor innanzi un dí non vissi mai:
Seco fui in via, e seco al fin son giunto,
E mia giornata ho co' suoi pie' fornita.

CCCLVII

Every day I long with growing greed
To follow my beloved and faithful guide
Who led me in this world and now does lead
Me on a better way out of grief's tide;

And I cannot be held back by the lies
Of the world, which I know; a light so clear
Inside my heart is sparkling from the skies,
That I begin to count the time and year.

Nor do I have to fear death and its threat,
Which our King suffered with the greatest pain
To make me face it strongly, without dread;

It did enter just now by every vein
In her who had been given me by fate,
And did not trouble her limpid forehead.

CCCLVIII

Death cannot render a sweet visage wry,
But a sweet visage can make sweeter death.
What need have I of other guides to die?
She guides me, who taught me every faith.

And He who was not chary of his blood,
Who with his feet broke the Tartarean doors,
With his own death seems to comfort my sores.
Then, come on, Death; your coming is my good.

Do not delay, because it is high time;
If it is not, it was the moment when
My lady from this life vanished away.

I have not lived a single day since then:
With her I walked, with her I end my climb,
With her feet I accomplished my workday.

CCCLIX

Quando il soave mio fido conforto,
Per dar riposo a la mia vita stanca,
Ponsi del letto in su la sponda manca,
Con quel suo dolce ragionare accorto,
Tutto di pièta e di paura smorto,
Dico:—Onde vien tu ora, o felice alma?—
Un ramoscel di palma
Et un di lauro trae del suo bel seno,
E dice:—Dal sereno
Ciel empireo, e di quelle sante parti,
Mi mossi, e vengo sol per consolarti.—

In atto et in parole la ringrazio
Umilemente, e poi demando:—Or donde
Sai tu il mio stato?—Et ella:—Le triste onde
Del pianto, di che mai tu non se' sazio,
Coll'aura de' sospir, per tanto spazio
Passano al cielo, e turban la mia pace.
Sí forte ti dispiace
Che di questa miseria sia partita,
E giunta a miglior vita?
Che piacer ti devria, se tu m'amasti
Quanto in sembianti e ne' tuoi dir mostrasti.—

Rispondo:—Io non piango altro che me stesso
Che son rimaso in tenebre e 'n martíre,
Certo sempre del tuo al ciel salire
Come di cosa ch'uom vede da presso.
Come Dio e Natura avrebben messo
In un cor giovenil tanta vertute,
Se l'eterna salute
Non fusse destinata al tuo ben fare?
O de l'anime rare,
Ch'altamente vivesti qui tra noi,
E che súbito al ciel volasti poi!

Ma io che debbo altro che pianger sempre,
Misero, e sol, che senza te son nulla?
Ch'or fuss'io spento al latte et a la culla,

CCCLIX

When my dear, sweet and faithful comforter,
To give a solace to my weary head,
Comes to sit at the left side of my bed
With that soft reasoning and cunning air,
Full of love and of pity, pale with fear,
I say:—Where do you come from, happy soul?—
She then draws out two small
Branches of palm and laurel from her breast,
And says:—From the clear nest
Of the high heaven, from that holy view
I departed and came to comfort you.—

In words and gestures then I thank my love
Humbly and I ask her:—How do you know
My state?—And she:—The sad waves of your woe,
Of which you never seem to have enough,
With your sighs' breezes through the spaces move,
Enter the sky and undermine my peace.
Does your sorrow increase
When I have left the human misery
And reached eternity?
This ought to make you glad, if you did care
As your looks and your words used to declare.—

I reply:—Only for myself I weep,
Who have remained in darkness and constraint,
Certain that to the sky you had been sent,
As of a thing one sees both clear and deep.
Why then did God and Nature want to heap
So much good in a youthful human heart,
If the eternal part
Of salvation were not meant as your goal?
O you, exalted soul,
Who among us one time loftily lived
And flew to heaven, where you are arrived!

And what else can I do but weep forever,
Wretched, alone, who without you am nought?
Had my cradle and milk condemned my lot

Per non provar de l'amorose tempre!—
Et ella:—A che pur piangi, e ti distempre?
Quanto era meglio alzar da terra l'ali,
E le cose mortali,
E queste dolci tue fallaci ciance,
Librar con giusta lance,
E seguir me, s'è ver che tanto m'ami,
Cogliendo, omai, qualcun di questi rami!—

—I' volea demandar—respond'io allora—
Che voglion importar quelle due frondi?—
Et ella:—Tu medesmo ti rispondi,
Tu la cui penna tanto l'una onora:
Palma è vittoria, et io, giovene ancóra,
Vinsi il mondo, e me stessa; il lauro segna
Triumfo, ond'io son degna,
Mercé di quel Signor che mi die' forza.
Or tu, s'altri ti sforza,
A lui ti volgi, a lui chiedi soccorso;
Sí che siam seco al fine del tuo corso.—

—Son questi i capei biondi, e l'aureo nodo,
—Dich'io—ch'ancor mi stringe, e quei belli occhi
Che fûr mio sol?—Non errar con li sciocchi,
Né parlar—dice—o creder a lor modo.
Spirito ignudo sono, e 'n ciel mi godo:
Quel che tu cerchi è terra, giá molt'anni;
Ma per trarti d'affanni,
M'è dato a parer tale; et ancor quella
Sarò, piú che mai bella,
A te piú cara, sí selvaggia e pia,
Salvando inseme tua salute, e mia.—

I' piango; et ella il vólto
Co le sue man m'asciuga; e poi sospira
Dolcemente; e s'adira
Con parole che i sassi romper ponno:
E dopo questo, si parte ella, e 'l sonno.

Rather than trying the lover's endeavour!—
And she:—Why do you cry as in a fever?
How much better it was to raise your wings,
And weigh the mortal things
And this deceiving sweet chatter of yours
With a balance that soars;
And to reach me, if you do love me so,
By plucking these fair branches where they grow.—

—I wanted to ask you—my answer says—
Those two branches of yours, what do they mean?—
And she:—In your own self this may be seen,
In you whose pen gives one honour and praise:
The palm is victory, and my young days
Vanquished the world and me; the laurel is
Triumph I do not miss
By the grace of that Lord who lent me vigour.
Now if another's rigour
Crushes you, turn to him as to a friend;
So that we be with him when comes your end.—

—Is this the yellow hair, the golden knot—
I say—that still holds me, and those fair eyes
That were my sun?—Err not with the unwise,
Nor speak—she says—according to their thought.
A bare spirit I am, to heaven brought:
What you look for has been earth many years;
But, to free you from cares,
I may still appear such; and still the same,
I shall more beauty claim
And be to you more dear, savage and kind,
The salvation of yours and of my mind.—

I weep; and my wet face
She wipes with her own hands, then sweetly sighs;
Into a rage she flies,
Using a language that would break a stone;
And after this she and my sleep are gone.

CCCLX

Quel antiquo mio dolce empio signore
Fatto citar dinanzi a la reina
Che la parte divina
Tien di nostra natura e 'n cima sede,
Ivi, com'oro che nel foco affina,
Mi rappresento carco di dolore,
Di paura e d'orrore,
Quasi uom che teme morte e ragion chiede;
E 'ncomincio:—Madonna, il manco piede
Giovenetto pos'io nel costui regno;
Ond'altro ch'ira e sdegno
Non ebbi mai; e tanti e sí diversi
Tormenti i' vi soffersi,
Ch'al fine vinta fu quell'infinita
Mia pazienzia, e 'n odio ebbi la vita.

Cosí 'l mio tempo in fin qui trapassato
È in fiamma e 'n pene; e quante utili oneste
Vie sprezzai, quante feste,
Per servir questo lusinghier crudele!
E qual ingegno ha sí parole preste
Che stringer possa 'l mio infelice stato,
E le mie d'esto ingrato
Tante e sí gravi e sí giuste querele?
O poco mèl, molto aloè con fele!
In quanto amaro ha la mia vita avezza,
Con sua falsa dolcezza,
La qual m'atrasse a l'amorosa schiera!
Che s'i' non m'inganno, era
Disposto a sollevarmi alto da terra:
E' mi tolse di pace e pose in guerra.

Questi m'ha fatto men amare Dio
Ch'i' non deveva, e men curar me stesso:
Per una donna ho messo
Egualmente in non cale ogni pensero.
Di ciò m'è stato consiglier sol esso,
Sempr'aguzzando il giovenil desio

CCCLX

That ancient, sweet and wicked lord of mine,
Being called to the presence of that queen
Who what is not terrene
In our nature ordains, ruling our prison,
I arrive there as gold by fire is seen
To refine, overcome by terror's sign
Where grief and dread combine,
Like a man who fears death and demands reason;
And I begin:—Lady, in my young season
I put my left foot first in his domain;
And nothing but disdain
And anger did I get; and such diverse
Pains I suffered and cares,
That in the end my long patience gave way,
And I hated this life's continuous fray.

Thus until now my time has passed in flight
Through flame and pain; how many useful measures
I scorned, how many pleasures,
To serve this undeserving flatterer!
And what talent possesses such rich treasures
Of words that could encompass my sad plight,
And the justified right
Of all the plaints that against him I bear?
O scanty honey, aloe of despair!
How bitterly he always used to treat
My life with his false sweet
Which drove me after the amorous throng!
For, if I am not wrong,
I was able to fly above and far:
He severed me from peace and gave me war.

This one made me love God less than I should,
And of myself take very little care:
Thinking only of her,
All other thought to me became a joke.
He alone was of this the adviser,
Always whetting my youthful longing mood

A l'empia cote, ond'io
Sperai riposo al suo giogo aspro e fero.
Misero! a che quel chiaro ingegno altèro,
E l'altre doti a me date dal cielo?
Ché vo cangiando 'l pelo,
Né cangiar posso l'ostinata voglia:
Cosí in tutto mi spoglia
Di libertá questo crudel ch'i' accuso,
Ch'amaro viver m'ha vòlto in dolce uso.

Cercar m'ha fatto deserti paesi,
Fiere e ladri rapaci, ispidi dumi,
Dure genti e costumi,
Et ogni error che ' pellegrini intrica,
Monti, valli, paludi, e mari, e fiumi,
Mille lacciuoli in ogni parte tesi;
E 'l verno in strani mesi,
Con pericol presente e con fatica:
Né costui né quell'altra mia nemica,
Ch'i' fuggia, mi lasciavan sol un punto.
Onde, s'i non son giunto
Anzi tempo da morte acerba e dura,
Pietá celeste ha cura
Di mia salute, non questo tiranno,
Che del mio duol si pasce e del mio danno.

Poi che suo fui, non ebbi ora tranquilla,
Né spero aver; e le mie notti il sonno
Sbandiro, e piú non ponno
Per erbe o per incanti e sé ritrarlo.
Per inganni e per forza è fatto donno
Sovra miei spirti: e non sonò poi squilla,
Ov'io sia in qualche villa,
Ch'i' non l'udisse. Ei sa che 'l vero parlo;
Ché legno vecchio mai non róse tarlo
Come questi 'l mio core, in che s'annida,
E di morte lo sfida.
Quinci nascon le lagrime e i martíri,
Le parole e i sospiri,
Di ch'io mi vo stancando, e forse altrui.

To his stone, while I would
Hope for relief from his oppressing yoke.
Alas! my clear and noble talent broke,
Why did I receive gifts from heaven's sphere?
Because I see my hair
Change, but I cannot change my stubborn will:
So utterly he still
Robs me of freedom, the one I accuse,
Who turned my bitter life to a sweet use.

He made me go in quest of foreign lands,
Wild beasts, rapacious thieves and shaggy nooks,
Rugged peoples and looks,
And all the traps that a pilgrim intrigue,
Mountains, valleys and swamps, and seas and brooks,
A thousand nooses laid in all those strands;
Winter in summer sands,
With danger always present and fatigue:
And this was with my enemy in league,
And though I fled, they never let me go.
If I did not sink low
Too early before harsh and cruel death,
Heaven did save my breath,
And not this tyrant who is merciless,
Who feeds on my despair and my distress.

Since he held me, no tranquil hour my soul
Has had or hopes to have; my nights ignore
All sleep, and can no more
With herbs or magic call it or renew.
By force and falsehood he comes to the fore
Of my spirits; never a bell did toll
At night, from distant knoll,
But I heard it. He knows that this is true;
Never a boring-worm did old wood chew
As this will gnaw my heart where he resides
And challenges death's tides.
Thence spring my tears and all my martyrdom,
My words and my sighs come,
That vex my heart and make me look so grim.

Giudica tu, che me conosci, e lui.—
Il mio adversario, con agre rampogne,
Comincia:—O donna, intendi l'altra parte,
Ché 'l vero, onde si parte
Quest'ingrato, dirá senza defetto.
Questi in sua prima etá fu dato a l'arte
Da vender parolette, anzi menzogne:
Né par che si vergogne,
Tolto da quella noia al mio diletto,
Lamentarsi di me, che puro e netto,
Contr'al desio, che spesso il suo mal vòle,
Lui tenni, ond'or si dole,
In dolce vita, ch'ei miseria chiama,
Salito in qualche fama
Solo per me, che 'l suo intelletto alzai,
Ov'alzato per sé non fôra mai.

Ei sa che 'l grande Atride e l'alto Achille,
Et Anibál al terren vostro amaro,
E di tutti il piú chiaro
Un altro e di vertute e di fortuna,
Com'a ciascun le sue stelle ordinaro,
Lasciai cader in vil amor d'ancille:
Et a costui di mille
Donne elette, eccelenti n'elessi una,
Qual non si vedrá mai sotto la Luna,
Ben che Lucrezia ritornasse a Roma;
E sí dolce idioma
Le diedi, et un cantar tanto soave,
Che penser basso o grave
Non poté mai durar dinanzi a lei.
Questi fûr con costui l'inganni mei.

Questo fu il fèl, questi li sdegni e l'ire,
Piú dolci assai che di null'altra il tutto.
Di bon seme mal frutto
Mieto; e tal merito ha chi 'ngrato serve.
Sí l'avea sotto l'ali mie condutto,
Ch'a donne e cavalier piacea il suo dire;

Be you the judge, who know myself and him.—

My adversary with loud plaints and cries
Begins:—O woman, hear the other side,
Where the truth does abide
Without a fault, from which this traitor strays.
This from his youth was to the art allied
Of selling little words or rather lies,
Nor does he realize,
Being brought from that dullness to my plays,
The shame of blaming me who tried to raise
Him pure and clean against his harmful will,
And complains of this ill
In a sweet life that he has called distress,
Borne to fame's happiness
Only because I raised his intellect;
He would never have reached that place elect.

He knows I made Atrides and the high
Achilles, Hannibal dire to your nest,
And another, the best
In virtue and in fortune among these,
As each was by his star diversely blest,
Fall in love with a maid's unworthy tie:
And for him I did spy
Out of a thousand ladies, and did seize
One who shall never walk in the earth's breeze,
Though Lucretia should come again to Rome;
Such lovely idiom
I gave her and a singing voice so sweet,
That no coarse, low conceit
Could ever have remained when she was there.
These are my falsehoods, that he had to bear.

This was the gall, this the wrath and disdain
Far sweeter than another's precious things.
And a good seed now brings
Bad fruit; thus the ungrateful will reward.
So well he had been guided by my wings,
That ladies admired him, and gentlemen;

E sí alto salire
Il feci, che tra ' caldi ingegni ferve
Il suo nome, e de' suoi detti conserve
Si fanno con diletto in alcun loco;
Ch'or saria forse un roco
Mormorador di corti, un uom del vulgo:
I' l'esalto e divulgo,
Per quel ch'elli 'mparò ne la mia scola,
E da colei che fu nel mondo sola.

E per dir a l'estremo il gran servigio,
Da mille atti inonesti l'ho ritratto;
Ché mai per alcun patto
A lui piacer non poteo cosa vile:
Giovene schivo e vergognoso in atto,
Et in penser, poi che fatto era uom ligio
Di lei, ch'alto vestigio
Li 'mpresse al core, e fecel suo simíle.
Quanto ha del pellegrino e del gentile,
Da lei tène, e da me, di cui si biasma.
Mai notturno fantasma
D'error non fu sí pien, com'ei vèr' noi;
Ch'è in grazia, da poi
Che ne conobbe, a Dio et a la gente:
Di ciò il superbo si lamenta, e pente.

Ancor (e questo è quel che tutto avanza)
Da volar sopra 'l ciel li avea dat' ali
Per le cose mortali,
Che son scala al fattor, chi ben l'estima;
Ché mirando ei ben fiso quante e quali
Eran vertuti in quella sua speranza,
D'una in altra sembianza
Potea levarsi a l'alta cagion prima:
Et ei l'ha detto alcuna volta in rima.
Or m'ha posto in oblio con quella donna
Ch'i' li die' per colonna
De la sua frale vita.—A questo un strido
Lagrimoso alzo e grido:
—Ben me la die', ma tosto la ritolse.—

I had made him attain
Such heights, that in the ardent talents' record
His name is glowing, and the flower of his word
Is plucked with fervour in more than one place;
He might have brought disgrace
To courtly sounds, like one of vulgar kind:
I exalted, refined
Him with the knowledge he learned from my school
And from her who was here the highest rule.

And, to keep for the last my greatest aid,
From thousand worthless actions I did save
Him, for he could not have
Endured or liked any thing that was base:
A modest young man, in his bearing grave,
And thought, when her sworn vassal he was made,
Who in his heart had laid
The seal of honour, raised him to her place.
Whatever is in him of charm and grace
He had from her and from me whom he scolds.
Never a night-ghost holds
As many fallacies as he for us,
Who did blessings amass
Since he knew us, from God and humankind:
And for this the proud one grieves in his mind.

Moreover (and this is what surpasses all),
I gave him wings to mount up to the sky,
Through mortal things to fly
On ladders to his Maker, by their laws;
For contemplating fixedly the high
And many virtues drawn in his hope's wall,
From one to other stall
He could have risen to the Supreme Cause:
And he sometimes said this in his rhymes' clause.
Now he has mine and her memory lost,
Which I placed as a post
In his frail life.—At this I raise a groan
Of anguish and I moan:
—He did give her, and soon made disappear.—

Responde:—Io no, ma chi per sé la volse.—
Al fin ambo conversi al giusto seggio,
I' con tremanti, ei con voci alte e crude,
Ciascun per sé conchiude:
—Nobile donna, tua sentenzia attendo.—
Ella allor sorridendo:
—Piacemi aver vostre questioni udite;
Ma piú tempo bisogna a tanta lite.—

CCCLXI

Dicemi spesso il mio fidato speglio,
L'animo stanco, e la cangiata scorza,
E la scemata mia destrezza e forza:
—Non ti nasconder piú; tu se' pur veglio.

Obedir a Natura in tutto è il meglio;
Ch'a contender con lei il tempo ne sforza.—
Súbito allor, com'acqua 'l foco amorza,
D'un lungo e grave sonno mi risveglio:

E veggio ben che 'l nostro viver vola,
E ch'esser non si pò piú d'una volta;
E 'n mezzo 'l cor mi sona una parola

Di lei ch'è or dal suo bel nodo sciolta,
Ma ne' suoi giorni al mondo fu sí sola,
Ch'a tutte, s'i' non erro, fama ha tolta.

—Not I—he answers—He who willed her near.—
At last, being both called to the just seat,
I with a trembling voice, he with a rude
Voice, our speeches conclude:
—Noble lady, I wait for your sentence.—
She smiles in our presence:
—I am glad to have followed your dispute;
But we need longer time for this lawsuit.—

CCCLXI

Often they tell me, the mirror I hold,
My weary spirit and my altered sight,
And my diminished nimbleness and might:
—Do not hide any more: for you are old.

To obey nature now is the best matter;
For any fight against it time will break.—
Then suddenly, as fire is quelled by water,
From a long, heavy sleep I seem to wake:

And I see well that our life runs away,
And that we cannot come twice to this spot;
And in my heart a word returns to stay

Of her, who now is loosed from her fair knot,
But in her day had so unique a name
That she robbed other women of their fame.

CCCLXII

Volo con l'ali de' pensieri al cielo
Sí spesse volte che quasi un di loro
Esser mi par c'han ivi il suo tesoro,
Lasciando in terra lo squarciato velo.

Talor mi trema 'l cor d'un dolce gelo,
Udendo lei, per ch'io mi discoloro,
Dirmi:—Amico, or t'am'io, et or t'onoro,
Perch'ha' i costumi variati, e 'l pelo.—

Menami al suo Signor: allor m'inchino,
Pregando umilemente che consenta
Ch'i' stia a veder e l'uno e l'altro vólto.

Responde:—Egli è ben fermo il tuo destíno;
E per tardar ancor vent'anni o trenta,
Parrá a te troppo, e non fia però molto.—

CCCLXIII

Morte ha spento quel sol ch'abagliar suolmi,
E 'n tenebre son li occhi interi e saldi;
Terra è quella ond'io ebbi e freddi e caldi;
Spenti son i miei lauri, or querce et olmi:

Di ch'io veggio 'l mio ben; e parte duolmi.
Non è chi faccia e paventosi e baldi
I miei penser, né chi li agghiacci e scaldi,
Né chi gli empia di speme, e di duol colmi.

Fuor di man di colui che punge e molce,
Che giá fece di me sí lungo strazio,
Mi trovo in libertate, amara e dolce:

Et al Signor ch'i' adoro e ch'i' ringrazio,
Che pur col ciglio il ciel governa e folce,
Torno stanco di viver, non che sazio.

CCCLXII

I fly to heaven, borne on my thoughts' wings,
So many times, that I almost believe
I am one of the souls who find reprieve
There, and who left on earth their tattered things.

Sometimes my heart trembles in a sweet frost
Hearing her, who makes colourless my face,
Tell me:—Friend, now I love and prize you most,
Because I see quite changed your hair and ways.—

She leads me to her Lord: and then I bow
And I pray humbly that heaven allow
Me to see either face and stay and wait.

They answer me:—Your fate cannot go wrong;
Though it be twenty or thirty years late,
It will seem much to you, but is not long.—

CCCLXIII

Death quelled the sun wonted to overwhelm
Me, and her perfect, wholesome eyes are dark;
Dust is the one who was my chill and spark;
Broken my laurels, these are oak and elm:

From this I see my good, and partly mourn.
There is no one to make frightened or bold
My thoughts, and cause them to feel warm or cold,
No one to make them hopeful or forlorn.

Out of the hands of one who soothes and stings,
Who in the past time left me lacerated,
I find freedom at last, bitter and sweet;

And to the Lord whom I adore and greet,
Who with his nod governs the holy things,
I return, tired of life, and with life sated.

CCCLXIV

Tennemi Amor anni vent'uno ardendo,
Lieto nel foco, e nel duol pien di speme;
Poi che madonna e 'l mio cor seco inseme
Saliro al ciel, dieci altri anni piangendo.

Omai son stanco, e mia vita reprendo
Di tanto error che di vertute il seme
Ha quasi spento; e le mie parti estreme,
Alto Dio, a te devotamente rendo,

Pentito e tristo de' miei sí spesi anni,
Che spender si deveano in miglior uso,
In cercar pace et in fuggir affanni.

Signor, che 'n questo carcer m'hai rinchiuso,
Trâmene, salvo da li eterni danni;
Ch'i' conosco 'l mio fallo, e non lo scuso.

CCCLXV

I' vo piangendo i miei passati tempi
I quai posi in amar cosa mortale,
Senza levarmi a volo, abbiend'io l'ale,
Per dar forse di me non bassi essempî.

Tu che vedi i miei mali indegni et empî,
Re del cielo invisibile immortale,
Soccorri a l'alma disviata e frale,
E 'l suo defetto di tua grazia adempi;

Sí che s'io vissi in guerra et in tempesta,
Mora in pace et in porto; e se la stanza
Fu vana, almen sia la partita onesta.

A quel poco di viver che m'avanza
Et al morir degni esser tua man presta:
Tu sai ben che 'n altrui non ho speranza.

CCCLXIV

Twenty-one years Love held me in his fire,
Happy in burning, hopeful in despair;
When my heart and my lady rose up higher,
Toward the sky, ten other years of care.

Now I am tired and reprimand my soul
For that error of mine that nearly slew
The seed of virtue; and my final role,
Supreme God, I devoutly offer you,

Sad and repentant for my wasted age
That should have been applied to better use,
To look for peace and to escape from woe.

O Lord, who have confined me in this cage,
Take me, save me from our eternal foe;
I know my sin, I look for no excuse.

CCCLXV

I go lamenting my past history
That I spent in the love of mortal things,
Without soaring up high, though I had wings,
So as to leave more worthy proofs of me.

You, who see my mistake worthless and bad,
King of the sky, deathless, invisible,
Give your help to a soul that strayed and fell,
Make his defects by your salvation glad;

That if I lived at war and in a storm,
I die in peace, in port; and if my stay
Was vain, that my departure may reform.

During the little life that I have left,
And at my death, let your hand not delay:
Of any other hope I am bereft.

CCCLXVI

Vergine bella, che di sol vestita,
Coronata di stelle, al sommo Sole
Piacesti sí, che 'n te sua luce ascose,
Amor mi spinge a dir di te parole;
Ma non so 'ncominciar senza tu' aita,
E di colui ch'amando in te si pose:
Invoco lei che ben sempre rispose,
Chi la chiamò con fede.
Vergine, s'a mercede
Miseria estrema de l'umane cose
Giá mai ti volse, al mio prego t'inchina;
Soccorri a la mia guerra,
Ben ch'i' sia terra,   e tu del ciel regina.

Vergine saggia, e del bel numero una
De le beate vergini prudenti,
Anzi la prima, e con piú chiara lampa;
O saldo scudo de l'afflitte genti
Contra ' colpi di Morte e di Fortuna,
Sotto 'l qual si triumfa, non pur scampa;
O refrigerio al cieco ardor ch'avampa,
Qui fra i mortali sciocchi;
Vergine, que' belli occhi,
Che vider tristi la spietata stampa
Ne' dolci membri del tuo caro figlio,
Volgi al mio dubio stato,
Che sconsigliato   a te vèn per consiglio.

Vergine pura, d'ogni parte intera,
Del tuo parto gentil figliuola e madre,
Ch'allumi questa vita, e l'altra adorni,
Per te il tuo Figlio, e quel del sommo Padre,
O fenestra del ciel lucente, altèra,
Venne a salvarne in su li estremi giorni;
E fra tutt' i terreni altri soggiorni
Sola tu fosti eletta,
Vergine benedetta,
Che 'l pianto d'Eva in allegrezza torni.

CCCLXVI

Virgin most lovely, who clothed with the sun,
Crowned with the stars, the great heavenly Light
Pleased so that he concealed in you his ray,
Love presses me to speak of your true height;
But to begin I need the vision
And help of you and of him who did stay
In you for love; you answer those who pray
And who call you with faith.
Virgin, if our lost breath
Inspired your mercy, and the sad decay
Of mortal things, hear my worshipping cry,
Bring comfort to my war,
Though I be straw,   and you queen of the sky.

Virgin most wise, who the glad group enhance
Of the blessed and prudent virgins all,
Being the first, and with a clearer lamp;
O mighty shield of any suffering soul
Against the blows of death and treacherous chance,
That makes us triumph over evil's clamp;
O coolness in the bright furnace and swamp
That foolish mortals know;
Virgin, those eyes that glow,
Which saw with anguish the pitiless stamp
In the dear limbs of your beloved Son,
Turn to my dubious state
That, torn by fate,   recites this orison.

Virgin all pure, in every part entire,
Of your lovable Child daughter and mother,
Who light this life, the other beautify,
For you, your Son and of the supreme Father,
O window of the sky, shining empire,
Came to save us in our last moment's cry;
And among all the dwellings that stood by
You were chosen alone,
Virgin who always shone
And did Eve's tears into mirth modify.

Fammi, ché puoi, de la sua grazia degno,
Senza fine o beata,
Giá coronata   nel superno regno.

Vergine santa, d'ogni grazia piena,
Che per vera et altissima umiltate
Salisti al ciel, onde miei preghi ascolti,
Tu partoristi il fonte di pietate,
E di giustizia il sol, che rasserena
Il secol, pien d'errori, oscuri e folti:
Tre dolci e cari nomi hai in te raccolti,
Madre, figliuola, e sposa;
Vergine gloriosa,
Donna del re che nostri lacci ha sciolti,
E fatto 'l mondo libero e felice,
Ne le cui sante piaghe,
Prego ch'appaghe   il cor, vera beatrice.

Vergine sola al mondo, senza essempio,
Che 'l ciel di tue bellezze innamorasti,
Cui né prima fu simil, né seconda,
Santi penseri, atti pietosi e casti
Al vero Dio sacrato e vivo tempio
Fecero in tua verginitá feconda.
Per te pò la mia vita esser ioconda,
S'a' tuoi preghi, o Maria,
Vergine dolce e pia,
Ove 'l fallo abondò la grazia abonda.
Con le ginocchia de la mente inchine,
Prego che sia mia scorta,
E la mia torta   via drizzi a buon fine.

Vergine chiara, e stabile in eterno,
Di questo tempestoso mare stella,
D'ogni fedel nocchier fidata guida,
Pon mente in che terribile procella
I' mi ritrovo sol, senza governo,
Et ho giá da vicin l'ultime strida.
Ma pur in te l'anima mia si fida,
Peccatrice, i' no 'l nego,

Make me, you have the power, deserve his grace,
O endlessly serene,
Who long have been enthroned in heaven's space.

Virgin most holy, full of every grace,
Who by a true and high humility
Rose to the sky from where you hear my prayer,
You gave birth to the spring of charity,
The sun of justice that brightens this place
And time, filled with thick error and despair:
Three dear and lovely names in you appear,
Mother, daughter, and bride;
O Virgin glorified,
Lady of the King who did our fetters tear
And did our world create free and serene,
In whose most sacred wound
I beg, make sound my heart, o blissful queen.

Virgin alone on earth, without compare,
Who with your beauties made the sky love you,
Of whom no like or second we shall see,
Holy thoughts, actions chaste, pious and true,
Raised to our God the temple and repair
Of your beneficent virginity.
Through you my life can reach felicity,
If, Mary, at your prayer,
Virgin sweet and fair,
Where once damage was spread, forgiveness be.
In my mind I bow down, my knees I bend,
And pray, be you my guide,
My wayward stride direct to rightful end.

Virgin all clear and eternally stable,
Of this tempestuous sea ever-fixed star,
Of every trustful pilot trusted guide,
Consider in what frightening stormy war
I find myself without a rule or label,
And I already touch the final tide.
And yet in you my soul is fortified,
Sinful, I do confess,

Vergine; ma ti prego
Che 'l tuo nemico del mio mal non rida:
Ricorditi, che fece il peccar nostro,
Prender Dio per scamparne,
Umana carne,   al tuo virginal chiostro.

Vergine, quante lagrime ho giá sparte,
Quante lusinghe, e· quanti preghi indarno,
Pur per mia pena, e per mio grave danno!
Da poi ch'i' nacqui in su la riva d'Arno,
Cercando or questa et or quel altra parte,
Non è stata mia vita altro ch'affanno.
Mortal bellezza, atti, e parole m'hanno
Tutta ingombrata l'alma.
Vergine sacra et alma,
Non tardar, ch'i' son forse a l'ultimo anno.
I dí miei piú correnti che saetta,
Fra miserie e peccati,
Sonsen andati,   e sol Morte n'aspetta.

Vergine, tale è terra e posto ha in doglia
Lo mio cor, che vivendo in pianto il tenne;
E di mille miei mali un non sapea;
E per saperlo, pur quel che n'avenne
Fôra avenuto; ch'ogni altra sua voglia
Era a me morte, et a lei fama rea.
Or tu, donna del ciel, tu nostra dea,
Se dir lice, e convensi,
Vergine d'alti sensi,
Tu vedi il tutto; e quel che non potea
Far altri, è nulla a la tua gran vertute,
Por fine al mio dolore;
Ch'a te onore,   et a me fia salute.

Vergine, in cui ho tutta mia speranza,
Che possi e vogli al gran bisogno aitarme,
Non mi lasciare in su l'estremo passo;
Non guardar me, ma chi degnò crearme;
No 'l mio valor, ma l'alta sua sembianza,
Ch'è in me, ti mova a curar d'uom sí basso.

Virgin, but deign to bless
Me, that your foe may not my pain deride;
Remember how it was our sin that made
God take a human shape
And find escape for us in your bower's shade.

Virgin, how many tears I had to pour,
How many flatteries, prayers void and blank,
To my own punishment and grave mischief!
Ever since I was born on Arno's bank,
Seeking now this and now the other shore,
My life has never been other than grief.
Mortal grace, gestures, words, have been the chief
Interest of my soul.
Virgin sacred and whole,
Do not delay, perhaps my time is brief.
My days running more quick than lightning-chains,
Between sin and decay,
Have gone away and only death remains.

Virgin, someone is earth and has condemned
To pain my heart, who living made it weep;
And of my thousand ills not one she knew;
Had she known them, the harvest I did reap
Would not have changed; if other wish had stemmed
From her, I should be dead and she untrue.
Lady of heaven, goddess of the few,
If to say this is fit,
Virgin of holy wit,
You see all, and what others could not do
Is a small thing to your great majesty,
My suffering to end;
For this will lend you honour, bliss to me.

Virgin in whom I lay every hope
That you may, that you will help my great need,
Desert me not in the ultimate place,
Look not at me, but gaze on Him who did
Create my life; not my worth, but His scope,
Which is in me, may redeem my disgrace.

Medusa, e l'error mio m'han fatto un sasso
D'umor vano stillante:
Vergine, tu di stante
Lagrime, e pie, adempi 'l meo cor lasso;
Ch'almen l'ultimo pianto sia devoto,
Senza terrestro limo,
Come fu 'l primo   non d'insania vòto.

Vergine umana, e nemica d'orgoglio,
Del comune principio amor t'induca;
Miserere d'un cor contrito, umíle:
Che se poca mortal terra caduca
Amar con sí mirabil fede soglio,
Che devrò far di te cosa gentile?
Se dal mio stato assai misero e vile
Per le tue man resurgo,
Vergine, i' sacro e purgo
Al tuo nome e penseri e 'ngegno e stile,
La lingua e 'l cor, le lagrime e i sospiri.
Scorgimi al miglior guado,
E prendi in grado   i cangiati desiri.

Il dí s'appressa, e non pòte esser lunge,
Sí corre il tempo e vola,
Vergine unica e sola,
E 'l cor or conscienzia or morte punge.
Raccomandami al tuo figliuol, verace
Omo e verace Dio,
Ch'accolga 'l mio   spirto ultimo in pace.

Medusa and my error made my face
A stone dripping in vain:
Virgin, now fill with sane
And holy tears my weary heart and base;
So that at least my last weeping be pure,
Without terrestrial mud,
As the first flood   was mad and insecure.

Virgin quite human and averse to pride,
Let love of common origin move you;
Have mercy on a heart contrite and shy:
For if a little piece of earthly glue
I can love with a faith that is so wide,
What shall I do with you, thing of the sky?
If from the state so low in which I lie
By your hands I escape,
Virgin, to your pure shape
I will devote my mind and style and sigh,
My tongue, my heart, my tears and all my skill.
Lead me to my reprieve,
And do believe   in my converted will.

The day is coming and soon it will start,
Time does so quickly run,
Virgin unique and one,
And now conscience, now death pierces my heart.
Recommend me to your Son, to the real
Man and the real God,
That Heaven's nod   be my ghost's peaceful seal.